NORTH STAR

NORTH STAR
A MEMOIR

PETER CAMEJO

Haymarket Books
Chicago, Illinois

First published by Haymarket Books in 2010
© 2010 Morella Camejo

Haymarket Books
P.O. Box 180165, Chicago, IL 60618
773-583-7884
info@haymarketbooks.org
www.haymarketbooks.org

ISBN: 978-1931859-92-9

Trade distribution:
In the U.S. through Consortium Book Sales and Distribution, www.cbsd.com
In Canada through Publishers Group Canada, pgcbooks.ca/home.html
In the UK, Turnaround Publisher Services, www.turnaround-uk.com
In Australia, Palgrave Macmillan, www.palgravemacmillan.com.au
All other countries, Publishers Group Worldwide, www.pgw.com

Special discounts are available for bulk purchases by organizations and institutions.
Please contact Haymarket Books for more information at 773-583-7884 or
info@haymarketbooks.org.

This book was published with the generous support of Lannan Foundation and
the Wallace Global Fund.

Cover design by Ragina Johnson. Cover photo courtesy of Morella Camejo.

Printed in Canada by union labor on recycled paper containing 100 percent
post-consumer waste in accordance with the guidelines of the Green Press
Initiative, www.greenpressinitiative.org

Library of Congress CIP Data is available.

10 9 8 7 6 5 4 3 2 1

To the thousands upon thousands of people who have worked with me through the years for peace, for social justice, against racism, and for human rights. I know that future generations will build on what we have done. And to the children, the future participants of mass social struggles who will make the Third American Revolution a reality

CONTENTS

PUBLISHER'S NOTE

Haymarket Books is honored to present this posthumous memoir by Peter Miguel Camejo. A friend of Haymarket Books, Peter shepherded the important book *Independent Politics*, edited by Howie Hawkins, which we published in 2006.

Matt Gonzalez brought the *North Star* manuscript to Haymarket, explaining that it was unfinished but that Peter had been working diligently to the end of his rich and active life to complete it. We responded immediately that we would be honored to publish the book. Peter had been writing the penultimate chapter on the day he went into the hospital for the last time. Peter passed away from lymphoma on September 13, 2008.

We extend our gratitude and appreciation to Morella Anzola Camejo for supporting Haymarket throughout this process. We would like to acknowledge the editorial work of Leslie Evans, who assisted Peter on the unfinished manuscript. Max Novick gave thoughtful comments on the early stages of the manuscript, and Caroline Luft and Dao X. Tran provided invaluable editorial assistance in preparing the manuscript for publication. Thanks also to Rachel Odes, Mike Davis, and Todd Chretien, who worked with Peter and helped make this project possible. Our thanks also go to Ralph Nader and his staff for their contribution to fact-checking the text.

CHAPTER 1

MIRACLE IN CALI

It was June 12, 1979. The day was beautiful and mild. A light breeze swept through usually humid and hot Cali, Colombia. Two Colombian friends were driving me to the airport, where I had a flight to catch to Cartagena, on the northern coast. I was wearing a bright yellow tee shirt, which—as it turned out—was rather significant.

Cartagena was the next stop on my speaking tour of Colombian cities. In my speeches I was addressing the latest developments in the overthrow of the U.S.-backed Somoza dictatorship in Nicaragua. I was looking forward to the trip to Cartagena, one of the most beautiful places I had ever been. For very little money I could stay at an oceanfront hotel and swim on one of the world's most beautiful beaches. After Colombia I planned to go on to Peru to support the presidential candidacy of Hugo Blanco, leader of the peasant uprisings of the 1960s and hero among the Peruvian people.

Little did I know that at the Cali airport Colombian secret police from the Administrative Department for Security (DAS*) were waiting to arrest me on orders from the CIA. To be arrested in Colombia is very dangerous—the rule of law is not one of Colombia's traditions.

---

* Editor's note: Camejo mainly gives the full name in its English translation and the acronym in its Spanish initials.

1

I arrived at the airport with my two friends and the three of us walked in. The airport was small, just a short walk from the entrance to the check-in counter. I handed my ticket to a young woman behind the counter, who did two peculiar things. In those days the check-in agent had a printed list of passengers and he or she circled the corresponding name as each passenger checked in. Instead of circling my name, this young woman made a circle in the air above the paper. I took notice of that but didn't recognize that something larger was under way. Next she took my small bag and instead of placing it onto the conveyor belt she hid it under the counter. Then she said, "Go pay your exit visa." My flight to Cartagena was, of course, a domestic flight so I responded, "I'm not leaving the country." She looked right into my eyes, really hard, and repeated, "Go pay your exit visa."

The exit visa was only one dollar so I thought … okay. As it turns out the secret police knew that I was wearing a yellow tee shirt. But my paying an exit visa would convey to the secret police, who were in the airport somewhere watching my yellow shirt, that I must not be the person they were seeking because they knew that Peter Camejo wasn't leaving the country. In fact, as I walked away to pay the exit visa, two police agents went up to the young woman and asked, "Is that him?" She told them, "No."

As I came up to the exit visa stand the man behind the counter turned and quickly walked into a back office. I could tell something was "off," but was unaware of what was actually happening: the airport workers had put into action a plot to save me. These workers were risking their jobs and possibly more to keep me out of the hands of the political police. As I stood at the counter waiting, a woman sitting nearby said, "Go upstairs. Your wife is waiting for you." I leaned over and said, "I'm not married." She repeated impatiently, "Go upstairs. They're waiting for you." One of my Colombian friends said, "Pedro, maybe someone knows you and wants to talk to you. Let's go find out. You have time."

A man was selling lottery tickets in the stairwell. I had a ticket I had bought for fifty cents somewhere and showed it to him to see if I had won. He said no. My friends and I continued up the stairs. The stairs turned left and we came to a door. Having no idea what else to do, I knocked. A woman stepped out and asked, "Are you Camejo?" I said yes. She responded, "Quick, come in here." We stepped into a room where flights were announced. Several workers in the room whispered, "Stay silent!"

Then it hit me. No one had to say a word. The three of us stood still. Between announcements of flights the employees filled in some of the details. The woman from the check-in counter explained that the secret police had said I was a drug dealer and was to be arrested, and that I would be wearing a yellow shirt. The airport workers told me they would wait until my flight to Cartagena took off, and then they would check to see if the secret police had left the airport.

After about twenty minutes word came from the airport director's secretary that she had overheard a conversation between the DAS police and the airport director. Apparently the secret police had determined that I had to be in the building and they were going to conduct a search. The bad news hit us hard. The airport workers said to me, "We can't hide you. But we'll take you to our union office so at least when they arrest you they won't beat you."

The union headquarters in the airport was a one-room office with two people inside. They greeted me, very friendly, and apologized, not knowing what else to do. I asked my two Colombian friends to remain in the airport but to stay far away from me so they wouldn't also get arrested. I gave them the telephone number of a good friend in New York so that efforts could be made to defend me.

The main thought that kept crossing my mind was to be thankful my companion, Gloria Najar, wasn't with me on that trip. The fear that something might happen to her was frighteningly strong in those days when the two of us traveled in Latin America. My other primary thought was that I would probably be in the same clothes for a long time, maybe weeks.

I asked the union leaders if there was a bathroom nearby. (Who knows when you'll be able to go once the secret police grab you?) "There's a bathroom right here," they said. I walked in and began urinating. I'm sure it could be heard clear as day in the main room. At that moment the two secret service police came into the office. They must have known the union leaders from working the airport beat. The men greeted each other in typical Latino macho style with some sort of joke. I paid little attention until I heard one of the DAS officers ask, "Who's in the bathroom?" One union leader responded, "Oh, so the queer wants to take a peek?" The secret service policeman made his own derogatory joke, denying any interest, and walked out.

To this day I am bewildered by the incompetence of the secret police and the influence of homophobia on their actions—that they would prefer to let a suspect escape rather than compromise their "masculinity." I rationalized later that maybe they assumed the noise was being made by another union member, since if a suspect were hiding in a bathroom, he probably shouldn't be urinating.

When I stepped out of the bathroom the union leaders held their fingers to their lips. One whispered, "There is a small chance. Your friends have driven their car to the door downstairs. When I tell you, run down the stairs and take off." Amazingly, the search was being conducted by just the two police officers, with no backup watching the stairs or the doors. As soon as they entered the next office, I was down the stairs in a second, out of the building, and into the car. We pulled away from the curb. I said, "Attract no attention, drive slowly." I lay down in the back seat. Within minutes we were away from the airport.

Hiding Out in Colombia

All the left groups in Colombia, as in the United States, are penetrated by police informers. My Colombian friends said the safest way to hide me was to put me up in a secret location. One of them knew a young professional who had a tiny apartment out of town.

In a diary that I kept at that time I refer to the person who lent me the apartment as Enrique. (For security reasons, I did not use last names in my diary and sometimes even the first names were fake.) Arrangements were made quickly, and once again cooperation was automatic. The sympathy and support I was receiving continued to amaze me—how these people kept stepping forward to save an American they didn't even know.

I was left alone in a tiny apartment. There was no food. I had no car or means of communicating with anyone. I fell asleep that night thinking of what steps I should take. First, I decided to try to call my father in Venezuela. The president of Venezuela at that time was a relative of my family by marriage— my father's sister, my Aunt Clara, was married to Humberto Campíns, a first cousin of Venezuelan president Luis Herrera Campíns.

We had never met. Some time earlier I had been invited by my Campíns cousins to meet the president, but I told them I would not meet with him while he supported the dictatorship in El Salvador. He sent me a message, delivered in a friendly inner-family way, that for his part he was waiting for me to stop supporting the "communist" guerrillas in El Salvador. My first hope was to see if my father could talk to President Campíns, and whether he might intervene for me.

The next morning my Colombian friends picked me up. We went out to eat and they said they had reached my friend Gus Horowitz in New York. Gus, one of the most brilliant people I have ever met, was my roommate at MIT. He went to work immediately to try to help me. I set out to call Venezuela and, as happens often, all the lines were down and I couldn't get through. At the time, I was unaware of what began to transpire in the United States. Meanwhile, Gus reached my mother, who entered the act with her usual energy to rescue me.

As soon as my mother learned of my predicament in Colombia she called my stepfather, Robert Ratner, who at the time was president of the U.S. branch of the United Nations Association, headquartered in New York. The call got through to Robert while he happened to be in a meeting with Cyrus Vance, then secretary of state under President Jimmy Carter.

The phone was handed to my stepfather right in front of Secretary Vance. My stepfather was so visibly disturbed as he spoke to my mother that finally Vance asked him, "What's wrong, Bob?" Robert explained, "I have a stepson who ran for president as a socialist and they are trying to arrest him in Colombia. He's hiding out."

Without hesitating Cyrus Vance told an assistant, "Get the Colombian government on the phone right now and ask them why they are trying to arrest Peter Camejo." That call must have shaken up the Colombians, to have the secretary of state of the United States, in the span of one day, calling Colombia on my behalf. They must have thought the CIA had made a mistake, or maybe that I was a high-level double agent or something like that. Whatever they thought, they weren't going to risk a confrontation with the United States. So the order for my arrest was lifted in Colombia. Of course, I didn't know that.

Not being able to get through to Venezuela I couldn't decide what to do. Going to the U.S. consulate would be ridiculous, since that would be the same as turning myself in to the CIA. I thought my only chance was to contact the Venezuelan consulate in the hope that Venezuela wouldn't hand me over. So I called the local consulate. The consul, Colonel Tomás Pimentel D'Alta, got on the line with me and said, "I know who you are. I know your dad. My cousin worked with him in Puerto La Cruz." Colonel D'Alta told me to come to his office, assuring me of protection.

At the consulate the excitement over my situation was palpable. Everyone wanted to hear what had happened. Then the Venezuelans started brainstorming how to get me out of Colombia. One consulate employee suggested getting an airplane and flying below the radar to Venezuela. Once again I was astonished at how, without hesitation, people stepped forward to help me.

The colonel came up with an interesting proposition. He said, "I'll make you an employee of Venezuela so they would be violating protocol to arrest you." Right then and there they knocked out a document, had me sign it, and with that I was a diplomatic employee of Venezuela.

Then the colonel announced that he would call the head of the Colombian secret service in Cali to find out what was happening. I was opposed to the idea, since that would reveal my whereabouts and seemed too dangerous. The colonel reassured me that he would not disclose my location. He made the call right in front of me. Immediately we were informed that the arrest order had been rescinded. The government of Colombia wanted to apologize to me for the "mistake." The head of the secret service asked if the consul could arrange for me to visit him so he could express his regrets personally and assure me of safe passage anywhere in Colombia.

At first I worried that this was just a ploy to arrest me. The colonel assured me that, given the normal relations between Venezuela and Colombia, it would be next to impossible for the Colombians to be openly lying in this case. With great trepidation I agreed. The colonel said goodbye and good luck.

My two Colombian friends drove to the secret service headquarters. When we reached the office I walked in slowly. The receptionist said I could go right in to see the director, Alberto Romero. As I walked down a hallway I passed a group of secret police, standing around so they could see what I looked like. I sensed that this was their way of letting me know they might not be taking me today, but they would be ready to go if the orders changed.

The secret service director looked a movie villain in charge of torturing people. He spoke calmly, saying, "A mistake was made. We apologize. You will not be arrested or bothered in any way. You are free to travel anywhere in Colombia." I thanked him and wished him a good day, turned, and slowly walked out. The agents were still there in the hallway, motionless, with no expression on their faces.

That evening at a coffee shop I met up with the young woman from the check-in counter who had saved my life. She returned my suitcase and told me that the CIA had released my passport photo to all the airports in Colombia in order to facilitate my arrest. Knowing who I was, she had recognized me at the counter and spread the word to the other employees, who set out to help me escape. We laughed over the fact I hadn't picked up on all the signals she had tried to give me. I suggested that perhaps I was so stupid it kept me from acting nervous and attracting attention. She told me to stop being so stupid and to be more careful. I thanked her profusely and asked her to thank all the others. "No, we thank you for what you are doing," she replied. Fortunately there had been no repercussions for any of the workers and they were all pleased I had escaped. When we said goodbye it was difficult not knowing what I could ever do for these hard-working people who risked their jobs to protect me.

So why would the CIA put out the completely fallacious story that I was a dope dealer and start a nationwide dragnet that could have gotten me killed? The reason, it finally emerged, was that the CIA was upset about my plans to go to Peru in support of Hugo Blanco's presidential campaign. At the time, amazingly, Blanco was polling about 25 percent, and the CIA was trying to prevent the left in Peru from unifying behind Blanco. I knew Blanco well and was known myself among some of the left leaders in Peru. To prevent my reaching Peru, the CIA decided to frame me and imprison me in Colombia.*

I will forever be thankful to Cyrus Vance for having intervened to protect me. But there is a lingering question. Did he order an investigation? Did he try to find out why the CIA was trying to arrest an innocent citizen of the United States? I suspect not. Or if he did, chances are the CIA got out of it as they always do, being an agency often exposed for its misdeeds but above the law when it comes to prosecution.

Having eluded the frame-up, I resumed my tour of Colombia as planned, continuing on to beautiful Cartagena. I stayed at the Hotel San Felipe. The day of my arrival, after a couple of relatively brief meetings, I was on a bus where a young person was listening to music from a small radio. As a sign of the times, suddenly the music was interrupted for an announcement: "This morning a guerrilla band attacked police, killing two and wounding four." The report described the guerrillas as belonging to one of the leftist groups in Colombia. To my surprise the entire bus began applauding.

---

* I did not go on to Peru, because by then I had talked to friends in New York and learned that Hugo Blanco had told them not to have me come. The word was out I would be arrested upon arrival. For more about Hugo Blanco, see chapter 11.

CHAPTER 2

MY FAMILY AND MY EARLY YEARS

I was born December 31, 1939, at 8:00 a.m. in Queens, New York. My name on my birth certificate is Pedro Miguel Camejo Guanche. At that time my family was living in Caracas, Venezuela, but my mother had experienced difficulties with the birth of her first child, my brother Daniel, and decided to have me in the United States.*

My mother's decision made it possible for me to run for president in 1976 and for vice president with Ralph Nader in 2004. During the campaigns I joked that my mother was psychic for having given birth to me in the United States.

My Grandmother Wins the Cinco y Seis

The other major reason my mother chose New York, aside from its excellent hospitals, was that her parents lived in New York and she had attended high school there. My mother's maiden name was Elvia Guanche. Her family had gone into exile during the Juan Vicente Gómez dictatorship in Venezuela (1908–1935). My mother's parents, Miguel and Adela Guanche, spoke out

---

* In addition to my older brother Daniel I have a younger brother, Antonio, born in 1942. Later in my life came a half-brother, Nikolas Camejo, born in Caracas in 1956, and a sister, Bettina Camejo, the only daughter of my father's third wife. My father adopted Bettina. From my mother's remarriage I gained a brother, Dan Ratner.

against the dictatorship and were forced to leave the country. When they emigrated to America they lost everything. My grandmother worked as a seamstress in the New York garment district, while my grandfather, who had been a judge in Venezuela, became a bank teller.

Miguel and Adela did not return to Venezuela until near the end of the 1940s. They were still very poor. Then something marvelous happened. In Venezuela there was a long-running weekly tradition of betting on the horses in the Cinco y Seis (Five and Six). Six horse races were run, and to win the Cinco y Seis you had to pick all six victors; if no one hit all six horses, the winnings went to those who got five of the six correct. All week long people discussed the horses competing, the jockeys, and who were the odds-on favorites. On Sunday the results aired on the radio (later, on television) and the whole country tuned in. You could make a very small bet, like fifty cents, and win twenty thousand dollars or more.

One Sunday my family's guardian angel was working overtime. My grandparents were sitting in their home, visiting with friends. They had the radio on and the announcer began reporting the winning horses for the Cinco y Seis. After each name my grandmother said, "I have that one." No one paid attention. By the end she had hit five—and no one in all of Venezuela had picked all six. With the winnings my grandparents were able to buy a large home. They divided it into three apartments, rented out two, and lived for the rest of their lives off that income plus my grandmother's social security.

I loved my maternal grandparents very much. My grandfather Miguel died of a heart attack in his early sixties, when I was sixteen. He was one of twelve children of Juan de Dios Guanche, an esteemed Venezuelan educator who founded and directed several schools, including La Escuela Superior and La Escuela Comercial, both of which were dedicated to the poor in the belief that education would help people get out of poverty. My great-grandfather also served as president and secretary of the Municipal Council of the city of Petare and was elected to the State Legislature of Miranda. His concern for the poor led to his becoming president of the Humanitarian Hospital of Charity. He is revered to this day in Venezuela and has a school, Colegio Juan de Dios Guanche, dedicated to his memory.

My grandmother Adela lived to be ninety-eight. Her mother, born in Paris, fell in love with a Venezuelan medical student doing his residency in France. They married and soon after returned to Ciudad Bolívar on the

Orinoco River in Venezuela. Adela wrote poetry, played the *cuatro**** and guitar, and loved to sing, skills she passed on to my mother. She delighted in cooking Venezuelan food for her grandchildren whenever we visited. In her later years my brothers Daniel and Antonio, who were living in Venezuela, looked after her. Our grandmother was an incredibly generous, energetic, and independent woman. When I was running for president in 1976 she sent a gift of a thousand dollars to help me out from the little she had. Late into her nineties Adela would horrify my mother by climbing up a wooden ladder onto the roof of her house to pick fresh mangoes from a tree in her small front yard.

A Family Tragedy

Like all Venezuelans my grandfather was brought up in a country where children are taught from infancy to believe in supernatural powers of all kinds. As he grew up he absorbed the Judeo-Christian creation myths. I have found that once someone is convinced the world is only four thousand years old and was created in seven days, they can end up believing almost anything. Along came a Christian Science preacher, who converted my grandfather.

I want to make it clear that I respect many people who are religious. There are countless very courageous people who have fought for social justice, equality, peace, and tolerance because of their religious beliefs. I have worked with religious people my whole life and have enormous respect for many of them. But I am an atheist and always have been. I make a distinction between religious people who are trying to do good things in this world and those religious people who promote hate and prejudice through their beliefs. Additionally, apart from social views, there is a risk that goes hand in hand with religious irrationalism and rejection of science—a risk of unintentionally inflicting harm, sometimes irreparable.

My grandparents had four daughters. One of them, my mother's sister Adela, named for my grandmother, became very ill. So my grandfather called the Christian Scientist, who came and prayed while my aunt's condition got worse and worse.[†] The other girls, watching their sister dying, finally broke down and called a doctor. But the doctor arrived too late. He turned to my grandfather and shouted, "I could have saved her! It was just blood poisoning." The Christian Scientist said, "No, it was God's will."

---

* A cuatro is a four-stringed instrument, similar to a small lute or ukelele.
† Traditional Christian Scientists believe in healing through prayer rather than medicine.

My grandfather pushed the Christian Scientist out of the house and then locked himself up in his room for about a week. When he emerged he gathered his family, all in tears, and told them, "Never mention religion again in my presence."

I was about twelve when my mother told me this story. She said, "I decided not to let anyone indoctrinate you kids with any religion, but to let you grow up and decide for yourselves." Not having been indoctrinated, early on I came to the logical conclusion that all the myths about the world's being only four thousand years old, made in seven days, woman created from the rib of a man, etc., were absurd. As an adult I have come to view as a kind of cruelty to children this practice of brainwashing young people with superstition and fear. I thank my mom every day for her wisdom and foresight.

My Family on My Father's Side

My grandmother on my father's side was an Anzola. This linked us to a huge extended family, all descendants of Miguel Anzola. Miguel Anzola was left as a newborn on the steps of the home of a Catholic priest named Anzola, in the small town of El Tocuyo, near Barquisemeto.* It is assumed the priest was the father. He gave the child his name, raised him, and sent him to Europe to be educated. I believe Miguel was half indigenous; my conjecture is based on pictures of him. Who his mother was is not known to me or, to my knowledge, to anyone else.

After the triumph of the revolution, led by Simón Bolívar, Miguel became the first governor of the province of Barquisimeto. He was a prominent attorney and later served as governor of the State of Lara. Miguel had fourteen children, one of whom, Amador, also had more than a dozen children. One of Amador's many children was my great-grandmother, whom I remember seeing when I was five years old. Another was my wife's great-grandfather. Thus my wife, Morella, and I are fifth cousins. Today there are more than six thousand descendants of Miguel Anzola in Venezuela. Every five years a few hundred of them attend a family gathering in Miguel's hometown of El Tocuyo. And all of us Venezuelan Anzolas love reading or spreading rumors about whatever happens to a member of our extended family.

---

* It is believed that Miguel was born in 1802; some sources state 1798.

Origin of the Camejos

According to my dad, who learned it from his granddad, three Camejo brothers came from Spain about three hundred years ago and settled in Venezuela. One went east, one went west, and the other arrived in the center of Venezuela. My family is descended from the Camejo brother who settled in the interior, near the city of Barquisimeto.

One of my Camejo great-grand-aunts, who lived in the port city of Coro, owned slaves at the time of the revolution. She freed her slaves to fight with Simón Bolívar. I have been told that one of them may have been named Pedro, and as a slave he would have carried Camejo as his last name. It is not clear whether this family lore is accurate, but what is certain is that a former slave named Pedro Camejo became a hero of the revolution. Nicknamed "El Negro Primero," or "the black leader," Pedro Camejo died at the last great battle for independence, the Battle of Carabobo in June 1821. Today the five Bolívar Fuerte bill (worth about one dollar) features a portrait of Pedro Camejo, and a statue of him stands in Caracas at the memorial to the Batalla de Carabobo. There are streets, buildings, parks, and monuments throughout Venezuela named for Pedro Camejo.

Ever since I was quite young I have felt proud to share his name. When I was a child people would stop to take my photograph because there are very few Camejos and, to my knowledge, at that time I was the only one in Venezuela named Pedro. I would have liked to have been named in honor of the revolutionary hero Pedro Camejo, but I was actually named after a grand-uncle whom I loved dearly.

At the age of ninety-two, seemingly out of nowhere, my father looked at me and said, "Pedrito, I want to tell you something. My grandfather told me the reason the Camejo name is so rare is that we were Jews that had to convert and pick a new name because of the Inquisition." This struck me as an amazing statement and I was glad my dad told me. I have no idea if it is true, but it would be odd for the story to have been passed down quietly for generations if it were not.

Barquisimeto

I was always happy when I visited Barquisimeto, as I was surrounded by relatives. They were so loving toward me and curious about my experiences growing up in the United States.

I had a special place in my heart for my grandmother on my father's side, Carmen Octavio de Camejo (nee Anzola). We called her Chita, short for Carmencita. She owned land, some of which she had inherited from her family, and the rest of which my grandfather had left her. My Aunt Milagro told me that Chita never collected rent from the peasants working her land. Rather, Chita called press conferences periodically to inform local reporters that she had decided to carry out her own "land reform" by giving away her land to the campesinos who worked it. In the end she gave away much of her land to the peasants.

When my grandmother was quite elderly, some peasants working on the land told her that they had found some pieces of old pottery in the earth. She asked them to keep looking for more and explained that she would buy it from them. (I suspect they just gave her most of it.) She built shelves in her house to store the dusty shards of pottery. I remember her telling me, "Pedrito, this pottery may be twenty thousand years old." We all said, "Yes, yes, grandma, that's great."

Then one day she was visited by an expert from the University of Caracas. To make a long story short, I've been told that my grandmother's collection turned out to be the greatest find of indigenous pottery ever in Venezuela. It is all in a museum now and a huge monograph was published, noting each piece, estimating the source and probable creation date. So I thank my grandmother for having had the foresight and perseverance to save these artifacts and then to donate them for posterity.

My grandmother was a figure from another place and time, like a character right out of *One Hundred Years of Solitude* by the famous Colombian writer Gabriel García Márquez. In Márquez's novel there is a grandmother with gold hidden throughout her house that no one can find. So it was with my own grandmother. While visiting Chita at her home in Barquisimeto in the early 1970s, I woke up to find a 1915 U.S. gold piece under my pillow. (My mother had the gold piece set into a tie clip for me; it is one of the few accessories I ever wore.) In the old colonial style, in Chita's house the rooms opened onto long corridors that met in a central courtyard. Hammocks hung from the bedroom walls. Chita liked to spend hours napping in a hammock.

My grandmother also slept with pictures of both Fidel Castro and Jesus Christ over her bed. I never asked about it but waited for her to offer an explanation, which she never did. My Aunt Milagro, the only political progressive in my family until I came along, told me, "She likes Fidel because he is good to the peasants."

Chita's husband, Daniel Camejo Acosta, died before I was born. My paternal grandfather was a surgeon and visited his rural patients on horseback. He often did not charge for his services, thinking it was hard enough on a person to be ill. One very grateful patient was a rich landowner, who left my grandfather a large parcel of land as payment. The estate was called Las Tunas and lay between the towns of Duaca and Barquisimeto. Daniel Camejo Acosta was considered a great orator and was regularly invited to speak at important occasions in his hometown of Ospino. A collection of his unfinished writings, entitled *Noticulas Truncas*, relates the times and tribulations of an itinerant doctor in rural Venezuela. He was highly esteemed and the main hospital in Barquisimeto is named in his honor, Hospital Daniel Camejo Acosta.

My Parents, Daniel Camejo Octavio and Elvia Guanche

My dad, Daniel Camejo Octavio, was born into a landowning family but did not inherit any money. After his father died, the family survived by selling off, bit by bit, plots of the land owned by my grandparents. Despite starting from scratch, my father became one of Venezuela's most innovative and successful developers of beach resorts.

My dad had a strong personality and a lot of guts. He met my mother, Elvia Guanche, at the swimming pool of Club La Florida in Caracas. At the time my mom lived in New York and was just visiting. After she had gone home, my dad somehow scraped together the money for passage on a ship and traveled all the way to New York to see her. He was madly in love. When he arrived in New York he told my mom how much he loved her and suggested that they get married that very day. They went out, found a priest, got married, and stayed out all night.

The next morning they showed up at my grandparents' house. Fortunately my grandfather Miguel wasn't armed or my dad's life might have been cut short. Daniel and Elvia explained that they were married and loved each other. Once my grandparents had calmed down, they gave their blessings. It took a little longer for my dad's family to accept my mom. They didn't approve of my father's marrying a "foreigner"—even though my mother was originally from Venezuela—not to mention a woman he had met at a swimming pool. (At least that's what my mom told me.)

In the early years of their marriage my parents struggled financially. While they were living in the small Andean town where my father attended college, my mother once had to sell some of her clothing to buy milk for my older brother Daniel. Soon after my birth in late 1939 our family moved to Texas, where my father earned a master of science degree in Municipal and Sanitary Engineering at Texas A&M. We lived in the town of Bryan in Brazos County, about ninety-two miles northwest of Houston, the nearest big city. My younger brother, Antonio Camejo Guanche, was born in Texas in 1942, when I was two. With the start of World War II we moved back to Venezuela.

My very first political act was at the age of five, staging a two-person picket line with my seven-year-old brother Daniel, holding up large banana leaves in protest. The green of the leaves was also the party color of the Venezuelan Social Christian Party, founded by our neighbor, Rafael Caldera.* Its members were known as Copeyanos, from COPEI, the initials of the main party committee. At the time there was a revolution brewing in Venezuela, led by the rival party, Acción Democrática (AD). Our banana leaf protest lasted only a few minutes before my mother told us to put the leaves down—she didn't want anyone to see us, as the other side was winning. Around the same time, 1945, Caldera's wife came over to our house to ask my mother to hide a revolver that belonged to Rafael. My mother put it under the floor of our living room. In that charged political climate all activists were suspect, especially if caught with a revolver. AD was a social democratic party, a member of the European Second International of socialist parties. I remember peasants going by our house with machetes to join the AD rebellion, which brought Romulo Betancourt to power in a coup in October 1945. Later AD became one of the most corrupt organizations in Latin America.

My parents were divorced in 1947, back when you had to go to Las Vegas to do it. My mom and we three children left Venezuela that year and came to live in the United States. We ended up in a small middle-class home in Great Neck, New York, but I would spend every summer with my dad back in Venezuela.

---

* Caldera later served as president of Venezuela from 1969 to 1974 and from 1994 to 1999. The second win came after running as an independent; Caldera won by a substantial margin, in large part because he promised to free Hugo Chávez, who was in prison at the time.

My Mom and My Stepdad

My mother was always there for us. After my parents' divorce we lived on a modest alimony from my dad. For a while my mom dated an ex-marine. We three boys were inspired by this and organized a Great Neck Junior Marines. The group included neighborhood children ranging in age from five to twelve. My older brother Daniel, twelve at the time, was our general. The five-year-olds were the privates. There were about twenty kids altogether, and we all had army surplus uniforms and rifles from World War II that sold for two dollars. The barrels were plugged so the guns couldn't shoot. Our parents thought we were cute, marching up and down the street.

A fort we built in the empty lot across the street from my house was the main site of our games. We played "war," usually against the Germans, sometimes against the Japanese. Once one of the kids came up with the idea that we should fight Stalin, but most of us didn't know who Stalin was.

My mom had a hard time with me and my brothers as we entered our teens. I remember lying down with about five other kids in a tomato garden on a hill just above a road, throwing tomatoes at cars as they drove by. Another prank was to station kids on each side of the road. As a car approached we pretended that we had a rope lying across the roadway and suddenly mimed yanking it taut in front of the oncoming car. We got in serious trouble for all this and more. What compelled us to do those kinds of things is not clear to me to this day—it seems almost universal for kids of that age—but I do wonder if that rebellious energy had something to do with all three of us getting involved with radical politics as we grew older.

When I was fourteen my mom married Robert Ratner, one of the kindest and dearest people I have ever met. He was of Jewish heritage yet was not observant, and his background added a whole new dimension to our cultural understanding. To this day I am friends with some of his old friends. He was very kind to my mom and the two of them had a wonderful life together. They went on cruises and loved going dancing.

Robert had served as president of the America-Israel Cultural Foundation and later became CEO of the United Nations Association (as mentioned in chapter 1). He worked closely with Robert Benjamin, who, with Arthur Krim, headed the United Artists movie studio from 1951 to 1981. In elementary school my best friend was Alan Benjamin, Bob Benjamin's nephew, who lived one block from our elementary school. We used to play canasta after school at his house. My memories of Alan are of a dear childhood friend. We went through those really early years together when you start talking about girls.

I met my very first girlfriend, Barbara Walker, in Coral Gables, Florida. My family lived in Coral Gables for about two years, when I was eleven until I was about thirteen. Barbara and I went to one movie together, but then I moved back to Great Neck because my mom was about to marry Robert.

Then I started liking a girl named Helene, who lived right near Alan Benjamin. Helene's parents had died in a Nazi concentration camp. All she had to remember her parents by was a little box made out of matchsticks. That made a deep impression on me. Living in Great Neck at that time and having many Jewish friends made me aware of the history of the Jewish people and of the discrimination and suffering they have endured.

In ninth grade I ran for class president and lost to a very nice boy, Neal, who ended up becoming Helene's boyfriend. So I lost the election and the girl. My brother Antonio did better in his early foray into politics, and was elected president of his class when he was a senior at Great Neck South High School.

My mother suffered increasingly as my brothers and I grew up and got involved in radical politics. She and my stepdad cared deeply for all of us, but my mom hounded me endlessly to stop being a radical, get married, get a job, and have kids. My stepdad was more measured and didn't criticize me, but I knew he agreed with her.

My Father, the Developer

It was great when I was young to spend summers with my dad in Venezuela. We lived in a small house my father rented—he always rented; he thought of his yacht as his home. My two brothers and I went swimming all day or sailed on little Sailfish boats my dad bought for us. Early on my dad worked to end malaria in Venezuela as a cofounder of INOS, the National Institute of Sanitary Works. After that he began his career as a developer, eventually obtaining a doctorate in Mathematics and Physics from La Universidad Central de Venezuela in Caracas.

His first resort project, started in 1950, was the Laguna Beach Club in the seaside town of Caraballeda, just northeast of Caracas. Almost sixty years later it is still there in good shape. Laguna Beach Club was one of Latin America's first condominium complexes—that is, each apartment was sold as real estate property. Laguna Beach Club stands next to a small lagoon and also has a beautiful sandy beach on the ocean. At the time of its construction it was the second-tallest building in Venezuela, fourteen stories high.

One day when I was about twelve or thirteen, we were spending the day at the pool at Laguna Beach Club. Sitting on the patio, my father pointed out two girls, maybe five or six years old, and said to me, "Look at those two little girls in the swimming pool, Morella and Nancy. They are your relatives, they are your cousins." One of those little girls, Morella Anzola, is now my wife.

From the start my dad financed his construction projects in an innovative way. He created a model of his building, developed all the plans, and then pre-sold some of the units on installment payments. Once he had a critical mass of contracts, he would then approach a bank about getting the financing to build. As he built, he kept selling contracts. My dad used a similar model of financing throughout his career, from Laguna Beach Club to the six-hundred-store Plaza Mayor shopping center in Puerto La Cruz, which he finished at the age of eighty. One of his greatest achievements is the Complejo Turístico El Morro (El Morro tourist complex), which encompasses some two thousand acres along the Puerto La Cruz coastline and helped to launch the Venezuelan tourist industry with its thirty thousand hotel rooms, restaurants, shops, marinas, and twelve miles of navigable canals.

Corruption was rampant in the Venezuelan construction industry and remains so to this day. It was common for builders to cheat on building requirements, pay kickbacks to politicians, and buy off the inspectors. My dad never cut corners. He built everything to code. After the devastating 1967 earthquake in Caracas, which killed hundreds of people and left eighty thousand homeless, countless buildings in the beach areas collapsed, some of them right next to my dad's projects. Remarkably, once the dust had settled it became apparent that all my dad's buildings had held firm with no damage, and no one in them had been injured. People realized that Venezuela had at least one honest developer who built to code—my dad—and this served as a huge boost to his career.

All three of us boys worked for my dad at one point or another. One summer my older brother Daniel, who was always looking to make money, got my father to hire him as a kind of accountant-paymaster for the various construction projects. Daniel was in charge of paying the workers each week. One evening during dinner my brother proudly announced that one of the workers had lost his pay, but for my dad not to worry because Daniel had paid him again. My brother lost his job. I think my dad found him something else to do.

I was a teenager when my father was working on Club Puerto Azul, a resort yacht club in the beach town of Naiguata. At the end of the workday, the younger workers would go to the beach to play soccer, and I usually played with them. Looking back, I'm sure that they took care not to knock me over or anything since I was the boss's son. But I remember the pain and confusion I felt as I made friends with these young people, who worked so hard all day and lived in slums. What they were building was exclusively for people of wealth. Their work made everything possible and yet the workers owned nothing, receiving only enough pay to survive.

When I was sixteen I climbed up on the roof of one of my dad's buildings, Bahía Del Mar, to watch the sun rise. To my left was the ocean and to my right the mountains. Along the mountainside I could see all the shacks of the working people. I looked out over the ocean and then I turned and looked where the working people lived. I made myself a promise. I actually said it slowly and out loud to myself: "I will spend my life fighting for them. This is not right, this is not right." I remember thinking very clearly, "On the day I die I want to be able to say to myself, 'I tried.'"

I Enter the Olympics

Whenever my father finished a project he took a break to go sailing. No one else in his family had ever been involved in sailing, but from an early age he had a love of sailboats. As an adult he bought himself a yacht and sailed all over the world. Over the years he bought larger and larger boats until he owned a beautiful eighty-five-foot ketch called the *Caribana*. At that time I was living in the United States in the slums on Manhattan's Lower East Side, subsisting on an income less than minimum wage, but occasionally I would take a vacation with my dad on his yacht. The contrast in lifestyles was astounding. It made me understand social classes clear as day. I didn't read about it; I lived it. Both sides.

My dad's racing boat of choice was Star Class—a two-person, 22.7-foot, sloop-rigged keelboat—and I sailed with him. In the late 1950s we raced in the South American Championship in Brazil and in the North American Championship in San Diego. Then he asked me to join him in the competition to qualify for the 1960 Summer Olympics in Rome, representing Venezuela. I was twenty years old.

We entered the qualification race at Lake Maracaibo and won easily, but a problem arose. Although I was a dual Venezuelan and U.S. citizen—all children born of Venezuelan parents are considered Venezuelan by law, no matter where they are born—I had no official proof that I was Venezuelan. At the last minute my dad was able to get my papers and so I was off to Italy for the Summer Olympics.

The sailing competitions were held not in landlocked Rome but in Naples, on the southwestern coast. The Soviet sailing team had come in dead last in the 1956 Olympics, so everyone took pity on them and made room for them at the start of the first race. But after they won that race by defeating several favorites, some entrants started trying to block the Soviets at the starting line.

Following each race the protocol was to take the boats out of the water. One day my dad and I walked past the Soviet boat and my dad, who was super-anti-anything having to do with socialism or Soviet Russia, said to me, "What a terrible boat they make." So I climbed into the Soviet boat, took a look around, and reported back, "Dad, their boat was made in New Jersey."

While I was in the Russian boat I noticed something intriguing. Next to the mast was a piece of paper with charts on it and a pencil hanging on a string. The following day I asked one of the Russian team members, "What are you doing with the paper, pencil, and charts next to your mast?" He said that they charted the wind so they could catch what direction it was shifting. Of course, if you could catch even a 2 percent shift and made a long tack in the right direction, you could turn that knowledge into many yards of advantage. I told my dad, "Let's follow the Russians."

There was only one race left. From the start Venezuela was right behind the Soviet boat. The Russians took a long tack while all the others, except us, went the other way, tacking back and forth following the Italians. Suddenly we were completely separated from all the other boats. It was just the Russians and Venezuela. The Russians were about fifty meters ahead of us. When we came upon the first buoy, sure enough, the Russians were in first place and we were in second, well ahead of everyone else.

The race course was to run three buoys two times. Running the wind, we continued to gain on the Soviets because we were lighter (at the time I weighed 120 pounds, a handicap for us when we were climbing the wind). At the halfway point the Russians suddenly changed course from what they had done before and one of them started waving and shouting furiously at us but we couldn't make out what he was trying to tell us. My dad thought that we should repeat what we did on the first leg. "Forget what they are doing now. It doesn't look right," he said, but I urged him to keep following the Russians.

As it turned out the Soviets knew that they had already won the overall gold, given the number of points they had accumulated in the combined races. They had been instructed to sail past a boat with a camera crew to get footage for Russian television. So rather than winning the race, what we achieved was an unintended appearance on USSR national television. As a result we came in twelfth or so. In the overall sailing competition Venezuela finished in the top half of the fifty-odd countries represented.

Competing in the Olympics was truly a once-in-a-lifetime experience. I only wish that I still had my Olympic jacket and my bronze participants' medallion. Unfortunately they were stolen out of my car in the late 1970s. I would do almost anything to have those mementos back to give to my grandchildren.

CHAPTER 3

POLITICS AND PEOPLE DURING MY TEENS AND EARLY TWENTIES

Discovering Socialism

When I was twelve years old, for reasons I do not entirely understand, I became interested in politics. I had heard at school that Russia was a dictatorship and treated people awfully. This, of course, turned out to be true enough. I wanted to do something about it and told my dad I was going to go to West Point when I grew up so I could help liberate Russia.

Not long after, at about thirteen, I was talking to my Aunt Milagro in Barquisimeto, and I told her I wished Venezuela were run by the United States because in the United States there were no poor people. She informed me that there were indeed poor people in the United States and that I had it exactly backward: people in Venezuela were poor because the United States did in fact run Venezuela by supporting our local dictator and controlling our economy.

I was taken aback by her comments. I loved, respected, and trusted my Aunt Milagro, yet that was not my dad's point of view or that of any other relative I had. She planted a seed of doubt in my mind. Then in ninth grade my teacher handed out some materials that depicted how terrible socialism was. An illustration showed a person being carried on a pedestal by working people who looked like slaves; the person sitting on the pedestal had a whip with the label "Bureaucrat." Under the illustration was the caption, "SOCIALISM." I, of course, assumed this was accurate.

But one day in the library I found a book called *Isms*. I borrowed it and at home discovered that it defined political words. When I got to the entry for "socialism," it read something like "production for use, not for profit, democratically run." I was stunned. That was so different from what I had been taught by my teacher. So I took the book to school and asked my teacher to explain why this book said something different from what he had taught us. He answered that socialists may claim to be for democracy and sharing, but that's not what they really do.

My curiosity was aroused. One day I saw an ad in the *New York Times* for socialist literature. It was a tiny ad sponsored by the Socialist Labor Party, an old, somewhat sectarian group, as I would learn later. Using my allowance money I sent away for a catalog of publications and then ordered some pamphlets. I started reading Karl Marx and Frederick Engels. I could hardly understand anything. But I took away these notions: socialists wanted people to be equal and they didn't like it that the rich got everything and working people were poor. These ideas fit exactly with what I had observed my whole life in Venezuela. I certainly didn't read anything that indicated opposition to democracy.

This made me very suspicious. I wanted desperately to understand more. While attending a folk concert in New York City with other teenagers—I think Pete Seeger was singing—I bought some socialist newspapers, including the *Young Socialist*. I kept ordering more literature.

At fourteen I told my mom I was now a socialist. She told me to go out and play. I asked permission to go from our home in Great Neck on Long Island to New York City to attend a meeting of the Socialist Union. To my amazement, as I look back, my mother said it was okay but that I had to be back by 10:00 p.m. I traveled alone on the Long Island Rail Road to my first meeting. I'd imagined that it would be in a huge hall with thousands of workers with red banners or something along those lines. As it turned out I was the first person to show up, so I sat and waited. Only about fifteen people came. I later learned that the Socialist Union, led by Bert Cochran, had broken off from the Socialist Workers Party in 1953. They were very nice to me. I couldn't understand anything they were talking about but I could tell they supported the poor and were in favor of equality. The small size of the meeting didn't turn me off. On the contrary, I thought, I need to find a way to help because the socialists are so outnumbered.

Jill Carlton

As a teenager my interest in politics was strong but more or less parallel with my other concerns—school, sports, and girls. One day the balance shifted pretty dramatically.

When I was sixteen I went to my friend Bruce Carlton's house after school. Bruce was smart and we tended to talk about math and science. As we walked through the front door I glanced into the living room and his fourteen-year-old sister Jill was lying on a couch reading. She looked up for a second to see who was coming in. Our eyes met and something extraordinary happened to me, I could feel my body changing. I didn't know what was happening—my blood vessels must have been constricting. I was in a panic. From that point on my brain stopped working. All I could think about were those eyes.

I couldn't let Bruce know. But after that Bruce and I became really close friends as I kept finding reasons to go to his house. Soon enough he figured it out and said to me, "You're after my sister." I replied, "You got that right."

Finally I was able to get up my courage to ask Jill to a basketball game. In 1956 you couldn't drive at night unless you were eighteen, so my mom had to drive us. It's different now, but in the 1950s America was a socially repressive place for youth. I couldn't tell Jill I liked her directly, so instead I shook her hand and held her coat. She knew immediately.

Jill and I lived a typical teenage life of the 1950s. We went to dance parties almost every weekend, saw movies, hung out with friends. Her parents owned a home on Martha's Vineyard and during the summer we had picnics on the beach, went swimming, and played tennis. Jill was extremely smart and could polish off the crossword puzzles in the *New York Times*, something I couldn't do at all.

I solved the no-driving-at-night problem by borrowing the driver's license of one of my best friends. Van Mow was Chinese and the two of us looked completely different. Yet when Jill and I went parking and the police checked up on us, they always okayed everything, even after looking at Van's license. They were unfailingly polite, flashing their lights and waiting a minute or two before approaching our car. They always told us to go home but then left us alone.

With Jill's permission let me just say that we became two very happy teenagers. To this day I thank her for making my adolescent life a blessing— together we avoided the confusion and suffering that so many other teenagers experienced because of the sexual repression and ignorance in our society.

I told my personal story of first love while running for governor in California to illuminate in an indirect way why we must support full rights for gays and lesbians, including marriage. As I said to the primarily young audiences, I had no choice. I was a heterosexual, period. It's no different for gays and lesbians. They look into the eyes of someone of their own sex and their brain stops working.

I'd say to the young people, "I know you are going through the same thing I went through. It's okay, you're fine, you're normal; it's our society that is wrong." The laughter and applause that exploded, not just from students but from adults in the audience too, were amazing. Being open about your own life experiences has a huge impact on young people when you relate on issues that are real and immediate to them but that many in our society deem unacceptable topics for conversation.

As an added benefit to my teenaged bliss, I also got to meet Jill's grandmother, Mina Eskanazi. She was a socialist and in 1922 had run for Congress as a socialist in the Sixth Congressional District of New York, receiving 7.26 percent of the vote. In 1956 there was a movement in New York to run a socialist for governor, which brought together various socialist currents including the weekly *National Guardian* newspaper, members of the Communist Party and the Socialist Workers Party, and many independent socialists. Jill's grandma invited me to go with her to a meeting of this unity effort.

That was the first time I met members of the Socialist Workers Party (SWP). That meeting would change my life.

Barry Sheppard

At school I did very well in math but not as well in English. On the SAT as a junior in high school I finished the math section well before anyone else. I got an 800, which was the highest score possible; I got about 650 in English. The math score helped get me accepted to the Massachusetts Institute of Technology.

When I entered MIT in Cambridge, Massachusetts, I knew no one. But soon I met Barry Sheppard, a senior and, like me, a math major. Barry had a broad range of interests beyond mathematics—I was amazed by his knowledge of world history, Marxism, theories of psychology, and much more. We sat around talking about all kinds of things and became close friends.

Barry was a member of the Young People's Socialist League. In December 1958 I joined the SWP Youth at a conference of supporters of its newspaper, the *Young Socialist*. SWP Youth was a bit to the left of the Young People's Socialist League. But Barry and I put aside our political differences to try to form a student socialist group in Boston. We called it the Greater Boston Socialist Student Organization. Eventually we had about twenty people of varying views in our little group.

Our efforts drew in two other MIT math majors. One was Gus Horowitz, my roommate at MIT. Gus and I spent endless hours talking, especially while he was reconsidering his religious views. I remember the day we went to lunch at a non-kosher place in Great Neck and he announced, "Okay, watch this. I am going to eat a hamburger." It was incredible to watch him break free of the strictures. The other math major was Ron Payne, an extremely dedicated and self-sacrificing individual. Ron and I were very close all our lives.

In 1959 I decided to join the SWP proper. Barry came with me to the meeting in Boston; we don't remember it quite the same way, but his memory is probably better than mine. The organizer of the SWP branch in Boston was Larry Trainer, a printer of Irish descent. He started the meeting with a long speech aimed at Barry and me, explaining that we had both asked to join the party, and then made a motion to accept us into membership. There were about fifteen SWP members in the room. As I remember it, Barry had just come to witness the meeting, but kept his mouth shut and joined anyway. He remembers it differently and insists that he did intend to join. Regardless, Barry and I worked together for many years. Political differences drove us apart for a time, but in recent years we have rekindled our friendship.

Soon after Barry and I joined the SWP, we dissolved our MIT student group. Most members joined us in forming a *Young Socialist* support group in Boston. In April 1960 we founded the SWP-led Young Socialist Alliance (YSA).

In 1961, Barry and I moved to New York to become the national leaders of the YSA. I knew I wanted to be a full-time activist, so I decided to leave MIT behind. Barry was elected the YSA's national chairman and I was the national secretary. At that time the YSA was a very small organization, with probably only about 150 members nationally. It would expand rapidly, both in size and influence, when the anti–Vietnam War movement began in 1965.

I Am Drafted

At twenty I was drafted into the army. When I went to be inducted I refused to sign the loyalty oath. That oath no longer exists. In addition to pledging to uphold the Constitution the oath required you to swear that you didn't belong to any of a list of about 150 organizations deemed "subversive," which had been selected arbitrarily by the attorney general. None of the groups on the list had the right to appeal its designation as "subversive." The whole process clearly violated the First Amendment so the army avoided ever letting it be examined by the courts.

Officials handed out the loyalty oath to about fifty inductees in the room. Then they told us where to sign. No one read it or had any idea what he was signing. I knew this was coming so I handed it back without a signature. About twenty minutes later a soldier came up to me and said, "You forgot to sign this." I said, "No, I didn't forget. I don't violate the law and that form is illegal."

A few minutes later a captain came to see me. I was surprised because the captain was a woman. (This was 1960.) Her first comment to me was, "I know why you did this." I thought she was going to say she knew I was a socialist. Instead she observed, "You've been to college." I almost laughed out loud. After giving me a "last chance" to sign she told me to go home and that I would hear from the army later.

After a time I received a letter stating that I had been rejected from the Armed Forces and given a 4-F status—unfit for military service for medical, psychological, or moral reasons. There was a certain stigma to getting a 4-F as it meant something was "wrong" with you, anything from asthma or flat feet to being gay. It did cause prospective employers to look at you more closely. But the army offered me an appeal if I wanted to serve. I wrote back saying yes, I wanted to serve, since it was illegal for them not to let me serve.

I was given a hearing. This amounted to a right-wing Cuban emigrant asking if I knew a list of people from Great Neck who, I figured, had been or were suspected to be members of the Communist Party. I didn't recognize any of the names, but even if I had I wouldn't have admitted it. A tape recorder in front of me had its power switched off to make it seem as though they weren't taping everything I said, although I'm sure they were, just from some other source. It did cross my mind to whisper to the Cuban in Spanish, "You're doing a great job. It wasn't easy for the Party to get you in," to get a laugh wondering how he would explain that to his superiors, but I stayed quiet. After the questioning I was told they would contact me. The army sent me another letter stating I was a 4-F and would not be allowed to serve.

The Cuban Revolution

In January 1959 the U.S.-backed Batista dictatorship in Cuba fell and the July 26 Movement, led by Fidel Castro, came to power.* In the summer of 1960 I went to Cuba in a delegation of six YSAers. For me it was a joyous experience to witness a country, brutally ruled for years on behalf of America's corporations, that was now in the hands of people who aspired to eliminate the corruption, exploitation, and poverty that had been the hallmarks of the Batista dictatorship.

The six of us YSAers got on a train and traveled from Havana to Santiago de Cuba for a huge July 26 rally. All the international guests going to the event were aboard the train. We made a sign to put in the window that said, "Americans for Cuba." At each station stop I climbed out onto the platform, overlooking crowds that came out to cheer the visitors, and gave a speech on behalf of Americans who believed in the right of the Cuban people to rule their own country. At every stop we got enthusiastic cheers.

In Santiago de Cuba the rally took place in a huge open field. We were led up to the stage. Sitting with us were some of the original twelve July 26 Movement survivors who started the revolution to liberate Cuba from Batista's pro-corporate dictatorship. Later Fidel Castro arrived and wanted to shake hands with all the international guests. Everyone lined up to shake his hand. I didn't because I thought it disrespectful to waste his time. Now I wish I had.

Two helicopters circled above us to protect the crowd and the Cuban leaders. There was constant fear the CIA would try to assassinate Castro or others. Of course the whole world knows they have tried but failed for many decades. With the helicopters buzzing you couldn't hear the speakers so the crowd started waving up at the helicopters. It took a while for the pilots to figure it out and fly off a distance so the rally could begin.

The commitment level of the youth we talked to was overwhelming. I was struck by their massive support for the revolution and how it must feel

---

* The July 26 Movement was named to commemorate an attack by anti-Batista rebels on the Moncado army barracks in Santiago de Cuba on July 26, 1953. Only twelve rebels survived, including Fidel and Raul Castro.

when people oppressed their whole lives suddenly had a government that aimed to represent them. I would wager that every one of them would have given their lives on the spot to protect what they viewed as their liberation from U.S. domination.

Public Speaking

In 1962 I toured the United States speaking in defense of Cuba. I had given the first speech in my life at the age of nineteen in Boston, while at MIT. With that very first speech I found I had a natural affinity for public speaking. I don't know exactly why, although I think it has something to do with the strong oral culture of Latin America. As the years passed I developed and deepened my ability to address a crowd with humor and persuasiveness. Many jokes have just come to me while I was speaking. But I have always prepared some jokes ahead of time too, ones I have tested and know will work with a crowd, because I have found that nothing does more to get people to listen to you than humor.

To me, public speaking is its own art form. In the 1970s a speech-and-debate teacher came to listen to me and said she found it very interesting that I violated a lot of what are considered the rules of speechmaking, but that my style was exceptionally effective. Through the years I have learned small but specific techniques—for example, that a moment of sudden silence will gather the audience's concentration, or that you can sense whether or not you are reaching people. You can feel it in the audience's physical movement. During a talk the audience is participating much more than they are aware. At rallies people really speak to each other through their responses.

One of the keys to effective political speaking is the use of what are called defensive formulations. With a defensive formulation, you base a position around something people already understand and support, such as people's battles for democracy and freedom, something positive and generally accepted. By doing so you can create a bridge from the audience's existing awareness to something that they might not yet understand or even have considered.

The Civil Rights Movement

The other great influence on my life in the early 1960s was the developing mass struggle against Jim Crow, the peculiar U.S. form of apartheid discrimination against African Americans and other people of color. As early as the age of fourteen I sent money from my allowance to Anne and Carl Braden, Kentucky-based white supporters of the African American civil rights movement. I remember writing them, "This is all I can send you but I will try to send you more." Years later, when I ran for president, Anne told me that she remembered my sending her my allowance and said, "I endorsed you just for that."

The two years that I lived in Coral Gables, Florida, from ages eleven to thirteen, I witnessed and lived Jim Crow as a white person. No African Americans were allowed in my school. No African American was allowed in downtown Miami after 6:00 p.m. It was a permanent curfew.

Once when I was on a bus the driver stopped the vehicle, stood up, and told a pregnant African American woman to get up so a white woman could sit. The pregnant woman had sat as close as she could to the "black" section of the bus, which was marked by a dotted line across the floor. The "black" section was full so the pregnant woman had nowhere else to sit. She got up and stood. I was twelve and sitting nearby so I got up and gave her my seat in the "white" section. I stood in front of her, between her and the bus driver. The bus driver stood still, looking at me with hate in his face, but after a moment decided not to do anything about it and went back to driving the bus.

When a black chain gang was working on our block, my mother turned to me and said, "This is just wrong, what they do to blacks in this country." I don't know where my mother got her views; she rarely spoke of race in any context, but she voiced her thoughts aloud to me that one day. In our home with my mother there was never any racism. Things were different in Venezuela, where the idea of white superiority was simply an accepted concept, although one seldom discussed in upper-class circles.

There was plenty of racism in Great Neck, too, just not as blatant as that of the South. When we moved back, my eighth or ninth grade teacher met with my mom, as she did with all parents. When she heard we had lived in Florida, she said to my mother, "They know how to handle Negroes in Florida."

At Great Neck North High School I played on the varsity soccer team, along with two of my best friends, Van Mow and his brother Maurice. One day our coach, Richard Chamberlain, kicked the Mow brothers off the team, presumably for being Chinese.

Van and Maurice were the children of General P. T. Mow, deputy commander of the Chinese air force during World War II under Chiang Kai-shek.

In 1952, while on assignment in the United States to buy aircraft parts for Taiwan, General Mow was accused by his government of failing to account for some $7 million. He denied the charge but had to go into hiding in Mexico for fear of being assassinated. When the affair blew over the Mow family moved to Great Neck. They clearly didn't have the millions their father was accused of embezzling. In fact, they had no resources at all so they started a small Chinese restaurant in Great Neck. It was not easy for this one Chinese family in a town of Anglos.*

Extremely upset by our coach's actions, I talked to the other players and got them all to agree to quit the team if Maurice and Van weren't allowed back. I thought that if we all quit, Great Neck North would have no soccer team and this would attract attention, maybe enough to get the coach fired. Instead the coach asked each player for a private meeting. When he met with me he said, "You know what Maurice is," meaning, of course, Chinese. I answered, "Yes, so what?" By the time he had met with the rest of my teammates, I was amazed and disappointed to discover that the entire soccer team except me had gone back on their promise to quit.

Van, Maurice, and I decided to form our own soccer team. We got a coach who lived a block away from me, recruited a handful of other players, and joined a league that played on weekends.

When I got to MIT, the first small socialist group that I cofounded was focused on supporting the struggle for civil rights. We picketed the local Woolworth's in sympathy with the ongoing protests and sit-ins at segregated Woolworth lunch counters in the South. Every weekend we mobilized people to picket Woolworth's as well as other stores that discriminated.

Before I joined the SWP in 1959, one particular aspect of the party that impressed me was learning that during the 1955–56 Montgomery bus boycott in Alabama, the SWP worked to help from early on, including donating station wagons to support the boycott and delivering them to Montgomery.

Selma, Alabama

Years later, in 1965, I went to Selma, Alabama, to take part in the third and last of the three voting rights marches to Montgomery that year. I walked

---

* Van Mow is now a highly regarded scientist and Maurice Mow teaches at Chico State University in California.

the fifty-four miles, much of the way no more than ten feet from Martin Luther King Jr. The march took five days and four nights. During all that time I never actually met King. As we marched I noticed that FBI agents were there to protect him. It bothered me since I did not trust them, but I was glad they were there nonetheless. Later it would be revealed that the FBI was working to destroy Martin Luther King, targeting him in one of their vicious programs against anyone fighting for social justice in America.

In the procession to Montgomery we passed a tiny school for African Americans. Jesse Jackson approached King and asked him to stop and circle the school to hold a prayer so the media would film the despicable conditions of schools for African American children. King looked at the FBI agents. They said no. Undeterred, Jackson recruited a small group of young people, ran over to the school, and started his pray-in. I was impressed by Jackson's defiance, his determination to tell the truth.

As we marched people stopped to watch along the roadside. White workers stood in silence, some showing hatred toward the marchers. African American workers stood on buildings and cheered for the marchers as we passed. The first night we slept on the grass of a large courtyard. During the night racists threw bricks at the sleeping demonstrators.

On the way back we were all jammed into station wagons. I was about three station wagons from the one driven by Viola Liuzzo, a thirty-nine-year-old white civil rights activist from Detroit with five children. A short while later that day she was murdered by a group of Ku Klux Klansmen who chased her car for twenty miles after she left our caravan to drop off some civil rights workers. In time it was revealed to the public that one of the people in the KKK car was an FBI informer. You have to wonder why the FBI couldn't have arrested those people before they killed Viola Liuzzo.

Malcolm X

In the early 1960s I got to know Malcolm X and became quite close to his assistant James Shabazz, with whom I went on several speaking tours. Malcolm X was not the widely admired hero then that he became after his death. The vast majority of the black movement was focused on the integrationist civil rights struggle, led most prominently by Martin Luther King. Most white liberal and radical organizations, as well as a large part of the African American leadership, didn't view black separatist groups like the Nation of Islam, to which Malcolm belonged, as contributing to the struggle.

The SWP was one of the first organizations comprised primarily of European Americans to make contact with Malcolm X while he was still in the Nation of Islam and to offer its support.

The Nation of Islam (NOI) had existed since 1930 but with little national prominence. As Malcolm X rose within its ranks, at the beginning of the 1960s the NOI began staging dramatic public actions, which included demonstrations against police brutality and big public meetings calling on American blacks to demand their own state or to return to Africa. The NOI also implemented regular street-corner sales of their newspaper, *Muhammad Speaks.*

SWP members came in contact with the NOI in several cities and admired their discipline, pride, and aggressive defense of the black community. In 1963 the SWP had a major discussion about black nationalism. Two of the older members, Robert Desverney, who was black, and George Breitman, who was white, argued strongly that the SWP should be supportive of black nationalism and in particular of Malcolm X and the NOI. SWP members were convinced. The party began a collaborative, continuing relationship with Malcolm that grew closer after his split from the NOI to found the Organization of Afro-American Unity in 1964. During that same time period most other mainly white radical groups continued to denounce the NOI as black racists.

I met Malcolm X on several occasions. I used to go to Harlem to hear him speak. The meetings were designated for African Americans only, so Malcolm set up a front row for "reporters" so that those of us who were not of African descent but supported Malcolm could attend. We sold the SWP paper, the *Militant,* at the meetings. The SWP members selling the paper included European Americans; sometimes there would be hostility expressed. But Malcolm would tell the audience, "Buy the *Militant.* They are the only people telling the truth about us." Sales always picked up after Malcolm spoke.

Malcolm's speeches were something to see and hear. The SWP helped contribute to his legacy by collecting many of his speeches in the book *Malcolm X Speaks.** It is still in print today and serves as a wonderful introduction to Malcolm's ideas and his passion. I would add, though, having been present at some of them, that the printed page can't convey the feeling that existed in the room. You can't feel the body language, how he stood so proudly, honoring the African people and the traditions of struggle in America against

---

* George Breitman, ed., *Malcolm X Speaks: Selected Speeches and Statements* (New York, NY: Grove Press, 1994).

racism. One of his many strengths was his ability to make African Americans proud of their heritage, explaining how their culture, history, and lives had been stolen from them. He would denounce Christians as the people who had enslaved, raped, and murdered Africans. The room would break out in cheers and applause and laughter as Malcolm described how Europeans had lived in caves, eating raw meat, while great cultures had thrived in Africa.

Malcolm held one belief in common with the SWP that, in particular, bonded the two groups: he expressed complete opposition to the two-party electoral monopoly of the Democratic and Republican parties. Over and over he would urge people never to vote for either of the two parties that had robbed them of their rights, that lynched them, that betrayed them day and night. His message was revolutionary. He wanted only the full truth—no compromise with injustice. He criticized Martin Luther King for calling only for nonviolent resistance. Malcolm X believed that people had the right to defend themselves by any means necessary.

Malcolm's assistant, James Shabazz, and I traveled together on speaking tours. Like Malcolm, James was clear in calling for complete and total equality—not tomorrow but right now. Repeatedly he would explain how the two-party system betrays and fools people into supporting injustice. It is one of the great misfortunes of America that the undemocratic electoral system—which does not allow for proportional representation or for runoffs that could permit an independent political force to be built—has led over time to African Americans becoming Democrats by a large margin.

Today most African Americans have ended up in the party that in the not-so-distant past championed slavery, racism, and Jim Crow segregation, solely because in their eyes the other party looked even worse. Until the late 1940s segregation still existed in many restaurants and in real estate dealings of the Democratic-controlled cities of the North. Into the mid-1960s, most northern Democrats continued to refuse to break with their openly segregationist fellow party members in the South. Most Americans do not know that, even as late as the Franklin D. Roosevelt administration, lynchings were announced on the radio and in newspapers. In some cases the railroad offered special train fares to a lynching. The NAACP begged President Roosevelt, the most famous Democratic Party leader of the twentieth century, to have the federal government intervene to stop lynchings. Roosevelt's answer was that he had no jurisdiction to intervene in state matters, in Alabama or elsewhere. During the 1950s, when Lyndon B. Johnson headed the Democrats in the Senate, he bragged that he had blocked discussion of discrimination in the South and had prevented the passage of any anti-lynching bill.

In 1965, when President Johnson tried to recover some of the political support he had lost through his war in Vietnam by finally backing a voting rights act for the South, most Southern Democrats bolted from the party and went over to the Republicans. This defection helped win a second term for Richard Nixon in 1972. It was only then that the Democrats shifted from being an openly racist party and accepted the end of Jim Crow.

The Democrats have continued to co-opt and sideline every serious protest movement for social justice. Our electoral system is set up consciously to prevent people from being able to gain representation by forming independent parties. When I ran for governor in the 2003 recall election in California, the ethnic group that gave the Green Party its highest vote was African Americans, with Latinos second. I firmly believe that if truly free elections were ever allowed in the United States, the Democrats would lose their Latino and African American base.

At the huge 1963 rally in Washington, D.C., at which Martin Luther King gave his "I Have a Dream" speech, the SWPers were selling an issue of the *Militant* with a headline that called for the formation of an independent African American political party. We sold every single one of the thousands of papers we had brought. I believe it was ten thousand copies. I remember digging through trash cans for discarded papers and reselling them.

It was a terrible blow to all of us in the SWP when Malcolm was assassinated in February 1965. I attended his funeral. Malcolm X had a profound impact on me and it was very painful to lose him. Malcolm's murder, like the murder of Martin Luther King three years later, was a great tragedy for America and a devastating setback to building a movement for social justice.

I should add that as the years have passed I have shifted a bit in my view of Martin Luther King. I see him now more clearly as a great figure for social justice, whereas in the 1960s his call for nonviolent resistance had bothered me. Today I understand better the necessity of that call, given the relationship of forces—the hostility of the power structure toward African Americans and the violence confronting the African American community. It is hard to grasp today the courage it took for him to protest the greatest crime of American history right in the heartland of the ignorance, violence, and brutality that racism has perpetuated throughout our nation's existence.

CHAPTER 4

I MOVE TO BERKELEY

Toward the end of 1965 the YSA sent me to Berkeley to help develop the organization in California.* In the four years since Barry Sheppard and I had moved to New York to head the national office, the YSA had grown a bit and some excellent leaders had emerged. The real standout was Jack Barnes, a Carleton College graduate who had joined the YSA and SWP in Minneapolis. Jack helped recruit a group of very capable leaders into the YSA, including Carleton classmates Larry Seigle, Dan Styron, and Mary-Alice Waters; while at graduate school at Northwestern, Jack brought in brothers Joel and Jon Britton, Lew Jones, and several more from the Chicago area.

Jack and his companion, Betsey Stone, entered the New York core of the YSA in 1964. By that time the San Francisco Bay Area was starting to emerge as a center of protest activity, and the YSA determined that I should go to California to help build the movement on the West Coast.

Meanwhile, Deborah Weinstein and I were married in New York in 1965. Debbie was the daughter of two SWP members, Nat and Sylvia Weinstein,

---

* I wish to emphasize that this is a memoir, not a history, including not a history of the Berkeley student movement for the years that I lived there. It is about some of the major experiences I participated in. Many other things happened in Berkeley in the sixties and I do not mean to understate or not recognize the participation of others in that tumultuous period.

who were among the most committed, hardworking SWPers I had ever met.* Debbie and I moved in with her parents to save money for our move to California. In a one-bedroom apartment in Brooklyn, this was rough on everybody. Her parents slept in the living room and Debbie and I slept in the bedroom. But that wasn't all: Debbie's sister Bonnie and her husband, Roland Sheppard (Barry's brother), also slept in the bedroom. As I mentioned: rough on everybody.

Working Overtime

To earn extra income for the move I got two jobs as a computer operator in Manhattan. One shift started at 8:00 a.m. and ended at 4:00 p.m. The other started at 4:00 p.m. across the street and ended at midnight. Afterward I would catch the subway to Brooklyn, fall asleep, and then wake up to rush back to work on Sixth Avenue. I only kept this up for about two months, but we were able to pay for our airfare to California.

I had first worked as a computer operator at Diners Club, the charge card company. At Diners Club the computer filled a large room yet had only about the computing power of a handheld calculator today. Programs were put in with punch cards and the computer worked off four huge tape drives. I often worked the night shift, which involved putting in a program and then waiting five hours for the computer to update files or print bills. People were awed by the computer. I once played a joke on one of the supervisors by inserting into the print memory the statement, "Ouch, don't close my printer so hard." Then I left the printer door slightly ajar and when the supervisor passed by I asked him to close it. When he did, the computer immediately printed the message. He was flabbergasted.

Until I was forty-five, my main occupation was working for the social justice movement at below minimum wage. But I also worked many other jobs at various times to make ends meet. My first non-movement job was filing cards for an insurance company for two dollars an hour. The other workers showed me almost immediately how to make a little extra by saying you'd work overtime. Once people had left the building you could take the cards you were supposed to file, hide them, handwrite a later exit time on

---

* Nat and Sylvia Weinstein were forced out of the SWP in 1983 in a political dispute, but both of them remained true to their beliefs throughout their lives. Sylvia died in 2001; Nat is still active in social justice work.

your time card—there was no time clock—and go home. The next day you could just file the cards you'd hidden.

I also worked for a period as a painter's apprentice, until I was asked to paint the ceiling of a church without a safety harness. I quit, preferring to stay alive.

Debbie and I flew out to California in late 1965 and rented a small apartment on Dwight Way in Berkeley. Debbie got a job and I started working for the movement. I registered at UC Berkeley as a history major. Some people think I was part of the Berkeley Free Speech Movement (FSM) * but I didn't move to the West Coast until nearly a year after the FSM protests of late 1964–early 1965. When Debbie and I arrived there were only about fifteen YSA members at UC Berkeley. A San Francisco chapter across the bay was about the same size. SWP membership was a bit larger and included some people who had been involved since the 1930s and '40s.

Berkeley already had a national reputation as a center for opposition to the Vietnam War. In May 1965 the Vietnam Day Committee (VDC), organized mainly by activist Jerry Rubin and math professor Stephen Smale, held a two-day teach-in on the war that drew thirty-five thousand people. I joined the Berkeley chapter of the Student Mobilization Committee Against the War in Vietnam (SMC), a national organization formed in the fall of 1966 as the youth affiliate of the various National Mobilization antiwar coalitions.

The SMC didn't require that its members hold any particular beliefs outside of wanting the United States to immediately withdraw from Vietnam. This open approach was supported by the SWP and the YSA, which worked to build up the SMC in cities with SWP or YSA branches. The SWP understood that the development of a genuinely united mass movement against the war was of crucial importance and that people didn't have to agree on the nature of capitalism, the two-party system, or other issues in order to work together to demonstrate against the war.

---

* The FSM, led by famed spokesman Mario Savio and other students, fought the UC Berkeley administration for students' right to free speech on campus. I met Mario Savio early on and had the greatest regard for him. We disagreed on some things but he was always the kindest person, respectful to everyone. In the late sixties during the antiwar upsurge in which I was very active one CIA agent called me "the Mario Savio of his day." I found that very flattering but the truth is that Mario Savio was such an exceptional and marvelous person that no one could compare to him.

In contrast, many left groups at that time mandated that potential participants agree with them on all manner of issues before joining a demonstration or antiwar action. For example, Students for a Democratic Society (SDS), briefly the largest left-wing student organization in the country, had called the first big national antiwar demonstration, in Washington, D.C., in April 1965. Later SDS abstained from large demonstrations and tried to assert its control over smaller, more militant actions that demanded agreement on many other issues. The Communist Party wanted to orient the antiwar movement to support what they called the "liberal wing" of the Democratic Party.

But at successive national conferences the SWP's open policy tended to carry the day as independent antiwar activists saw the SWP as defending their right to be part of a movement without having to agree to a broader agenda.

When we leafleted to form chapters of the SMC, the response was excellent. Some of our own members argued that working to build this other organization represented a failure to go out and publicize the YSA itself. But by working intensely with hundreds and soon thousands of students angry about the war, we drew a number of them to the YSA. Young people respected our competence as SMC activists and grew interested in our interpretation of the roots of the war. We explained, student by student, the illegal history of the war, how both parties—the Democrats, who were in power, as well as the Republicans—supported the war while the whole world opposed it. Some became interested in learning more and attended classes organized by the YSA. Many chose to join the organization.

Part of what made us attractive was precisely our support for a single-issue, united antiwar movement. Of course, our positions against racism, for social justice, and opposition to totalitarianism whether in Latin America or in Stalinist Russia, were always presented up front in our literature and speeches. When I spoke as a representative of the antiwar movement I limited myself to the issues around Vietnam but presented them in such a way that audiences could see the broader connections between the war and monied interests.

One of the SWP's older national leaders, Tom Kerry, was the first as I recall to promote the concept of a united-front antiwar movement in the SWP. Our initial inclination in the YSA had been to suggest that antiwar committees take a stance against the Democratic Party, which was obviously sponsoring the war. Tom argued that our primary task was to help build a massive popular opposition to the war. He explained that a by-product of that effort, independent of the antiwar movement, would lead to people being open to our advocacy to break with the two-party system. Without the SWP many of the massive, united antiwar protests that occurred all over the United States might not have taken place.

I was out speaking publicly against the war almost immediately upon arriving in California. At first the meetings were small, only twenty or thirty people. As time passed the meetings got bigger until there were audiences of thousands. The crowd usually kept growing as I spoke. I would take a microphone onto an open campus area outdoors and just start talking. I threw in a lot of jokes, which always helped. One of my crowd-pleasers described casualties in Vietnam. I would say, "When casualties are reported every night you will notice that on one side they say a nationality, the United States; on the other they say an ideology, communists. For instance they will say 20 Americans were killed, but they killed 1,500 communists. If they were consistent and gave an ideological breakdown, it would be something like 30 conservatives, 42 liberals, 155 socialists, and 250 apoliticals were killed and 4 existentialists were missing."

Students would break out in laughter as they recognized that the reports in the media were heavily shaped by propaganda. To report, day in and day out, that Americans killed *Vietnamese* in Vietnam would bring home who was the aggressor. The word "communist" was used to stop people from thinking about what was really happening. Today there are slightly different terms, such as "insurgents" or "terrorists," used for the same purpose—to avoid having to say Americans killed *Iraqis* in Iraq.

I would describe how the United States had airplanes to bomb and kill, they had tanks and bulletproof jackets, while the Vietnamese freedom fighters had no tanks, no airplanes, nothing but rifles. The truth was that the people in Vietnam did not support the United States. The overwhelming majority was against the imperialist U.S. invasion and for the National Liberation Front (NLF). That was why the Vietnamese could sustain immense casualties and still continue to fight for their country's independence.

As the American public, on campuses and across the country, became increasingly aware of the reality of the war in Vietnam, there was a massive transformation of public opinion. It was the first time in my life, at least in the context of campus politics, that those of us who opposed the war and strongly opposed U.S. policy found ourselves in the majority.

Stop the Draft

Students in Berkeley began reaching out to draftees, urging them to refuse to fight an illegal, murderous war. In the summer of 1965 the Vietnam Day Committee (VDC) had begun demonstrating along the train tracks that brought recruits to the Armed Forces Induction Center in Oakland. Students tried to stop the troop trains and leafleted the arriving GIs. This effort continued in various forms via multiple groups, leading to a massive explosion in Oakland in October 1967.

Numerous student antiwar groups called for a Stop the Draft Week of demonstrations to begin on October 16, 1967, in Oakland. In preparation they planned to hold an organizational meeting on the Berkeley campus. The Alameda County Board of Supervisors voted to ban the meeting. Such a ban, of course, was in violation of the U.S. Constitution. The university formally took the position that they disagreed with the supervisors but would respect their decision, and proceeded to padlock the hall where the meeting was to have been held.

The response on campus and throughout the Bay Area was angry. As evening approached, students began milling around the plaza in front of Sproul Hall, where the campus administrative offices were located. We in the YSA discussed the situation and decided to set up a microphone—a precious asset we owned—on Sproul Steps. The microphone went up around 9:00 p.m. and we opened it to anyone who wanted to speak. The rally began to grow and soon there were several thousand in attendance. In all some 135 people spoke that night, including about 35 professors. I spoke around midnight and stayed at the rally all night. Being twenty-seven, a bit older than most students, I was exhausted by daybreak. I remember suggesting to others, "Let's call another rally for tomorrow night and plan what to do later." But the audience by this point was made up largely of high school students and young college students, and they had no intention of stopping. Chants broke out of "Let's march on Oakland!"

I could feel the gathering intensity and knew that a march was inevitable. The YSAers at the rally declared our support and so did every other group present. Spontaneously a few thousand people, a very young crowd, began marching toward downtown Oakland, where draftees would be arriving. As the marchers entered the city the Oakland police were mobilizing and calling for assistance from other police forces. Word had gone out through the grapevine and, I believe, on the radio and TV. Young people along the way ran up to join the demonstrators. The police didn't know how to confront the growing crowd because students began spreading out across many blocks, leaving the police with only thin lines to confront them.

I watched as several students commandeered a bus parked on a slight incline. They put the bus in neutral, released the parking brake, and began pushing it so it would roll down toward a line of police. Other students quickly surrounded the bus to stop it. Movement leaders, including us in the YSA, had no control over what was happening. The demonstration had become a spontaneous outbreak of anger against the war and the draft.

Some protestors threw rocks at the police. Others argued not to use violence. The police began beating students as well as reporters, who had started popping up all over the place. The reporters must have assumed the police would respect their press badges, but I saw at least one get beaten.

Incrementally a tactic developed that would be used extensively a year later in the battle for Telegraph Avenue. To shake off police advances, groups of students divided into three contingents as they came to a street corner, running in different directions. That had the effect of forcing the police to choose one direction or to separate. If they separated, their numbers dwindled. Before long they would be way outnumbered. This began happening all over and in all directions. Gradually the downtown area of Oakland was paralyzed and there just weren't enough police to do anything about it.

The angriest young people continued throwing rocks at the police, who had no way to defend themselves. Another tactic developed that would be used in later demonstrations. Students threw rocks way up in the air above the police, who had to look up to avoid being hit. While the police were looking up, other students threw rocks straight at them. The police were unprepared for this onslaught and began to retreat, trying to regroup.

The demonstrations continued all day into the afternoon. I remember being exhausted but exhilarated to see the courage and defiance of youth raised against this inhumane, murderous war. In the late afternoon, as most demonstrators began to leave, I finally went home.

The Student Elections

Then a new issue arose. In the wake of the demonstration, the university announced that they were going to suspend eleven students. The charge was nonsensical: allegedly the microphone used at the evening rally on Sproul Steps had not been preapproved. The eleven suspended students had all spoken at the evening rally. My name was among them. The university seemed to be trying to target leaders of the antiwar movement but their selection was haphazard. Many years later I would read an incredible article by Seth Rosenfeld in the *San Francisco Chronicle* explaining that then-Governor Ronald Reagan and the FBI had created a joint project with the aim of removing antiwar student leaders and professors from the Berkeley campus. The attack against the eleven students appears to have been part of that program.

We called a meeting on campus and began organizing to defend the eleven. There were huge disagreements as to how to handle this struggle. Some wanted to call a general university strike in support of the eleven. Other students didn't think that was wise. What we decided to do was to run the eleven as a slate for the ten seats on the Student Senate. Student election voting at Berkeley was done in a democratic manner, following the general concept of instant runoff voting, in which the voter selects a first, second, third choice, etc. So it was not a problem that we were running more candidates than the number of seats. The election was in a few weeks, at the end of November.

All the students charged, I recall, were European Americans except myself, a [white] Latino, and Patti Iiyama, a Japanese American. Patti was extremely brave. At that point in her Berkeley career she had only one more quarter to go to receive her masters. In the end it took her four years to get her graduate degree because the university suspended her three times. Each time she continued her political activity, putting everything at risk. Patti came from a working-class family. Her parents had been interned during World War II when all Japanese Americans in California were rounded up and put in camps. At a meeting to discuss the student elections, I remember saying something along the lines of, "The eleven are all white; we need to reach out more to the African American students." Patti yelled out, "Excuse *me*!!" The whole room broke out laughing at me.

In the meantime the administration started holding hearings for each student charged. Certain students were told if they apologized, they would not be suspended. Some did apologize and charges were dropped. For me that was not an option. When brought before the committee and questioned I immediately accused them of opposing the rule of law and violating the First Amendment of the U.S. Constitution. I compared our struggle to that of African Americans who were denied the right to vote and due process.

The committee asked me, "Would you do it again?" I answered, "Of course! Would Martin Luther King do it again? It is the administration that should be tried for what they are doing." Naturally, these answers were not popular among the professors and some moderate students involved in the so-called hearings. Patti Iiyama and others also stood up to the committee and said, "No, what we did was right; free speech is the law, not your inquisition." As the Student Senate elections drew closer everyone knew the balloting was about this issue. The administration was starting to feel the pressure of public opinion.

The night before the student elections in late November of 1967 there was a knock on my door at 2:00 a.m. I went to answer it and three policemen came in. They told me to get dressed, I was under arrest. They followed me right into my bedroom where my wife Debbie was sleeping. I told her not to worry but to spread the news once I was gone.

When I was handcuffed and inside the squad car one officer asked me, "Peter, what have you done?" I said, "I have no idea. You are the ones arresting me." Then another policeman explained that the warrant for my arrest stated only, "For Good Cause." They had no idea why I was being arrested.*

At the jail the police asked me to pick any cell I wanted. They all looked the same so I just picked one and sat down to wait. Soon the media started arriving and, amazingly, the police let TV crews right in to interview me. Early that morning the news was already on the radio and TV: "Peter Camejo has been arrested for unknown reasons." At about 5:00 a.m. a reporter from the *Oakland Tribune* telephoned the judge who had issued the arrest order, woke him up at home, and asked, "Why did you have Camejo arrested?" The judge's answer, according to the *Tribune*, was not specific. Once that comment was out the judge was in deep trouble.

I was taken to court about 10:00 a.m. the morning of the student election. I had no lawyer but when my name was called a whole group of lawyers stood up—they had heard about the arrest and had all come to defend me. The lawyers caucused among themselves and decided that the head of the ACLU would represent me. In the courtroom the ACLU attorney stated for the judge the limits under which a person in the United States can be arrested, which include having violated the law, having jumped bail,

---

* The police in Berkeley were always polite to me, as I was to them. My reputation among the police in Berkeley was that I meant no harm to them as individuals.

etc. He asked the judge, under what law did you have Mr. Camejo arrested? The judge answered, "I had my reasons. Case dismissed."

Well, that settled the result of the student elections. I won in a landslide.

The Truth About UC Berkeley

The election results were a clear victory for us. Six of our eleven candidates were elected, giving the antiwar slate control of the ten-seat Student Senate. Some of the other four student senators also voted with us on issues. During the campaign I had pledged that if elected I would use the power of the Student Union, including the $250,000 we had in the bank and our ownership of two campus buildings, to help organize the antiwar effort.

The next day UC Berkeley announced the results of the hearings: two students were suspended until the following September, myself and Reese Erlich.* Reese was a leader of SDS and very well respected. If I remember correctly the rest of the eleven were relegated to a parole-like "twilight zone," in that if they did anything else the university disliked, they too would be suspended.

Then, over the Christmas holiday break, the regents of the University of California proceeded to confiscate all student-owned university property and funds. This action was clearly in violation of the law. Official university materials, distributed to all students upon admission, stated in no uncertain terms that the students owned property, including two campus buildings. Those properties had been paid for by the ten-dollar Student Union fee paid by each student; the fees went directly to the Student Union, which was controlled by elected bodies of the students.

I wrote a column published in the *Daily Californian*, the on-campus student paper, calling this one of the greatest heists in the history of California. Administrators then threatened the student editors with reprisal if they ever ran another article like mine. Very susceptible to pressure, the editors capitulated and would not print any more articles from me.

Around this same time a student who was an aspiring reporter—and as such had a tape recorder attached to his phone—called the university and by accident was connected to a call between two very high-ranking administrators. The two administrators referred to students as "peasants" and spoke

---

* Today Reese is a journalist. His whole life Reese has defended social justice and democracy. Reese was also one of the Oakland Seven, arrested during the Stop the Draft Week demonstration of October 16.

openly about professors and students they wanted to eliminate. This student immediately called me and told me what had happened. I rushed to his apartment and heard the tape. I told him we needed to find the best way to go public with it—this would make history. My biggest mistake was not making a copy. We went to the *Daily Californian* and played the tape for the editors, expecting they would publish a transcript and a story on their front page. The editors were shocked by the tape. But then they betrayed us by calling the administration to warn them. The administration immediately confronted the student who had made the tape and told him he could go to jail for what he had done. He capitulated and destroyed the tape. The *Daily Californian* editors, even having heard the tape, refused to print anything about it.

Many people have the image of UC Berkeley during the 1960s as a hands-off, permissive university. That is not how it was. The regents and the top administrators at Berkeley, who controlled the university system, were generally pro-war right-wingers, clearly unconcerned with their violations of our Bill of Rights. In one ploy after another they tried to stamp out free speech and dissent on campus.

One employee in the university administration accidentally came across a very peculiar file and told me about it. There was a file under my younger brother's name, Antonio Camejo. All that was in the file was a warning that should he ever apply to the University of California system, he was not to be admitted because he was my brother.*

Governor Reagan Gets Scammed

Ronald Reagan launched his political career by attacking Berkeley students when he ran for governor of California in 1966 on a platform of promising to "clean up the mess at Berkeley." He referred to the campus as a "hotbed of communism and homosexuality" and later denounced me in his 1968 list of "the 10 most dangerous people in California." So it was poetic justice when we were able to turn his pro-war, anti-student views to our advantage.

---

* At the time Antonio was teaching at Merritt College in Oakland. Antonio was in the SWP. Along with Froben Lozada, an SWP member originally from Brownsville, Texas, Antonio was among the pioneers of Latino and Chicano studies in California. After a student campaign supported by black, Latino, and Anglo students at Merritt College, Froben Lozada became chairman of a new Latin and Mexican American Studies Department and my brother one of the instructors. "Third World" studies soon spread throughout the state as a by-product of the sixties radicalization and particularly the Third World Student Strike at UC Berkeley in 1969.

To raise funds for the antiwar movement we held dance parties with bands, some of which, like Jefferson Airplane, went on to national fame. At one planning meeting people were sitting around complaining that the last dance hadn't drawn enough people to make much money. A freshman stood up and announced that he had a great idea for how we could get a huge turnout but he didn't want to say aloud what he was planning to do.

He sent an anonymous telegram to Governor Reagan to warn him that there would be "nude dancing and pot smoking" at our upcoming antiwar committee dance. The governor fell for it hook, line, and sinker. Outraged, he denounced our dance in a press conference. The resulting publicity for us was phenomenal—demand for tickets soared. The day of the dance the place was packed, including university administrators and undercover police, keen to make sure there would be no illegal activities taking place.

I ran around trying to be sure no one did anything that would result in arrests or in closing down the dance, since then we would have to return all the money. Suddenly, in the middle of the psychedelic light show, I noticed that projected on the walls of the dance hall were photos of a half-dressed female. I won't give her name, since I don't have her permission, but a well-known activist was running the light show for the dance that night. She figured that the university rules hadn't mentioned anything about nude photos. It was her way of saying "to hell with you" to the establishment. Nothing happened, everyone laughed, and we raised a lot of money that night, thanks to Governor Reagan.

Marijuana ... and Jerry Rubin

In the late 1960s large numbers of youth in Berkeley smoked marijuana. Smoking marijuana was seen as an act against the "establishment," which, for those in the antiwar movement, meant the culture of those who supported the war in Vietnam.

A much more addictive drug, one that did much greater damage, was openly and legally promoted in Berkeley with the full approval of the University of California—tobacco. Students were hired to hand out free cigarettes to fellow students as they arrived for classes.* The tobacco companies knew that it takes only about two weeks to addict a person to nicotine, and after

---

* My son and daughter-in-law told me that when they went to Berkeley in the 1990s free cigarettes were still being handed out to students by the tobacco companies.

that they had an addict at their mercy. Just as today, tobacco companies had both the Democrats and Republicans as defenders and promoters of drug addiction in the name of profits. In the 1960s we had a rough idea of the dangers of smoking but the topic was rarely discussed even among the left.

So, as our society set out to addict as many people as possible to one of the most damaging and addictive drugs of all, it cracked down on a non-addictive, far less dangerous drug, marijuana. Marijuana can be habit forming, but it is not addictive like tobacco. The right way to handle it would be through education starting early in life and through programs to help those who misuse it—treating its misuse as a medical and social issue, not a criminal one. Unlike tobacco, the plant from which marijuana comes, the hemp plant, has dozens of industrial and agricultural uses, documented throughout history. Our backward society has decided that the massive worldwide promotion of tobacco is acceptable, whereas using marijuana is a terrible, criminal sin, and has legally outlawed growing the plant.

In the 1960s I had nothing against people smoking marijuana any more than I have today. But within the YSA and SWP we prohibited having anything to do with any illegal drug, including marijuana, as a matter of security for our members. We realized that the police, especially the FBI, could and would use the information to victimize antiwar or civil rights activists and make selective arrests. Over time as we discovered paid FBI informers inside our organization we noticed that often they tried to get members, especially among the younger ones, to smoke marijuana.

When the SWP was building groups within the army of soldiers that opposed the war in Vietnam, eight GIs were imprisoned in North Carolina. In prison one of the eight offered marijuana to the others. Some of the soldiers present were SWP members and immediately recognized that the GI offering the marijuana could be a cop. Sure enough, it turned out he had been planted by the military.

I have never smoked marijuana. One person in Berkeley who was continually upset about this was Jerry Rubin, cofounder of the Vietnam Day Committee (VDC), visionary activist, and all-around remarkable person. Jerry would blow marijuana smoke in my face and say, "Inhale, inhale, you've got to try it." It was a testament to my willpower that I never did—Jerry was such a persuasive personality. For instance, we YSAers held the first screening of the movie made about Vietnam Day, the giant May 1965 teach-in at Berkeley, which also included footage of the Hells Angels attack on a VDC demonstration on October 16, 1965. Even after we leafleted the entire campus, only about 150 people showed up. Soon after, Jerry did a promotional campaign for the same film and packed an auditorium with thousands.

Jerry was a never-ending cultural act with a mission. He and some of his close friends in Berkeley, including Stew Albert, spearheaded the whole countercultural rebellion that got under way at many different levels in the late 1960s. He cofounded the Youth International Party, the Yippies, which ran a pig for president in 1968 as a kind of antiestablishment joke.

Jerry thought of himself as being far more radical than I was. But after he saw me stop a policeman from arresting a student, he changed his mind and said publicly that he had underestimated me. We often disagreed sharply and at times I was upset by positions he took within the movement, but we always remained friends. One day I explained to him that I believed humans would someday live in peace; there would be no rich or poor; people's values would be totally different, with no racism or hate. He looked at me and said, "No wonder you don't need drugs. You're permanently on a high."

After the Stop the Draft Week demonstrations in Oakland of October 16, 1967, seven demonstrators were indicted. These included extremely active and well-known leaders of the movement at the time, primarily from SDS. Known as the "Oakland Seven," they were Terry Cannon, Bob Mandel, Reese Erlich, Jeff Segal, Steve Hamilton, Mike Smith, and Frank Bardacke.* Reese Erlich, of course, was the student expelled with me.

The effort to victimize and imprison them was lost by Frank J. Coakley, the district attorney of Alameda County, who was backed by Dan Mulford, the Republican representative from Berkeley. In today's world no Republican can be elected anywhere in the area around Oakland/Berkeley. But not so back in the sixties.

---

* For an account of their battle with the judicial system, see W. J. Rorabaugh, *Berkeley at War: The 1960s* (New York: Oxford Press, 1989). Frank Bardacke has an incredible story to tell of his own. After his time in the Bay Area he went to help organize immigrant workers in Watsonville, California, among other very laudatory efforts. Frank and I first met in the early sixties in Boston. Bob Mandel remains a person I have seen on occasion, still fighting the good fight. I was especially close to Steve Hamilton and Mike Smith, who were both involved in every major effort that took place while I was in Berkeley. Terry Cannon, the editor of the *Movement*, a civil rights paper, and Jeff Segal were both very respected activists and leaders but I did not know them as well.

My Brother Is Imprisoned in Mexico

At the same time as I was fighting my suspension from Berkeley in late fall 1967 an article appeared in the *New York Times* announcing that four teen people had been arrested in Mexico. One of them was my older brother, Daniel Camejo. The fourteen arrestees were accused of being part of a guerrilla organization.

Later Daniel explained to me that he didn't know any of the others except one person he had met in passing. When he was arrested the police focused on only one thing. They wanted to know where he was printing a pro-labor newspaper. At the university, my brother had answered.

The police began beating Daniel in his cell. Sometimes they would take him out, over to a desk, and ask him questions. They showed him files with information about him. The papers were all in English—this was the CIA at work.

The truth was that a printing press had been hidden in the home of a poor peasant. This man had a family with children. My brother wouldn't tell the police where the printing press was no matter how long or hard they hit him. He knew what would happen to that family if the police identified them. Finally at one of the torture sessions, which had lasted two-and-a-half days a policeman pulled a gun and cocked it. They told him, "Tell us where the press is or we will kill you." My brother never told them.

I have often wondered what I would have done under the same circumstances. I cannot express in words my respect for my brother and how I admire him for his courage. The peasant family was never arrested.

About six months earlier Daniel had been living in the United States, where he had lived most of his life, but unlike me he held only Venezuelan citizenship. He began to fear that the U.S. government might deport him to Venezuela, where leftists were being killed in prisons. The military forces of then-President Raúl Leoni had clashed sharply with the guerrillas of the FALN (Armed Forces of National Liberation) and Leoni was rounding up actual and suspected FALN supporters. Daniel had made a film about the struggles in Venezuela, including footage of the guerrilla movement. The name of the film was *The FALN*. Even though he had used a pseudonym for the film, Daniel thought the CIA might know he was the filmmaker. So he moved to Mexico to avoid being deported to Venezuela.

When I heard about the arrest in Mexico I assumed it was related to the FALN film and I feared for my brother's life if he were deported. I called my father and asked him if he could intervene with the Venezuelan government to save Daniel. My father told me he was in a very difficult position since the brother of a high-ranking Venezuelan government official had just been killed by the guerrilla movement.

I flew to Mexico City. After a quick update from Daniel's friends, I approached one of the major daily newspapers and gave an interview in which I claimed that I had made the FALN film, figuring it would be much harder for the police to arrest a U.S. citizen. I also hoped they might lift the charges against my brother. I assumed the reporter interviewing me was connected to the police.

When I went to visit Daniel at the prison, I brought some money and wore extra clothing so I could leave him some. I hid the money in my sock, but as I neared the security checkpoint I saw the police were making people take off their shoes and feeling the bottoms of their feet. With only two people in line between me and the police I moved the money out of my sock and into a pocket in my jacket. When they searched me they said, "Empty your pockets." I went through the motions, but when my hand went into the pocket with money I just pulled out a piece of paper and left the money in there. I took off the jacket and held it under my arm as they patted me down. They never checked the jacket or felt the pockets and I got through with the money.

Daniel was in the same clothes he had been arrested in a couple of weeks earlier. He was sleeping on a cold concrete floor in the chill of Mexico City. When I passed him the money, he assumed it was for all the political prisoners. "No, this is just for you," I told him. "Please keep it." It wasn't very much. I had next to nothing in those years. Then I took off most of the clothes I was wearing and gave them to him. I walked out of the prison clad in only my undershirt, pants, and shoes with no socks.

A few days later I went back to the prison to see him but was told that he had been sent to court. My fear was that they might be shipping him to Venezuela. Immediately I set off for the court to find out. On the way out there was an open yard within the prison property and then a door to the outside. I was so anxious to try to save my brother that I started running and jumped through the door.

Two secret service police were waiting on the other side of the door. Unaware, I went flying past them and headed for a taxi about half a block away. The plainclothes cops ran after me without my knowing it. Suddenly they overtook me and we all fell to the ground. They had their guns out and ordered me to get into a car. The two police officers and the driver were all dressed in civilian clothes. I had no idea who they were. In my bag they found my American passport, which they examined with great interest. Then one of the officers asked the driver to stop near a pay phone. We were parked for about half an hour while the officer made a call. During the entire experience they asked me very few questions and told me nothing. When the policeman came back from the phone call he said to the other one, "Guess what—he's a North American."

Years later, when I got copies of my massive CIA files, exactly corresponding to the date of this event there was an entry stating, "Pedro Camejo is an American citizen not a Venezuelan."

We continued to drive, heading into the countryside. This made me very nervous—if they were taking me to a normal prison it would be in the city. Suddenly we took a turn and pulled up in front of a large government building. Inside they sat me down in a chair. No handcuffs or anything. After a while someone came and got me, took me to an office, and sat me in front of a young man who said, "They're just going to deport you back to the United States, but you have to sign a form that allows them legally to deport you by stating that you have violated Mexican law. If you do not sign it they will put you in jail and bring charges." The young official leaned forward and whispered, "Sign it. I'm not lying to you. All they will do is deport you."

I didn't have a problem with it. Given that I had just been kidnapped and had done nothing illegal, I thought, sure, I'll sign anything. If it meant I wouldn't go to prison, it was definitely worth it. So I signed without even reading the form.

Immediately I was put into another car with police officers and driven to the airport. No time to get my suitcase or anything. I was given a ticket and boarded on a flight to Texas—Dallas, I think. On the plane I was seated apart from other passengers. The stewardesses were very cautious. It was too complicated to try to explain to them that I was not a criminal and was no threat to anyone; I doubt they'd have believed me if I'd tried.

In the Texas airport the immigration officials asked, in a friendly tone, "Why are you being deported ?" I explained the facts in some detail. The agent was completely sympathetic. He said, "They arrest anyone down there. You're lucky they didn't throw you in jail." He asked if I had money on me to buy a ticket to go home. I said, "No." I was allowed to make calls and arranged for a one-way ticket to San Francisco. At the time I was so relieved to get home that I didn't reflect on the true oddity of my situation: it is very rare that Latinos get deported *from* Mexico *to* the United States.

Later that week I learned that my brother had not been deported to Venezuela but remained a prisoner in Mexico. In Mexico there are no jury trials like the United States. All that happens is your lawyer writes up your arguments and the police prosecutor writes up their position and a judge, usually corrupt, rules for the police. The key in Daniel's case was for him to be sentenced to five years or less because then they let you out of jail on appeal; in the case of my brother, he would be immediately deported.

All the others arrested with my brother were given more than five years. One was killed "trying to escape." My stepfather and my mother went to work using their connections to save Daniel. Since my stepdad was Jewish, they tried to get Israeli citizenship for Daniel so he could be deported to Israel if he got less than five years. Israel didn't accept the proposal. My mother went down to Mexico and displayed a photograph of her shaking hands with President Lyndon Johnson to prison officials. She got a mattress into my brother's cell so he could sleep, plus some clothing.

My parents never provided the details but they told me they had succeeded in getting to President Johnson regarding my brother's case. What LBJ did is completely unknown to me. Nevertheless, after two-and-a-half years in jail, my brother was sentenced to five years. In the Mexican system, this meant he would then be deported. But given the utter incompetence of the police in Mexico they deported him to Colombia. Upon his arrival in Colombia the local officials asked Daniel why he was in their country. They wouldn't believe his story, so they kept him in jail for about three weeks until they were clear he was Venezuelan. They then deported him to Venezuela.

By that time the Venezuelan political climate had calmed somewhat and danger to Daniel was reduced. Also, a family member who will remain anonymous held a position in the Venezuelan government that, in part, determined what would happen to people like my brother. After about two weeks they just let Daniel go.

Of all the amazing coincidences, my brother was imprisoned in Mexico City's main prison in the same cell that had been used for Leon Trotsky's murderer.

CHAPTER 5

THE BATTLE FOR
TELEGRAPH AVENUE

Brainstorming in a Coffee Shop

Plans began in a coffee shop on Telegraph Avenue in the late spring of 1968. I was seated with several other YSAers and we were talking about recent events in France. University students had led massive strikes and demonstrations that were joined by workers, spreading throughout the country and eventually turning into a general strike. For a moment it appeared as though the French government might collapse and the strikers, with majority support, could have ushered in a real democracy in France. The crisis had become so profound that French troops stationed in Germany were mobilized to march on their own country in order for the government to regain control.

The year 1968 was a high-water mark. January saw the Tet Offensive, later regarded as the turning point in the war in Vietnam, in which the NLF dealt a stunning blow to the U.S. occupation despite having no air cover or tanks. In May and June Paris was in the hands of revolutionary students and workers. In Czechoslovakia the Prague Spring was under way in defiance of the Soviet overlords, and continued in underground conferences and resistance after the Soviet invasion in August. And in October thousands of protesting Mexican students were shot at and many killed in the Tlatelolco Massacre. It was a year when the old order was shaken around the globe. Radical change was in the air.

I asked the other YSAers in the coffee shop what they thought we could do in support of the French students. Derrel Myers, one of the most courageous and active YSAers, made a suggestion. He told me he doesn't remember making it, but I do, because I loved the idea immediately and started brainstorming how to put it into action. Here was Derrel's idea in a nutshell: Hold a demonstration on Telegraph Avenue. The avenue, which starts on the south side of the Berkeley campus, had special relevance for the antiwar movement. In April 1966, a VDC rally on Telegraph Avenue in which we had all participated was brutally attacked by the police. Two years later, that attack against a peaceful demonstration was still on the minds of antiwar activists and many ordinary citizens of Berkeley.

There were so many actions going on in Berkeley at any given time that simply calling for a rally in support of the French students and workers would probably not make much of an impact; however, holding it on Telegraph Avenue could generate publicity and substantial support. I remember suggesting a strategy: "We need to get ourselves positioned in a defensive manner, making it clear we are just seeking our right to demonstrate. Let's ask the city council to close the street to avoid any danger for the demonstrators and we will make sure no one violates the law." Telegraph Avenue, or more specifically the four blocks of it nearest to campus, was often closed for events, including just about every football game.

We predicted that the city council, made up of primarily conservative, pro-war Republicans and Democrats, would turn down our request to close the street. Their "no" vote, we calculated, could lead to publicity and attract a large turnout for the rally. The easy first step was to request a sound permit, the only permit required by law to hold a public meeting on a public sidewalk. We got the sound permit without a problem. But the street was another matter.

I went to the city council to request the closing of Telegraph Avenue and made the obvious arguments: the street was closed for all kinds of events; the majority community of students had the right to use the street; safety was of paramount importance for all involved; we would cooperate with the police, have plenty of monitors present, and make sure no one got hurt; there would be no property damage, etc. I pointed out that streets were closed all over California for Democratic and Republican candidates so they could hold political rallies, and that we represented the majority opinion in South Berkeley, where Telegraph Avenue was located. I also mentioned that Ted Kennedy had recently spoken in Berkeley without a sound permit, had blocked two streets, and had even stopped a train; no police had interfered, nor was any protest registered by the city council.

They played right into our hands. With the arrogance of power, the city council said "NO!" to the closing of Telegraph Avenue. They could barely suppress their desire for a confrontation. The Berkeley *Gazette*, controlled by a friendly right-winger, ran stories about the coming clash. I assured the media that we would not violate the city council's decision, but we asked that the council reconsider. The police forces, like characters out of central casting, began gearing up for a confrontation; unbeknownst to us, they were even drawing up plans to test the use of tear gas for the first time in Berkeley.

Word of the action went out. In spite of the predictions of violence, a rally in support of the students and workers battling in the streets of France would be held on Friday, June 28, 1968. We warned people of possible danger and requested that, unlike at many other antiwar demonstrations, no children be present.

The action was initiated by the YSA, but as plans took shape we reached out to other groups to create a coalition. With each development we called an open meeting to discuss how we would proceed. Anyone who showed up was allowed to speak and to vote. At each turn the overwhelming majority endorsed our approach: to ensure everything we did was legal, to keep Telegraph Avenue clear, not to provoke the police—and to insist on our right to hold our rally. Many students began to volunteer to work as monitors for the demonstration.

As Friday the twenty-eighth approached, we tried to anticipate every possibility. We assumed that the police would plant undercover agents among the students. A major concern was that the police might confiscate our sound equipment, so we had a large group of monitors at the ready to guide our sound truck, which had a speakers' platform and audio equipment, out of the demonstration as soon as was necessary. Predicting that the police would cut the wires of our sound equipment as their first line of attack, we set up a backup PA system in a second-floor apartment with a balcony overlooking Telegraph. The students who lived there not only gave us the use of it for the evening but let us barricade the door so the police would be slowed down in their pursuit.

The Battle Begins

This was probably one of the most preordained confrontations of the 1960s. Each side was waiting for the other to make a move. The police assumed we would give them a pretext for attacking. We had every intention not to give them one, so they would have to make a blatantly unprovoked assault. As the demonstrators began gathering, we had scouts on motorcycles check the site where the police were assembling. They reported hundreds of police massing nearby. We soon saw policemen occupy the roofs across the street from our truck with the sound equipment.

I was MCing the event. Speakers at the rally, according to the SWP *Militant*, included Paul Jacobs of the Peace and Freedom Party; Eldridge Cleaver of the Black Panther Party; Jack Bloom of the Independent Socialist Club, who worked with me closely during the whole battle; Ralph Schoenman of the Bertrand Russell Peace Foundation; and Paul Boutelle, the African American vice presidential candidate of the SWP. Anyone seeing that list today would probably notice that the speakers were all men. It was not unusual in the 1960s for women to be excluded from leadership positions or speaking opportunities. It was not because they were not leaders or were uninvolved; it was due to the depth of sexism in our society, which influenced even the most radical groups on the left, including our own movement.

As the rally unfolded I noticed the mayor of Berkeley, Wallace Johnson, and Chief of Police William Beall standing close to the speakers' platform, watching the activity. Although not closed (as we were all too well aware), the street was empty because the police had closed it off further down, at the intersection of Telegraph and Dwight Way, about five blocks down from the university. Suddenly several students walked into the street and sat down. Monitors immediately swept in and in a friendly way asked for the students not to do that, and told them why. The students agreed, got up, and moved back to the sidewalk.

The police leaders thought that was a clear enough provocation. With loudspeakers they began announcing that this was an illegal rally and everyone should leave. I responded from the microphone, "Look, there is no one on the street. You, the police, have closed the street. Let us finish our rally and there will be no violence." Then I turned to my left and called on Mayor Johnson and Chief Beall to join me on the platform. The mayor walked off. But the chief of police came forward and could see from our platform that no one was in the street. Photos from that day show Telegraph Avenue completely empty and a huge line of monitors standing arm-in-arm the entire length to keep the street clear. I pleaded with him. "You have no reason to attack us. Let the rally finish." Chief Beall was quiet. After a bit he said, "Okay, let me consider this for a couple of minutes and I'll be back."

I realized immediately that he was not in charge. He had to get permission from higher-ups to call off the attack, presumably since the city had already made a big financial commitment to breaking up the rally. Meanwhile I stayed on the microphone, announcing, "Look, everything is clear. No one is in the streets, and no one is violating the law except the police, who are saying they have the right to disperse a legal gathering of citizens." I kept pounding the message. "If they attack us, slowly move out of their way. Avoid direct confrontations but stand up for your right to demonstrate. As long as the police are in the streets so will we be." We offered no provocation. We were holding a legal rally, protected by the Constitution of the United States, yet the police were discussing whether to violate the law.

Chief Beall came back and said, "This is an illegal gathering. You have to leave." I repeated the decision for the crowd, continuing, "You, as the chief of police, by making this announcement are committing a crime. If the police attack a peaceful rally, they are the criminals." As I spoke, a policeman from a rooftop across the avenue threw a glass bottle at me, missing narrowly. If it had hit me on the head, it could have killed me.

The police began moving in. A line of ministers stood in the way, pleading with the police not to attack the students, insisting that no law was being broken. The police pushed them aside. Suddenly our sound equipment was cut off. As planned, the sound truck took off immediately and I ducked into the apartment building where our microphone now appeared on a small second-floor balcony. The door was bolted and barricaded behind me and courageous students, including, as I recall, Mike Smith and Steve Hamilton, held off the police as they tried to break into the building.

From the balcony I could see the police flanks advancing. I repeated to the demonstrators, "You are within the law. The police and state troopers are violating the Constitution of the United States. You are totally within your rights to continue to demonstrate, but avoid direct contact. Slowly move back and when you hit street corners go in three directions." I could see hundreds of youths moving back, little by little, with looks of deep, palpable anger.

It is hard today for many people to understand the fierceness of the anger underlying the antiwar sentiment. It was that anger that really motivated youth to engage in open battle with the police, state troopers, and, in this case and others, the National Guard. The mood regarding the war in Vietnam was very different than it is today regarding the wars in Iraq and Afghanistan. There was genuine mass sympathy for the people of Vietnam and the forces fighting for its national liberation. Today, confusion about the sectarian violence in Iraq and the use of terrorist methods have made the antiwar sector hesitant to express the same kind of sympathy that antiwar forces of the '60s felt for the Vietnamese liberation forces fighting the U.S. occupation.

Holding Our Ground

Now the police began launching tear gas grenades. Students responded by flinging stones at the police. Just as in Oakland the year before, some threw stones high in the air so the police would have to look up to try to dodge them while others threw straight at the police. Some students retreated to the north, where a huge bonfire blazed on campus. More and more spontaneous initiatives sprang up throughout South Berkeley as people continued to join the demonstration and refused police commands to leave.

Not long after introducing the tear gas, the police managed to occupy Telegraph Avenue past my post on the balcony. In the apartment I had a change of clothes so that I might be able to escape notice. I thought my chances would be better if I left the scene alone. Wearing an unfamiliar jacket I stepped outside and walked right between two policemen. Neither seemed to recognize me. In a matter of seconds I reached Dwight Way and walked west, past the police lines, which were all focused on the barrage of stones coming their way.

Within minutes I met up with someYSAers, who formed a small defense cohort to travel with me to protect me from arrest. The police were closing Berkeley down as they continued to spread out and shut down more streets. Any young person was viewed as the enemy and was a target for assault, including students who were simply leaving a house or crossing a street. A frat party in an apartment was broken up by the police, who then beat some of the partygoers. Young members of the community who stood in front of their homes to watch what was happening were assaulted and in some cases the police even followed people into their homes and beat them. The police had also begun to employ a new tactic that was difficult for students to defend against. A squad car traveling at forty miles per hour would bear down on demonstrators and police would launch tear gas grenades at the youths as they ran out of its way.

The first person arrested, as I recall, was Dianne Feeley, a YSAer. Many students were arrested before the night was over. As the hour grew late, I realized it was too dangerous for me to go home, as the police might show up with an order to arrest me. So for the next five nights I slept at five different locations, moving around on a motorcycle. As I learned later, the State of California had in fact ordered the Berkeley police to arrest me. Apparently they responded by asking under what law. That is all the information I was given.

At night I tuned in to radio talk shows to see how the situation was being presented to the public. The first night it was bad news—the media was playing up the contention of the police that we had taken over the street in violation of the city council's decision and were throwing stones at police and so forth. Callers were overwhelmingly hostile. Our version of events was completely missing from the discussion. On top of it all, the police were claiming that 20 percent of their forces had to go to the hospital.

The next morning we talked to the media to try to get our side out. Unfortunately much of their coverage of our side focused on me almost exclusively, rather than on the illegal aggression of the police or on our struggle for civil liberties. The San Francisco *Chronicle* ran a piece with the headline, "Who Is This New Student Leader?" Many leaders from other groups felt left out and asked me to include them at press conferences. I was glad to, and implored the media to cover what the others were saying. Through the years I have noticed how hard it is to effect, in the end, what reporters put into words. In this case they continued to focus on me, but at least the other activists understood it was not my doing.

To determine our next move, the YSA continued to bring other groups and movement leaders into the discussion. I remember having two conflicting trains of thought. One was that we would not win people over by backing down, and the other was we needed the public to understand we were not the cause of the violence. Most people seemed to be similarly torn. Some maintained that we had fought well but could never do it again—another demonstration would no doubt be smaller and would show weakness. Others disagreed, fueled by fury at the police and the bad media coverage. We compromised by calling a public gathering for 5:00 p.m. at the foot of Telegraph Avenue, in front of the campus. We voted that if more than five hundred people showed we would retake Telegraph Avenue immediately, declare our right to assemble, and challenge the police, who would probably attack again.

Early in the public meeting, I could sense that the audience mood was a proactive one. Various movement leaders evaluated the situation and offered their recommendations as to what we should do. I offered my view that there was no clear "right" thing. One deciding factor would be whether people cared enough to come. I repeated our consensus on the five-hundred-person rule. If fewer than that showed, we would not take Telegraph Avenue. More than five hundred, we would. At a predetermined time we started a head count. Four people each counted a quadrant of the audience, and when they were through they added their totals. It defies belief, but anyone who was there can vouch for this fact: the number of people present totaled *exactly* five hundred!

Most of those present were between eighteen and twenty-two. They were fearless and had that beautiful purity of youth, the need to stand up for the truth regardless of the consequences. They wanted us to fight for our rights. It was the more experienced and slightly older people like me who were more cautious. I knew if we put it to a vote, there would be no turning back. I went to the microphone, announced the confounding figure of five hundred even, and said the only way to resolve this was to let those present vote on it. Cheers and applause broke out. The vote was overwhelmingly in favor of action. As we swept onto Telegraph Avenue, the news was already on its way to radio and TV reports: "Berkeley students have taken Telegraph Avenue again."

The students marched five blocks down to Dwight Way and started erecting a barricade. I saw my close MIT buddy and YSAer Ron Payne carrying wood and asked, "Where are you guys getting this stuff?" Ron said, "A construction site nearby." I thought, oh no, now we have destruction of property on top of all the other charges they are going to bring. Plus, the police could come from any direction, so one barricade wasn't going to help much.

Drawn by the news reports, a mass of new forces came out to support us and cheers rang out all over. "Telegraph Avenue is our community! It belongs to us!" Soon we had more than two thousand people on Telegraph Avenue. This time there were no monitors. People were getting ready for a battle. Students were loading up with stones; some, I feared, had Molotov cocktails. Militant demonstrations and courage before police abuse sent one message. Throwing Molotov cocktails and injuring policemen would send another. It was our goal to come out of this demonstration with our movement strengthened by broader popular support. I didn't want anyone on either side seriously injured or killed.

Mayor Johnson showed up before the police arrived. He proposed that we move the demonstration to an empty lot where he would debate me on the issues. I recognized immediately that this was a co-optation tactic, similar to what the Democratic Party has done to every social justice movement. The mayor's proposal was nothing but an attempt to disorient us, to try to co-opt the protest, and to demobilize people who were standing up for their rights. So, at a microphone, I called all the demonstrators together and told them of the mayor's proposal. We let him speak to the students directly. I counter-proposed that, instead, he tell the police to leave, and there would be no violence—we would hold our rally and then disperse. The students put the mayor's proposal to a vote. (This was lesson one for the mayor, that movements cannot be betrayed unless their leadership assists in the betrayal.) Hardly a soul voted for his plan except some plainclothes cops in the crowd and a few parents.

After a moment a man came up to the mayor, said, "Let's go," and hustled him off. The attack was about to begin. The police could have approached from the west, the east, or the north without obstruction. Instead they went with the most dramatic option, attacking our one barricade, at the south. Students quickly set the barricade on fire and retreated as the police charged through the blazing pile of wood.

The fighting was different this time. More ferocious than the night before, youths began spontaneously breaking store windows, striking out at the corporate symbols of a society that endorsed police attacks while the media was allowed to lie, the same corrupt society that was complicit in the murder of children in Vietnam. Anger seemed to have penetrated mass consciousness among the students, and I worried that the chances of injury were now very high. One of the first windows to go was at a Bank of America branch right on Telegraph Avenue near campus. In a poorly thought-out campaign, that bank branch had decided to offer a credit card to any Berkeley student who wanted one. The resultant unpaid charges were a disaster for the branch. I have no idea how much the bank lost in the end, but I do wonder how much of the money drawn against those cards was donated to the antiwar cause.

The battle the second night was shorter but more violent. Again passersby were beaten by the police, who attacked anyone who looked young. Again the police advanced and students dispersed, spreading the battle throughout the town. The city of Berkeley was in chaos. In response to the escalation, the city council declared a military curfew and called on the National Guard to occupy Berkeley. Democrat Ron Dellums, generally considered a progressive, sided with the establishment and voted in favor of the occupation.

That night on the radio I could tell we were still losing the battle of public opinion, but a shift had begun. Talk shows were now questioning the arrests of people who had nothing to do with the demonstrations, since the number of arrests had climbed rapidly. Callers asked, "Was all this really worth not letting students use Telegraph Avenue for a rally about France?" Thinking people were starting to speak out.

Victory or loss in this fight would be decided by public opinion. If public opinion turned against the police and the city government, the effort would be a victory for us and for the movement in general. But not everyone in the movement understood this.

Turning Point

We called a public meeting for the next day. Beforehand, a negotiating committee of movement "elders," myself included, met with the mayor, vice mayor, and the city manager, who had officially called for the curfew. Among the group were some individuals whom I admired and respected greatly: Peter Frank, an attorney with the Peace and Freedom Party; Max Scherr, the editor of the *Berkeley Barb*; and Bruce Rappaport, a sociology graduate student. We had agreed to take the results of our conference with the city leaders to the public meeting, which had already amassed a crowd of nearly a thousand.

Our negotiating committee argued with the city officials for two hours but they wouldn't concede anything. We offered that if they lifted the curfew we would cancel demonstrations for the day. (I didn't like this offer and was glad when it was rejected.) We asked that they agree in principle to let us have Telegraph Avenue for a rally and proposed the date of July 4. They refused that as well. As the session ended, several members of the negotiating committee rushed to the public meeting so they could be the ones to report the results. By the time I arrived the report of our conference was already under way. Some of the speakers lacked the credibility with the rank and file to have their views prevail, and that concerned me. I waited until they finished. When I spoke, I focused on the turning point ahead, emphasizing that we needed to act carefully in order to win the public over to defending our right to assembly. The majority of the leadership and the ranks of the movement agreed. I suggested that we march out of the meeting, go outside the curfew boundaries, and start a demonstration in front of city hall to protest the mayor's refusal to compromise with us. Then, if we had enough support, we would march into the curfew area.

This last street demonstration, on June 30, was smaller than the previous two. But it showed we would not be silenced by the curfew. The police and National Guard spent that evening arresting people all over town and beating people who had nothing to do with the demonstration. Radio talk shows definitely began to shift in our favor. That night I decided the time had come to focus on the city council: their betrayal of the people of Berkeley and of the U.S. Constitution. I saw an ideal opportunity to focus public opinion on a simple choice—respect the Constitution or continue violence. The onus was on the city council. In this way, people could see more clearly that we had only asked that rights be respected; the city council had caused the violence and suffering by their refusal to allow free speech.

We called off all demonstrations for Monday, Tuesday, and Wednesday, July 1–3. We devoted all our energies to preparing for a July Fourth rally on Telegraph Avenue. The plan was a step-by-step repeat of the original effort: we would go to the city council and ask for Telegraph Avenue. We held a mass meeting on campus—outdoors, because we were not permitted to have a room—at which this strategy was approved. The meeting was the largest yet, as many as 1,500 students. Keep in mind that during the summer the university had a registration of only about 9,000.

Meanwhile the curfew continued. There were no demonstrations, but people were still being arrested and beaten on the streets of Berkeley. Public opinion was swiftly moving in our favor and the city council was becoming politically isolated. Radio talk shows were now overwhelmingly on our side. I could feel the shift in the political mood of the city.

Our next step was to attend the city council meeting the next day. Under pressure the mayor agreed to schedule a larger room than usual. But that wasn't room enough—the turnout was so massive the meeting had to be moved to an even larger hall. Never before had a thousand citizens attended a city council meeting! The meeting was historic. It lasted eight hours. As many as a hundred people spoke—and about 95 percent expressed support for the movement's proposal to close Telegraph Avenue for July Fourth. The city council was hearing not just from students but also from ministers, parents, lawyers, doctors, and countless eyewitnesses to police brutality. The pressure on the city council was palpable.

Methodically the case became clear to all those present, including the media, that if the city council did not meet our demands, the response would be so massive and widespread they would be in deep trouble. I could see victory was near if we kept the pressure up and maintained a position of uncompromising determination for our right to public use of Telegraph Avenue.

When it was my turn to speak something peculiar and serendipitous happened. I had the floor for only a few minutes and I had prepared my speech carefully. About a third of the way through, I stated, "On July Fourth you will vote to give us Telegraph Avenue with no conditions or ..." and paused for effect. I was going to continue by saying that the consequence of any violence would be on their hands as we had the right to assembly, and so forth. Instead, there was a moment of absolute silence in the room, and then from deep in the back some young person shouted out, "WAR!!" Of course that would not have been the term I would have used, but the hall burst into applause. My mind was racing. If I resumed speaking it would be a total anticlimax. Slowly I turned around to look at the applauding mass of people, especially at the youth in the room, and walked off, my back to the city council, with everyone cheering. The city council got the message.

When the issue finally came to a vote the city council tried one last maneuver to deny us our rights. They agreed to lift the curfew but voted five to four not to give us Telegraph Avenue on the Fourth, offering an alternative site for a rally. There was an immediate outcry.

That evening, in the very same hall, close to two thousand people came to our mass meeting—the largest we had ever held, and one of the most memorable in my life. The Independent Socialist Club members suggested we accept the alternative location for July Fourth. I took an unambiguous, opposite position: Telegraph Avenue was the symbol and July Fourth was our date with destiny. This combination was now a symbol of our right to dissent, to fight against the war, to protect our constitutional rights. There would be no compromise. I told the gathered activists, if you stand firm, if you do not show division, we will win! I looked at the audience and said slowly, "I promise you this, if you stand firm tonight, the city council will capitulate."

I will never forget the overwhelming vote for my motion and the hugs and cheers I received as the meeting ended. I went to sleep that night knowing the council would meet again the next morning. I couldn't see how we could lose. They would capitulate—or we would have the most monstrous demonstration ever in Berkeley on July Fourth.

The next morning I got the call and knew immediately from the excited voice on the other end of the line. "Peter, we won, the city council reconsidered and voted 5 to 3 to grant us Telegraph Avenue for July Fourth and that no police would be present, period."

July Fourth

The Fourth of July was a celebration. We didn't have to do much; the event organized itself. Bands made arrangements to perform and tables were set up all along Telegraph Avenue for any group that wanted one. The street was so packed with people you could hardly move.

There were no police and therefore no violence, just joy. This crowd was very young and the victory was in their hearts. The joy was infectious. You could feel it. Youths were smoking pot. One group set up a huge sheet as a canopy and danced nude underneath. Somewhere in the middle of everything we held a political rally, but most people just wanted to enjoy that Telegraph was ours, that we had triumphed. Lots of reporters were walking around, taking notes, talking to people. I knew the euphoric mood was affecting the reporters and hoped that the media reports would be positive. I was still a bit stunned the next day when all the reports were favorable. The TV stations and newspapers across the board recognized July Fourth on Telegraph Avenue as a victory for the student movement and reported that there was no violence, no one arrested, no property damage, and that freedom was in the air.

Of course this was but one small victory in an ocean of struggle nationally and internationally and—seen from that perspective—not all that important. But it showed me, as well as countless others, the importance of winning over public opinion and having the courage to stand up for your rights in the face of seemingly insurmountable odds.

It is important to note that the Berkeley city council never opened an investigation of the crimes committed against its citizens. No charges were

brought against the police for attacking peaceable, legal rallies or for beating random young people in the streets. Once again the two-party system
went to work, with the Democrats acting as though they supported the antiwar movement while they maneuvered to turn antiwar sentiment into
electoral support for a party that would not only demobilize the movement
but betray it.

Drawing Conclusions

The battle for Telegraph Avenue had a profound impact on me and
sparked a change in my thinking. It would take some fifteen years before I
would be able to articulate what I started to think and feel in July 1968.

Joel Britton, at that time the organizer of the Los Angeles SWP, came
up to Berkeley to lend a hand after the victory. He quickly arranged a huge
banner in front of the YSA headquarters in Berkeley that said "One, Two,
Many Berkeleys," a slogan playing on Che Guevara's call for "two, three,
many Vietnams." He set up a table with materials that urged youth to join
the YSA. Since it had been all over the media that the YSA had led the Telegraph Avenue demonstrations, many people, perhaps a hundred or more,
signed up in short order.

That evening as Joel told me how well our recruiting effort had gone I
knew it wouldn't last. Yes, some of those people would join and become active
but most would not. I had an inkling of the reasons that would be the case
but I couldn't articulate at that time how the problem could be overcome.

What I sensed was how out of touch the left, and the YSA in particular,
was with the reality of what it would take to build a mass current for social
justice. The disconnect seemed to be tied to world events of the last fifty
years, mainly the rise of Stalinism that had dominated and destroyed the
world's left and with it the great current within the United States for social
justice. Stalinism had associated the left with a totalitarian, inhuman, un-
just, anti-labor state and a horrendous dictatorship. Our current, the SWP,
was among the groups that had fought Stalinism and tried to maintain the
ideals of the world socialist movement, but our contemporary approach
was as a faction of the gigantic internal struggle within the international
socialist movement.

When you walked into our headquarters there were posters and pictures of people from all over the world, but few of the great heroes and hero-
ines of the United States who had fought for the rights of labor, against

slavery, for racial and sexual equality, and for civil liberties. I don't think a single member of our organization or any of the others on the non-Stalinist left could name the first candidate of the Liberty Party, the original third party in American history, founded in 1840 to oppose slavery; nor had any of them ever read the *North Star*, the great abolitionist newspaper founded in 1847 by Frederick Douglass. But they could tell you a great deal about Lenin, the rise of Stalin in the Soviet Union, the negative role played by the Communist Party in the Spanish Civil War of the 1930s, etc. Instead of seeing ourselves as a continuation of the abolitionist, populist, and socialist organizations that made up our people's historic struggles for justice, equality, and freedom, we asked new members to digest a huge amount of history about the rise of Stalinism and how it had destroyed the left. We were so disconnected from our own history that to join our organization and remain active, a member had to become interested and invested in the internal factional struggles of socialism in Russia and Europe. This was important but couldn't serve as the framework for a mass movement for social change.

This issue is complex but crucial to understanding why no mass left organization came out of the 1960s or even the 1930s. It is not a question of placing blame. It is a question of understanding the destructive impact that the rise of Stalinism and its domination of the left had on the possibility of building a progressive, revolutionary movement.

I can remember thinking about this topic late at night but finding no answer, no way to get around it. I consider this the main quest of my life, to try to comprehend how we could build a movement to help bring about what I believe will be an inevitable Third American Revolution. The Third Revolution will continue and complete what the First and Second Revolutions, for independence from Britain and for the end of slavery in the Civil War, showed might be possible; that is, equality and social justice within a framework in which humans do not allow exploitation or any of the irrational, inhumane practices now so common throughout our planet. The Battle for Telegraph Avenue planted in my mind questions that would take fifteen years for me even to begin to answer.

CHAPTER 6

FELONY CHARGES, A TRIP TO CUBA, AND PEOPLE'S PARK

After the victory in the battle for Telegraph Avenue, I had become fairly well known and well respected among antiwar students, and infamous among the pro-war forces in the university administration and city and state governments. In the fall of 1968 another campus battle led to felony charges being brought against me and two other student leaders. Alameda County district attorney J. Frank Coakley, who also prosecuted the Oakland Seven, allegedly promised his friends that he would put me and Jack Bloom in prison for at least three years.

My role in the events that resulted in an indictment for conspiracy was almost accidental. Eldridge Cleaver, at the time a leader of the Black Panther Party (BPP), had been invited through student initiative to teach a ten-lecture course at UC Berkeley. The course had faculty approval. Originally the administration had agreed to issue course credit for participating students but was now going back on its promise. (In the meantime Governor Reagan wanted the course eliminated completely and was urging the Board of Regents not to pay Cleaver's salary.) A group of students, largely made up of SDS members, had been leading a struggle to demand fair treatment for the course.

I was not involved. To be honest, I was ambivalent about Cleaver and the direction the BPP had taken since its founding in Oakland in October 1966.

Initially there had been more overlap between the BPP and the SWP—one of their original core members had also been a member of the SWP, and the first issues of the Black Panther newspaper were stored at the SWP headquarters. That changed quickly, as the SWP disagreed strongly with the BPP on several issues. Of major concern was their top-down organizational structure with no internal democracy. We also did not agree with some of their formulations or their support for Maoism, which we saw as glorifying a Stalinist regime.

Once I shared the platform with a BPP speaker at Berkeley High School. The meeting was held during lunch hour, outside in an area where the high school students hung out. I spoke first and gave a primarily antiwar talk. Then the BPP member, who was quite young, took the platform. A few minutes into his speech he announced, "This is the answer to the struggle," and pulled a revolver from his pocket. At the time, that kind of slogan was becoming popular among some BPP members, as well as Mao's saying, "Power comes from the barrel of a gun."

I couldn't help thinking with sadness that if Malcolm X had not been assassinated, he might have been able to influence this new generation of African American youth in a more democratic, more politically effective way. The BPP had grown fast and attracted the most radical young African Americans because of its message of the right of African Americans to self-defense. The SWP, of course, supported the BPP's right to defend their community against racist attacks, whether from the police or from individuals. Most of my personal involvement with the BPP consisted of speaking out on their behalf to defend them from police abuse and, in some cases, the outright murder of their members.

The Occupation of Moses Hall

On October 22, 1968, 121 students sat in at Sproul Hall, the main administrative building, to protest the administration's refusal to offer full credit for the Eldridge Cleaver lecture series. The sit-in was nondisruptive; the students sat quietly along the hallways. Nonetheless, the administration ordered the police to arrest all the participants. Students reacted angrily, and the mood spread quickly beyond the original group.

The next day a rally was called on Sproul Steps. I had no intention of becoming involved, but some of the leaders of the effort asked if I would lend my support by speaking out on the issue. I agreed to speak but have little recall of what I said. Since it had only been a few months since the battle for Telegraph Avenue, the media was bound to focus on my comments. As the rally on the steps drew to an end, student leaders began calling for the group to occupy Moses Hall, where the Cleaver lectures were to be held. The leaders again asked for my support   if students saw that I was taking part, it would drum up support for the cause.

Without thinking it through I agreed to help lead the group of about a thousand students to Moses Hall. We walked through the gates out of Sproul Plaza to the center of the campus. Several hundred of us entered Moses Hall, only a short distance away. The others encircled the building, began singing protest songs, and announced to passersby that Moses Hall had been occupied, which drew more supporters and onlookers. Gradually the crowd outside grew to about three thousand or so. I had climbed to the top of the building and was watching the gathering expand when a young student ran over and said, "Peter, you'll want to hear this." He set a small radio in front of me as the announcement was made: "Peter Camejo has occupied Moses Hall along with thousands of students." This is not good news, I thought. I'll end up doing time for this.

The students in the building immediately viewed me as the leader of the action. Fortunately other student leaders were there to help coordinate, and together we spread the word not to destroy any property. A small group ignored this directive and began barricading the front door and breaking furniture. Others came to me with the news that someone had offered to get weapons to help us resist the inevitable police attack. I found it hard to believe that anyone could be so wrongheaded. I rejected the suggestion outright and urged them to let me know if anyone had weapons because we would physically remove any such individuals.

In pretty short order we were able to get unanimous approval from the students to abstain from violence and destruction. We set up a sound system on the roof. Around Moses Hall bonfires were started to keep the students outside warm as they prepared to defend the building from the police. As evening approached, discussion intensified as to what our strategy should be. A demand went out for me to address the students outside on how they should respond to the police—whether to resist physically or passively.

As I saw it, the problem was that if any police officers were seriously injured, it would gain us nothing and yet would make for much more serious charges against those inside. So, speaking from the roof to the crowd below I emphasized the right to self-defense but tried to make it clear that the enemy was the administration, not the individual police. The administration was denying the rights of students and faculty to choose a course and grant the participants appropriate credit. Again I asked that no weapons be used but added that the students had every right to stand in the way of a police advance.

Radios were scattered throughout the crowd, so everyone was made aware when the police began broadcasting that they would soon be taking action to remove the students occupying Moses Hall. No attack came. Then another broadcast. Still no attack. Each time a broadcast was made the tension would build. Then no attack would come. We had been informed by students on the outside that a huge number of police had gathered in front of Sproul Hall. It dawned on me that the police leader was quite psychologically astute. He announced every half hour that they were going to attack, yet each time they did nothing, playing with our expectations. This was mentally and physically exhausting. The police seemed to assume that the students would eventually get tired and leave. As the night wore on some participants did begin to drift away.

We held another meeting inside. I proposed that when the police entered, all the demonstrators should be seated in a classroom with photographers in the back of the room to document the occurrence. That way it was unlikely anyone would be hurt, and the police could not claim we attacked them and bring additional charges. I told the students that they should all expect to be arrested, adding that they could possibly be convicted on trespassing charges, which could mean about 180 days in jail. If they didn't want to take that risk, I said, there was no shame in just leaving. It was easy to depart through an open window in the back of the building. Some students left, but a group of seventy-six remained inside.

Close to 5:00 a.m. I knew the attack was coming soon because the police could not risk attacking during university class hours. If even a few hundred students resisted at the entrance and thousands more were about, a serious confrontation could develop. Sure enough, some time before 6:00 a.m. a well-disciplined wall of police officers, six across and almost a hundred men deep, advanced toward Moses Hall. The scene looked like a Roman legion on the march in a '50s movie epic. Few students remained outside but those who had waited all night were very militant.

I watched from the roof. Some students threw firecrackers as the police came closer. Hearing the pops of noise, the front line of police dropped to the ground, thinking it might be gunfire. The rows behind kept moving and tripped over them. That stopped the advance for about half a minute.

As the police reached the front door of Moses Hall I told everyone to go sit down in the classroom. We had three photographers in the back. I stood alone by the front door. Suddenly a policeman opened the door, poked his head in to look around, then just as quickly closed the door. A couple minutes later a different police officer opened the door and said, "Hi, Peter." We shook hands. He asked, "Is everybody okay?" I said, "Yes." Carefully and politely the officer explained that we would all be arrested and taken to Alameda County jail in a police bus.

When we got to Santa Rita Jail, the lockup for Alameda County (which includes Berkeley and Oakland), I was separated from the others and placed in a solitary confinement cell, barefoot. After a few hours one of the top prison officials came to my cell and asked if they were going to have "any problems" with us. He was putting on a tough front but it was obvious the prison staff was concerned that we might have a plan, for instance, to start a hunger strike.

At the time of arrest the police had divided us by gender. I would say about half the students arrested were women—I have an old copy of a defense brochure with a photograph on its front cover that shows the women being led out of Moses Hall with police lined up on both sides. They are all holding their fists up in the air.

All the arrested students were charged with disturbing the peace, malicious mischief, and most important, trespassing—the last of which was undoubtedly true. Eventually the first two charges were dropped and the students pleaded guilty to trespassing. They were given ten days in jail with an additional eighty days suspended sentence and a restitution fine of $300 each for expenditures claimed by the university administration, including damaged furniture. On personal orders from the chancellor, fifty of those students were also suspended from UC Berkeley—the largest mass suspension in university history.

Three of those arrested—Paul Glusman, a twenty-two-year-old history major; Jack Bloom, a doctoral student in sociology; and myself—were instead charged with conspiracy to commit a misdemeanor, which is a felony and carries a possible sentence of three years and a $5,000 fine. The D.A.'s complaint specified three overt acts.* Only Jack and Paul were charged with

---

* A summary of the charges and the events leading up to them was published in a brochure distributed by the Berkeley Defense Committee, which included a long list of sponsors: sixty professors, most from Berkeley; unions; well-known individuals; and progressive journals. Among the sponsors were the editor of the Daily Californian and a few famous people, such as Dr. Benjamin Spock.

anything that resembled conspiracy, and even then the charges themselves were rather ridiculous. At the Sproul Hall rally, Paul and Jack were said to have advocated with no less than "loud-speaking equipment" that people move to a "building on the campus of the U.C. in Berkeley and physically occupy portions of that building." The charges against me were different but no less ridiculous. I was accused of having directed meetings after we were already inside Moses Hall. I do not understand fully how one can conspire to commit a crime after one has already committed the crime. But rational thought was not one of the D.A.'s strong points.

The trial for Moses Hall would not take place for almost another year.

Trip to Cuba

As 1968 closed I went to Cuba with a YSA delegation to celebrate the tenth anniversary of the revolution. I stayed for three months. The United States would not allow American citizens to travel directly to Cuba, so the rest of our delegation was flying to Mexico first. But because I had been legally banned from Mexico* following my deportation in 1967, my trip started with a flight to Spain on December 25 from New York's Kennedy airport.

About three hours out over the Atlantic one of the left engines caught fire. I could see the flames coming out of the wing. Many of us wonder, when we fly on an airplane, what our reaction would be if a catastrophe were to happen. I can tell you firsthand. My immediate feeling was of deep depression—not panic, but a profound sadness. I thought I was about to die.

The pilot came on the speaker system with a calm voice and said something like, "One of our left engines has caught on fire. We can't put out the fire so we will begin to return to Boston for an emergency landing. The stewardesses will prepare the plane for this situation. Please cooperate with them." He was amazing. His voice was utterly calm and unhurried. Next thing I knew, the plane dropped rapidly until it was just above the water. I knew you couldn't last long in the North Atlantic even if you succeeded in getting into the water alive.

A flight attendant became overwhelmed and the others sat her down and buckled her up. Then they began removing seats from the exits so people could deplane more rapidly. A woman seated in front of me started

---

* A permanent ban on my visiting Mexico was legally established by my deportation; sometime later I just went back to Mexico and it was as though the ban had never existed.

praying, not too loud, but I could hear her; at first it annoyed me. But then a feeling of sadness and compassion for all the other passengers, especially the children, came over me. I found this interesting because in the first moment my depression had been only about myself. After another twenty minutes of steady, relatively uneventful flight I could feel my body chemistry change as hope that I might live entered my head.

The entire time everyone remained quiet. The pilot started taking the plane back to a higher altitude. During all this I could see the flames licking around the dead engine. After about an hour or more the pilot came back on the speaker and explained that the plane no longer had brakes so it couldn't land in Boston. Instead, he said, we would have to head back to Kennedy airport in New York, where we had started.

It took about another hour to reach New York City. As the plane approached the landing strip I could see fire trucks moving alongside the airplane at a high speed. Even before the plane touched the ground, firefighters, looking like gunners in a World War II movie, fired sheets of foam at the flaming wing. Before the airplane hit the ground they had put the fire out.

In the early hours of the morning we boarded another aircraft and took off for Spain a second time. I had known it would be a challenge to get to Cuba, but this was more than I had bargained for.

I thought it remarkable that I could get to Cuba from a country run by fascists, but not from the United States. The flight to Cuba from Madrid was actually routed through Canada; imagine flying to Europe and back, just to arrive ninety miles south of Florida. When we arrived in Cuba, at 3:00 in the morning, customs officials took our passports and kept them. I retired to the Habana Libre hotel, where I had a great room—these many years later I still remember it was room number 716.

The next day, New Year's Eve, I met up with the other YSAers in the delegation. According to my diary this included Joel Britton (from the L.A. branch), Robin Maisel, Linda Wetter, Danny Rosenshine, Evelyn Kirsch, Maureen Jasin, Dave Prince, Paul McKnight, Derrel Myers (from Berkeley), Will Reisner, Derrick Morrison, and two others from Madison and Cleveland whose names I did not write down. Later that day Eva Chertov, an SWPer living in Cuba, joined us, as did Robert Scheer, one of the many North Americans visiting Cuba at that time. In the evening we all went to the Copacabana, where we stood and sang the *Internationale* as the clock

struck midnight. That marked the end of one of the greatest and most tumultuous years in history, 1968; it was also my twenty-ninth birthday.

I stayed in Cuba until early March 1969, traveling throughout the island, visiting factories, farms, and the very site where the liberation forces
of the July 26 Movement launched their guerrilla war to end the Batista dictatorship and U.S. control over their country. Prior to the Cuban revolution
approximately 60 percent of Cuba's territory had been owned by North
Americans or Canadians.

On Sunday, January 5, 1969, the YSA delegation had the opportunity
to hear Fidel Castro speak. It was outside Havana, with a crowd of mostly
agricultural workers. I wrote in my diary:

> Castro started talking at 5:30 p.m. His talk was excellent. His style reflects
> such deep conviction, sincerity, and honesty. He does not talk down to
> the people but is extremely honest. He came down real hard on the real-
> ities of that region. Giving facts on how little existed and how little had
> been accomplished and the problems and concepts of how to change it.
> He speaks with the confidence of someone who feels full support in the
> masses for his position. It rained heavily … We were all full of mud. Got
> back at 11:45 p.m. We ate and went straight to sleep.

At the time of my visit Cuba was, as it remains today, a society run by
a one-party system. I raised this issue with Cubans I met throughout my
stay on the island. Their responses were interesting—no one claimed it was
a good thing. Rather, they maintained it was a necessity, due to the ongoing
terrorist attacks and threats of invasion by the United States, as well as the
never-ending U.S. blockade of Cuba. They argued that if the system were
to be opened up, the CIA would pour in billions of dollars to organize an
opposition and eventually would stage an invasion or incite a civil war in
order to retake Cuba. As it turns out that is exactly what the United States
did when its puppet dictator, Somoza, was overthrown in Nicaragua. So the
argument has a great deal of validity.

Our delegation met with lower-level officials of the Cuban Communist
Party. I posed the question whether it would be a good thing for the Chinese
government to let their people read the writings of Che Guevara. The party
officials responded, yes, of course. Then, I countered, why not allow the
people in Cuba to read the writings of Mao? Their response was that, unfortunately, Cuban realities were complicated. I took that as a reference to
Cuba's dependence on the Soviet Union for survival in terms of oil, arms,

and more; of course the USSR was in heavy conflict with China. No one, neither party officials nor ordinary citizens, seemed hostile as I asked these questions. Over and over what I witnessed was a deep commitment to the creation of an egalitarian society, and a genuine sense of solidarity with all working people across the world, especially the Vietnamese.

Throughout my travels I was struck by the real-life practice of this egalitarianism. What follow are some examples that stood out when I recall this trip. I attended a trial for a young woman who had stolen shoes from a store. The judge explained to her that, unlike in most other countries, in Cuba no one person could own hundreds of shoes while others had few or none. She needed to understand that stealing was not allowed because all Cubans were sharing what was available. She was permitted to keep the shoes but was required to work on an agricultural project for two weekends to compensate the economy for what she had taken. The sentencing judge worked alongside her and others.*

The city of Havana had developed block committees to deal with very local issues. One of the block committees' innovations was to station two people on each block to sit outside at night as a neighborhood watch. I believe they were armed, because Cuba had armed its people to be able to resist a U.S. invasion. So a person walking alone at night in Havana was protected on any given block by citizens sitting outside to make sure no crime was committed. I think Havana became the safest city in the world.

I visited a tobacco factory. Workers received full pay if ill and full pay after retirement. There was one month of paid vacation each year. In all the factories I visited, decisions were made by workers' committees along with the management appointed by the various government departments that coordinated the economy. No corporations existed, no stock market, and no owners.

On the very spot where the guerrilla war for liberation had begun, I met a peasant whose home had been given to him by Castro. In the early days of the revolution the peasant had risked his life to help the guerrillas, and in return Castro had promised him this house. It was beautiful. He lived with his doors wide open and chickens running around inside.

---

* What a difference from California, where a seventeen-year-old, Santos Reyes, received a sentence of one year in prison for stealing a radio and, later in life, was sentenced twenty-six years to life for cheating on a driver's license test (he had taken the written test for an illiterate cousin). See more about this case in chapter 20.

Nelson, one of the Cubans who drove me around during my stay, had fought against the U.S. invasion at Playa Girón in April 1961 (also referred to as the Bay of Pigs invasion). He took me there to show me the museum and the battle site. Visiting the Museo Girón was a profound experience for me, as I could see so clearly that the people back home in the United States had no idea of the truth. During the invasion the U.S. media had reported nothing but lies prepared by the CIA. Adlai Stevenson, the liberal Democrat serving as U.S. ambassador to the United Nations, got up in front of the UN and lied, denying that the United States was attacking Cuba—while it was happening.

I was deeply moved to learn what had happened at a small children's school on the very beach of the invaders' landing. Teachers had packed the schoolchildren onto on a bus and driven them away from the beach to safety. But a group of teachers refused to abandon their school. They all had rifles and military training, and they were determined to hold back the invaders until reinforcements could come. Tragically they all died in the attempt. One teacher, with his blood, wrote "Fidel" on the wall as he died. The first reinforcements on the scene were young recruits from a police training school. They had only light weapons but fought off the invaders until Cuban army troops arrived. Those Cuban army troops included Fidel Castro himself.

I left Cuba on March 4, 1969, and flew back to Madrid to make a connection to Brussels. There was no burning aircraft on this leg of the journey, but I had a tough time getting back as well. At the airport in Madrid there was an eighty-cent charge to board a plane, an "airport exit charge." I had run out of money and had only sixty cents. I asked the official to please let me on the plane for sixty cents because I was physically, materially unable to pay the remaining twenty cents. The official refused to let me board. Finally the person behind me said, okay, for God's sake, here is the other twenty cents, let him on the plane.

When I arrived in Brussels, Barry Sheppard met me at the airport. I had one cent on me.

People's Park

I only spent three more months in California after returning from Cuba. But that last short period was anything but peaceful. In May, a struggle broke out over a small community park—one that took on historic importance as it foreshadowed more deadly violence yet to come. This was the famous fight for People's Park.

People's Park is a small plot of land just south of the UC Berkeley campus, bounded on the east by Bowditch Street, on the south by Dwight Way, on the north by Haste Street, and on the west by Telegraph Avenue, with a half-block stretch between the avenue and the edge of the park. In 1967 the university had exercised eminent domain to take the land, at that time a part of the surrounding residential/commercial neighborhood. They evicted local residents and bulldozed their houses, with the plan to build a student parking lot. Then the project ran out of money and, into 1969, the land sat as a muddy, unutilized mess.

Starting in April 1969, some students and neighborhood store owners conceived the idea of trying to create a community park on the empty lot. With advice and help from a landscape architect, neighborhood residents and students cleared the ground and began to plant trees, flowers, and shrubs. The university announced its disapproval but promised that no sudden action would be taken. For several weeks the park flourished as a kind of student-community center with as many as a thousand people, students and citizens of Berkeley, working on the gardens and enjoying the park.

Early in the morning of May 15, Governor Ronald Reagan ordered 250 California Highway Patrol officers and Berkeley police into People's Park. The forces rolled in at 4:45 a.m., destroyed most of the garden's plantings, and facilitated the construction of a high chain-link fence around the perimeter of the park. To Reagan the park represented the great evil of the youth radicalization that was taking place not just in Berkeley but also around the country and the world. He was openly hostile to the student antiwar movement and the counterculture, and was not about to let a successful community project get in the way of enforcing property rights.

The response to Reagan's operation was rapid. That very day three thousand people gathered on the Berkeley campus. At noon my friend Michael Lerner was holding a public demonstration on the Israeli-Arab issue but, recognizing the immediate importance of the park crisis, Michael turned over the rally to the People's Park movement. Student body president Dan Siegel called on the audience to take back the park.

As mundane life events would have it, that same day I was at home recovering from the removal of my widsom teeth. I had not been involved in the founding or tending of People's Park. Many of the park participants were part of the counterculture (also sometimes called hippies or flower children). At the time I was firmly rooted within the more traditional socialist current and viewed the counterculture as diverting people from the real struggle at hand.

Looking back, forty years later, I have modified my opinion. I think the two currents, socialist and countercultural, reflected two different aspects of the radicalization in progress. The countercultural rebels were among the first to advocate the rescue of our planet from ecological destruction. They were environmentalists long before those in the pro-labor, socialist current acknowledged the importance of other species and their interrelation with our own. The counterculture also tended to be more outspoken on behalf of the rights of women and gays. They reflected a break with Christianity and other traditional religions that they saw as limiting human happiness and potential. They were pro-sex and antiwar while traditional religions were pro-war and antisex. The famous slogan "Make love not war" originated within the counterculture before it was popularized throughout the overall antiwar movement.

So the destruction of a small community park right in the center of Berkeley, an oasis created and enjoyed by anyone who wanted to participate, became a symbol for what was happening to our planet and to humanity.

The primarily young crowd supporting People's Park swelled to about six thousand people. Reagan's chief of staff at the time was Edwin Meese III,* who had previously been the district attorney of Alameda County. Meese ordered additional police to defend the occupation of the park. The police, in full riot gear, taped over their badges so they could not be identified. For the first time ever in Berkeley the police were given orders, apparently with Reagan's approval if not at his initiative, to shoot people. The worst were the Alameda County sheriff's deputies, who carried shotguns loaded with double-ought (00) buckshot shells, rather than the usual birdshot used for crowd control in extreme circumstances. The impact of double-ought buckshot shells was described recently on a shotgun aficionado website as "essentially equivalent to getting hit with a nine-round burst from a submachine gun."†

---

* Meese would later become U.S. attorney general under Reagan, during which time he was involved in the Iran-Contra scandal and resigned in disgrace after allegations of corruption.

† See http://www.internetarmory.com/shotgun_ammo.htm.

South Berkeley erupted in confrontations between unarmed demonstrators and the various police forces, who then began shooting. Shortly beforehand I had stopped off at the SWP headquarters on the second floor of a building on Telegraph Avenue. I was looking out the open window at the demonstration below when I saw a group of officers raise their shotguns and start firing. I assumed they were shooting into the air to scare people. Someone in the office grabbed me and yelled, "Peter, get back!" It may have been in that exact round of shots that the deputies blasted a group of unarmed people, seated on the roof of the nearby Telegraph Repertory Theater, watching the action. James Rector, a student, was mortally wounded. He lingered in critical condition in a hospital for a few days. Alan Blanchard, a carpenter, was blinded. Both were just spectators on a rooftop. The deputies then began firing tear gas and double-ought shotgun shells at the demonstrators in the street, many of whom were hit in the back as they tried to run away. Many people were seriously injured; 128 people were reportedly hospitalized.

The next day, May 16, in my diary I wrote, "Listened to KPFA [Berkeley public radio]. Demonstrators marched around town all day. Police and National Guard avoided confrontation. Demonstrators leaderless. No transitional demands. Meeting announced for tonight." I was still in pain from the removal of my wisdom teeth and added, "Swelling seemed to be back almost as bad as yesterday morning."

The YSA leadership asked me to get involved to figure out how we could help with People's Park. We definitely were not trying to take the helm of this movement, but wanted to build as broad a coalition as possible behind the park while respecting those who had founded it. At the meeting that evening, the YSA proposed a mass demonstration to denounce the occupation and show support for the park. Some people were strongly opposed to the idea because it seemed too cautious—they were so furious at the police that anything that resembled a moderate approach seemed wrong. Instead the group voted in favor of a proposal by Bob Mandel* to shut down businesses on Shattuck and Telegraph Avenues. But many people began to understand that what we were aiming at was to show the breadth and strength of the support the park had in our community. Lew Jones, who was heading our intervention, decided against making a motion that

---

* Bob Mandel was also one of the Oakland Seven arrested during Stop the Draft Week in 1967.

could have carried but might have been divisive; instead he chose to wait for a better opportunity to propose a mass march with broad support.

Within days Reagan had summoned 2,700 National Guard troops to occupy Berkeley. I wrote in my diary on May 17, "We must avoid leadership of this situation. Also avoid demoralization in our own ranks." Although events had made it possible to get a massive response against the occupation and in defense of the park, we did not want to alienate the people who had been behind this issue from the beginning. The efforts had to be unified for an action to work effectively. Our own people were also deeply frustrated that we could not find a way to help more effectively.

On May 18 I went to see the park, now occupied by the National Guard, and then to a meeting of YSAers at Patti Iiyama's home. Lew Jones and I spoke about the situation, describing what we viewed as disorganization and lack of political orientation among the park founders, but emphasizing the need for unity in action. The meeting seemed to raise morale among our own people. Thinking back I now believe Lew and I were essentially right in what we said at that meeting, but I think we were a bit too harsh on the park founders.

The countercultural current in Berkeley found its own ways to respond to the situation. One tactic was for young women to approach the National Guard soldiers, who were predominantly young men, to try to explain the issues. Soldiers tended to be much less aggressive in front of women than men. When the young soldiers were inside the park surrounded by the wire fence, as though they were imprisoned, some young women danced in front of them, stripped naked to the waist. In addition to being a tremendous distraction—the soldiers hung on the fence and their officers couldn't get them to stop watching—the women were also trying to send a message to the soldiers. The message was simple: there is another, happier, world; you don't have to be doing the evil you are being ordered to do; the demonstrators are not your enemies.

Today a lot of people would understandably take issue with this approach, but in Berkeley of the late 1960s this was considered okay, clever in fact. In all peace movements women have played a major role in trying to reach the troops, who often respond with less hostility toward women than toward men. In Berkeley young women would put flowers in the soldiers' rifles, a tactic first employed at the antiwar demonstration at the Pentagon in October 1967. As the National Guard units patrolled through Berkeley people sometimes gave them cookies laced with marijuana. The strategy was to try to win over the ranks of the guard. The police forces were generally crueler and politically to the right of the younger guardsmen and seemed out of reach.

On Monday, May 19, in my diary I wrote, "At 10:12 p.m. James Rector died." To my knowledge none of the sheriff's deputies or police officers who murdered James Rector and shot civilians in the back were ever investigated. Certainly none ever faced charges. Officials in city government, Democrats along with Republicans, continued to accept and overlook these crimes by law enforcement, which now included murder.

That same day Leah Schuman, a close friend of mine, came over to tell me about what she described as an "insane" meeting at Bill Miller's house to discuss what to do about People's Park. I liked Bill, a countercultural rebel, who had run for mayor of Berkeley with a poster of himself nude from the back, sitting down. The YSA executive committee decided to try to intervene at a city council meeting set for May 20, although we didn't expect too much. I got through the National Guard surrounding city hall but the police stopped me, saying the city council chamber was full and no more people could enter. Only three hundred people were allowed into the meeting; by contrast, there were four hundred National Guards surrounding the building. The mayor would not permit an open meeting.

On May 21 a memorial rally was held for James Rector on the Berkeley campus. While the rally was in progress, National Guard soldiers, wearing gas masks and with bayonets mounted on their rifles, surrounded the students. The soldiers pointed their rifles in toward the crowd. Suddenly helicopters zoomed in and dropped tear gas on the trapped students. The gas was so extensive that it drifted into a nearby hospital and wreaked havoc on the inpatients and staff.

That same day my brother Antonio came rushing to my home to tell me he had just heard that our brother Daniel had been found guilty in Mexico, but had only been given five years. In the midst of the tragedy and turmoil in Berkeley, this was a bright spot of good news.

Thursday, May 22, I attended a mass meeting of more than five hundred people in Berkeley to consider what to do next on People's Park. There we succeeded in getting unanimous agreement to start planning a mass march for Friday, May 30. We called the planning group the Big Friday Committee. Big Friday was only eight days away. I was elated, and I could see the morale of our supporters rapidly improving—now we had a project to put our efforts behind without running the risk of alienating anyone.

This action was not counterposed to anything else happening. The aim was to show that there was massive public support for People's Park and equally massive opposition to the police and National Guard occupation of Berkeley, the arrests, shootings, and murder.

The march on Friday, May 30 was enormous, probably the largest march ever in Berkeley proper. I estimated thirty thousand to fifty thousand people. Public opinion was swinging strongly in support of People's Park. The Berkeley City Council voted 8 to 1 against the military occupation. The park was now empty and at night young people climbed over the fence to plant flowers. Each day the National Guard would be ordered to destroy them.

The massive show of strength in the march, the continued resistance to the military occupation, and the spontaneous efforts of thousands of people throughout Berkeley eventually wore down the establishment. In the end the university relented and accepted that the park would remain.

The Felony Trial

My felony trial started on October 20, 1969, nearly one year after the occupation of Moses Hall. I had left Berkeley in June and moved to Boston, so I flew back to appear in court with the other defendants, Jack Bloom and Paul Glusman. For me it was a noteworthy experience, never before having faced a jury trial on felony charges. A rally in support of the three of us was held in Berkeley with about four hundred people attending.

The first and arguably the most important step in a jury trial is the selection of the jury. We realized that if even one movement person got onto the jury they could stop a conviction, since in a criminal case a unanimous verdict is required. Of course, any students in the jury pool were eliminated immediately by the prosecution. Other machinations didn't work—one young woman promised a fellow member of the jury pool, a well-dressed young man, that she would consent to go out with him as long as he promised to vote "not guilty" on our behalf. Neither of them got selected. Some members of the jury pool stated outright that they hated demonstrators, so our side knocked them off. An African-Asian woman said she could never convict us so she too was eliminated.

Once the twelve members of the jury had been selected, I performed a little test. I looked at each juror straight in the eyes for several seconds. If a person looks at you for more than about three seconds it begins to mean something. On a subway it means you might be a nut. At a party it means you're hitting on someone. At a trial I assumed it would mean, Are you for us? Most of the jurors looked away after a couple of seconds. But one African American woman stared back at me calmly. As the seconds passed I had to conceal my joy at knowing one person seemed to be on our side.

The prosecution, naturally, was led by Alameda County D.A. J. Frank Coakley. Coakley, as mentioned, was publicly hostile to the movement in general and to me and Jack Bloom in particular. Our defense was led by Art Wells, a Berkeley attorney. Art defended a lot of movement people throughout those years. Our fundraisers did so poorly we could hardly pay him. I have always felt bad about that.

Each day of the trial students would drop in to watch the proceedings. The prosecution's case for conspiracy was quite weak. An undercover policeman posing as a reporter had interviewed me inside Moses Hall during the occupation. At one point, with a tape recorder running, he had asked me how we had planned the action. On the tape it was impossible to make out what I said. A third voice could be heard, shouting, "Hey, Peter, what's happening?" so loudly that my response to the "reporter" was drowned out. I have no idea what I answered.

At one point a police officer testified for the prosecution. During the cross examination Art Wells asked him, "Do you know who Peter Camejo is?" He answered, "Yes." Wells then asked a variation of his question, elaborating, "Camejo is well known and you have seen him before so you would have no problem identifying him?" The police officer again answered "Yes." Then Wells turned to the jury and said slowly, "Well then, explain why when you came in today you turned to the prosecutor and asked him who was Peter Camejo." The policeman answered something like, "What? I didn't ask anyone who Camejo is." Wells responded, "No more questions."

It was decided that the three of us would not testify because our defense figured that the prosecution had failed to prove conspiracy ("beyond a reasonable doubt" is the legal standard for a jury to convict). Art Wells thought it best to not take the risk that some unforeseen detail might come out in testimony that could give the prosecution any advantage. We got some media coverage, so every other day Jack, Paul, and I were out speaking publicly about the trial. Paul and Jack seemed a lot calmer than I was. They tried to scare me by joking that once we were all in prison they would sneak in some pot to smoke. It worked, it scared me.

The trial lasted almost two weeks. On October 30, 1969, the night of the jury's decision, I wrote in my diary,

> I played chess … More and more people came to hear verdict. Finally we went to dinner. County Clerk joined us. We were a little nervous. The word—through bailiff—was a majority were against us. We worried for Paul Glusman. Finally at 10:30 p.m. the judge brought down the jury and asked how they were doing. The foreman said they were divided on two defendants but agreed on one and implied a conviction by saying, "The problem is can you have a one-man conspiracy?" Everyone's heart sank. About 100 were present. I felt mad and bitter—preferred to be found guilty if Paul was found guilty. Jury went out and came back. They read the verdict. It was for me not Paul and it was "not guilty." The clerk could not finish reading as everyone jumped up applauding and shouting. The jury hung 4 to 8 on Paul and Jack. We all went to Dave's [Dave Warren]* house for drinks. Everyone was happy. Jack and Paul will go for a hearing Nov. 3rd.

At the hearing Jack and Paul pled guilty to trespass. They were sentenced to five days in jail but were released after three.[†]

My diary continues, referring to my opinion that we needed a more political defense—more focused on civil liberties—to convince the jury. Still, I was glad to see Berkeley again, even if only for a few weeks while facing a hostile prosecutor. I wrote, "It's all over. I'm leaving Berkeley now for good. It was a happy two weeks and I'll miss Berkeley terribly."

---

* Dave and Penny Warren were great friends to me in Berkeley and afterward.

† Jack Bloom, a sociology doctoral student, had been a leader of the American Federation of Teachers union on campus. He was suspended because of Moses Hall and had already been blackballed from three California State colleges because of his political activity. Through support from his department chair he was able to keep his TA job, but didn't finish his PhD until 1980. Paul Glusman, only twenty-two and a history major, was dismissed from the university because of Moses Hall. Paul later wrote articles for various progressive journals including *Ramparts* and the *Express Times*.

CHAPTER 7

THE ANTIWAR MOVEMENT

From the past few chapters it might seem as though much of my time in the 1960s was spent in confrontations with the Berkeley police. That is only part of the picture. Most of the time I was working to build civil rights actions or the anti–Vietnam War movement and, concurrently, to help build the YSA and the SWP. The student antiwar movement expanded rapidly in the years after 1965 and grew to massive proportions by 1969–70. Outside of civil rights actions it was the first time in my life that I was involved in a genuine struggle of millions of people.

As with the entire book, this section on the antiwar movement is not meant to be a history. Recollecting my own experiences, I also want to outline the major political issues within the movement and my views on them both then and today. In addition to my recollections and diary I have drawn on Fred Halstead's *Out Now: A Participant's Account of the American Movement against the Vietnam War.** I knew Fred Halstead personally for years.

---

* (Anchor Books, 1978; Pathfinder, 2001.) Halstead's 729-page book offers an outstanding documented history of the Vietnam antiwar period, focusing on the periodic huge national demonstrations, mostly in Washington, D.C., New York, and San Francisco, and the organizations and conferences that built them. It is mandatory reading for anyone who wants to understand the events of that time. While Halstead wrote from a particular point of view, one with which I agree, he tries very hard to present accurately the views, opinions, and actions of currents with which he disagreed.

A member of the SWP, he played a crucial role in the leadership of the major national demonstrations against the war and was the SWP's presidential candidate in 1968.

Differences within the Antiwar Movement

Depictions of the antiwar movement of the 1960s most often feature protestors with signs proclaiming "Out Now!" But it took several years of struggle to get that position accepted. We had to overcome the influence of liberals, mainly from the Democratic Party—the party in power—who were against unequivocal opposition to the U.S. war. The liberal Democrats tended halfheartedly to support the U.S. invasion under the guise of fighting "communism" but favored negotiations to end the conflict.

Throughout the lifespan of the Vietnam antiwar movement, internal differences were constant and at times quite divisive. This tends to be the rule, not the exception, in movements for social change. But understanding the differences can be very useful (especially in those experiences of the 1960s and early 1970s) and teach us about building a massive pro-peace movement. Looking back some forty years later, I remain convinced that without the SWP/YSA current, the antiwar movement in the United States would have been weaker and its effectiveness limited.

Single Issue versus Multi-issue

When the first antiwar committees began appearing, as early as 1963–64, YSA members instinctively wanted to propose the passage of a resolution that opposed voting for either of the two parties supporting the war—the Democratic Party in particular, due to its greater influence among the left. This was my initial instinct too. But a debate broke out within the YSA/SWP over this issue. It was decided that we would be undermining the possibility of a united, massive movement against the war if we started pushing for other issues within it. Successfully opposing the war would in and of itself be an immense victory. If we could help create such a movement and played a nonsectarian role it would reflect well on our organization and people would become more open to listening to us on other issues.

During the antiwar era, there were three major political currents in the struggle against the Vietnam War. One approach was to orient the movement to work inside the Democratic Party. At certain times this current supported united mass actions, namely in non-election years. These groups included the Communist Party and its youth wing, the W. E. B. Du Bois Clubs; the Social Democratic organizations; and the liberal wing of the Democratic Party itself.

I belonged to the second current, a broad coalition. It called for a united, single-issue antiwar effort in order to reach the most people. At the same time all the groups in the coalition were free to promote their broader agendas separately—setting up literature tables, leafleting, or carrying banners for their particular views—but not to impose those views on others as a precondition for working together against the war.*

The third, rather loose, current I called "ultraleft." They tended to oppose mass actions, which they viewed as a waste of time, focusing instead on street theater or open confrontations with the police to attract media attention. This current drew many of its supporters from the burgeoning counterculture, although the counterculture was infinitely broader than this specific, antiwar segment. Eventually, frustrated radicals rose to the leadership of the ultraleft. They insisted that limiting a mass demonstration to a central antiwar position was intrinsically wrong and that other issues—usually openly revolutionary ones, such as calling for a victory for the Vietnamese NLF and defeat of the United States—had to be included.

On occasion this third current called their own actions but the turnouts were generally dismal. When they tried to form coalitions based around multi-issue platforms, the coalitions fell apart almost as fast as they were assembled, since the only unity they had was an opposition to the big antiwar marches. Gradually some among the ultraleft turned to unprincipled strategies. When demonstrations were called with an agreed-upon, public policy of nonviolence (on the basis of which many participants chose to come), some ultraleft groups tried to stir up confrontations with the police in order to "revolutionize" the large demonstrations. In many instances they stormed the speakers' platform, took the microphone from the organizers, and harangued the audience about their views. Their effect was often counterpro-

---

* It amazes me that, even today, progressives within the movement still have a problem comprehending the value of actions with unity around an important issue. When millions of Latinos and their allies marched throughout the United States in 2006 in the largest demonstrations in our country's history, it was around the issue of immigration and the persecution of undocumented workers. No one in their right mind would have demanded that they also agree with other very important concerns in order to participate in a united action, such as calling for single-payer health care, abortion rights, gay marriage equality, opposition to the war in Iraq, opposition to the Democrats, and so on.

ductive and tended to play right into the hands of pro-war forces, since the fear of violence made many people hesitant to attend antiwar marches. Undercover agents inside the movement, which included FBI as well as local police, used the same tactics of promoting disunity through confrontational politics as a way to weaken the movement.

This third current was supported by most of the leaders of SDS, which had begun life in 1962 as an extremely moderate student group. SDS had lurched to the far left after its successful Washington march in 1965, eventually shattering into rival fragments that included various Maoist groups and the Weather Underground. This current also included people such as Jerry Rubin and Abbie Hoffman from the counterculture.

The pacifists were divided among all three currents, although some, like the highly respected pacifist leader Dave Dellinger, tried hard for a long period to form a bloc with the ultraleft in an attempt to develop pacifist mass civil disobedience.

Berkeley's Vietnam Day Committee

When I arrived in Berkeley in 1965 the principal antiwar group was the Vietnam Day Committee (VDC), founded by Jerry Rubin and Abbie Hoffman. The VDC had come to national attention with its May 1965 teach-in at UC Berkeley that drew a crowd of thirty-five thousand, as well as its troop train demonstrations around the Armed Forces Induction Center in Oakland. The VDC almost disappeared in 1966 when most of its founders turned their attention to the Democratic Party in support of antiwar activist Robert Scheer's campaign for Congress.

In April 1966 the VDC called a demonstration against the Vietnam War for April 12 on Telegraph Avenue (see chapter 5). The "antiwar" Democrats in the Scheer for Congress campaign criticized the VDC for calling the protest, concerned that it might affect Scheer's chances in the election. The VDC refused to cancel the protest. They requested a permit from the City of Berkeley, which was refused. Four days before the demonstration the VDC headquarters was bombed; four people were injured and the office was destroyed. On April 12, four thousand people gathered on Telegraph Avenue near Moe's Bookstore. Just as we would do again in 1968, we had set the microphone for the rally on the second floor of a nearby apartment and barricaded the door. I was speaking from the second floor when the police attack began. Fortunately the police never drew their guns and no one was seriously injured.

After the police waded into the sea of demonstrators, YSAer Patti Iiyama led a contingent of a hundred women from the action to march on city hall in protest of the police action. About half the remaining demonstrators followed. As the marchers moved toward the center of Berkeley, the police assailed them. Afterward, Robert Scheer denounced the demonstration to disassociate himself from the students and the VDC.

A week after the demonstration the VDC held a meeting to evaluate what had happened. About 120 students were present, including Jerry Rubin, who had left the VDC to support Scheer's campaign but had subsequently broken with him. Former members who were supporting Scheer stayed away. The anger toward the Scheer campaign was palpable. People were furious at having been attacked by those who were supposedly our allies. A rumor spread that Scheer himself might come to the meeting to denounce us; he never showed. During the elections for a new steering committee one young woman made a motion to send a message to Robert Scheer "to go fuck himself." We didn't vote on that motion, but it definitely would have passed.

The VDC elections strongly favored those of us who supported continuing antiwar actions regardless of what liberal Democrats like Robert Scheer wanted. Of the fifteen members of the new steering committee three were in the YSA, including Syd Stapleton, who had a played a major role in the Free Speech Movement of 1964; myself; and Jaimey Allen. Jerry Rubin was nominated but did not receive a majority. When someone nominated Bettina Aptheker,[*] a leader of the Berkeley Du Bois Club (the CP youth wing), which held a pro–Democratic Party position, the whole room broke out in cynical laughter.

These elections reflected the depth of the radicalization in Berkeley. Students began to reject voting for either of the two parties supporting the war and were absolutely furious at politicians telling them to shut up and stop protesting. But those of us in the YSA did not refuse to work with Democrats, Bob Scheer in particular,[†] where we agreed on opposition to the

---

[*] Bettina had played a major role in the Berkeley Free Speech Movement of 1964. She often fought for unity around issues such as opposing the war and was generally not factional toward the YSA and SWP.

[†] I respect Bob Scheer for many of the efforts he has made through the years to tell the truth of what is happening in the world. He wrote what is probably the best pamphlet against the war in Vietnam. As a journalist for the *Los Angeles Times* he covered issues no one else had been willing to raise. The last time I saw him was in Los Angeles at a meeting opposed to the death penalty.

war. Working with Democrats, including elected politicians, on issues on which we agreed—such as demonstrations—was considered fundamentally different from directing people to vote for candidates in the Democratic Party.

In these struggles within the VDC the Independent Socialist Club (ISC) and the YSA formed a bloc together. Some of the antiwar current that could be described as countercultural also blocked with us; they supported keeping the antiwar movement independent from support of the Democrats even if they as individuals supported candidates such as Bob Scheer.

Soon the VDC made an effort to reestablish a united antiwar movement among all the currents calling for opposition to the war. A well-attended meeting was held in San Francisco on June 23, 1966. It succeeded in bringing about unity, with only the CP abstaining. The new coalition was eventually named the United Committee to End the War in Vietnam, and the VDC declared itself the Berkeley student wing of this broader organization. The new, united antiwar formation focused on demonstrations scheduled for August of that year.

This process—argument, division due to differences, and then later, usually after elections, reunification—became the norm, and it was during those periods of unity that the most massive and effective antiwar demonstrations were built.

FBI Disruption

The FBI planted provocateurs in all the antiwar groups. (Through the Freedom of Information Act some of their activity has later come to light.) One of their objects was to try to undermine the SWP/YSA call for unity around the slogan "immediate withdrawal." As part of their larger goal of destroying the antiwar movement, the FBI sent out fake letters, distributed fake leaflets, and made false accusations that some activists were FBI informers.

Here is an excerpt from a letter sent to SWPers in early 1966 by the FBI, pretending to be criticizing the SWP from the "left," in an attempt to turn them against their own organization:

> Presently, you've been struggling with your party in its efforts to become part of the greatest ground swell of opposition to this country's imperialist policies that has ever existed … this was an unprecedented opportunity to militate against Washington and Wall Street. But, true to the SWP's history

of sectarianism, you witnessed the young "Trots" promote a divisionary and undermining line of "immediate withdrawal" at these conferences ...*

The goal of this letter to SWP members was to demoralize them, to try to convince them that their efforts to win support for the slogan "immediate withdrawal" were leading to defeat and disunity.

The FBI sent fake letters to the CP claiming to be from the SWP and fake letters to the SWP claiming to be from the CP. They handed out fake leaflets at demonstrations to incite infighting among groups. They planted informants inside all the organizations and used the information they collected to harass individuals or to get leaders fired from non-movement jobs. I was fired from one job in San Francisco unquestionably as a result of their work. The paid FBI informants inside these groups distributed illegal drugs in order to be able to arrest active members on drug charges. The arrested individual would never know that they had been illegally entrapped by the FBI due to their antiwar activity.

No one has ever been arrested, charged, or imprisoned for any of these criminal acts. Undoubtedly law enforcement officials knew of this criminal activity since they were the very ones carrying it out.

Denial of Constitutional Rights

Throughout my life's work I have experienced, time and again, nationally and locally, the ways in which the U.S. government continually violates the law in order to prevent political opposition from exercising their constitutional rights. While these violations are carried out, the media is responsible for sustaining the public's belief that they live in a law-abiding, democratically run nation.

The most egregious historical example of the denial of legal rights to American citizens is, of course, the treatment of African Americans well into the 1960s. A more extreme form of this illegal treatment existed in the Jim Crow South with the tacit support of the national government. During the antiwar movement some of the most outrageous illegal acts also occurred in the South. In Georgia, Julian Bond, an African American leader

---

* From an undated anonymous letter headed "An Open Letter to Trotskyites," written by the FBI and released as part of an SWP lawsuit. In Nelson Blackstock, *Cointelpro: The FBI's Secret War on Political Freedom* (New York: Pathfinder Press, 1976), 120.

of the Student Nonviolent Coordinating Committee (SNCC), was elected to the state legislature. But on January 10, 1966, the established legislators voted 184 to 12 not to seat him because he had endorsed SNCC's statement opposing the Vietnam War.

Federal, state, and local police agencies, as a matter of policy and with a large commitment of personnel and resources, worked to undermine political activities explicitly protected under the First Amendment of the Constitution. As in the McCarthy period of the 1950s, at the end of the 1960s the police tried to get activists fired from their jobs, to frame them on flimsy or nonexistent charges, or to discredit them publicly through false accusations.

Before the war ended some antiwar demonstrators would be killed. Some were murdered by private individuals, and some were murdered by official agencies of the government. In a few cases right-wing extremists carried out terrorist attacks on antiwar forces. In some instances this involved setting bombs. On May 16, 1966, a right-wing terrorist entered the Detroit SWP headquarters and shot three YSAers, killing Leo Bernard, who was also an activist in the United Committee to End the War in Vietnam. The 1969 murder of James Rector and wounding of demonstrators by Alameda County sheriff's deputies horrified Berkeley and the nation. The massive explosion in student antiwar activity in the early 1970s occurred in large part as a response to the murder of students by police and National Guardsmen.*

The Student Mobilization Committee

On December 28 and 29, 1966, a conference was held in Chicago to launch a new organization, the Student Mobilization Committee Against the War in Vietnam, otherwise known as the "Student Mobe" or SMC. This new organization experienced the usual infighting and growing pains, but by the turn of the decade it began a massive expansion and played a powerful role in building the antiwar movement.

The idea behind the SMC came from Bettina Aptheker. Bettina favored working inside the Democratic Party and supporting liberal Democrats. But

---

* On May 4, 1970, Ohio National Guardsmen shot unarmed students at Kent State in Ohio, some of whom were protesting the U.S. invasion of Cambodia, wounding nine and killing four. Later, on May 14–15, at Jackson State College in Mississippi, students protesting the Kent State tragedy and historic racial intimidation were met by police and state troopers, resulting in the killings of two students and woundings of numerous others. See more later in this chapter.

unlike many of the other youth associated with the CP, she was also committed to working with all forces possible, including the YSA, to build mass demonstrations. Forty years later this may seem logical but in 1966 it took a lot of courage for her to maintain such a position. Thanks to Bettina's flexibility on tactics, a general consensus was achieved: representatives from the three major political currents among radical students—the Du Bois Clubs, YSA, and SDS—agreed to work together, at least for the moment.

Thus began an organization that a few years later would become the largest antiwar student organization in the United States, growing to a membership of as much as one hundred thousand with an even broader base of supporters. The YSA viewed the SMC as reflecting its line of unity and action around the struggle against the war and threw itself into building local chapters.

From the beginning many unaffiliated students were drawn to the SMC as a vehicle to express their opposition to the war. YSAers leafleted the Berkeley campus calling for the first SMC meeting of the year, but by accident only two of our members showed up. No one from the other left political currents attended. The turnout was large, beyond our expectations. Our two members helped to lead the meeting, a steering committee was created, and work began in support of the next major antiwar actions. Similar events were happening across the country. As the SMC grew, so did the YSA's influence and support.

This created tension within the SMC's national leadership. The SMC had moved its national office to New York after the founding conference in Chicago. The national office staff was comprised of the same elements as the adult antiwar coalition—radical pacifists as the largest group, with smaller representation from the YSA and the CP. The YSA representatives in the SMC national office were Syd Stapleton and Kipp Dawson. Outside of New York, the YSA's influence within SMC was much larger than its representation in the official national leadership. This arrangement worked fairly smoothly during 1967 and into the spring of 1968.

At that point several individuals who had agreed to the original idea of the SMC as a united, non-exclusionary antiwar group began to press for adding other issues. They hadn't decided what all the new issues should be, but they began to resent the YSA's insistence on staying focused on Vietnam and the next big street demonstration. The majority in the national office started holding secret meetings to deal with the "YSA problem." This group, led by Linda Morse and several other radical pacifists as well as members of the CP, decided they wanted to transform the SMC into a multi-issue organization with various focuses such as antiracism, campus civil liberties, anti-draft work, and more. They just didn't understand that the SMC was growing so fast exactly because it was not a multi-issue organization. By focusing solely on opposition to the war, it could unite the antiwar sentiment on campuses around the country. There were already many multi-issue groups but none of them was growing like the SMC.

Their solution was to push the YSA out of the national leadership, declare the SMC an organization based on many issues, and overnight have their own large multi-issue organization. The radical pacifist–CP wing of the New York SMC, using several shifting rationales, fired YSAers Syd Stapleton and Kipp Dawson, consequently excluding the YSA from the SMC national leadership. The exclusion prompted a reaction around the country and SMC chapters began filing protests. Even the Student Senate in Berkeley passed a resolution demanding non-exclusion. The Berkeley Student Senate did not include any YSAers but it represented exactly the politics the YSA supported—united mass actions, non-exclusion, and rank-and-file democracy.

A meeting of the SMC national continuations committee was called in New York for June 29, 1968. Some four hundred people attended. About ninety of the participants were YSAers or SWPers, but they had overwhelming support from the independents in the delegations from outside of New York. Before any votes were taken Linda Morse led a walkout, supported by Jerry Rubin. Those that favored the walkout charged that the SMC had become a YSA front. They set up a new organization called the Radical Organizing Committee, which collapsed within a few months.

The SMC, reasserting that its policy continued to welcome all students against the war, immediately called for a national conference of all the SMC chapters for the first week of September to assure members that the organization remained an internally democratic and non-exclusionary movement. In the years ahead the SMC experienced its greatest growth and influence, quickly becoming the mass-oriented left wing of the movement.

The October 15, 1969, Vietnam Moratorium

In 1969, concerned about the growing antiwar sentiment, the Democrats made a move to try to become a force within the movement and, in doing so, to present their electoral perspective as the answer to all issues. A Vietnam Moratorium was called for October 15, 1969, in cities across the country and around the world. Business as usual was to stop, making space for demonstrations and teach-ins about the war. The moratorium organizers, several of whom had worked on the 1968 primary campaign of Eugene McCarthy, had initially planned for a similar event to be repeated on the 15th of each month "until there is American withdrawal or a negotiated settlement." The premise was that the moratorium would be a forum in which to discuss and consider what our nation should do about the war. Clearly the Democrats wanted those participating, especially youth, to conclude that they needed to get involved in electing Democrats. The moratorium was not supposed to be a protest of the war, exactly, just a discussion about it. They wanted to be able to control a mass mobilization through which they could promote their policy of getting off the streets and, instead, supporting their candidates. But almost everybody involved and the public at large saw this as antiwar activity.

When the moderate supporters of "peace" presented this idea in very moderate language, even elected officials began to support the moratorium. The SWP/YSA and in turn the SMC saw this as a huge opportunity. Now the media—instead of denouncing us and refusing to support or even announce antiwar demonstrations—shifted into a neutral stance, with some national media outlets officially supporting the moratorium. We immediately got behind the demonstrations while openly calling for an end to the war.

When I left Berkeley in June 1969 I first went to New York and then moved to Boston, where our movement showed great potential. Quickly I became involved in the Boston branch of the SMC. On October 2 we called a Boston-area organizing meeting to prepare for the impending October 15 Vietnam Moratorium at Boston Common. Expecting about two hundred people, we had reserved a hall that could seat about six hundred. But the turnout was much larger than even the hall could hold and the crowd overflowed, with students milling around outside. We had no place to break up into committees as we had planned. At a loss for what else to do, I got up and gave a ten-minute talk on the war and the SMC. Then we did our best to get people organized to help build the October 15 demonstration.

At that time there were twelve active campus SMC chapters in Boston with nine more in formation, as well as several high school chapters. The SMC leafleted all the Boston campuses for the moratorium march to Boston Common. Our plan was that the individual campus marches would merge into one giant march as they approached the common. We called for the formation of contingents at each of the campuses and printed banners and placards calling for immediate withdrawal.

We designed a little SMC button—with just the letters "SMC." During the buildup for the October Moratorium we sold our Boston allocation of two thousand in three days. On October 9 I noted in my diary that we had also sold eight thousand October 15 demonstration buttons. On October 11 I wrote, "Lots of young kids all over [SMC headquarters] painting signs. We had to make 1,000 signs. Takes a lot of work. Made sure they all said SMC on them." On October 13 I wrote, "Joyce says my pamphlet sold out—they ordered 10,000 more." This referred to a pamphlet I wrote, "How to Make a Revolution in the United States," inspired by the May–June 1968 events in France. It explained how a general strike, as developed in France, can become a battle for control of the nation—by working people or by the rich. I also mentioned, "Boston Globe attacked me on page 2." The *Boston Globe* had called for excluding the SMC from the upcoming rally and tried to pave the way for the conservative wing of the Democrats to capture the moratorium.

The Democrats exercised tight control over the larger moratorium planning meetings, especially the makeup of the speakers' list. We accepted, of course, that the Democrats' point of view would predominate, but fought to allow the Out Now current and the student movement also to have speakers. The situations varied throughout the country but in Boston the Democrats fought hard against allowing the SMC to have a speaker, despite its mass influence among students. Grudgingly, at last they asked who the SMC wanted on the speakers' list. When the SMC said "Peter Camejo," the Democrats were apoplectic. In the end they accepted my speaking with one proviso: I would be the very last speaker. It was clear they figured that these rallies went on so long there wouldn't be much of a crowd left by the end.

The march was huge. The SMCers from the Greater Boston area led the mass student contingents from each campus, which in turn gathered into an enormous flood of humanity marching toward Boston Common. Slogans were overwhelmingly for immediate withdrawal, "Out Now!" being the most popular.

The rally at Boston Common was estimated at one hundred thousand people, the largest moratorium event in the nation. Senator George McGovern, a leading liberal who became the Democratic presidential candidate in the 1972 elections, received a standing ovation when introduced. In my diary, I described how "young people applauded anything that sounded antiwar, even the mention of politicians like Kennedy and [Eugene] McCarthy." The audience was far more antiwar than the speakers' platform. Most of the presentations toed the Democratic Party's line of avoiding a call for immediate withdrawal. Naturally many speakers ran over their allotted time, so by the time my name was announced one would have assumed only stragglers would still be there. But people stayed, interested to hear the whole program.

When I was finally introduced I could sense that the tone of my message evoked an immediate response. I noticed people who had started to depart returning to the rally. My speech began to be interrupted by burst after burst of applause, including standing ovations. I remember in particular alluding to the moderate wording of the call for moratorium by stating, "We are not here to *discuss* or *consider* the war …" Instead, I said, "… We are here to end the war, to withdraw our troops, and not tomorrow but today." The loudest applause came after the line, "This movement is not for sale now, not in 1970, and not in 1972," referring to the coming congressional and presidential elections.

One of the moratorium organizers, Ken Hurwitz, who had been opposed to my speaking and was politically opposed to me later, wrote the following in his book *Marching Nowhere*:

> [T]he last speaker of the day [was] Peter Camejo, the Venezuelan revolutionary who had had us all ready to write a press release of disassociation. Still a step or two away from the microphone, he started in on his speech. He didn't want a single person to leave the Common before he had a chance to work his spell. The words came in a high pitched, staccato cadence, and his whole body vibrated to the rhythm.
>
> "Vietnam, he said, isn't a mistake but an absolute inevitability of the system.
>
> "And to those politicians who are joining the bandwagon," he continued, "this antiwar movement is not for sale. This movement is not for sale. This movement is not for sale now, not in 1970, and not in 1972." I expected the next shot of the crowd [the rally was televised] to show five thousand people sitting in front of the platform and ninety-five thousand people heading for the Park Street subway station. But that wasn't so. People were listening and responding. Certainly the majority wasn't agreeing entirely with the revolutionary stance, but they were listening … It didn't matter whether we were socialist revolutionaries or not. He made us hate the war perhaps more than we ever thought possible. It was a scourge, a plague—

there could be no "timetable" for ending it, it had to be ended now. Camejo spoke with such easy power, it was demagogic and frightening. This was a day of peace, but he made me see just how close the peace in the antiwar movement always is to something far more charged and militant. Our own latent emotionalism and contempt surprises us all. Camejo ended his speech at the peak, and the crowd applauded until their hands were weary.*

October 15, 1969, had changed the antiwar movement. Millions of people had turned out for marches, rallies, and teach-ins across the country and around the world. As Fred Halstead described it, "... the antiwar movement for the first time reached the level of a full-fledged mass movement. Before that there had been huge demonstrations, but only a large vanguard of the whole population of the country was directly involved. On October 15, millions of ordinary Americans were out in the streets demonstrating, canvassing door to door, picketing, leafleting, and so on."† *Life* magazine reported, "It was a display without historic parallel, the largest expression of public dissent ever seen in this country."‡

Those who had opposed the single-issue focus on unity through mass action were now relegated to the sidelines.

How We Handled the Ultralefts

The success of the mass movement, and of the SMC in particular, caused resentment among some of the extreme left groups, who now decided to target the SMC. This was particularly true of the Progressive Labor Party (PL), a Maoist group that had been working inside SDS until SDS splintered in 1969. The SMC experienced physical attacks against members as well as more frequent attempts to seize the speakers' platform at mass rallies. One such episode unfolded at a demonstration at Boston Common, one in a series of large Boston-area demonstrations that took place immediately after the Kent State massacre of May 4, 1970. We had expected about five thousand people but outrage at Kent State resulted in an explosive increase

---

* Ken Hurwitz, *Marching Nowhere* (New York: W. W. Norton & Company, 1971), 143–44. While this excerpt appears to be supportive of the crowd's reaction to me it reveals a great deal about the mentality of Hurwitz and other Democrats. Hurwitz refers to me repeatedly as a "revolutionary." I never used that word or any similar term, nor was my talk in any way about "revolution." In his analysis he seems to fear me because I was definitive about ending this war, a war that his party had started, supported, and—unfathomably—still thought might have some redeeming features.

† Halstead, *Out Now*, 488.

‡ *Life*, October 24, 1969.

and about twenty-five thousand people took part on May 5, 1970.

PL had recently attempted to seize the speakers' platform at the large, second moratorium in Boston on April 15 and had succeeded with a strong-arm squad at the moratorium event on the same date in New York. So we knew we were in for a fight on May 5. We wanted to avoid a pitched battle with them, knowing that if one occurred the media would focus all its coverage on the violence within the peace movement rather than on the real issues.

We had to devise a way to block PL from attacking us. So we set up a microphone on the steps of a large building next to Boston Common and positioned about thirty monitors with SMC armbands in front of it. The ultralefts began gathering right in front. They brought in about three hundred people and must have figured they could easily storm the platform and take over the rally from the SMCers.

What they didn't know was that the setup was a decoy. In the middle of Boston Common was a metal power box with an outlet, which enabled us to wire another microphone. We brought in a second, low platform that lay flush with the ground so no one noticed it. A large number of monitors without armbands surrounded the platform, looking to the world like people just milling around. The crowd facing the setup across the street grew to a huge size. Then, when the event was to begin, we suddenly elevated the platform, plugged in our sound equipment, and started the rally. The crowd quickly shifted toward the sound and moved to gather around our new platform, creating a massive block for the ultralefts, who were now on the outside. The monitors drew tightly together around our platform and, at last, put on their armbands.

The maneuver worked beautifully. It was gratifying to see the faces of the PL toughs when they realized we had fooled them.

A much uglier incident occurred a few weeks later at a meeting of the Boston SMC at MIT. Some fifty or sixty members of PL launched a physical attack. The SMC monitors fought them in the hallways to prevent them from entering the meeting hall. Several people were injured including one SMC member, John McCann, who was blinded in one eye. He was seized by a group of PL thugs, dragged down the hallway, knocked down, and stabbed in the eye with the pin of a political button. This violent, Stalinist approach—using physical force to prevent people they disagreed with from holding meetings—was exercised on several occasions and by more than one ultraleft group. At some rallies the ultralefts actually brought the proceedings to a complete stop. Once in control of the platform they shouted their hostile views over the loudspeakers. It was not as though they had no other option—all groups were welcome at the large rallies if they agreed to participate peacefully, and each group was allowed a speaker regardless of their politics. In general the ultraleft groups refused and would not help build the movement. Their own demonstrations were ineffectual in comparison. For example, two wings of the collapsing SDS, Revolutionary Youth Movement 1 and Revolutionary Youth Movement 2, held their own marches on October 11, 1969, as an alternative to the National Moratorium, advertising them as "Gigantic National Actions." They attracted about three hundred people to each.

November 15, 1969

The main adult national antiwar coalition, the New Mobilization Committee to End the War in Vietnam ("New Mobe"), had set November 15, 1969, as the next big action, to take place in Washington, D.C. The politics of this march were very different from the October 15 Moratorium. In the interim the Nixon administration had gone on an all-out offensive against the Democrats who had supported the moratorium. They also unleashed a huge propaganda campaign against the upcoming effort. The Democrats, instead of fighting Nixon's pro-war stance and standing up to the red-baiting charges, with few exceptions capitulated and distanced themselves from the upcoming demonstration. Thus the November action was led almost exclusively by forces independent of the Democratic Party.

On November 13 and 14 I spoke in Minneapolis, Cleveland, and Detroit, then headed for Washington. On the evening of the 14th I spoke to students at George Washington University, a few blocks from the White House. My diary reads, "Spoke to 1,500—tired—talk came hard—but I got a standing ovation. Went outside—spoke for 5 minutes to 500 people."

Saturday, November 15, 1969, witnessed the largest demonstration in our nation's history. In my diary I described it: "Demonstration was I think 500,000 to one million. Bourgeois press claiming 250,000. They at least admit it was the largest ever. Composition was still basically student movement and older antiwar middle-class types. This was a heavy mobilization of those forces." To have propelled that number of people to Washington, D.C, the movement nationally must have had at least ten million to twenty million in overt supporters and millions more sympathizing.

On November 16, I added, "The demonstration was a success. The red-baiting featured us—we should recruit from it. The [antiwar] coalition will undoubtedly fly apart as we enter 1970. We will see.—Meanwhile ... no escalation and no end to the war."

Sure enough, once the congressional elections for 1970 got under way, the Democrats would again promote working for their "peace" candidates as opposed to building mass demonstrations, which hurt our ability to maintain as broad a coalition. But, as it turned out, different events were about to ignite a massive explosion of antiwar activity.

A Few Days in the Life of an Activist

After the success of November 15 I wrote, "We had a lot of fun driving home except we had 8 in the car and it took 14 hours." At that time the activists were young, most under thirty years of age. I had turned thirty the year before. There was nothing more rewarding for all of us than making progress toward ending the cold-blooded mass murder of the Vietnamese people. The joy of the young is special; there is an exuberance and drive to it. Antiwar work made all of us feel that there was a real meaning to being alive. It gave us hope that regardless of the odds against us and the enormous power of the pro-war, exploitative forces around the world, we were starting to defeat them—at least as far as this war was concerned.

In general the radicalized youth were really busy, really happy people. The young activists had full social lives, usually with others in the movement, dating and partying as well as organizing. Everyone was engaged in something that they believed in and that they saw as changing the world for the better. Radicalization among the young reached far and wide, incorporating segments you might not expect. I even met a Playboy Bunny at an antiwar meeting—I tried to get her reading radical literature and encouraged her to change her line of work. In my diary I wrote this poignant note: "Bought Doris a flower and left it for her." But I was successful only on the political front.

My days were filled morning to night with organizing meetings or else I was traveling, giving talks about the war, or doing ideological battle with the ultralefts or the moderates who wanted to divert the movement into the Democratic Party. Sometimes I traveled a few times in a day. Describing events around the April 15 second moratorium, in my diary I mention that I held a meeting at Boston University, then "... I drove as fast as I could to

Cambridge. Ran up to podium as I was being introduced. Spoke for 15 minutes, went quite well. Took off for airport … Slept on plane. Arrived at 5 pm [in Washington, D.C.]. Went to demonstration. Lots of Ultras acting like ultras should, burning American flags, shouting waving flags, etc. Spoke, some harassment from ultras. Attacked them—talk went over well. [Arthur] Waskow chairing. Should have hit ultras harder."

I was always pushing myself. On April 30 I spoke to five hundred students at MIT in the morning; in the afternoon I took off for a speech at Amherst, a two-and-a-half hour drive. I spoke from 7:15 p.m. till 9:35 p.m. and stayed after to talk to a few students interested in joining us. Driving home I was totally exhausted and fell asleep at the wheel. Just as I was going off the road the car jarred a bit, it woke me up, and I was able to avoid having an accident. I pulled over and slept for an hour, getting home at 1:40 a.m. The next morning an MIT professor asked me to come back to speak again but I had to catch a flight to Detroit at 11:30 a.m. After holding several meetings with the Detroit YSA I took a nap, then later debated Zolton Ferency, a professor, former Democratic Party state chairman, and founder of the short-lived Human Rights Party. The following day, May 1, I was back in Boston working to get a referendum on the ballot on the war. In my diary I wrote, "Talked to Mike K. then held [YSA] antiwar steering committee meeting at my place. Gave all the comrades a big pitch on referendum. Hope I'm right. They agree—but fail to have the same enthusiasm I do … We have undertaken a mammoth job. I wonder if we can do it—to get 100,000 signatures requires getting 8,000 per week."

I kept going like this day after day, month after month, year after year, while I was in my twenties and thirties. I was so intense I didn't even own a record player for about five years.

The Student Antiwar Tsunami

In early May 1970, events triggered a sudden surge in the already intense antiwar activity. First was the U.S. invasion of Cambodia and its extension into Laos, which hit the news media May 1. As demonstrations erupted across the country, the outrage deepened with shock as four students were shot to death by National Guardsmen on May 4 at Kent State University in Ohio, and two students were killed by local police at Jackson State College in Mississippi on the night of May 14.

The day after Nixon's expansion of the war into Cambodia and Laos, students went into action throughout the nation. At Kent State it started small but built each day. On May 2, two thousand students marched on the Kent State ROTC (Reserve Officers' Training Corps) headquarters. Someone set the ROTC building on fire. The National Guard had been called out with orders to shoot if anyone cut the firemen's hoses. No one was shot that day. At an evening rally downtown windows were broken.

On Monday, May 4, a student strike was called at Kent and a thousand people gathered on campus. The police declared the gathering illegal and ordered it to disperse; students refused and some responded by throwing rocks at the police. The National Guard arrived and started using tear gas. Students retreated but did not disperse, and many threw the tear gas canisters back at the guard. A group of National Guardsmen suddenly raised their rifles and began shooting into the crowd of student demonstrators.

No one had anticipated this could happen. Students were stunned as they realized the U.S. army was now shooting to kill. When the shooting stopped four were dead, one crippled for life, and many others wounded. The four who died were Allison Krause, nineteen years old; Jeffrey Glenn Miller, twenty; Sandra Lee Scheuer, twenty; and William K. Schroeder, nineteen. That evening the national news began reporting the story, and an entire nation went into a state of shock.

The National Student General Strike

Within a few days 350 campuses were on strike nationwide. In all 536 universities were taken over during this period. Strikes, takeovers, or demonstrations took place in the majority of the 1,350 college-level institutions across the country. It is estimated that 60 percent or four million of the seven million total U.S. students participated.* All over the nation students poured out of their classes into spontaneous demonstrations. This current quickly caught on in the high schools, with students marching from one high school to the next, drawing out strike supporters in huge numbers.

The SMC called on campus groups to occupy facilities for mass antiwar organizing. That is, rather than going off campus to set up picket lines, students used the university facilities to send activists out into the community with antiwar leaflets and posters. Fearing the universities would be transformed from controllable institutions into organizing centers for the antiwar forces, California governor Ronald Reagan ordered the whole

---

* Halstead, *Out Now*, 561.

state-owned university system, including Berkeley, closed until May 11. On May 7 the SMC held a press conference calling for all campuses nationwide to join the student strike. Before long it was clear that the majority of students in U.S. higher education were on strike. In New York all major college campuses were on strike. At Princeton the vote to strike was 4,000 for, 200 against.

In the face of this groundswell, even members of the Nixon cabinet began questioning the administration's war policy. On May 8 Nixon promised to have all the troops out of Cambodia by the end of June. On May 9 at 5:00 a.m. Nixon went out to talk to some of the young antiwar activists encamped near the White House. The Democrats, always adept at figuring out how to co-opt and derail a movement, began pushing for students to get involved with the elections. One obstacle in their path was that most students were not yet able to vote, since the voting age at that time was twenty-one. So the Democrats began promoting the idea of moving the voting age to eighteen.

Labor and the Antiwar Movement

On Friday, May 8, at the corner of Broad and Wall Streets in Manhattan about a thousand high school and college students held a memorial for the students slain at Kent State. Peter J. Brennan, president of the Building and Construction Trades Council of Greater New York, called a counterdemonstration of construction workers nearby in support of the war. Between two hundred and four hundred construction workers, divided into groups so that they approached from all four directions, waded into the student memorial wielding clubs and crowbars. Joined by several hundred pro-war thugs, they beat not only the students, but also neighborhood office workers who had come out to try to shield the students. Seventy people were injured. The pro-war crowd also descended upon City Hall, where—on orders of the mayor—flags were flying at half mast in honor of the Kent State dead, and raised the flags to the tops of the poles.

After the May 8 events Brennan organized two weeks of daily construction worker demonstrations in support of the war. The workers were paid for their time on the marches and their unions required their participation to be paid. This culminated on May 20 in a pro-government rally of some fifty thousand people, likely the largest pro-war demonstration on Vietnam. Peter Brennan was rewarded for his efforts by being appointed secretary of labor after Nixon's 1972 reelection. Up to that point the AFL-CIO's national leadership had been almost solidly in support of the war, regardless of whether Democrats or Republicans were heading the government.

Antiwar forces in the labor movement responded with a demonstration numbering about twenty-five thousand, for which the workers were not paid. About a dozen unions participated, including the hospital workers, the American Federation of State, County, and Municipal Employees, garment workers unions, and the progressive International Union of Electrical Workers. The division within the labor movement would continue, but at last worker organizations had begun to join the antiwar movement in larger numbers.*

Killing Black Youth

As the antiwar wave swept the country black colleges held many demonstrations. The police began to act in a particularly vicious manner at these gatherings of African American youth. On May 9 a sixteen-year-old African American was beaten to death in the Richmond County jail in Augusta, Georgia. A tense standoff at an Augusta demonstration on May 11, during which police had their guns trained on the speakers, erupted into civil unrest over a wide stretch of the city. The police shot six African American protesters to death; many others were wounded.

Then on May 14 the police murdered two African American students and wounded fourteen at a protest at Jackson State College in Jackson, Mississippi. The dead were Phillip L. Gibbs, a junior at Jackson State, and James Earl Green, a senior at Jim Hill High School.

High school students in New York forced a closing of all the city's high schools in protest over the killings at Jackson State. But only about fifty colleges nationwide held special actions in support of the Jackson State students, and many of the sympathetic institutions were historically black schools. After seeing the gigantic explosion of protest over the murder of the white students at Kent State, African American youth became bitter over the much smaller response to the killings at Jackson State.

The falloff in response was due in part to factors not related to race. The protest wave that crested after the May 4 killings had begun to recede. Yet of course the lesser response to Jackson State also reflected the deeply

---

* See Halstead, *Out Now*, 544–45.

ingrained racism of our country, and it weakened the call for unity among all students to fight the war and to stand up against the vicious criminal attacks on antiwar students.

The Chicano Moratorium

The wave of deep radicalization had also taken root among Chicanos and other Latinos. The power of this movement added a new dimension to the antiwar movement. In different areas of the country several influential groups had developed and begun to work together.

One of the most astounding was a political party of Chicanos called El Partido de la Raza Unida or, more commonly, La Raza Unida (RUP). La Raza Unida was born in the mind of one of my dearest friends and political allies during the 1970s, José Ángel Gutiérrez (known by his initials, JAG). He earned his doctorate from the University of Texas at Austin and did post-doc work at Stanford. Projecting that a Chicano party could capture control of a large part of South Texas, JAG founded La Raza Unida in January 1970 in Crystal City, Texas. RUP then spread throughout the Southwest to California and later even moved eastward. The rise of RUP authored a new chapter in Texas history as several counties came under its control.

In Los Angeles various Chicano-led organizations grew rapidly during the late 1960s and early 1970s, including the Center for Autonomous Social Action (CASA), founded in 1968. CASA offered legal aid to undocumented Mexican workers in California and, over a ten-year period, broadened into a national organization with a program of international solidarity, civil rights, and antiracism.

The year 1970 also saw the formation of the antiwar National Chicano Moratorium, supported by a wide spectrum of Chicano organizations, ranging from the mainstream, such as the Congress of Mexican-American Unity, the Mexican American Political Association, and GI Forum (Mexican American veterans), to more progressive groups like La Raza Unida. But the base of the movement was students organized through El Movimiento Estudiantil Chicano de Aztlán (MEChA), the Chicano Student Movement, a broad umbrella organization founded in 1969.

The National Chicano Moratorium called for an antiwar action in Los Angeles for August 29, 1970. This was the first mass Vietnam War–focused action sponsored by a racial minority in the United States. Proportional to population Chicanos continued to take the largest casualties in Vietnam of any U.S. ethnic group. This moratorium was a powerful attempt to mobilize the Chicano community to defend itself against the damage this war was doing to their people.

During the large demonstration (estimated at twenty thousand to thirty thousand people) the police attacked the protestors, killing four people and wounding many others. Most famous among those killed was *Los Angeles Times* reporter Ruben Salazar. Coincidentally, as I sat writing this chapter I noticed an announcement on the front page of the *San Francisco Chronicle* that a stamp was being issued in honor of Ruben Salazar. This is the way things work in the United States. Innocent people are murdered by authorities, no one is tried or goes to jail for the crimes, and then forty years later a stamp is issued, making it appear as though all those things are behind us.

The GIs Help Bring the War to an End

After the wave of demonstrations in the 1970s the antiwar movement gradually declined with the public's growing impression that the war was coming to an end. In part that could be attributed to another aspect of the youth rebellion and the overwhelming opposition to the war—the rise of militant opposition to the war by the troops themselves.

The GI antiwar movement began slowly with some very courageous soldiers who protested the war from within the army. Almost always they were brought up on charges or expelled from the military. I was not involved personally in the organizing of this aspect of antiwar activity, although the SMC was vital in helping to distribute information sheets and newsletters put out by antiwar GIs. These materials appeared at army bases all across the country and helped to build connections to the SMC.

As the antiwar movement in the streets continued, albeit on a smaller scale, the number of GIs joining the demonstrations grew rapidly. I remember one demonstration led by about two hundred GIs, who came in full uniform, refusing to accept the army's regulation that prohibited demonstrating in uniform. These young men were among the most courageous of all Americans in their opposition to the war.

Inside Vietnam the United States started losing control of its own armed forces. This is one of the great secrets of American history. Soldiers began to refuse orders, trying to find ways that would not result in their being immediately arrested or shot. One extreme solution appeared: when officers tried to force soldiers to advance against their wills, the rank and file killed their officers. Such killings became known as "fragging," in reference to taking a fragmentation grenade and throwing it into a commander's tent during the night. American RadioWorks, a major U.S. public radio documentary service, in 2008 interviewed Professor Terry Anderson, a Texas A&M University historian who specializes in the 1960s and the Vietnam War. Anderson told them, "The U.S. Army itself does not know exactly how many … officers were murdered. But they know at least six hundred were murdered, and then they have another fourteen hundred that died mysteriously. Consequently by early 1970, the army [was] at war not with the enemy but with itself."*

Vietnam became the first war the United States lost. For bringing the killing in Vietnam finally to an end, significant credit must be given to all the youth in America who rose up against the war, and to the antiwar GIs who changed the relationship of forces, making a reality of what had appeared a military impossibility.

There are so many heroes in the battle for peace in the world that most of their stories never get told. The monument in Washington to the 58,256 American soldiers who died in Vietnam does not state the most important message the American people need to hear. These young Americans were murdered by U.S. imperialism; they are victims not of the Vietnamese but of the Democrats and the Republicans, of the corporate rulers in America.

It is hard to express in words the feeling we all had when we held demonstrations against the war with GIs on the front lines and on the speakers' platform. As the war finally ended, with the American pullout from Saigon on April 30, 1975, it was an immense political lesson for me personally. I learned that what appears impossible is sometimes possible and that people who at first appear unreachable can be reached.

---

* Available at http://americanradioworks.publicradio.org/features/vietnam/us/movie. html, accessed June 2, 2008.

CHAPTER 8

THE SWP AND
THE FOURTH INTERNATIONAL

A generational transition within the SWP took place formally on May 14, 1972, when Farrell Dobbs resigned as national secretary and Jack Barnes, just thirty-two at the time, was elected in his place. Barry Sheppard became the organizational secretary, and I took a position on the Political Committee.* The central group of younger leaders, most in their early thirties or still in their twenties, was quite large. Among them were Mary-Alice Waters, Gus Horowitz, Joel Britton, Lew Jones, Betsey Stone, Doug Jenness, Caroline Lund, and Larry Seigle. This is only a partial list—at the height in the early 1970s more than a hundred people were employed full time at the SWP's national office and print shop at 410 West Street on Manhattan's west side, next to the Hudson River. There were also critical leaders in the branches of other

---

* The SWP was structured in branches, usually a single branch in each city where the party had the necessary minimum of ten members. In New York there were branches in several boroughs. Each branch elected an executive committee and the executive committee elected or recommended to the membership a branch organizer, treasurer, and secretary. Each branch also elected delegates to a national convention, usually every two years. The national convention elected a National Committee (NC) that would be the highest body nationally and would meet periodically, usually twice a year. The NC, which numbered about forty people, would elect a Political Committee (PC) that numbered about seven or eight to coordinate its work on a day-to-day basis. The PC resided in New York.

cities. In my life I never met a more committed group of people, more self-sacrificing and respectful in their personal interactions, than the generation coming out of the 1960s in the SWP.

The central core of the older party leadership had consisted mainly of several men who had all been involved since the early 1930s. In addition to Farrell Dobbs, who had led the Minneapolis Teamster strikes of the mid-thirties, and Tom Kerry from the seamen's unions on the West Coast, these leaders included Joseph Hansen, who had been Trotsky's secretary and was the SWP's main writer on international politics;* George Breitman from Detroit, who undertook the publication of Trotsky's collected writings as well as the speeches of Malcolm X; and the party's principal intellectual, George Novack. A slightly younger second tier included Fred Halstead, Nat Weinstein, Harry Ring, and Ed Shaw. All these men remained active in the SWP after the transition to the younger team. The SWP's founder, James P. Cannon, had retired to Los Angeles in 1952 but occasionally sent his comments to the New York leadership until his death in 1974.

With the rapid growth of the SWP and the YSA during the antiwar movement, an ideological crisis had manifested itself within the SWP. The older, primarily worker-based segment of the party had grown concerned that the SWP would be changed by its newer members, most of whom were middle-class youth. Many of the older members opposed our support for what they saw as contemporary issues, such as gay liberation, and in general were nervous that the SWP might abandon its roots in Trotskyism and begin to alter its "program."

I had begun to sense these problems back in Berkeley, during the days after victory in the battle for Telegraph Avenue. The crisis had begun in 1970 over which way the SWP would go: forward, evolving into an organization connected with the realities of the national and international living struggles of real people; or inward, self-isolating from realities because those realities did not correspond to a preconceived idea ordained as the unchangeable truth.

---

* On a plane trip back from Europe I had a chance to talk to Joe Hansen. He told me the story of how he had become Trotsky's secretary and bodyguard in Mexico at the age of twenty-seven. One of the primary reasons was that Hansen had been a national rifle shooting champion in the United States. Joe was the person who heard Trotsky cry out from his office as Stalin's agent, Ramón Mercader, struck him with an ice axe. Joe ran in and threw Mercader to the floor, breaking his arm. Trotsky yelled to Joe, "Don't kill him!" On the way to the hospital, Joe told me, Trotsky said, "This time they got me."

The Trap for Trotskyism

At one point SWP national secretary Farrell Dobbs told me, "The program has been developed. Our job is to implement it." In one form or other I heard this idea repeated by many SWPers, old and new. This struck me as contrary to the essence of Marx's writings about the materialist basis of science and how it applies to economic and social relations. Science is a process, not a discovery or revelation by a genius. Not only is a political program an evolving concept, but it also requires continuous discussion and debate in order for it to be effective. And it must, most important of all, be tested against reality. In other words, the program of an organization trying to bring justice to the world must be a process rooted primarily in the living mass struggles of the people. It is not a written document put together by intelligent people in the past.

This concept of the "program" was a defining aspect of Trotskyism. Born as a faction opposing the Stalinist degradation of socialism, the Trotskyist movement defended the founders of the socialist movement while at the same time rejecting the cult-like deification of Marx and Lenin. Thus the Trotskyists became caught in a framework that focused not only on the correct interpretation of Marx and Lenin but also on the correct interpretation of events within Russia. This led to the rapid development of rigidity in how they viewed and approached the world around them. Groups of Trotskyists across the globe focused on the internal debate over the degeneration of the Soviet Communist Party and its worldwide influence, rather than on the expressions of the living struggles of their own country.

The early Trotskyists were aware of this dilemma and saw their primary role as trying to win people over from the mass Communist parties in order to fight for a return to the values of the socialist movement prior to its Stalinist degeneration. Gradually this fight led to a solidifying of the idea that the Trotskyists were the defenders of the true "program." This idea of the defense of the program became detached from the real, material developments in the mass movement. Among Trotskyists the idea of the true "program" gradually became its own icon to be defended.

In making these points I am, of course, generalizing and oversimplifying. The battles in which small groups of Trotskyists fought against Stalinism will go down in history as heroic. Trotskyists were murdered in tremendous numbers in Russia and were persecuted in other countries as well. They faced not only enormous hostility from the huge mass base of the Communist parties, but also endured attacks from pro-capitalist forces.

As an instrument to revive the mass world movement for social justice, however, I think that Trotskyism had historical, internal, sectarian limitations that blocked it from being able to become a critical force for social change. But during the early 1970s I can see in my diary that I still thought it was possible that the Trotskyist movement would gradually, and with occasional opportunities for explosive growth, come to replace the influence of the Stalinists and social democrats.

The Fourth International

After the huge wave of antiwar activity of 1970 I had moved from Boston back to New York, and into the center of the SWP leadership. Much of my focus going forward was on international work, primarily in Latin America and Europe. "International work," in addition to being out of the country, referred more specifically to my helping to build the Fourth International (FI). The FI comprised all the Trotskyist organizations throughout the world that had banded together in support of socialism, but against Stalinism and social democracy.

When Stalin took over the Third International or Comintern (Communist International), comprised of all the Communist parties, a new group calling itself the Fourth International was founded at a congress in Paris in September 1938.* The FI suffered a damaging split in 1953 over disagreements as to how to relate to the much larger Communist parties and social democratic parties. A reunification congress in 1963 established the structure as it was when I was became involved with the FI.

The SWP was affiliated to the FI but the American SWP did not have formal membership. This was due to anticommunist legislation in the United States, specifically the 1940 Voorhis Act and the 1940 Smith Act, which made it illegal to belong to an international radical organization.

At the FI's Tenth World Congress in 1974 it was claimed that the FI had sections in forty-one countries. Most sections had memberships ranging in number from less than a hundred to three hundred. Exceptions were the United States, France, Argentina, Mexico, and Spain, which had up to

---

* The First International was founded in 1864 and disbanded in 1876; the Second International, which dissolved at the start of World War I, was founded in 1889. The Third International, or Comintern, was dissolved in 1943.

few thousand each. The central body of the FI was the United Secretariat, which met in Paris and was responsible to a larger International Executive Committee (IEC), which had representatives with delegations depending on the size of their organizations. During my involvement the principal figures in the United Secretariat were the Belgian Marxist economist Ernest Mandel, supported by Pierre Frank of France and Livio Maitan of Italy, with some younger leaders emerging primarily from the French section following the May–June 1968 upsurge.

Differences in the FI: Foquismo

Just as I was coming into the political leadership of both the SWP and the FI, a sharp difference in approach arose that threatened to divide the movement. According to the traditional view, in each country we would try to build mass parties through work in the living movements, especially within the working class (such as in the trade unions). But with the triumph of the Cuban Revolution in 1959, a current had appeared in Latin America calling for a very different approach.

This approach was called *foquismo* and it was associated with Che Guevara, the heroic Argentinean leader of the Cuban Revolution, who was assassinated by the CIA after his capture in Bolivia in 1967. Foquismo held that where dictatorships existed it would be possible, through an armed struggle, to establish a small nucleus—or *foco*—of rebels in the mountains or rural countryside. The foco would then launch a war that could lead to triumph, echoing the events that had led to victory in the Cuban Revolution. In Argentina, Uruguay, and Brazil variations on foquismo developed into urban guerrilla warfare, promoted by the Brazilian revolutionary Carlos Marighella.

The international debate over this issue continued into the 1980s. In the SWP we were completely opposed to foquismo. I wrote several documents arguing against it, including a pamphlet called *Guevara's Guerilla Strategy.**
The SWP's position was that guerrilla warfare, as seen in the Cuban Revolution, was a tactic that could be effective in a rising mass movement, but that a general strategy of trying to start guerrilla wars with small groups would almost certainly lead to defeats in most cases. This stance was rejected by most of the European sections and their Latin American supporters. The

---

* Peter Camejo, *Guevara's Guerilla Strategy: A Critique and Some Proposals* (New York: Pathfinder Press, 1971).

SWP's major statement on foquismo was an April 1971 article Joseph Hansen wrote for the International Information Bulletin titled "In Defense of the Leninist Strategy of Party Building." In a sharp fight at the FI's Tenth World Congress in 1974, a slim majority (55 to 45) voted to support the strategy laid out by the Guevarists. The minority, which included the SWP, opposed that policy and continued to support the traditional strategy of building a vanguard party through mass work.

The Sallustro Kidnapping

In Argentina the local Trotskyist group had split in two. One splinter group supported the general position of the SWP while the other supported armed struggle. The two groups had diverged from a party called the Revolutionary Workers Party (PRT in its Spanish initials) and distinguished themselves by appending the names of their newspapers: the pro–guerrilla warfare group was the PRT *Combatiente* and the mass work group the PRT *Verdad*.

The pro–guerilla warfare group was ready for action, not just talk. They formed a military wing called the Ejército Revolucionario del Pueblo (ERP—Revolutionary Army of the People) and began engaging in armed struggle against the Argentinean dictatorship. Unlike the July 26 Movement in Cuba, which had a huge popular base of support, the ERP's base was quite limited. Their approach quickly became very different from that of the original Cuban movement; ERP's tactics included kidnappings and assassinations, actions historically rejected by the Marxist movement and labeled as terrorist.

I was making regular trips to Argentina primarily to meet with the mass work–oriented PRT *Verdad*. On one of those trips I also requested to meet with the ERP. At first they refused to see me, but eventually a meeting was arranged. I agreed to stand on a certain street corner in Buenos Aires to wait for a pickup. A car pulled over and I got in. The people in the car told me to look down at the floor the whole time, the rationale being that if the police were to arrest and torture me I wouldn't be able to reveal what I hadn't seen. The car stopped and we all got out. Again they asked me to look down at the ground, which I did, and in a short time we entered an apartment.

A portable radio was hung on the doorknob with soft music playing so that someone walking by would not be able to overhear the conversation. In the apartment were two men representing the ERP. I will call one Luis and the other Marcos, since I didn't know what names they were using or what their real names might have been. They knew who I was and we began talking, primarily about why we had differences as to how to fight the dic tatorship. They were both very polite.

There was a knock on the door and another person entered. Marcos and this person talked for a while near the door. I couldn't hear them, as I was sitting at the other end of the small apartment on a wide ottoman. After a little while Marcos came over to me and asked me to stand up. He opened the ottoman I had been sitting on and to my amazement it was packed with U.S. $100 bills. I don't know how many $100 bills would fit in about a four-foot by two-and-a-half-foot chest, but I would guess it had to be about a million dollars. Marcos took out a few bills and gave them to the third person, plus a revolver. Then the third person departed, and Marcos resumed the conversation with Luis and myself.

About two hours into the conversation we agreed to end the meeting. They drove me back to the pick-up spot and we said goodbye. My reaction was sadness—I believed that they would die fighting the dictatorship. Despite our disagreements I could not help but respect the personal sacrifice they were making to try to end the tyranny.

On March 21, 1972, the ERP kidnapped Oberdán Sallustro, director general of the Fiat auto plant in Córdoba, Argentina. It was front-page news in Argentina and was reported in many other parts of the world, particularly in Italy, which owned the Fiat plant. As Sallustro was being driven to work in Córdoba his car was cut off by two ERP cars. His chauffeur was wounded in a struggle and the Fiat executive was hustled into one of the waiting vehicles and driven off. The ERP then announced they would execute Sallustro unless Fiat agreed to rehire a group of fired strikers and the government released fifty imprisoned ERP members, paid the ERP an indemnity, and distributed a billion pesos' worth of clothing and school supplies to poor people near the Fiat plant. Fiat agreed to the terms but the government refused.

During these negotiations I flew to Buenos Aires and requested a meeting with the ERP. They quickly agreed. I was surprised at how different this meeting was from the first one—it took place in an office in a large building with five or six people present. I made a short and very direct plea that Sallustro not be killed and instead be set free. I agreed that he was probably a terrible person who had committed many abuses against workers but that kidnapping and killing him would end up hurting the struggle rather than helping.

The ERP representatives were very polite to me throughout the meeting. But one of them—no one used a name—attacked me politically. He said that they got no real support at all from "people like [me]" (meaning groups like the SWP), and added that even the Russians were providing them with arms. When it was appropriate for me to respond, I warned them not to trust the Russians, explaining that they would doubtless provide the ERP with weapons but once they had penetrated the organization, the Russians would then betray the ERP for a deal with the dictatorship. After my observation there was a brief silence. Then the person who had criticized me said something dismissive of my warning about the Russians.

They gave me some underground newspapers, thanked me for coming, and led me out of the building into a car that dropped me off near a subway station. In circumstances such as these, you should never keep on your person any materials you are given, and I had come prepared. In my briefcase was a stamped envelope addressed to New York. The first thing I did was to find a mailbox to mail myself the materials I had just received.

As it turned out, at about 1:00 a.m. security forces stopped the taxi that I was in for what seemed to be a random check. My mind blanked on whether I had mailed the materials earlier. The police took me out on one side of the taxi and asked me where I was going. They also asked the taxi driver. I feared the worst and tried not to show it, remaining still and speaking only when asked a question. Then they took my briefcase and went around the other side of the car to examine it. In a matter of minutes they returned my passport and briefcase, and said, okay, you can go. Looking back I have often reflected on how I would have been toast if the Internet had existed in those days—a simple search would have instantly turned up all sorts of information about me. The world was a different place in the 1970s.

After more than two weeks of searching, on April 10 the Argentinean police discovered where Sallustro was being held and tried to free him. The ERP members holding Sallustro shot him dead and three of the four escaped; the fourth, a young Brazilian woman, remained in the house and surrendered when the police broke in. Sometime later in Paris I was told that the person who killed Sallustro was Marcos—the host from my initial meeting with the ERP—and that he had later died in an airplane crash in

Paris. Luis, I was told, was captured by the army, tortured, and killed by being dropped from a helicopter.*

Immediately after Sallustro's death the SWP wrote a public statement that denounced the killing and reiterated the traditional Marxist view opposing terrorist acts. The major European groups of the FI, in contrast, defended the killing of Sallustro. This episode was but one in an endless series that intensified the differences within the FI, which were becoming increasingly sharp.

Cultism within the Left

Stalinism, to justify its mindless top-down rule, had turned Marx, Engels, and Lenin into icons. These three had revealed the truth. And those who correctly interpreted their writings were ordained to lead the world, while disagreement with that interpretation was tantamount to heresy. Like a religion, the Stalinists persecuted those who dared to dissent, and proper interpretation of the written divine guidance could only be made by a priesthood that was guided by the ordained cult leader, Stalin.

This freezing of the writings of earlier leaders into scripture marked the transformation of a materialist philosophy into an idealist one, with all the trappings of a cult. When differences appeared among Stalinists, as between Stalin and Mao, then two currents, both claiming to be the true interpretation, developed. Each denounced the other for its misinterpretation, inevitably explained away as the evil influence of those with false beliefs.

Within the Trotskyist movement differences arose over the correct interpretation of events within the Soviet Union and over the exact analysis of the nature of Stalinism. In time sects and cults developed that identified themselves as Trotskyist, some amazingly bizarre. A extreme case was the Latin American leader Juan Posadas, whom I met in 1960, who espoused the theory that extraterrestrials supported his movement and that UFOs were proof of socialism on other planets.

---

* As it is more than thirty years later and the government of Argentina is no longer a military dictatorship I do not see how this information could affect anyone. Nonetheless I debated whether to include this story given that the CIA was undoubtedly a part of activity supporting the dictatorship, as the agency has been involved in supporting and opposing regimes throughout the history of modern South American politics.

The Moreno Cult

The Argentinean group allied with the SWP in this debate, the PRT *Verdad*, was led by Nahuel Moreno. Moreno's real name was Hugo Bressano—almost everyone called him Hugo. He ran the PRT *Verdad* like a cult. Whatever he thought became policy and he was very open to sudden shifts if he saw an organizational advantage. Since he had proven able to build an organization of about a thousand members in Argentina he began sending organizers to other Latin American countries to take over their little groups. He called this international operation the Bolshevik Tendency.

Moreno was generally successful, especially in Colombia, with its history of volatility on the left. Moreno's Bolshevik Tendency was instrumental in starting the Bloque Socialista in Colombia in 1976. The name changed in September 1977 to Partido Socialista de los Trabajadores (PST—Socialist Workers Party). The following year a second group had formed, the Liga Comunista Revolucionaria (LCR—Revolutionary Communist League), which began allying with the American SWP and changed its name to Partido Socialista Revolucionario. I was particularly fond of the leaders of this latter Colombian movement.

Moreno's cult-leader status reached its zenith with the Simon Bolivar Brigade, the group with which in 1979 he infiltrated the Sandinista movement in Nicaragua, an astonishing and disgusting maneuver that I will detail in a later chapter.

Spain

In contrast to many of the other trips, I enjoyed my visits to the FI section in Spain. The Spaniards seemed open-minded. When I first arrived I had some problems understanding their pronunciation (European Spanish is quite different) and a lot of the idioms. For instance, I spent a few weeks confused as to why in meetings the Spaniards kept making references to someone named Ostia, who was not present and whose name seemed to be invoked only out of exasperation. This proved to be the word *hostia*, the Catholic host—the communion wafer—and the expression is used like the English interjection "Christ Almighty!"

Spain was completely different from the rest of Europe in that until the death of Francisco Franco in November 1975 and for a brief time afterward it was governed by a fascist dictatorship, one that had relatively good relations with the United States. In Spain it was illegal to hold a meeting, period.

It was illegal to print a newspaper or to hand out leaflets. Yet the opposition to the fascists was organized and immense. A key reason was that the Catholic Church had abandoned its support for the regime and had itself moved into opposition

Early on I recall learning that in churches a priest would leave a window open so the underground could "steal" its mimeograph machines (for those not old enough to remember, mimeographs were the messy, aromatic ink-and-stencil copiers of the '60s and '70s). The church could then report the "robbery" and buy new machines, as the church was allowed to have duplicating equipment.

In Spain I traveled under my own name as a U.S. tourist. I learned quickly that every hotel reported the names of its registered guests to the police but it took three days for the mail to reach the police. So I moved hotels every three days. Interestingly, when I later gained access to my CIA files, they referred to the peculiar fact that every three days I switched hotels. In Barcelona, my usual destination, I traveled by subway. One of the simple techniques to avoid being followed was to get on the subway, travel one stop, get out, cross the platform, and catch the subway going the other direction. It wasn't too hard to notice if someone was following you.

The FI supporters in Spain were overwhelmingly new members and very young. Many of them had been already imprisoned by the government for one reason or another. Since all meetings were illegal, holding a national gathering was not easy. About a hundred people holed up in a house for three days. No one went out, except for a few people who bought food or other necessities. For the first time in my life I slept with other males in one bed. And that was a luxury—the fact that I got to sleep on a bed instead of on the floor was because I was an international guest.

With the exception of my visits to Spain, over time I began to dislike having to go to Latin America and Europe to talk to the various Trotskyist groups. It was a very tiring and rather lonely task to be traveling all the time. Much of the work felt futile. Yet I want to point out that most of the groups were involved in supporting struggles on specific issues for workers' or students' rights, not just the extremes I have touched on here. The rank and file in most cases were deeply committed people like the SWPers in the United States.

But every section was caught up in a quest to defend the correct "program," defined in abstraction from practice, which required a leader who had the true interpretation. So inevitably multiple groups developed, each supporting a local guru who represented the correct "program" and historical interpretation. These relatively small groups then tried to plead their individual cases to larger groups in other countries to become the foreign group's representatives in their homeland. In France three relatively strong organizations became centers for smaller groups throughout the world. The disconnect between reality, activity, and each respective "program" was complicated further by the fact that the Stalinist parties remained dominant on the left and large social democratic formations also were present in many countries.

Given that most of these groups have dissolved or changed their positions over the years I think it unnecessary to review the particular opinions and formations that existed while I was working with them as a representative of the SWP, which itself suffered from similar symptoms and was evolving slowly in a direction I no longer supported.

CHAPTER 9

THE 1970 CAMPAIGN FOR U.S. SENATE AND THE 1976 CAMPAIGN FOR PRESIDENT

In 1970, during the height of antiwar activity, the SWP proposed that I run for the U.S. Senate from Massachusetts. The idea was to take advantage of my popularity among antiwar young people to speak out against the war in Vietnam as well as to address other important social issues. We didn't expect much to come of the campaign, since meeting the stringent requirements for ballot status would be impossible, but figured it could help raise the profile of the SWP and generate more awareness of the growing opposition to the war.

One way to prompt the media to cover my campaign was for me to debate incumbent Senator Edward (Ted) Kennedy. Given that I was at zero in the polls, a socialist, and a write-in candidate, debating Kennedy would not have seemed to be an option. But with some artful and fearless strategizing I was able to debate Ted Kennedy three times, albeit unofficially. Here is how we did it.

Kennedy was scheduled to address a group of students at Boston University (BU) on September 13. That evening we mobilized campaign supporters and leafleted at BU as people arrived for the meeting. At about 7:45 p.m., when the hall was packed, we noticed that the microphone was set up and ready to go but no one from the Kennedy campaign had yet arrived.

I walked to the front of the hall, took the microphone, and introduced myself. From the outset I made it clear that I respected fully that this was Ted Kennedy's meeting and that as soon as he arrived I would step down; but, I added, so rarely did the American people ever get a chance to hear from anyone aside from Democrats and Republicans, I just wanted to pose some issues for them to think about when Kennedy spoke. The audience, naturally, seemed somewhat nervous. In my speech I focused on the war in Vietnam and pointed out that we would all be voting on an initiative in November but that Kennedy had not yet taken a position and we should urge him to call for a vote against the war. After this brief presentation I left the stage before Kennedy or his campaign people showed up.

When Kennedy entered I was struck that he hardly had anyone with him. One of his young nephews sat with him onstage. Kennedy did not get the usual standing ovation when introduced, I think in part due to my remarks that he had not taken a clear stance against the Vietnam War. In his talk he criticized "campus violence," which also didn't go over too well. During the question-and-answer period, I wrote in my diary, he "gradually weakened his standing before the overflow audience."

Near the end of the event Stu Singer, a leading SWPer, got up and said that Peter Camejo, the socialist candidate for Senate, was in the audience and asked whether Kennedy would allow Camejo a few minutes of speaking time. To my amazement and that of everyone else present, Kennedy immediately responded in the affirmative, saying, "Sure, come on up, Peter." I don't think he knew who I was. Given Kennedy's lack of security personnel and the fact that his two brothers had been assassinated, I didn't want there to be any tension as I approached the stage. I was nervous walking up there and kept both hands in front of me and visible to him. His young nephew suddenly stood up and ran out of the hall. I felt really sorry about that and I think Kennedy did too but he said nothing.

Kennedy held the microphone out for me to speak but kept it in his hand, obviously being cautious. I urged him to join with all of us in opposing the war in Vietnam and asked him to declare how he would vote in November on the referendum. The audience applauded loudly in support. Kennedy allowed me some more time to raise a few other issues and then gave his reply. He said he had not made up his mind yet on how he would vote on the war initiative. Then he let me speak again. He seemed to realize that I was speaking respectfully, and that I acknowledged fully that this was his meeting.

Once again I urged him to join with the majority of the people of Massachusetts and around the world in opposing the war. I thanked him for his openness in having allowed me an opportunity to address his meeting. Again the audience responded strongly, mainly as a way to urge Kennedy to declare against the war. We shook hands and I thanked him again (off-mike) before exiting the stage.

The entire time I was, of course, astounded that Kennedy had allowed me to speak at all, under the circumstances. There was never any question that he was going to win the election; nevertheless, by letting me speak even for ten minutes he had demonstrated an openness that few Democratic Party candidates shared. The next day the *Boston Globe* reported that Kennedy had debated socialist Peter Camejo at Boston University. The *Globe* did not, however, include a single word I had uttered, covering only Kennedy's remarks. That day I appeared on local news Channel 56 for fifteen minutes to point out that fact. A few days later, on September 17, the *Boston University News* ran a solid article on the Kennedy–Camejo debate.

About a week later I got a call from the *Boston Globe*. They had arranged for a reporter to spend the day with me on October 8; the article was slated to run on page 3, in the same spot as the article on the debate with Kennedy. The reporter who covered me was Bruce McCabe. After a few short campaign events and a two-hour interview, we went to Northeastern University to hold an open outdoor rally at the same location as Kennedy had earlier in the campaign. The police didn't allow rallies there and we aimed to make the point that Kennedy could get away with it but that they would likely arrest me. I drew a crowd of about three hundred students. Sure enough, the police showed up, disconnected our sound equipment, and told me to leave or I would be arrested.

I didn't leave but continued speaking, explaining to the students what was happening. The police arrested me for "trespassing" and took me to a nearby station to be booked. I was arraigned at about 2:30 p.m. McCabe, the reporter, was pleased to have an interesting, action-packed article, accompanied by photos of my arrest and the students booing the police. He told me, "This is all I need, Peter. Thanks."

On October 9 I went to another Kennedy event, hoping to debate him, and brought with me the article from the *Boston Globe* showing my arrest. Again Kennedy invited me to speak. The debate was filmed for national television by CBS. I showed everyone in the audience the photo of my being arrested while following Kennedy's example. Ted laughed and said, "You're getting more publicity than I am." On a piece of paper I had made a list of issues I hoped to raise. Ted let me go over all the points, which I did quickly in about five minutes, then asked me, "Peter, can I borrow your list?" I said sure. Then Kennedy took up each one, giving his respective opinions. The next day the *Globe* ran an article titled, "Kennedy, Camejo Meet in Natick."

As the years have passed I have often thought about how nicely Kennedy treated me and I wish I had made more of an effort to get to know him. Although I often disagreed with him politically his generosity and kindness gave me respect for him.

The evening of October 14 I debated the Republican senatorial candidate, Sy Spaulding, at Boston University. Spaulding was very polite and we debated a couple times before the last debate with Kennedy, a three-way match that took place on October 19 at Holy Cross College in Worcester, Massachusetts. Again the format was fair and everyone was courteous. Later that day I spoke to an audience of two hundred at Holy Cross, then ran off to do a radio show for an hour, and, still later, raced over to Northampton to talk to supporters—a typical campaign day.

On October 25 the conservative *Boston Herald-Traveler* ran a front-page article by Gordon Hall in which he red-baited me. We talked to Sy Spaulding's campaign office to get their support against the red-baiting attack. At Tufts University later that day we were scheduled to have another three-way debate with representatives but no one showed from the Kennedy campaign. Of the approximately 250 students in attendance, 67 signed up for a class on socialism.

The afternoon of October 26 I met with Crocker Snow of the *Boston Globe*, who explained to me that Robert Healy was the person at the *Globe* trying to block the coverage of my campaign. That evening I addressed 125 students at Stonehill College. The next day I spoke at Amherst and Holyoke, where the campus papers endorsed our campaign.

As the campaign entered its last week the media interest escalated. Incredibly, on Monday, November 2, the day before the election, the *Boston Globe* ran an article entitled "Candidate Camejo Ignored by Media." The piece was quite favorable.

On election night we held our campaign party at a church, which had a polling station in the basement. Wearing a suit and tie I went down to the basement after the polls had closed and found one poll worker still at the station. I asked him how the election had gone. He answered, no problems, about the normal turnout. Without telling him who I was, I asked if people had written in any candidates. The man paused for a moment. Then he actually reached into the wastebasket next to him and pulled out a wad of paper. We both looked through it and there were about seven or eight write-ins for me. I asked him what would happen to those write-ins. As he wadded the paper back up and set it on a desk, he said, "We mail those to the voting center."

The 1976 Presidential Campaign

In mid-1974 Jack Barnes, the SWP national secretary, informed me that he had polled all the SWP branches and it was unanimous that they wanted me to run for president in 1976.* As it turned out, Barnes himself was opposed to my running, as Barry Sheppard has told me. I had figured as much and told Barnes I would have to think about it.

There were certainly more than a few factors to consider. First it crossed my mind that, afterward, being a former presidential candidate without a college degree might make it very difficult for me to get a regular job if I ever were to quit or be expelled from the SWP. Beyond that, I was concerned about what kind of campaign would be run. I thought we should try to run an inclusive campaign, not explicitly socialist, built around the key issues affecting working-class people and other sectors, such as racial discrimination and equal rights for women and gays. In other words, I hoped to build a campaign that would not be focused on recruiting more members for the SWP, but one that would reach out to broader forces in the aim of making a real impact.

At the time my views seemed to be a one-person minority within the SWP. I suspected that Jack Barnes, who knew I did not see eye-to-eye with him, would try to control the campaign and limit its scope. He and others in the SWP leadership wished I weren't quite so popular among the membership, but Barnes was astute enough to sense that the party could use my appeal to its advantage.

My popularity in the SWP was deceptive. The membership sensed that, unlike the other party speakers, there was something unique in my presentations that attracted new people to the SWP. However, most people did not realize that it was the nonsectarian manner of my approach—they

---

* At the time I was only thirty-four years old, but would be thirty-six by the time of the election; the Constitutional requirement to run for president is thirty-five.

just thought it was because I was a good speaker, a sort of political stand-up comic who used a lot of humor to illustrate points and keep the audience entertained.

I had another major concern about undertaking a presidential campaign. I had developed a medical condition, now called irritable bowel syndrome, then referred to as "spastic colon." It is a disorder of the intestinal tract, exacerbated by stressful situations, that causes abdominal pain and other inconvenient digestive problems. The doctors gave me pills to try to control it.

My companion, Barbara Thornton—my wife,* for all intents and purposes—said she would support whatever I decided but emphasized that everyone in the SWP was asking that I run. Before I agreed to run I told Barnes that Barbara should be assigned to the campaign and allowed to travel with me, as she was more than qualified to be part of the campaign staff. Barnes would not consider it, despite the fact that when he traveled for international work his companion, Betsey Stone, was also assigned to international work to travel with him. I had the feeling Barnes wanted me to press the issue so he could retract my candidacy by explaining to the SWP that I had made unreasonable demands. I asked Barbara how she felt and whether she thought I should push the issue. At the time she was working a full-time job in New York as well as taking on all kinds of assignments for the movement. We decided to drop the issue; I would run. To this day I have mixed feelings about that decision.

Willie Mae Reid, an African American SWPer from Chicago, was nominated to run as the vice-presidential candidate. She was one of the most self-sacrificing and committed persons I ever met. I was very happy with the choice and enjoyed campaigning with Willie Mae, even though much of the time we were on separate tour schedules. She was an excellent communicator and added a great deal to the slate.

Campaign Launch

The campaign was announced at a YSA convention in St. Louis on December 27, 1974. Our campaign literature hadn't arrived in time so we had to make replacement copies early in the morning in order to have our materials ready for the announcement. As it turned out the SWPers driving the truck from New York had gotten in at 4:00 a.m. but didn't realize the

---

* Debbie Weinstein and I divorced in 1970.

press materials were in the truck. During all the stress and strain over the missing literature, they were catching up on sleep.

Many reporters showed up to cover the announcement. They wired me for recording while I was seated. When my candidacy was announced I tried to stand up, but because of the wiring the reporters barked at me, "No, you have to stay seated!" so I did. The next day widespread press interest continued—we were getting press for both the YSA convention and the campaign as separate stories.

On December 29 I addressed the convention of about a thousand SWP delegates and members. Before it was my turn to speak I had to leave the podium twice because of my illness. But the speech went fine, in part because of the supportive audience, most of whom had heard me speak before. I opened my speech with a tongue-in-cheek line: "This campaign is a very serious matter so I will not be cracking jokes, making you laugh, or entertaining you anymore." The whole room broke up laughing. It was downhill from there as I poked fun at the Democrats and Republicans, talking about Watergate (Nixon had resigned in August) and all the major issues before us.

On the roster before me were Nan Bailey and my running mate Willie Mae Reid, who both gave excellent speeches, as well as my campaign co-manager Ed Heisler, about whom I wrote in my diary "was also good." It would be nearly two years before we learned that Ed was a paid FBI informant.

A Typical Day

From the outset the campaign was intensive. I started doing national tours right away. In every city with an SWP branch a committee was set up to coordinate the election effort. As the campaign progressed, advance teams traveled ahead of me to help YSA locals build meetings and set up tables on campuses before I spoke. These teams were usually very young people with a car. They weren't paid, just given funds to cover minimal expenses. Back in New York we had a central campaign staff that numbered less than a dozen, counting both paid staffers and volunteers.

In a typical morning I visited unemployment offices and shopping centers, where I shook hands, talked with people, and gave out our brochure called the "Bill of Rights for Working People,"* in which we proposed eight rights:

---

* Available online at http://www.marxists.org/history/etol/writers/camejo/billof rights.htm.

the right to a job,
the right to an adequate income,
the right to a free education,
the right to free medical care,
the right to secure retirement,
the right to know the truth about economic and political polities
    that affect our lives,
the right of oppressed minorities to control their own affairs,
and the right to decide economic and political policy.

The response was generally very positive, especially if any media were present. We learned quickly that the presence of a camera tends to make the public curious and persistent. They seek you out and are more willing to speak out about the injustices of our society.

In the late morning or early afternoon I spoke at colleges and universities, sometimes two in a day. Some of the rallies on campuses, especially outdoors, grew from several hundred to occasionally a thousand or two. Late afternoons I taped radio interviews or gave TV interviews. We found that setting up specific appointments with the media worked better than press conferences, although we did some press conferences too, especially later in the campaign. In the evenings we held public events to bring together campaign supporters and potential donors.

At the start of the campaign tour, I stayed overnight with friends in each city we visited. Unfortunately that translated into sleep deprivation, because—despite the enjoyment of being with people you know and love—staying with friends is the equivalent of adding another meeting or two to the schedule, every day. Friends want to be good hosts and ask a lot of questions about how things are going. After a few months of losing sleep I implemented a new plan for my accommodations. Each SWP chapter recruited a volunteer whose sole campaign duty was to stay elsewhere for the night in order to lend me his or her apartment. Once this plan was put into action I was able to get more rest.

The campaign routine remained intense, an effort that would stretch out for the better part of two years. Although I became exhausted—a state made worse by my illness, which got me down to an alarming 117 pounds—I found it inspiring to reach new people almost every day and to witness all the hard work that supporters were contributing throughout the country.

Venezuelan Support

One of my first press breaks happened in a roundabout way. While visiting me in New York my father had picked up some of our campaign literature. As a well-known figure in Venezuela, he was often met at the airport by media representatives looking for an interview. This time he handed the reporters our campaign materials and announced that his son was running for president of the United States, which got us front-page, supportive coverage in the Venezuelan papers. After all, in South American politics to run as a socialist did not have the same connotation it had in the United States. A well-known Venezuelan poet wrote a poem backing me, which was published in the major Caracas dailies. This was no doubt due in part to my sharing the name Pedro Camejo with the legendary Venezuelan liberator.

Later on my grandmother Chita held a press conference in Barquisimeto, in which she told reporters that if I got elected I had better be good to the peasants and the poor. Otherwise, she announced, "It would be better that he come back to plant potatoes in Rio Claro." She also told the press that even if I lost the election, I would win a seat in the Senate, which is the way the electoral process works in Venezuela. I am quite sure the reporters knew better but they had fun with the interview and featured a photo of my grandmother. My uncle Amador got students in Barquisimeto to plaster the entire city with my campaign poster. When I visited afterward, people walking down the streets of Barquisimeto recognized me from the publicity.

All told though I think I got better press in Venezuela than in the United States. I even suggested to my campaign staff that we should consider having me go to Venezuela to do some serious media in the hope that it would be picked up by the U.S. press, but I couldn't get the campaign committee behind the idea. This reflected larger problems within our organization.

Mass Media

We had succeeded in 1970 in drawing some attention to my Massachusetts senatorial race by having me debate Ted Kennedy. But in a national campaign it would be much harder to break into the mass media. One of my ideas was to challenge all the major presidential candidates to a debate. We didn't expect anyone to agree but it wouldn't hurt to ask. To our amazement the Democratic Party candidate at the bottom of the polls at that time, Jimmy Carter, wrote back to say that he agreed to debate me.

Our reaction was—wow. Several universities offered almost immediately to sponsor the debate but then Carter's poll figures starting rising and the universities changed their minds. Carter was impressively honest, because when reporters called his campaign to follow up on my assertion that Carter had agreed to a debate, his staff confirmed it was true.

Incredibly, no mention that Carter had agreed to a debate with Camejo appeared in the media, either due to reporter disinterest or, more likely, to censorship. So that became part of my statement to reporters: that they would not be allowed to report the story. Finally in Minnesota a TV crew came to film a piece on our campaign and I told them about the Carter debate letter. They demanded to see it so I showed it to them. They still wouldn't believe it so they called the Carter campaign and had it confirmed. They shot footage of the letter, asked me to comment on it, and told me to watch the 7:00 p.m. news so I could see that in America there is a free press. I assured them they wouldn't be able to run the piece. We waited, turned on our TV, and watched as the 7:00 o'clock news hour passed; no report on the Carter debate.

Arrested in Atlanta and Houston

A ripe opportunity for some publicity occurred in Atlanta, where President Ford was speaking on February 3, 1975. I went to Ford's talk to support a civil rights protest led by Hosea Williams of the Southern Christian Leadership Conference. A group of us were arrested for not moving when the police told us to. I was put in the police wagon and assumed that our New York office, alerted by the Atlanta campaign, would be tipping off the media that a presidential candidate had been arrested.

When I was released later that night I was shocked to learn that the New York central campaign office, managed by Doug Jenness, had done nothing. They didn't think we should push it. The following day I participated in a press conference with Hosea Williams but the national campaign staff continued to do nothing. Even the next issue of the *Militant*, our SWP newspaper, didn't mention that its presidential candidate had been arrested. As the word of my arrest got around among SWP members, I noticed that few of them asked me why it had not been reported.

I knew, of course, that the resistance was coming from Jack Barnes, whose concept of the campaign was rather limited. Jean Savage, who worked in the New York campaign office, kept me informed about things she overheard. A few days after my Atlanta arrest Jean called to tell me that Doug Jenness thought we shouldn't use a quote from Ted Kennedy referring to me as "a worthy opponent" because it made us sound as though we were a little pro-Democratic. That kind of quibble made it clear to me that Doug Jenness's views were sectarian as well as just plain illogical, but they reflected the direction in which Barnes was taking the SWP.

I thought we should run a campaign that tried to unify people fighting for peace, for social justice, on labor issues, against racism, and more—a campaign that would help people see the reality of the two-party system and the nature of our corporate-controlled press. While it might seem hard to believe, insofar as anyone was willing to challenge the two-party system the SWP was among the strongest groups; our level of campaigning, including the final vote, demonstrated this.

Throughout the campaign I did not express my concerns, except on narrow, specific issues, or hold meetings with SWP members, even close friends. (At the time I considered this as evidence of my discipline, but looking back I see it as a deficit.) The overwhelming majority of the SWP leadership saw the campaign merely as an opportunity to reach a slightly larger audience to try to recruit to the SWP. Anything beyond that simple orientation was considered a waste of time—an attitude of self-importance that, at its essence, strikes me as elitist.

My perspective on these issues was not as clear as it is today or I would never have agreed to run. The national SWP office persistently tried to limit the scope of the campaign while regarding me as an instrument for recruitment but also as a threat. After the lack of action regarding the Atlanta arrest I didn't say much but began thinking about how to get the campaign director changed.

A little more than a month after the Atlanta events, on March 11, a Houston city police car started following the car I was in with three campaign workers named Juan, Sylvia, and Armand. Suddenly the police pulled us over. They ordered everyone out of the car but me. I got out too, to try to find out what was happening. One police officer said, "Did I tell you to get out?" elaborating with profanity. I refused to get back in the car so he jumped on me, twisted my arm, and told me I was under arrest. Then he added, "You're the commie running for president." Since one officer was preoccupied with me and there was only one other, I urged the three campaign workers to run in different directions and to call the campaign office when they reached a phone. They took off immediately with the police officers shouting "Stop!" The police did not pursue them.

I was taken to the police station to be booked. When we arrived a very young cop began yelling that he was going to kill me. Two older cops pulled him back. I made note of his badge number: 2208. This time after I got out of jail I went to the FBI to file a report on the threat on my life, the illegal police trailing, and the false arrest. Once again the campaign missed an excellent opportunity for media coverage, although the New York office at least expressed its concern.

In June a steering committee took over the campaign, increasing the number of decision makers and giving me the opportunity to voice my ideas a bit more aggressively without hurting anyone's feelings. But that didn't last long. Without consulting me, the SWP leadership chose Andrea Morell, who was even more stubborn than Doug Jenness when it came to these issues, as the new campaign manager. Later in the campaign Morell and some others started bad-mouthing me to SWPers they thought would align against me.

On June 10 the trial took place in Houston. In my diary I described the trial: "The cops lied quite a lot. But the most amazing testimony was the local shopkeeper's testimony. They claimed I went to hit the cop … The jury took only a few minutes and returned a not guilty ruling." The New York Times and Houston Post each had a reporter on the case all day. A few radio stations came, as well as Channel 2 TV. That evening we held a victory dinner party with about fifty campaign supporters.

Latino Activists

During the campaign I made a special effort to visit Latino leaders and activists. For the first time in American history a Latino was running for president, and in general Latino leaders, activists, and students tended to be extremely supportive. When I spoke to a meeting of Chicano students in East Los Angeles, half of them signed up to work on the campaign.

From my efforts on the campaign trail I developed a wonderful relationship with the farm workers' leaders in Texas and Ohio. Baldemar Velásquez, president of the Farm Labor Organizing Committee, and I became lifelong friends. I also met Juan Mari Brás, the leader of the movement for Puerto Rican independence, whose paper Claridad ran a very positive article.

Juan José Peña from Las Vegas, New Mexico, was the leader of the New Mexico La Raza Unida Party (RUP). A good friend, Juan worked with me during the campaign and afterward. The New Mexico RUP endorsed me for president and Juan spoke with me at rallies and other events. Manuel Archuleta in Albuquerque was also a close friend and a key figure in the movement.

The most important of these relationships was my friendship with José Angel Gutiérrez, the central leader and founder of RUP in Texas. JAG and I have been friends for more than thirty years. He had first met my brother Antonio when they worked together on some pamphlets on the historic rise of the Chicano party in Texas. To my amazement JAG got RUP in Texas to endorse me for president, and I believe I actually won a majority in several South Texas counties because of RUP's endorsement.

The SWP versus the FBI

In November 1975 I had to fly east on short notice to testify before a congressional hearing as part of an investigation into the FBI. In 1973 the SWP had filed suit against the FBI on behalf of members of the SWP and the YSA, demanding an injunction against harassment and compensation for damages sustained during the FBI's decades-long, illegal Counterintelligence Program (COINTELPRO). Officially formed in 1956, COINTELPRO targeted leftist organizations, in particular the SWP, with surveillance, infiltration, harassment and blackmail of party members, and disruption of legal political activities, among many other criminal acts.* With the help of the Political Rights Defense Fund (PRDF), information about the FBI's extensive illegal activities—including a specific "SWP Disruption Program"—began to come to light. These revelations spurred media interest in the SWP and in our presidential campaign.

Hundreds of stories on the FBI investigation and the SWP's lawsuit appeared in major papers. During 1975–76 I was mentioned in more than a dozen articles in the New York Times and finally made their front page on March 29, 1976, as part of an article titled "F.B.I. Burglarized Leftist Offices Here 92 Times in 1960–66, Official Files Show."

I cannot confirm the details, but in regard to COINTELPRO an amazing and disturbing story came to my attention. During the pretrial period a former top FBI official, William C. Sullivan, contacted the PRDF committee. Sullivan had headed the FBI's domestic intelligence division and had been

---

* The lawsuit proceeded over the course of thirteen years. In 1986, Judge Thomas P. Griesa ruled in favor of the SWP and awarded $264,000 in damages. See also Blackstock, *COINTELPRO*.

the third-highest-ranking official in the FBI until he retired in 1971 over disagreements with J. Edgar Hoover about the bureau's violations of citizens' civil liberties. He met privately with a few reporters and told them how disgruntled he was with the FBI's criminal activity. He was slated to testify in a number of cases.

According to my source Sullivan requested a secret meeting with the PRDF in Iceland. The meeting actually took place and Sullivan divulged some of the tricks the FBI was using, in violation of the Freedom of Information Act, to hide COINTELPRO documents.* Not long after the Iceland meeting Sullivan was shot to death, on November 9, 1977, in New Hampshire in what was called a "hunting accident." The shooter was the twenty-two-year-old son of a state policeman. To this day there is considerable suspicion that Sullivan was murdered to shut him up.

Informants in the Campaign

The judge in the case of the SWP versus the FBI was Thomas P. Griesa, a conservative Republican federal district judge. He seemed taken aback to learn that the FBI had investigated and harassed an organization that in forty years had never broken the law and was not expected to do so. The SWP's lawyers told the judge that they suspected the FBI had planted paid informants among my campaign staff around the country. In disbelief the judge asked the FBI's attorney if it were true. The FBI requested a week to respond and when the time was up, they announced that there were indeed paid informants among the campaign staff—sixty-six in total. The judge was shocked and ordered the FBI to remove all the informants on a specific date.

Within the SWP we set a simple trap. We stated officially that no members could resign on that date; therefore anyone who did would reveal themselves to be FBI informants. To my amazement this included Ed Heisler, the co-chair of my campaign.

We had occasionally discovered paid FBI informants in the SWP over the years, but not on this scale. Over time we had noticed that the FBI tended to place one informant per branch. Although there were accidental revelations, the most common means of unmasking came via the U.S. Postal

---

* An example of such tricks, revealed earlier in the investigation, was to label COINTELPRO files "Do Not File," and to prepare them without the usual filing numbers—therefore an inspection of regular FBI files would reveal no filing numbers out of order.

Service. The FBI required the informants to send regular, handwritten reports to a P.O. Box, with no return address on the envelope. Once in a while the FBI forgot to renew a particular P.O. Box and an informant's report was opened by postal workers in an attempt to find a return address for the letter. Since most of these reports looked like minutes of a meeting, and specifically of the SWP, the post office forwarded the report to us.

In one case we were forwarded a copy of a report with a fake name signed at the bottom. We knew only that it came from Minneapolis, so we had all the members in that chapter fill out a questionnaire. Then we hired a handwriting specialist to identify the informant by his handwriting. It was an older worker, a member since the 1930s. He confessed when confronted, claiming the role was harmless and he needed extra income. We expelled him. In other cases we knew who it was but took no action so the FBI wouldn't send in a new informant.

The San Francisco "Scandal"

In June 1976 while campaigning in the Bay Area I was told that Asher Harer, one of the long-time leaders of the San Francisco SWP, had in his possession some old microphones and wires that he had found hidden in the ceiling of the SWP office back in the 1950s—recording equipment undoubtedly placed by the FBI to monitor SWP meetings. The equipment was to be sent to New York as evidence in our lawsuit.

I took a look at the microphones and wires and thought, old as the story was, if it were linked to the SWP lawsuit and all the new revelations of FBI criminal activity, we might be able to parlay it into some Bay Area press coverage. So I called the *San Francisco Chronicle* and offered them an exclusive if they put the story on their front page and included a photo of me with the microphones.

Sure enough, the article came out on the front page of the *Chronicle* on June 27, 1976, with the photo after the jump. We put out a press release the morning the *Chronicle* story hit, so they got their exclusive. The TV and radio media then jumped on the bandwagon, so we got a good response in the media. I thought this was a nice little coup for us, not only promoting the campaign but also helping to shed light on the FBI harassment of progressives and the SWP in particular.

That day or the next Jack Barnes arrived in San Francisco. His face was angry and, as best I can recall, his first words to me were "I have never been so embarrassed as to see an article on the front page of a daily newspaper where it says that the SWP is anticommunist." Internally I had to restrain myself. I think I replied, "Really?"

In passing the article stated, "SWP leaders say they descend from the U.S. Socialist Party, support civil rights, and oppose the Communists." This was obviously one reporter's effort to boil down a complex description. We were against the Stalinist government of the Soviet Union and strongly opposed the official Communist Parties, although we usually explained that we were the real communists and that communism was supposed to be democratic. The reporter interviewing me was not up on this exact formulation and he had abridged it to make the point that we were against the Communist Parties.

I thought to myself, "We've got a hopeless sectarian here." Barnes thought it was embarrassing—"horrendous" was another word he used—for us to land the front page of a major daily paper, spreading the story about the FBI harassment and getting publicity for the campaign, simply because the reporter didn't get the anti-Stalinist formulations exactly right. After this exchange Barnes and I went to lunch with Farrell Dobbs, the great labor leader from the '30s and the SWP's national secretary for decades. It was obvious to me just from Farrell's body language that he sided with Barnes.

Ballot Status

One of the most remarkable achievements of the SWP's 1976 campaign was winning ballot status in—I believe—more than thirty states. The biggest challenge was California. All our signatures were collected by volunteers. As August 1976 approached we feared that we wouldn't reach the 150,000 signatures we had set as our goal. The California requirement at that time was about 100,000 signatures, but we aimed to have a large safety margin in case some of the signatures were rejected, which was inevitable. It was clear that a campaign leader would need to be on the ground in California to reinforce the volunteer effort and organize an additional contingent of young activists to help.

I proposed that the campaign director, Andrea Morell, go out to California for three weeks to lead the stepped-up effort. She refused, countering that if I wanted to see California on the ballot I was the one who should go. Having just campaigned in California in late June, it was the last thing I should have been doing as the candidate, but I went. I arrived in Los Angeles on July 24, 1976. On July 25 we had a special meeting with the campaign committee and the local SWP leadership. Our goal for the 150,000 signatures was August 6, before the annual national gathering of the SWP at Oberlin College in Ohio. Some SWPers, especially leaders dealing with the day-to-day work, had doubts we could make it. I advocated bringing in help from other cities, lowering our goal to 130,000, and then submitting whatever we could gather by the deadline.

Two days after our meeting, Sam Manuel called to tell me his car had been stolen—with 14,000 petitions in the trunk. No one, I thought, would steal Manuel's old, worn-out car. My thinking was that the petitions were probably stolen by the FBI. Earlier that month an FBI informant, Tim Redfearn, had been arrested for burglarizing the SWP's Denver office. We had also recently learned that in 1968 the FBI had stolen SWP presidential candidate Fred Halstead's briefcase. So to go to the media and float the possibility that the FBI had stolen the signatures did not seem too far-fetched.

At 3:00 p.m. on July 27 we met with the ACLU director, Ramona Ripston, who was very supportive. She said the ACLU would consider helping us. We went ahead and called a press conference for the next day. Back in New York, the reaction from campaign director Andrea Morell was typical: "We'll see if anyone shows up for the press conference tomorrow."

Our press conference was a success, with Channels 4 and 7, the *Los Angeles Times*, radio, and *El Express* all filing stories. I flew to Oakland to meet with local campaign leaders, and the very next morning got a call that the L.A. police had returned the car. They claimed they had found it in the San Fernando Valley and that it had been used for a homicide. All the petitions were still in the trunk. Of course there is no way to know if the police story were true but I suspect it was pure fabrication.

By August 2 we had attained 140,000 signatures and went ahead with submitting them in the various parts of the state in which they had been collected. We knew that we could still collect more if too many of these were declared invalid. In Los Angeles we submitted 92,000 signatures on August 4. Then I flew to San Diego and back up to San Francisco* to hold

---

* Because other third parties were also submitting their petitions, in San Francisco I ran into Gus Hall, the CP presidential candidate, who referred to me and the SWP as an FBI operation. This I found unconscionable, especially in light of our ongoing struggles with the FBI. Regardless of political disagreements, the SWP defended the CP's right to their views and defended their members against illegal harassment and persecution—at that time being a CP member was quite dangerous in terms of holding or getting a job—yet in return for our support we were accused of being FBI agents.

more press conferences, which were increasingly successful, and to submit more signatures.

In the end we got on the ballot in California.

The Home Stretch

As we entered September the issue of the presidential debates came to the forefront. All too predictably I had to argue with Andrea Morell and other SWP leaders even to permit campaign staff to work on demanding that we be included in the debates. In my diary I wrote, "The sectarianism on these kinds of things is amazing—always tied to the 'we can't really do that' attitude." At the time I still hadn't connected the sectarianism to the general methodology and underlying rigidity of the SWP's outlook. We simply seemed to be on a permanent collision course.

I pushed hard on the subject of the debates and they finally yielded, giving Jean Savage the okay to start working on the issue. Jean was effective almost immediately: the next day we got a front-page article in the *New York Post* about the legal steps we were taking to be included in the debates. The fact that Carter had agreed in writing to debate me was finally more of a story. I proposed that perhaps we could find a radio TV station that would give me equal time right after the debate between Ford and Carter. This did not come to pass, but I think with more effort it could have been accomplished and would have reached a wide audience. As expected we were not permitted to take part in the official presidential debates, but that was not the sole endpoint—raising public awareness of the exclusionary nature of the two-party system and adding our voice to the conversation, even from the outside, was the larger goal.

We had been getting good media coverage in the context of the ongoing FBI revelations and I thought there was more ground to be gained in that area. At the beginning of September I was able to request my own highly censored FBI file. It revealed that the FBI had been following me since I was eighteen years old. They even included in some reports what time I turned off the lights in my apartment to go to sleep. But the SWP leadership still couldn't grasp the potential of publicizing any of these FBI divulgences, including the fact that there had been informants in my campaign. On September 8, exasperated, I wrote in my diary, "Larry [Seigle, director of the SWP Political Committee] was incapable of understanding why we should make an issue of the 66 agents!"

Liberal Exclusion Policy

In Cambridge, Massachusetts, on September 11, 1976, a meeting was held by the women's liberation movement in Kendall Square. The women leading the event had invited me to attend and speak, but behind the scenes the event was organized and controlled by Democratic politicians. The list of speakers was broad and I was, of course, pro-choice and a supporter of the Equal Rights Amendment to the Constitution (ERA), not to mention the only presidential candidate in attendance. But the Democrats did not want me to speak.

Quite a few leaders of the women's movement were also SWP members working on my campaign. On the spot they wrote a petition asking that I be allowed to speak and got the overwhelming majority of people at the rally to sign it. When all the other speakers had finished they handed the petition to the organizers. The Democrats running the rally just ran away. Then we approached the mayor of Cambridge, who was up on the speakers' platform, and he physically tried to push me away from the podium. Since the rally was over I climbed onto the stage and announced to the remaining crowd what had happened. Naturally the majority opposed exclusionism; I have found this always to be true. The people want openness and don't want views suppressed, but "liberal" leaders are always working to exclude anyone not in favor of the Democratic Party.

The Final Leg

As we entered the last fifty days of the campaign I continued to tour throughout the nation. The news around the FBI continued to increase our media coverage and our campaign events drew increased turnouts. I don't have an exact figure as to how much money we raised but it was substantial; adjusted for inflation I would estimate anywhere from half a million to a million dollars altogether.

We reached a large mainstream audience with the late-night talk show, *Tomorrow with Tom Snyder*. Snyder gave me a half hour to make up for the time they had given the major candidates. The show came off great—I recently had the chance to listen to a sound recording of the episode, and I was surprised at how much faster my mind worked at thirty-six than it does today. I had speedy responses to all Snyder's questions, with economic and other data to back up my statements, and everything was presented with humor and in a friendly, relaxed manner. After one commercial break I held up a four-page handout called something like "The Truth about Carter." I announced that if people sent a donation of any amount to the campaign, we would mail them a free copy of the brochure. Over the next week or so we got more than 3,300 letters, most including contributions, out of Snyder's viewing audience of about six million.

On October 17 I appeared on *Meet the Press* along with other third-party candidates. On the show I spoke for fifteen seconds in Spanish; later I learned that they were very concerned about what I might have said, since no one on the production staff knew Spanish.

In the very last days of the campaign I debated Michael Harrington, the leader of America's social democrats and exponent of "lesser evilism." He, of course, supported the Democrats. The SWP printed a transcript of the debate in a collection* and Harrington called to protest our making money off his name. I'm not certain but I recall that we offered to give Michael half the profits if he agreed to pay half the losses when the book didn't make money. Needless to say he dropped the issue.

It was emotional for me to visit cities for the last time as part of the campaign. I loved going back to Las Vegas, New Mexico, where Juan José Peña's RUP office was overflowing with our campaign literature. At an event in Phoenix in October I met a young Pakistani activist, Agha Saeed, who would become a dear friend and political ally for the next three decades.† On October 27 we held our final meeting at UC Berkeley, where about a thousand people attended. Being back in Berkeley made me quite nostalgic; in fact, I still feel that way every time I am near Telegraph Avenue or Sproul Steps. We held the wind-up rally in New York on October 30, 1976, with five hundred supporters.

The Vote

On election night the television networks reported only the votes for the Democrats and Republicans with the exception of the State of Texas. Television stations in Texas hired students and sent them to polling stations throughout the state to call in the votes for all candidates, including myself.

---

* *The Lesser Evil? Debates on the Democratic Party and Independent Working-Class Politics* (New York: Pathfinder Press, 1977).

† A central figure in the Pakistani, Muslim, and Arab American communities, today Agha is chairman of the American Muslim Alliance and is one of the most courageous spokespersons against discrimination.

All night long, as each polling place reported its vote totals, the candidates' totals increased respectively. According to these reports, our vote came in at about seventeen thousand statewide.

But when Texas published its official results my vote total was reported as only 1,700. It is my speculation that individual counties opt not to report the third-party votes, or else they award them to their favored party. My immediate reaction was that this was too good to believe: the stealing of votes was now meticulously documented and following up would be easy. Since the TV stations had collected the results by counties, if we simply looked at each county's results and identified ones where officials had us at zero but students had called in votes for us all night long, we would have proof of fraud.

To me this was an obvious opportunity to generate publicity and to drive home once again all the points we had been making about the two-party system. When I made the suggestion to Jack Barnes, he replied, "Absolutely not."

The final nationwide vote credited to us was just under a hundred thousand, more than the totals for the Citizens Party, Libertarians, and the Communist Party. I believe there is no way to ascertain exactly how many people voted for me or for other third-party candidates in 1976. Although in general we know the number couldn't have been too large given the spoiler system,* "lesser-evil" voting, and other factors, the total may have been somewhat larger. There has been overwhelming evidence in recent years that votes are regularly manipulated, altered, and stolen. For instance, in San Francisco the dead always vote Democratic, election after election. One would think some medical school might be interested in investigating why dead Republicans vote for Democrats.

As small as this campaign may appear within the broader political arena, it was the largest and most successful in scope for the socialist movement in decades. We reached large numbers of people and it surprises me how many still walk up to tell me, "I voted for you in 1976."

---

* In a "spoiler system" a minor-party candidate is viewed as taking votes away from a major-party candidate, thereby "spoiling" a close election. The two-party system of the United States is set up such that any third-party candidate is portrayed as a potential "spoiler." This phenomenon discourages voters from supporting third-party candidates and promotes "lesser-evil" voting. The "spoiler effect" can easily be avoided by allowing for runoff elections. For more on the "spoiler system" and "lesser-evil" voting, see chapter 19 and others.

Postscript

To balance my recollections and commentary I should note that the SWPers who disagreed with me during the campaign were always very civil. I respected them for their commitment and dedication. For the overwhelming majority of the SWPers I worked with on the campaign I have nothing but respect and admiration. The self-sacrifice and hard work among the campaign participants at all levels was truly impressive. Most of what I did, of course, could never have happened without them, including especially my running mate Willie Mae Reid. By the end of the campaign I had so many friends and so much respect for our collective achievement. I especially want to thank my companion, Barbara Thornton, who was always there for me, from all the problems of my illness to the issues of stress, constant travel, and our being apart.

CHAPTER 10

SAN ANTONIO NATIONAL IMMIGRATION CONFERENCE

When the 1976 presidential campaign ended Barbara and I took off to Venezuela for two weeks for what turned out to be one of the happiest short periods in my life. In Puerto La Cruz we sailed around the small islands right off the shore and enjoyed the beautiful weather. We rented a VW microbus with sleeping berths in the back and drove to Barquisimeto to visit my grandmother Chita and other relatives. At my uncle's hacienda, Botucal, we had fun riding horses and just being out in nature. Some reporters tried to interview me but I opted not to do any media—I needed some time off.

While in Venezuela I started thinking about my next move. Occupying my thoughts were the many Latinos I had met during the presidential campaign, primarily Chicano leaders in the Southwest. I hoped to get the non–Democratic Party radical current of Latinos to work together by organizing a national conference in support of undocumented workers and, through those efforts, to form a new coalition with potential for expansion.

Barbara and I had decided to relocate to California. At that time the SWP had divided the country into six or so districts and I was made the district organizer for the Southwest. On January 25 we left New York in a caravan consisting of a truck with all our stuff and a car. Coming along for the move were Frank and Bianca Grinnon, close friends whose plans happened to match our own. We had also packed all the furniture and boxes for two older SWPers who were retiring out West, Tom Kerry and his wife Karolyn. As soon as we got beyond the New York city limits, the truck ran out of gas; the gauge didn't work.

The road trip was slow going. In Texas we got stuck in a snowstorm. In New Mexico we went off to see the Carlsbad Caverns. We finally reached Los Angeles on February 3 and started unpacking. As soon as I could I started arranging meetings with Chicano leaders about my idea of a conference in support of the undocumented.

José Angel Gutiérrez

Key to these meetings was José Angel Gutiérrez (JAG), the founder and leader of the Texas RUP. He liked the idea of a conference but was thinking more along the lines of calling for a national march on Washington. I thought his idea was too ambitious for the time being; in any case, a national conference could be a stepping-stone toward a national march. I proposed to base the conference out of Texas. After a few discussions JAG and I agreed to start meeting with other Latino leaders to assess the level of support.

Those meetings took place in March of 1977. In Austin I talked with Armando Gutiérrez, a professor and leader of the RUP, who was very close to JAG. I met with SWP forces in San Antonio and other Texas cities to propose that the conference be held in Texas, where the RUP was strong. A San Antonio SWP leader, Pedro Vasquez, helped me set up meetings with Chicano leaders in the area, including Paco Cantu, who brought ten people over to his home to discuss the idea.

Generally we encountered nothing but support. Mario Compean, the leader of the RUP in San Antonio, was one of the most enthusiastic in this initial phase. He gave me consistently good advice as to how we should work together and form a coalition to run and organize the conference. As I continued to travel, and as people JAG and I had talked with began talking to other people, the support kept growing.

In Los Angeles I met with Sister Maria Barron, who gave me the names of religious people who would support us. In Texas the Mexican American Cultural Center, a Catholic organization, wrote a front-page article in their paper defending the SWP from attacks made by individuals within the Colorado Chicano movement. During this project I came to work with priests, nuns, and other representatives of the religious community, who were among some of the most committed people I have ever met. They were extremely kind to me and did whatever they could for the movement, all the way up to the conference.

The Northern California SWP had Chicano leader Froben Lozada within its ranks as well as my brother Antonio, who helped launch the first bilingual education program in the California public schools and later, with Lozada and Victor Acosta, helped establish the first Latin and Mexican-American Studies Department at Merritt College in Oakland. Juan José Peña and the New Mexico Chicano groups around the RUP endorsed the conference. Chicano groups in Salt Lake City signed on. In Arizona the support came primarily from younger Chicanos, who proposed to build a car caravan to attend.

On May 2, 1977, we held a leadership meeting in Los Angeles at which JAG urged everyone to unite in support of the conference. This was a crucial gathering because it assembled many of the leaders in the Southern California region, such as Herman Baca, who gave the opening statement. I made special note of Baca's support as well as that of Antonio Rodriguez of the Center for Autonomous Social Action (CASA).

Soon after this initial show of unanimity, however, divisions began to appear. There was some conflict between two important forces in Los Angeles: on one side was the RUP of California, led in part by Raúl Ruiz, the editor of *La Raza* magazine and a professional photographer, especially of movement events; on the other side was CASA, led by Antonio Rodriguez. CASA was quite militant, strongly nationalist, and influenced somewhat by the CP, which lent them a strong anti-Trotskyist prejudice. They were very committed people and out of that current would come many future leaders within the Chicano community, including the mayor of Los Angeles as of this writing, Antonio Villaraigosa; speaker of the California state assembly Fabian Nuñez; and Gilbert Cedillo, who was elected to the California State Senate in 2002.*

Looking at the proposed immigration conference from CASA's point of view I could see that the influence of the SWP—a primarily Anglo organiza-

---

* I worked with Cedillo, a good friend, in the period after the year 2000 fighting to regain driver's licenses for undocumented workers. Gil has led an endless and lonely battle on this issue.

tion not rooted in their community—was an issue that bothered them. CASA decided to react in a sectarian manner, fighting the non-exclusion policy of the conference, and demanded that the SWP not be allowed to participate. They quickly gained the support of many leaders in the Southern California area in a campaign against the SWP. I wanted to meet with them to see if we could come to agreement based on our common ground on the issue of a pro-immigrant policy. We certainly wanted their inclusion in the conference at a central leadership level. But they made it a policy not to talk to us and physically attacked SWPers if they were selling the *Militant* in the Latino community.

There was already conflict between CASA and the RUP. In Los Angeles and throughout the country the RUP chapters defended the right of the SWP, especially its Latino members, to participate in the conference. There was a lot of goodwill toward the SWP as a result of my 1976 presidential campaign and the continuing support the SWP had given the RUP. In any case it was to the advantage of the Latino movement to draw in people from other communities, such as African Americans, labor, the churches, and Anglos in general. Many people caught in the middle tended to side with us for a non-exclusionary policy but some were scared by the red-baiting aspect of the CASA attacks.

The conflict became very serious when Mario Compean of the RUP in San Antonio, who had been so instrumental at the outset, began backing the CASA campaign against the SWP. In this fight José Angel Gutiérrez maintained a very principled stance. JAG would not allow anyone to be excluded who wanted to support the purpose of the conference. He made it clear to all those demanding the SWP's exclusion that he wouldn't go along with it and considered it a form of red-baiting.

Another obstacle to CASA's campaign was the critical role played by SWP members in making the conference happen. I was traveling almost continuously throughout the Southwest, meeting with groups to distribute the conference call written by JAG. In San Antonio a group of SWPers and rank-and-file independents were the backbone of getting the mailings out, raising money, generating press coverage, creating the leaflets and posters, and handling all the critical key details. The SWP team included many Latinos, such as Miguel Pendas, Pedro Vasquez, Antonio Gonzalez, and Andy Gonzalez. Some of the independent Chicanos and Chicanas working with us on the project also joined the YSA.

Among the young independents working with the SWP was Gloria Najar. I met Gloria at an antiracism party on September 3, 1977. She told me about growing up in a South Texas working-class Chicano home. We hit it off immediately and became close friends, a connection that later evolved into a personal relationship lasting six years.

Gloria kept in touch with people who were being influenced by the divisive campaign and informed me about shifts in opinion. On a day-by-day basis CASA was not such a problem, but we all suspected that they were mobilizing to try to take over the conference or to damage it beyond repair.

Division in the SWP

Simultaneous with these problems within the Chicano movement was a growing opposition to the conference—and to my promotion of it—from the leadership of the SWP. At the outset their attitude had been one of token support, with the implicit assumption that the project would never get off the ground. But as the conference grew some of the central SWP leaders began to become downright hostile. Once again Jack Barnes saw something that promoted my standing in the SWP—Latino SWPers were excited that we were helping to build a Latino-based conference and we had begun to recruit more Chicanos to the YSA in several cities. In order for the mainly Anglo SWP leadership to express their hesitancy and to impose the limitations they wanted to put on the work being done in San Antonio, they needed a Latino or Latina to be their spokesperson. It was very sad for me to see Olga Rodriguez, a member of the SWP National Committee, take on the role of defending the leadership's attacks on the conference.

Unlike during the presidential campaign, this time I took a harder line. I sent the SWP leadership in New York a letter demanding their support for the conference, including a request that two full-time, experienced leaders be sent to reinforce our work for the final couple of months in San Antonio. Then I met with them in New York and told them I wanted the mailing list of the donors to my presidential campaign, which had included many Latinos, so that we could send out a conference funding and participation request. Their answer to me was "absolutely no"; the list belonged to the SWP and could not be used to help build the conference. They also opposed my request to send some leaders to San Antonio. Among those going along with this refusal to support the conference were leaders such as Barry Sheppard, Mary-Alice Waters, Larry Seigle, Gus Horowitz, and of course Jack Barnes.

At the time, they knew I would not go public with these differences. In truth I never told anyone. The SWPers working day and night in San Antonio and in many other cities never had a clue as to how the SWP high command was acting. The real dynamic would have come as a shock to many of the people involved and would have demoralized those working on the conference. In New York their main concern was the reaction that Latinos within the party might have to the almost entirely Anglo leadership taking such a position. Thus they used Olga Rodriguez to make the official reports on the conference, which downplayed the impact of the work being done. I never protested this; in general Olga was cautious about the extent to which she openly opposed what we were doing.

In one instance we needed to make copies of JAG's conference call for distribution. Olga insisted that we only print two hundred. I had to stand up and say, no way; we will print two thousand just to start.

The truth was that the standing and acceptance of the SWP among Latinos within the movement was growing due to the conference work. For instance, at a coalition meeting of thirteen groups in San Antonio, chaired by Mario Compean, everyone unanimously accepted my making the motions that were to be adopted by the conference. Problems arose only when CASA made an issue of the SWP's presence. The attacks went only in one direction. We did not respond in kind. We called for CASA's right to participate, along with anyone else who agreed with the conference's goals.

In the last stages we suddenly got some information about CASA's strategy. One of Gloria's closest friends was the roommate of the girlfriend of a CASA leader. Through her we learned that CASA, realizing they couldn't win a majority, planned instead to try to block any decisions at the conference. Apparently they had established an alliance with Mario Compean.

At the Conference

The National Immigration Conference was, all told, a success. At its peak the participants filled an auditorium seating a thousand people. On Friday, October 28, there was a smaller meeting to decide some final issues and to approve the schedule. CASA, carrying out their plan to create chaos, opposed the schedule. Of the three hundred attending that meeting, including all the people who had worked so hard to build the conference, CASA could muster only forty votes. When this relationship of forces revealed itself and with José Angel Gutiérrez present, Mario Compean backed down and voted to approve the schedule.

Media coverage was favorable at the beginning, as they were impressed with the breadth of groups participating. Later the focus shifted to the infighting, which had an understandably negative impact on public opinion. On Saturday, October 29, we held a key rally with several leaders speaking. Each speaker had a time limit of ten minutes. Antonio Rodriguez, the head of CASA, was one of the first presenters. He spoke for exactly forty-seven minutes. The chair was afraid to interrupt him. Rodriguez's talk was full of rhetoric but low on content. He was clearly fishing for a major ovation but didn't get one, in part because of his lack of content but also because he had alienated many of the conference participants with his divisive campaign. When JAG took the floor there was an immediate huge ovation. He laid out the key issues in the injustices perpetrated against Mexican immigrants: abused at the border, abused on their jobs, underpaid, rejected for many of the rights their taxes were paying for, and subjected to cultural discrimination. Yet the immigrants were needed economically and the corporate world wanted to keep the border open to recruit the essential labor they couldn't otherwise get for their businesses.

I spoke toward the end and focused on how easy it would be to solve the existing abuses and on the lie that the United States faced an "immigration problem." I addressed the failure of the two major parties to end the mistreatment of our people. When I finished there was a prolonged standing ovation.

At the action plan workshop CASA tried again to vote everything down but lost 80 to 45. Rumors had started to sweep the conference that CASA was planning a physical attack on SWPers the next day. The SWPers wanted to prepare a defense guard around me, figuring if these rumors were true, I would be a target. Early in the morning on Sunday, October 30, we had a caucus meeting of all the SWPers and YSAers at the conference. In total we numbered only about forty so the idea that we controlled the conference numerically was ridiculous.

In the various workshops CASA focused on red-baiting and disruption. They even voted against issues they supported in protest that the SWP had been allowed to participate. A motion calling for an open border passed overwhelmingly—CASA voted against it. CASA's strongest showing was in a vote on the action platform: the vote was 264 for the conference proposal we backed to 226 against. The threat of physical attacks never materialized.

At the end of the conference I wrote in my diary, "Conference slowly dies out. (Compean also spoke out against disunity—good speech). Adjourned about 7 PM. Media eats up infighting. Amparo attacks SWP to press, etc. CASA leaves as a group. We hold fraction barbecue. JAG stops by to socialize. Tired."

Balance Sheet

The first national conference of its kind failed in its objective. Our goal had been to start a broad united national coalition by first holding a gathering of the more militant forces independent of the Democrats. Had the conference succeeded in solidifying a progressive coalition our aim was to try to broaden out to our whole community, including the mainstream groups, without letting ourselves get taken over by the Democrats. In this we failed. And as negative as CASA's sectarian actions were, they were not the fundamental reason that the effort did not succeed.

The great radicalization of the late sixties and early seventies that had created the RUP and CASA was coming to an end. Right after the conference José Angel Gutiérrez told me the RUP was now on the defensive as the Democrats were working to crush it. In the areas controlled by the RUP, the Democrats made sure to cut off all funding from federal and state programs. To regain the funding the RUPers capitulated and switched to the Democrats in some areas. The RUP's bedrock, Crystal City, held out as long as it could but even it was eventually overwhelmed in 1977.*

Back in Los Angeles CASA began having internal problems and had largely collapsed by late 1978 or early 1979. The young people in CASA went in all directions. Most joined the Democratic Party and achieved positions as mentioned above.

The October 1977 conference in San Antonio was a turning point, an idea formed too soon to have succeeded. But the work helped to inspire the dream of a united mass movement defending the Latino community. On November 4, 1977, as I left to return to Los Angeles I wrote in my diary, "It

---

* The story is detailed in José Angel Gutiérrez, *The Making of a Chicano Militant* (Madison, WI: University of Wisconsin Press, 1999). See also Ignacio M. Garcia, *United We Win: The Rise and Fall of La Raza Unida Party* (University of Arizona Mexican American Studies Research Center, 1989).

is sad to leave S.A. But CA is in bad shape and it's best I go back, etc. etc."
The truth really had little to do with Los Angeles or San Antonio but a lot
to do with Gloria Najar. That's what my "etc etc." meant.

Postscript: Where They Are Today

Nativo Lopez

A young CASA member who participated in the conference, Nativo
Lopez is now my very close friend. Although he remains on good terms
with many of the former CASA people, Nativo went in a different direction,
working with the famous Chicano leader Bert Corona, the elder statesman
of the 1970s Chicano movement in Los Angeles. After Bert's death in January 2001 Nativo became executive director of the movement Bert had
started, Hermandad Mexicana Nacional, now called Hermandad Mexicana
Latinoamericana, a community service and advocacy organization for
Mexican American immigrants.

Around 2003 Nativo also became the central leader of the Mexican
American Political Association (MAPA), which includes Mexican Americans of all political views. Through his efforts MAPA opened up to more
than the Democrats and Republicans, in 2006 even endorsing the state slate
of Greens that I headed. Nativo became a Green and worked closely with
me as we tried to move the Green Party toward more of a focus on Latinos,
other minorities, and working-class people.

In May of 2005 Nativo called for a general strike of Latinos against the
mistreatment of undocumented workers, specifically the denial of driver's
licenses. Nativo's call spread across California and on the day of the strike,
schools in L.A. Latino communities were half or even almost completely
empty and Latino-owned stores were closed throughout the state. Demonstrations appeared spontaneously, organized by local people in city after
city. The number of Latino workers who refused to go to work is unknown
but it was a very large number. Gil Cedillo told me that he was in his office
at the state Building when he saw thousands of people marching by so he
ran and got in the march, to cheers from the crowd. Everyone was amazed
by the success of Nativo's call.

After the general strike Nativo came to the Bay Area and held a meeting of leaders of a range of Latino organizations to review the strike's effect. Nativo invited me and Matt Gonzalez of the Greens to to give our views along with Miguel Araujo (who also helped organize the meeting); Luis Magaña, leader of the movement for undocumented workers in Stockton; and other representatives of our community.

Nativo was at the center both in Los Angeles and nationally of organizing the immense 2006 demonstrations in support of undocumented workers, which exploded across the nation. He was the main media representative of the movement to legalize undocumented workers and fought to block a vicious, anti-immigrant bill introduced in Congress in 2005.

I went to Los Angeles to join the March 25, 2006, march of a million people. This demonstration was possibly the largest protest ever within the United States. At one of the coalition meetings I ran into former CASA leader Antonio Rodriguez, now almost thirty years after the San Antonio conference. I walked up to him and shook hands, just saying "How are you?" He was cordial. I wanted to talk to him more but we didn't get a chance.

Antonio Gonzalez

The forces on both sides of the 1977 San Antonio conference, even though they have aged, are still active. One of the most remarkable is Antonio Gonzalez. He was a nineteen-year-old SWPer at the time. Antonio was from San Diego but decided to stay on in Texas. Along with Andy Gonzalez we became roommates for a short period in San Antonio in 1978.

In San Antonio, Antonio started working with Willie Velasquez, who sought among other things to get the Latino community registered to vote. Willie created the Southwest Voter Education Project, and his efforts spread throughout the nation. After his death the William C. Velasquez Institute was formed. Antonio became the leader of both of these institutions and developed them into strong national organizations. In 2005 Antonio was named one of *Time* magazine's twenty-five most influential Hispanics.

Although Antonio works with all the established mainstream Latino organizations, he has fought for inclusion of the currents outside the Democratic Party. After the mass demonstrations in 2006 Antonio established what is now known as the National Latino Congreso, which holds national conferences each year to unify the Latino community. Antonio told me that we finally got our national coalition of the entire community, just not exactly the way we had planned in 1977.

CHAPTER 11

INTERNATIONAL WORK: HUGO BLANCO; NICARAGUA

After my return to Los Angeles in late 1977 I resumed my focus on international work. I was almost always traveling, either to Latin America or to Europe. In retrospect I am amazed that I was still trying so hard to see if anything positive could be created out of the Trotskyist groups in Latin America. The various groups lived in a state of permanent internecine warfare, each trying to prove to itself and others that it had the right interpretation of the Marxist bible. I was caught in the middle, an outsider attempting to figure out who was right, who was rational, and how something real could be created.

To others around me in the SWP leadership these small Trotskyist groups were extremely important: the idea was that if we could just get it "right," then we could re-create a force that could help bring about revolutionary change. The more Jack Barnes thought of himself as the new Lenin the more he pushed to carry out this international work. Even though to some extent I was still a believer they all sensed my doubts and therefore their doubts about me kept increasing.

The one outstanding exception to all this was Hugo Blanco and his work in Peru. He was an inspiration and an important figure in my life. It was his cause that brought me into the crosshairs of the CIA in 1979.

Hugo Blanco and the Peruvian Peasant Revolution

Born in Cusco of an Anglo father, a lawyer who defended poor peasants, and a Quechuan mother, Blanco earned a doctorate in agronomy in Argentina. In the early 1960s he returned to his hometown, the one-time Inca capital, deep in the interior of southeast Peru and joined the growing peasant movement. The most militant peasant unions were developing in an area near Cusco called Chaupimayo.

As had been the case since the European invasion, Quechan peasants worked for the landowners for free. Just as in medieval France, the indigenous peasants worked on the owner's land three days a week as a concession for being allotted a parcel of land for themselves, which they could work three days a week. If the peasants failed to meet their obligations, the landlords' private police flogged the offenders with whips.

Blanco went to the areas near Cusco known as Valle de La Convención and Lares, where some strikes had already been attempted. Barefoot, he asked a landlord for work and was hired. Connected to a small Trotskyist underground in the cities, he began trying to organize the peasants with whom he worked. He raised the concept of a general strike, proposing that if the peasants struck in massive numbers and refused to work the owners' land, it could bring an end to their oppression. A secret underground militia of about twenty youth was formed to protect the peasant farmers from police reprisals. All they had for arms were some old rifles and a few revolvers.

Then it began to happen. One day in 1962 peasants in La Convención rose up and refused to go to work on the owners' land. It started slowly, with just a few hundred. When the landlords' police went to investigate they were confronted by armed peasants telling them to drop their weapons and leave. Soon thousands of peasants were on strike. In a few days the strike had grown to a hundred thousand. Ultimately that strike wave receded and failed, but soon another wave began to swell, breaking through and spreading throughout the region. Eventually the Peruvian government declared an end to serfdom and granted the right of people to be paid for their work.

During the strikes a policeman was killed in a confrontation with the peasant militia. The media labeled Blanco a murderer and called for him to be brought to justice. He was captured by police while staying in the home of a peasant. The Peruvian government charged Blanco with murder and sought the death penalty. He spent three years in solitary confinement before the case went to court.

Meeting Hugo Blanco

An international movement of solidarity helped save Hugo Blanco's life. In Chile the entire Chamber of Deputies voted to call for amnesty for Blanco. In Belgium forty-three members of parliament called for his release. The Italian Confederation of Labor, sugar workers in India, Amnesty International, Jean-Paul Sartre, Simone de Beauvoir, ten British MPs, four hundred scholars in the United States, seven thousand trade unionists in Canada, London engineers, and large sectors of the population of Peru, to name but a few, joined the worldwide campaign for Blanco.

In New York I worked on the English edition of Blanco's book describing his experiences with the peasant struggle, *Land or Death*,* which he wrote in prison. Eventually he was moved to El Frontón, an island prison near the port of Callao. The very first North American to visit Blanco in El Frontón was Kitty Cone, a courageous woman who led the U.S. fight for rights for people with disabilities.

In early 1970 I went to Peru to meet Blanco. On January 23, after an early morning meeting with his lawyer, I boarded the official visitors' launch for the trip to El Frontón, about a half-hour boat ride. Blanco knew I was coming and had heard a little about me. It was such a joyous moment for me to meet him in person. We sat together and talked about all kinds of things, especially the international campaign on his behalf. At the time we had no idea that one day Hugo would not only be free, but also elected to the congress and later to the senate of Peru. For the moment it was just the two of us sharing our lives and our hopes in that cold, windy prison off the coast.

Unfortunately visitors were only allowed one hour. The guards strode through the jail, announcing that the visitors' boat was about to leave. I was not about to limit my meeting with Blanco to a single hour, so I hid in the prison until they left. Since the guards had not even counted the visitors upon arrival, they had no idea one remained behind. Blanco told me, "Don't worry, they won't arrest you. There is a prison guard change at 4 p.m. and you can get on that boat and leave." We talked for several more

---

* Hugo Blanco, *Land or Death: The Peasant Struggle in Peru* (New York: Young Socialist Alliance, 1967; Pathfinder Press, 1972).

hours, completely unnoticed by the guards. That was the beginning of a close friendship and political collaboration.

It is a challenge to convey the immense courage of this man. While imprisoned he published reports on the beating, torture, and murder of inmates in that very prison, naming the officers who committed the crimes. Suffice it to say by doing so he risked his life. For example, on September 12, 1968, in the magazine *OJO* he reported that two prisoners had been slowly beaten to death and named the officers who had committed the murders— three captains, two lieutenants, two sergeants, and a corporal of the Guardia Nacional. Year after year Blanco continued to speak out regardless of the danger to himself.

Hugo Is Freed

On December 22, 1970, in a general amnesty Hugo Blanco was freed. A rally of ten thousand was held in a soccer stadium in support of all the released political prisoners. I was in the United States at the time but numerous Peruvians who were there have described it to me. When the prisoners—many of whom had risked their lives fighting for democracy and social justice—entered the stadium one by one, the audience responded with rounds of applause. And when it was finally Hugo Blanco's turn, the crowd exploded with joy. They wanted to touch Blanco. The chants went up from all over, "Hugo, Hugo, Hugo." Unhurried, Blanco walked the perimeter of the stadium, reaching out to people with tears in their eyes, thousands of people overjoyed that the man who had helped free the peasants was himself finally free.

Lamentably the amnesty did not extend to many other political prisoners, including two Argentineans who had been working with Blanco, Eduardo Creus and Daniel Pereyra. We received word that a certain politician claimed he could secure freedom for Eduardo Creus if we paid him a sum of money. I brought the funds to Peru but the situation seemed peculiar— perhaps a pardon was coming for Creus and a corrupt politician was trying to benefit. I don't recall all the details, and the descriptions in my diary from the time are intentionally sketchy, since I carried it with me. The end result was that Creus was freed without our having to pay the bribe.*

---

* Eduardo Creus was freed on January 20, 1971, while I was still in Lima. He was immediately deported to Argentina. I met him in Buenos Aires a few days later to congratulate him on his freedom and hear about his experiences.

As part of that trip I went to the main prison in Lima, where most of the political prisoners were held. Upon my arrival many of them came to hug me—I guess they had heard about the work on behalf of political prisoners I was involved with in New York. They were thrilled to hear about those who had been released. We talked at length about how they were being treated and whether their sentences might be commuted. It broke my heart—not hard to do, I will admit—as I saw some of the prisoners without shoes, many of them with torn clothing, suffering in the cold.

I still had more than a thousand dollars in cash on me. Only by a miracle was that money not in the hands of a corrupt functionary. It had been raised for the freedom of Peruvian prisoners. So I made a decision on the spot and handed the money over to one of the central leaders of the political prisoners—in front of the others, for obvious reasons—to be used to buy clothing, food, and whatever else they needed. (In Latin American prisons, with money you can buy just about anything.) I explained how I happened to have the money on me and how by fate I had not turned it over to the con man. The response was silence. A thousand dollars was a large sum in Peru in those days, especially for these prisoners who had nothing. This was a very welcome gift from the Spanish-speaking Gringo who they all knew was really a Venezuelan.

After being freed Blanco was deported from Peru a couple of times. For a period he lived in Chile and later in Sweden, returning to Peru in 1978. I visited him in Chile and remember my fear for his life when I heard of the military coup against Allende on September 11, 1973 (the first "9/11.")[*] Thankfully Blanco was able to seek refuge in the Swedish Embassy. Had he not found safe haven, I believe he would have been killed.

In August 1978 I was in Lima with my companion, Gloria Najar, to help with Blanco's campaign for parliament in Peru. We were supporting his efforts to create a coalition among various groups within the Peruvian left. At internal meetings I spoke alongside Blanco to try to unify the left. Our work was opposed by the sectarian followers of the Argentine Trotskyist cult leader Nahuel Moreno, the Morenistas, who tried to destroy or over-

---

[*] A close friend of mine was killed the day of the coup, the leader of a group of Brazilians called "Grupo Grande." He could have fled but he waited for his wife at home. The police arrested and killed him that night. His wife, the daughter of one of the military dictators in Brazil, spent years searching the prisons of Chile for her husband. That was in part, of course, the work of the CIA.

take any movement they could not control. As relations among the Peruvian left groups strengthened, the police also took note of the participation of the Gringo-Venezuelan and my close relationship with Hugo. In my diary I described the events of August 25, 1978:

> Flew to Tacna with Blanco, Alfonso, and Gonillas. Also on the plane was Hernan Cuentas, FOCEP-POMR [Worker Peasant Student and Popular Front–Revolutionary Workers Marxist Party] deputy [congressperson] & Diez Canseco V.R.-UDP deputy. About 200 people received Blanco [at Tacna airport] ... Then to a press conference. Hundreds of people packed in listening. Then we led a march to a mass meeting. Somewhere between 10 to 15 thousand people were present. In a town of 70,000 population! Massive sympathy for FOCEP. Diez Canseco spoke well ... POMR Cuentas calls for Constituent Assembly to power. Blanco spoke for 1 ½ hours. Excellent speech. Huge sympathy. Not all—thousands listened intently but not all applauded ... Youth so enthusiastic—we take collection, 15,500 soles [Peruvian currency]—FOCEP collection prior 6,000 soles ... Five thousand go with Hugo to open new headquarters. Then to a dinner in a Barrio. At 2 AM Hugo leaves in taxi for Arequipa and then Cusco.

Here is another glimpse of work with Blanco, from Sunday, August 27, 1978:

> Spent day going to slums to do interviews & take pictures. Almost universal support for Hugo Blanco. Many for FOCEP—one open Trotskyist found by chance ... Slums terrible conditions—no water, no electricity, no toilet facilities, no way to wash. Etc. etc.—they use river, have to walk to get water. These are factory workers, employed workers!

When I stayed in Lima I rented a hotel room that cost two dollars a day. Taking a shower was possible but occasionally I got an electrical shock because the water was warmed with a small electric heater. Anything of value left unwatched would be stolen. I carried everything with me in a valise and slept with it under the bed. An American friend of mine, SWPer Mike Kelly, had his typewriter swiped when he left it for a couple of minutes.*

Spending time with Blanco was rewarding, not only in terms of the work, but because he could also be very funny, often unintentionally so.

---

* Mike Kelly's track record in Peru was not great. He also took a photo of his girlfriend that happened to show a Peruvian tank accidentally in the background; consequently he was arrested as a "Chilean spy." With the help of his congressional representative from Boston we eventually got Mike out of jail. He was deported and ordered never to return to Peru. The next time I visited Peru, there was Mike. I remember telling him, "Please be careful, Mike. What's the matter with you?"

One day we were walking and I got really hungry. I said, "Hey, Hugo, let's stop at this little restaurant. I have to eat something or I'm going to die." Hugo looked at me and replied, "Pedrito, I can't eat in a restaurant. What would people think if they saw Hugo Blanco enter a restaurant? We have to eat out here in the street like all workers." What could anyone say to that? So we ate from a street vendor, even though I knew I would most likely get Montezuma's Revenge, caused by bacteria the locals are used to but for which foreigners have no defense. (I often got sick while traveling in Latin America, especially in Chile. Never have a salad in Chile.)

When Blanco was first elected to the Peruvian congress there were many threats against his life. I bought him and his bodyguard bulletproof vests in the States and took them down to Peru. With regular jackets over them, the bulletproof vests were undetectable. Blanco told me that while he was walking through the congress building one of his fellow deputies slapped him on the back, paused for a second, and said, "Uh-oh. I won't tell anyone."

When I purchased the vests I also had the presence of mind to get a bulletproof jockstrap. But I bought only one. The argument between Blanco and his bodyguard—regrettably I can't remember his name—over who should get the jockstrap was priceless. Naturally the argument began with each of them laying out why he thought he should have it; then after a few minutes, with typical Latino machismo, they were arguing why the other one needed it more. I was on the floor laughing.

For helping Blanco in his 1979 race for president of Peru the CIA tried to have me arrested, as described in this book's opening chapter. The entire episode still strikes me as incredible. As it turns out, even though the plot against me failed, the CIA still got its way. The Peruvian left did not unite, and a divided movement was unable to win. The time had not yet come.

On January 22, 2006, Blanco attended the inauguration of the new president of Bolivia, Evo Morales Ayma, the first indigenous person to become president of that overwhelmingly indigenous country. In recent years Bolivia, Brazil, Argentina, Chile, Uruguay, Venezuela, and even Paraguay have all elected governments that to one degree or another have sought to assert their independence from centuries of economic and political domination by the United States. Unfortunately Peru remains among the minority of South American countries that continues to suffer from the traditional corruption and abuse that is part of the U.S. sphere of influence.

I have not had contact with Hugo Blanco for many years, but occasionally I hear about him from friends. Now in his seventies, Blanco was quite ill a couple of years ago. I hope that circumstances will allow me one more chance to see him.

Nicaragua

In the summer of 1979 the long struggle of the Sandinista National Liberation Front (Frente Sandinista de Liberación Nacional, or FSLN) against the U.S.-backed Somoza dictatorship triumphed. At incredible sacrifice a massive movement had swept throughout Nicaragua, growing into an armed insurrection to remove the bloody tyrant. This was of great interest to me and I wanted to understand how the revolution had occurred.

I was not alone—the entire global left started talking about Nicaragua and the Sandinistas. Within the Trotskyist current debates raged as to what the Sandinista victory meant and what attitude to take toward it.* In 1977 the SWP had started a Spanish language bimonthly, *Perspectiva Mundial* (*PM*), edited by my friend José Perez. *PM* ("World Watch" in English) was written in the least sectarian manner of any publication produced by the SWP. It struck me that it might be useful to circulate *PM* in Nicaragua as well as to step up its reporting of Nicaraguan events.

The idea arose in the SWP for me and Fred Feldman, one of the SWP's major writers, to go to Nicaragua. On July 28, 1979, Fred and I traveled to Costa Rica to try to enter Nicaragua as reporters. We were able to cross the border but there was no conventional transportation available to Managua. A truck driver delivering pamphlets to the Sandinistas let us climb on top of his cargo. Unfortunately that truck got a flat, but we had the good fortune at 7:30 p.m. to catch another truck, this one loaded with bananas. We sat atop the bananas and rode into Managua, where we were deposited at the central marketplace.

It was night. In the distance we saw the InterContinental Hotel and decided to walk there, even though it was quite a stretch. As we passed through

---

* The guerrilla tactics used by the FSLN had reopened the argument in the FI over armed struggle versus mass action, with many factions refusing to support the FSLN on ideological grounds. The SWP was split on this issue. Although I had formerly been a staunch opponent of foquismo/armed struggle, I saw the Sandinistas as representing a new kind of movement, one that refused to let Stalinism or any other force block it from developing a mass base to fight for democracy and social justice in Nicaragua.

an upper-middle-class neighborhood we suddenly heard shots. Someone was shooting—at us. Suddenly a voice nearby, invisible behind three feet of high grass, shouted, "Get against the wall and don't move." With no idea what was happening, we froze against the wall.

The shooting stopped. Then a man in a Sandinista uniform came out of the house right next to us. He called out to the man lying in the grass, "Did you see him?" The man in the grass, who turned out to be a young Sandinista soldier, called back, "Still can't see where he's shooting from." Then the older Sandinista pointed at us and asked the man in the grass, "Who the hell are these people?" He replied, "Beats me."

We had our suitcases in our hands and explained we were foreigners trying to get to the hotel in the distance. The older Sandinista took us into the house, which, we discovered, was a Sandinista army headquarters. The house had belonged to Luis Somoza, the deposed dictator's brother. A sniper—some were still active—had been firing at the Sandinistas and three soldiers were in various areas of the grass, trying to pinpoint the sniper's position to try and kill him.

The house was full of young Sandinista soldiers. They gave us space on the floor, food, and cushions to sleep on. We sat down and started listening to the conversations, which were fascinating. I remember clearly that there was talk about a three-way rift among the Sandinistas. One of the older soldiers stopped by and reminded the others, "We're unified now, let's not talk about this anymore."

Getting Organized

The next morning we continued on our journey and ended up at the Hotel Camino Real. I started looking for a place to live for the two of us and for the others we expected might be coming. Fred began covering the near-daily government press conferences.

Nicaragua was alive as the revolution worked to organize the people: new unions were springing up, Sandinista-run ministries were forming, the army was consolidating and making sure there was food, running water, and transportation for the people. The FSLN leaders must have been working twenty hours a day.

On August 3 Fred and I joined a demonstration of fifty thousand people. On August 5 I flew back to the United States to meet Gloria in Louisiana, and we drove together to Oberlin College, site of the annual SWP convention.

At the SWP convention I gave a report on the situation in Nicaragua. The enmity toward me from the SWP leaders was becoming more and more open. Doug Jenness attacked me for suggesting that we should wait for the FSLN to decide their next moves. His view was that we knew better what to do in Nicaragua and should start saying so. I disagreed strongly.* Gloria, witnessing the hostility toward me for the first time, was shocked. She warned me, "These people hate you." I tried to argue otherwise. She told me not to be so blind.

The FI Response and the Simón Bolívar Brigade

Reactions among Trotskyist groups to the developments in Nicaragua were diverse, ranging from sectarian viciousness against the FSLN all the way to support for the Sandinistas. In the SWP, the leadership soon shifted toward backing the FSLN. For the moment Jack Barnes and I agreed on Nicaragua. The Europeans were sectarian and started sniping against the FSLN in their media.

The worst was direct disruptive activity on the ground in Nicaragua. The Morenistas, followers of Argentine cult leader Nahuel Moreno, tried to take advantage of the situation by attacking the FSLN.

Earlier in the struggle Moreno had seen an opportunity for his Bolshevik Tendency and started a group called the Simón Bolívar Brigade (SBB), a group of his followers in Colombia. SBB members put on the armbands and other paraphernalia of the Sandinistas and went out into the streets of Columbia to raise money to build the SBB, which—they professed—was going to help the Sandinistas. Moreno did this without the FSLN's approval and the money raised was taken by his group.

The SBB gathered about two hundred young volunteers and sent them to Costa Rica. From there they began negotiations with the FSLN. For their part, the FSLN welcomed the SBB, thanked them, and proposed to integrate these international volunteers into the units they were forming to open up a southern front. The Somocista army had entrenched itself along the border with Costa Rica to prevent the FSLN from doing so.

---

* I remember in San Francisco the SWP put up posters in the Latino district, the Mission, saying the main problem in Nicaragua was the Sandinistas. I was in charge of coordinating our work defending Nicaragua at the time, and arriving from New York, was shocked to see this. I held meetings with local Nicaraguans to apologize. But that this could even happen indicated the depth of the "we know better than anyone" sectarianism that had become part of the culture of the SWP and the Trotskyist movement in general.

The SBB leaders refused, announcing that they would operate only as a separate unit with their own leadership; moreover, they could not be sent to the front lines given their lack of experience, limited armament, and outsider status. The FSLN said "thanks but no thanks"—there was no way any battle units would be led by anyone outside the FSLN.

The SBB waited. The FSLN at great sacrifice opened up the southern front, pushed the Somocistas back, and finally took Managua, overthrowing the dictatorship. At that point, in the confusion and chaos immediately after Somoza's fall, the SBB made their move, entered Nicaragua, and set up their operation in Managua. During this time the SBB began "helping" to organize trade unions. What they were doing in actuality was trying to build their own political current while the FSLN was preoccupied with a thousand issues. Soon the SBB called demonstrations against the FSLN— the first ever— around some secondary trade union issues. The FSLN assessed the situation and surmised that these people were either idiots or CIA agents trying to disrupt the revolution. Of course the SBB were idiots, unapologetically sectarian operators trying to undermine the living movement in Nicaragua.

The FSLN moved to deport these foreigners and redoubled their efforts to try to stop the disruption from Maoists and "Trotskyists." These events created utter confusion inside Nicaragua toward the SWP and our aims; fortunately many of the leaders of the FSLN understood the differences between currents. Many FSLN leaders were in favor of our being in Nicaragua and making *PM* available because they feared the influence of the Stalinists. The FSLN newspaper *Barricada* even ran a pro-SWP article explaining that these various groups calling themselves Trotskyists were not all the same. Meanwhile Moreno began to refer to the FSLN as the "bodyguards of Somocistas."

For me this was one of the most shameful periods to be associated with the world Trotskyist movement. Ernest Mandel in Europe and many of the FI-affiliated groups, the British consistently being the worst, tried to defend the SBB's disruptions of the Sandinista movement, which had defeated the dictatorship after decades of struggle and sacrifice. I was disgusted. If the SWP had not shifted toward a pro-FSLN position I would have quit right then and there. In my diary I quoted Gloria, who asked me, "Are you going to go crazy?" I was in a serious state of confusion.

To my relief the SWP took the lead in opposing the sectarianism within the FI and made a concerted effort to establish good relations with the FSLN. Several central SWP leaders came down to Nicaragua, including

Barry Sheppard, Doug Jenness, and even Jack Barnes. Other international leaders arrived as well—Hugo Blanco came in from Peru and several arrived from Mexico, including an old friend of mine, Manuel, who actually ended up voting for sectarianism and broke my heart.

Once the airlines were functioning again Gloria flew to Managua and took charge of getting *PM* placed on newsstands, at FSLN offices, on campuses, and at hotels. We were pleasantly surprised to see that the paper sold out almost immediately. Orders kept climbing. Teachers started using *PM* in their classes. Unions took bundles to sell in factories. I asked for more copies. The magazine was paying for itself but the SWP leadership in New York refused to increase our allotment.

Almost Deported

I was in the middle of the whole Trotskyist/Nicaragua crisis, flying back and forth to New York and Europe to deal with the madness, when the extremist factor started attacking me personally. One of the craziest of the sectarian groups was the Workers Revolutionary Party in England, led by Gerry Healy, whose followers were known as Healyites. They had been allied with the SWP in the 1950s but had opposed the 1963 reunification of the FI and were on a campaign to malign the SWP as a group of police agents. They printed a paper in Spanish and distributed it all over Managua with a photo of me on the front stating that I was a CIA agent operating in Managua.

In November I went back to Europe for the World Congress of the FI, largely a waste of time with all the rhetoric against the FSLN. On November 21 Fred, Gloria, and I boarded a plane to return to Nicaragua. Five leaders of the FSLN armed forces were on the flight with me. I spent some time talking to the head of Nicaragua's air force, Raul Venerio. According to my diary I also spoke with General Joaquín Cuadra, the army chief of staff.

I was going through customs in Managua when I was told to return to the airplane. There was an order for my deportation. I called out to the FSLN leaders I had been talking to on the plane to see if they could stop my being deported. In my diary I wrote, "Cuadra stopped them." What Cuadra did was tell them to put me in jail overnight and then, in the morning, take me to the Ministry of the Interior to work things out. He apologized to me profusely and said he was sure it was some sort of mistake. A young soldier of maybe twenty named Manolo was assigned to accompany me. Once the officers had left, Manolo turned to me and said, "I know you from L.A. I could never put you in jail. Go home and go to the ministry office tomorrow." I thanked him and I left with Fred and Gloria.

It took three days to get this issue straightened out. The next day Fred and I met with Enrique Schmidt, a half-German, half-Nicaraguan cabinet-level official at the Ministry of the Interior.* Enrique apologized and explained, "This is the kind of mistake the security forces make because they don't know one group from another." To finally settle my status they had to consult with Tomás Borge and Henry Ruiz, central leaders of the FSLN.

Living in Nicaragua

Gloria was forced to make a very difficult decision. She went back home to Texas to decide whether she was going to finish her education or come to stay with me in Nicaragua. On September 10 I spoke with her mother, who informed me that Gloria would not be coming back to Nicaragua. I was destroyed. Two days later Gloria called to say, "I'll come back—forget school." She returned to Nicaragua.

In October Gloria and I flew to Miami and on the return leg of our trip one of the oddest things happened. We disembarked the airplane at the wrong stop, in La Ceiba, Honduras. We waited for our luggage at the baggage claim and noticed it wasn't there. Suddenly it dawned on me that we were at the wrong airport in the wrong country, and flights ran only three times a week. Our plane was already slowly pulling away. I ran out onto the runway in front of the plane and waved madly at the pilot. The plane braked and they let down the stairwell, and Gloria and I got on the plane. The passengers were all laughing. Needless to say, today you would probably get shot for trying to do something like that.

While we lived in Nicaragua we had no hot water, nor washing machines or dryers for our clothes. The house we lived in was wide open with a central yard. All kinds of animals lived with us, mainly large lizards. We got used to taking cold showers. We washed all our clothes by hand and hung them out in the blazing Managua sun to dry. The clothes came out completely different than out of machines. They felt good and smelled good. I loved wearing clothes dried by the sun. As for the cold showers, well, that was a bit different. You just jumped around a lot while showering.

---

* Enrique was killed in October 1984 in a battle with the U.S.-funded Contra terrorists.

On November 7, 1979, we attended a huge FSLN rally in honor of their central leader, Carlos Fonseca Amador. He had been murdered exactly three years earlier by the Somocistas, and the FSLN held a mass wake and reburial at the Plaza de la Revolución in the center of Managua. Gloria climbed up to the roof of a four-story building to get some good photos. I was at the front of the crowd near the speakers' platform when I noticed her up there, hanging off the edge of the roof with her camera. I waved but I think she realized I was scared for her, so about twenty minutes later she popped up next to me where most of the media was standing.

After all nine of the FSLN top commanders had finished their speeches they picked up the coffin, which was clearly very heavy, and began to walk out. They procession route was to pass about thirty feet from where we were standing. Just as they were even with us, one of the nine pallbearers let go of the coffin. He ran over to Gloria, put his arms around her, and gave her a big hug. The huge audience started laughing as the other eight pallbearers yelled at him to get back in position.

I tried to hide my jealousy and just froze. The place was full of teenagers with machine guns. I wanted to go punch the guy but could only imagine the laughter. So I did nothing. I looked at Gloria and she was smiling, the center of attention. I asked, "Are you okay?" She just smiled.

Tipping Point

Sometimes even a small event in life can bring about much greater understanding. I had such an experience in Nicaragua, one that started a change in my life.

The FSLN gathered people together for block meetings by setting a tire on fire as a way to let everyone on the block know that a meeting was about to happen. One day I came across such a meeting by accident. I can't remember who was with me but we decided to stay. A young man, probably no more than twenty-four, stood on a box and began speaking to the whole neighborhood that had come out to listen.

As he spoke it dawned on me. The way he communicated, the message he gave, was what I had always tried to say; but he used only clear, understandable words and his message built on the living history of Nicaragua and the consciousness of the workers and their families who were listening.

He explained how Nicaragua belongs to its own people. How rich foreigners had come and taken their country from them but that they were the people who worked and created the wealth of their nation. They had the right to run it and to decide what should be done. He spoke about the homeless children in the streets and how under the U S.-backed dictatorship nothing was done for them. He described in detail how the FSLN was trying to solve each problem. That it would take time. That Nicaragua was still in danger of foreign intervention. To never forget those who gave their lives so that Nicaragua could be a free nation. At each mention of the departed, the crowd shouted, "*Presente*," to affirm that the missing ones were still with them, here. At every meeting of the Sandinistas, regardless where it was held, someone would read off the names of people from that block, school, or union who had given their lives for freedom. Everyone at the meeting would shout "*Presente*."

My mind began to race. Of course this young man was not going to use terms that would lead to confusion; he would place these issues in the culture, history, and language of his people. It dawned on me—that is why this movement had won. They didn't name their newspaper after some term from European history; they didn't speak of "socialism" or "Marxism." While the rest of the left of the 1960s and '70s was in decline throughout Latin America, caught up in the rhetoric of European Marxism and the influence of Stalinism, the FSLN had delivered a great victory for freedom.

I thought about the United States—the great traditions of our struggles for justice, our symbols, our language—and how disconnected the left was from that reality. I am not sure if it was on that night or another that I had the concrete thought, "We need a paper called the *North Star*," the greatest symbol of our nation's struggle for freedom. I remember keeping these thoughts to myself. I didn't talk to Fred about it. Possibly I told Gloria, I can't remember. But etched in my memory forever is that block meeting with the fire in the middle of street and some unknown youth changing my life.

CHAPTER 12

WORK AND THE LEFT
IN THE EARLY 1980S

The work we had been doing in support of Nicaragua was brought to a halt as the SWP decided that kind of work was "middle class" and that a "proletarian" approach had to be discovered. Jack Barnes and his grouping were convinced that the new wave of radicalization would occur in the industrial sector. In formal resolutions adopted by the SWP leadership, Barnes asserted that "gigantic battles for power" were imminent and that the radicalization of the working class was just around the corner.

But reality pointed in a different direction. Unions, which at one point had organized 33 percent of American labor, had shrunk to just 12 percent. No major political opposition appeared. Yes, there were many defensive struggles as the industrial unions were weakened by corporate and governmental attacks, which had been stepped up under Reagan. But labor had no labor party or any kind of effective defense strategy. By the early 1980s the industrial working class and its unions had been in a sharp decline for two obvious, interconnected reasons. First was the growth of globalization; second was the union capitulation to the Democratic Party. At every level the unions, pushed by the Democratic Party, were capitulating, supposedly a necessary step for U.S. corporations to be competitive in the global economy.

There was vital political activity occurring at the time, such as the struggle for democracy in El Salvador. A new environmental movement was also starting to gain momentum. But instead of getting involved the SWP abandoned all its mass-oriented political work in favor of embedding members in the various industrial unions. Barnes's industrial theory—known as "the turn"—was like the second coming. *Sooner or later labor will rise and we need to be there.* Consequently if you questioned the view that the center of all politics was now in the industrial unions you had obviously fallen from the true faith. I saw the development of a workerist, ultraleft line in the SWP, but as I did not have a clear understanding of the problem I was hesitant to fight. I actually voted to support the industrial theory. In part, I did so because I knew that if I were to vote against such a resolution, there would be a campaign against me and an attempt to isolate me from the membership. More practical SWPers sensed the madness and left the organization.

Working in the Garment Industry

After Gloria and I returned to the United States from Nicaragua, as crazy as it sounds, I decided to test the SWP's official theory for myself. So I went to work in the New York garment district. I got a job at Bill Blass, a line of women's clothing. My job was packaging and shipping the final products. I claimed to have experience and faked that I knew what I was doing, but it was the kind of work you could learn to do in one day.

My fellow workers were in general depressed and demoralized. Privately they would admit conditions were bad, the pay was bad, and the union did nothing. Politically nothing was happening.

All the products we made carried the International Ladies Garment Workers Union label. Supposedly we could join the union after six months. When I had been at the job long enough to qualify, I went to the union center. They told me point blank that the shop I was working at was a nonunion shop. Two people out of the entire shop were admitted into the union so the management could use the union label. There was nothing they could do. All of this was explained calmly, as though it shouldn't be a shock that the union label was just a lie.

At another nonunion garment shop my job involved pushing the clothing carts to the shipping warehouse. If you have ever been in New York's garment district you have seen workers pushing those carts through the streets. Some shop workers became suspicious of me because they noticed I could speak English without a Spanish accent and I could type.

Over time on that job I became friends with José, a young Puerto Rican guy about nineteen years old.* He told me how he lived in a small apartment with lots of relatives, all trying to survive by splitting the rent and food costs. I asked him how he made ends meet on his low pay and one day he told me. He had three incomes. Once a month he would vanish during lunch, shoot over to New Jersey, and collect an unemployment check under another name. Then, he told me, once a week he would throw one of our products in the trash can where scrap paper piled up, pushing the garment down to hide it under the paper. Later, the trash collectors would arrive and take the can downstairs. There was a tiny coffee shop on the street level. The trash men would hand over the garment to the coffee guy, who in turn would sell it for a third of its cost to a mafia person who came by to pick up the stolen goods. José got a small piece of that action.

As he told me this, I remembered the owner of the shop counting units one day and saying, "Oh my gosh, another piece has disappeared."

One day José and I were pushing some garment carts through the streets in the dead of winter. Mounted police patrolled the area on horses so the gutters were full of horse manure. A huge gust of wind flipped over our cart and all the clothing fell out, landing in the horse manure. We tried to clean it off with newspapers we found lying on the sidewalk. When that was futile we decided just to go to the delivery point to see if they would accept the damaged products. As it turned out, the guy working there had a cold and couldn't smell anything. Those garments were probably on store shelves within a day. We joked that people probably liked the items even more because the leather parts smelled genuine.

I Depart from the Socialist Workers Party

Gloria also worked in garment with me and for a while drove a Frito-Lay truck. Together we decided this was madness. Our industrial jobs had nothing to do with politics and we needed to rethink everything. The SWP allowed members to take a leave of absence and be inactive for a period of time. So I reported to Olga Rodriguez that I wanted to take a leave. Olga then reported in writing to the entire leadership of the SWP, clearly with

---

* Even though it has been twenty-seven years, I will use a pseudonym and alter a few facts lest by some chance I should do "José" any harm by telling this story.

Barnes's complicity, that I had informed her of my resignation. This was not a misinterpretation of intent—I kept a diary at the time and wrote these things down. Sadly, lying seemed to have become part of the regular process in the SWP. In fact, once while I was translating for Jack in Europe I refused to continue when he just started fabricating.

Even my MIT friends Gus Horowitz and Barry Sheppard were buying into utterly absurd positions. The SWP had gradually separated itself from all political activity, rendering the membership passive. Finding union jobs in auto, steel, or another industry allowed some members to maintain the illusion they were doing something political. But the SWP leadership went so far as to dictate that members should not be teachers, work for a library, or take any sort of "middle class" job, and there was not to be any more student movement work. This disconnect from reality led to internal conflict, factionalism, and expulsions, until the SWP was reduced to a sect, a cult around Barnes.*

The Barnes cult added a distinctive twist. They decided to refer to themselves publicly as "communist," which they do to this day. In the world of political sects this is a conscious effort to remain isolated. It assures their few followers that they stand alone, that they will prove right and everyone else wrong. The cult leader has mystical inherent knowledge that no one else is able to attain except by becoming a follower.

The one thing the Barnes cult does have is money. They own some very valuable real estate purchased by the SWP in the late 1960s, which should keep them going for a long time.

Building a Hyatt

I needed to get a job. My brother Daniel was building a hotel in in Puerto La Cruz, Venezuela, the first Hyatt in Latin America. My father's creditability as a developer had allowed Daniel to get a Venezuelan guarantee on a loan from a British bank for about $15 million to build the thou-

---

* During the crisis in the SWP I met with James Percy, the leader of the Australian SWP (their name later changed to the Democratic Socialist Party.) At an international gathering Jim told me the Australians had also come to the conclusion that the American SWP had turned into a Barnes cult. He made it clear that they wanted to work with me and hear my views on these issues. Throughout the 1980s I made speaking tours to Australia, even traveling to Perth on the West Coast. My close friendship with Jim Percy unfortunately ended when he died in 1992 at the age of forty-four from colon cancer.

sand-room hotel, to be named Puerto Camejo after our father. For the time being Gloria had gone home to Texas to see her family.

I went down to Caracas and started working for my brother. The hotel was about half-finished when I got there but Daniel was running out of money for the project. Interest rates were at record highs due to the financial crisis that had gripped all of Latin America during 1980–82 and banks were cutting off loans or folding altogether. At 20 percent the debt to the bank over two-and-a-half years took half the capital needed to build the hotel. Daniel went to the Venezuelan government and argued that if the hotel failed all would be lost, but if it were to be finished, rising inflation would mean that the debt could be repaid over time. He needed about another $10 million to complete the construction. The Venezuelan government approved the plan and offered the British bank a governmental guarantee.

Just as Daniel was preparing to fly to London to sign the new contracts, Argentina decided to retake the Malvinas Islands, which the British, under the name "Falklands," claimed as their own.

Naturally all of Latin America, including Venezuela, had declared in support of the Argentines. The British bank contacted Daniel to inform him that they could no longer make loans to Venezuelans. Immediately the corrupt world of Venezuelan development saw an opportunity to take over a half-finished thousand-room hotel. The sharks began to circle. It was a personal and financial disaster for my brother.*

This left Gloria and me without jobs. We went back to Miami, where Daniel had some prepaid, unused furniture intended for the hotel. He proposed that we sell it off, so I set up a little company named after our grandmother, ADELA, and began liquidating the furniture at rock-bottom prices. My brother let us collect some of the profits and for a short period Gloria and I had a little bit of money. Soon the sharks arrived and the remaining furniture came under their control.

Return to California

As the SWP was melting down several members who had quit—or who had been expelled, a rapidly growing phenomenon—contacted me. Why

---

* The beautiful hotel, now called Mare Mares, was finished by another company. It is located in the El Morro project created by my dad.

hadn't I fought the Barnes group? Some of my closest friends back in the Bay Area asked me to come out to California so we could see if anything could be salvaged.

I felt that I had let down many friends who had worked with me throughout the years in the SWP. I should have fought harder. Now, out of the movement for the first time since 1959, I had no college degree and no resume, no way to make a living. This was not just putting a strain on me but also obviously affected Gloria and our relationship, which at that point I should have made my number-one concern.

Gloria and I had been together for about four years and had lived in Texas, New York, Nicaragua, Venezuela, and Miami. Now we were moving to California. We moved literally every year. She had lost the opportunity to finish her college degree; she could have become a doctor like her brother. And every time she started making plans to go back to school I was telling her we had to move again.

The poverty, turmoil, and other mistakes on my part slowly destroyed our love. In California she met a professional about her age, they fell in love and I lost her. While that was one of the most difficult moments of my life, I was still happy for her; I knew it was probably the best thing that could have happened.

The North Star Network

In California I gathered some of the ex-SWPers and we formed a new group called the North Star Network and launched a magazine, *North Star*. A major focus of our activity was on helping the people of El Salvador in their struggle against the U.S.-backed military dictatorship. Numerically the response was a pleasant surprise—about 1,500 people were associated with us. I recognized, however, that many of these people were older, tired ex-members of groups. There was a wide range of opinions as to how to proceed. A lot depended on me, yet I was too exhausted, depressed, and broke to do much at the time. Another small group, led by Steve Hiatt, merged with the North Star Network and Steve became our magazine editor.

Ray Markey, a union leader in New York, and I had been good friends in the SWP. We worked together in building the North Star Network, and I often stayed at Ray's apartment when I went to New York. Ray had been the most outspoken in the New York union movement for the formation of a labor party. He was repeatedly reelected as president by the members of his union and everyone accepted his determined stand for independent political action. When the SWP leaders told him to give up his position as leader of the New York Public Library Guild (AFSCME Local 1930) he told them to go to hell. To meet with people joining the North Star Network around the country I did a little bit of traveling. While visiting Utah I met a woman named Cherie Lopez and we started dating, a challenge given that I was living in Berkeley and had no money. Cherie had a four-year-old daughter called Nickie, and I fell in love with that child. I talked to her on the phone for long periods of time about her Barbie dolls. In San Francisco the three of us went to an anti-apartheid march and little Nickie was shouting right along with the demonstrators. We were chanting "No apartheid!" but Nickie was shouting "No part time!"

In a terrible turn, at age five Nickie died suddenly from an inherited disease. Her mom was devastated, and our relationship ended. Nickie's death was very hard on me. To this day I keep a photo of her in my office at home.

El Salvador

A new generation stepped up to lead the North Star's work in helping the people of El Salvador in their struggle against the dictatorship. These leaders were youth compared to many of the North Star supporters and they referred to us as "the sixties people." As we worked together I developed the highest respect for these young people, some of whom have become my life-long friends.

An amazing woman, Heidi Tarver, became one of the central leaders of this new solidarity movement. I first met Heidi at a demonstration in Los Angeles. She was a little nervous about me, understandable given all the chaos the movement was facing from "sixties people." Heidi's two sisters, Lisa and Rebecca, were also deeply involved; Rebecca took a bullet in El Salvador but survived. I consider all three of them very special people. This new generation risked their lives to support the struggle of the peasants and workers of El Salvador for democracy and the rights of working people.

Michael Wyman, a bit older than the others, would become one of my closest friends. In Washington, D.C., Mike worked tirelessly at the Washington Center for Central American Studies (WCCAS) as editor of *El Salvador On Line*, an English-language newsweekly. Unlike anyone else I have ever met Mike lived in a permanent state of poverty while he used his own money to help fund the El Salvador solidarity movement and other progressive efforts.

At the same time Mike's future sister-in-law,* Sylvia Rosales, was involved in trying to set up discussions between the Farabundo Martí National Liberation Front (FMLN—the revolutionary coalition) and the Salvadoran government to bring about an end to the civil war. The dangers for the FMLN to participate in such discussions inside El Salvador were too great. Even to suggest such talks could incite an attack from the death squads and result in the murder of the FMLN representatives.

Amazingly, five talks were organized by WCCAS: two in Washington, D.C., two in San Francisco, and one in San Jose, Costa Rica. Eventually these talks led to a settlement that ended the civil war and prepared for the election of a government that marked an end to the period of open dictatorial rule. The evolution of this process, the isolation of the extreme right and the start of a new era in which the FMLN could function legally, is a little-known story in which the WCCAS played a major role, especially Sylvia Rosales.†

Also among this generation of leaders was a whole group of Salvadorans. Three that I worked with closely were Luis Flores, Alicia Mendoza, and Ramón Cardona, who is now a member of the parliament in El Salvador, representing Salvadorans living in the United States.

The Rainbow Coalition

At the time the North Star Network was formed I made a major political mistake. A new sense of possibility had emerged when Jesse Jackson started the Rainbow Coalition and ran (as a Democrat) for president in 1984. Within the North Star there was a desire to get involved in supporting Jackson's organization. While there were various points of view, mine being clearly opposed to the Democratic Party, I let myself be influenced into seeing the Jackson movement as a possible beginning of a real reform movement (similar to the nineteenth-century "barnburners") or an actual split with the Democrats.

This error on my part lasted until I came to my senses and realized that, with few exceptions, the Rainbow Coalition was just another name for keep-

---

* I officiated at the wedding of Mike and his wife Carolina in their backyard in Corte Madera, California, October 1, 1998. It is legal in California for anyone to officiate a wedding. I was terrified but everything went off as planned.

† Today Sylvia works in the East Bay for the AnewAmerica Community Corporation, which she helped start. The foundation helps immigrant entrepreneurs fund microbusinesses and provides business education. Her efforts have turned the foundation into a resounding success.

ing progressives in the Democratic Party. Jesse Jackson was a hard-core Democrat and remains so today.

In Oakland the Rainbow Coalition was led by an extremely dedicated
man, Wilson Riles, Jr., the son of the first African American elected to
statewide office in California. Wilson, a Democrat, had been an Oakland city
council member, and through the Rainbow Coalition it was decided that he
should run for mayor. The mayoral election was a nonpartisan race and I
felt very comfortable working to help Wilson, as did all the other people involved in the North Star Network or the Rainbow Coalition. He was running
against a mainstream, pro-corporate Democrat, also African American. We
all felt Wilson had a good chance if we could put together a powerful campaign. His platform was clearly pro-labor, pro–social justice, and pro-peace.

Jesse Jackson was scheduled to come to Oakland and we thought this
could be a real opportunity to gain support for Wilson Riles. To our shock and
amazement Jesse Jackson, without talking to Wilson or to the Rainbow Coalition, held a press conference to endorse the mainstream Democrat against
Riles. I will never forget the anger it created. Wilson stood up to Jackson and
publicly attacked Jackson's open break with the supposed platform of the Rainbow Coalition. Wilson lost the election in part due to Jesse Jackson's betrayal.
Years later Wilson Riles, Jr., resigned as a Democrat and joined the Green Party.

After this betrayal most of the Oakland members of the Rainbow Coalition changed their attitude toward Jesse Jackson. Over time Jackson worked to
end the Rainbow's independent organizational structure, putting it under his
direct control as he more openly opposed allowing the Rainbow Coalition to
be an organizing center for people who favored independent political action.
Only in Vermont did the coalition break with Jackson to form an independent
political current, called the Progressive Party, which still exists. It has its own
representatives in the state legislature but does also endorse Democrats.

Decline of the Sixties Left

The left was unraveling throughout the country. As Stalinism collapsed
in Russia, Stalinist groups splintered in turn. A group called the Committees
of Correspondence broke with the U.S. Communist Party and a later evolution produced another group, the Line of March. I checked out these new
formations and became friends with some of their leaders. They were welcoming but it slowly dawned on me that none of these groups had the
faintest idea what they had been doing by supporting Stalinism.

They couldn't understand the connection between their liberal, pro–Democratic Party views and the influence Stalinism had over their politics. In their minds they considered the two things separate. Many admitted that they had vicariously supported horrible crimes but all that was dismissed as "mistakes" that had been made in Moscow. They just couldn't see the link; that Stalinism had oriented the world "left" to support the rule of money over people as a strategy for alliances and trade with the Soviet Union. They also didn't seem to realize how extreme the totalitarian regimes in Moscow and China were. Most continued to think that Stalinism was part of the workers' movement but had committed missteps. They failed to understand that Stalinism was not just a political current but a socioeconomic current that defended a brutally anti-labor privileged sector.

The founders of the North Star participated for a period with the former Line of Marchers in publishing a magazine called *Crossroads*. But all these efforts eventually resulted in these groups' gradually dissolving into liberals within the Democratic Party. Often they maintained seemingly radical stances on some international issues but their position was always to support the Democrats politically.

During this period of realignment I went to the library at UC Berkeley and, on microfilm, read every single issue of the nineteenth-century abolitionist newspaper *North Star*. I was eager to learn how that movement had handled the two-party issue. Reading the *North Star* was a very emotional experience for me. I felt such a connection with that heroic earlier generation. It was surprising to me how they faced many of the same issues we face today. Although we paid homage to them we had not really listened to them closely or tried to learn from their struggles. The revolutionaries of the Civil War—the Second American Revolution—had among them endless differences. They were divided and forever arguing, an inevitable aspect of any real mass social movement.

Finding Work in California

I still needed a job. After my return to California at first I delivered sushi to small retail units. That didn't work out. Then through the grapevine I learned that the San Francisco post office had been found guilty of discrimination and was consequently required to hire more Latinos. I took the test, got hired, and went to work in the main San Francisco post office. It was quite eye-opening to learn how hard postal workers actually work, in contrast to all the stereotypes. I made eleven dollars an hour as a postal worker, a big step up from zero. But I had a back problem that eventually forced me to look for a different line of work.

In Berkeley three dear friends reached out to help me. Dave Warren, a computer programmer, proposed to teach me his trade and was even prepared to vouch for me in the meantime so I could take on programming work right away. Years earlier he had done the same thing for my old MIT friend Ron Payne. Derrel Myers had a small business painting houses and offered to make me part of the team.

The third person who tried to help me was Alan Hicks.* In a way Alan saved me from the predicament I was in by coming up with a simple rationale. He said, "Peter, your strength is in your ability to speak to people. You are very convincing." So he proposed that I go to work for Merrill Lynch, the investment firm.

Alan was very knowledgeable about finance but I still thought his idea was a little far-fetched. And if I were to get the job, I feared people would think I was selling out, a socialist working for an asset management company. Alan reasoned that working for Merrill Lynch was a sales job like any other and I would learn it fast, make some money, and not hurt my back.

My resume had two things on it that were actually true: my name and telephone number. At my interview they gave me a short, simple math quiz, which was easy enough. The office manager asked me if I knew anything about finance and I answered, "Not really. That's why I want to work for Merrill." They offered me a job starting with a guarantee of $2,000 a month. I got nervous that if I accepted the job on the spot they would think I needed money and that wouldn't fit with the resume I had handed them. So I told them I couldn't accept it but would think it over since I wanted to learn about investing.

My friends all yelled at me, "Take the job!" A day later Merrill called and offered me commissions on top of the $2,000. I accepted the offer and started work at Merrill Lynch in downtown San Francisco in July of 1985. This would change my life on several levels. Mainly I started making money.

---

* During his SWP years Alan had worked diligently on Latin American causes, heading up the L.A. chapter of the U.S. Committee for Latin American Political Prisoners, aiding Hugo Blanco, organizing concerts in support of the Sandinistas, among many other efforts. He received an award from the Nicaraguan consul after Somoza was overthrown.

Left and below: Peter as a young man; above: Peter, age nine

Above: Protesters erupt in anger during the 1967 Stop the Draft Week in Oakland, California; right: A campaign poster for Peter's 1976 bid for U.S. president with the Socialist Workers Party, reprinted in a front-page story in a Venezuelan newspaper

Above: Edward Kennedy interviews Peter at Boston University, September 1970. Peter is holding up a newspaper report of his arrest after speaking at a protest against the war in Vietnam; below: Peter appears on *Meet the Press* with three other minority party candidates for president in October 1976.

Right: Peter speaking to a rally at the University of Wisconsin, Madison's Union Concourse during his 1976 presidential campaign; below: pictured with his running mate, Willie Mae Reid, in St. Louis, Missouri.

Right: Peter preparing to speak at a San Francisco antiwar rally in October 2001

Below: Peter with his family (clockwise from top left): son Victor Baquero; Peter; son-in-law Charlton Lee; daughter Mari Baquero-Lee; wife Morella, holding grandson Daniel; and daughter-in-law Kelly Moreno Baquero, holding grandson Andrew

Peter autographing copies of his book, *The SRI Advantage: Why Socially Responsible Investing Has Outperformed Financially* in 2002

Left: Peter and Morella holding their grandson Oliver, 6 weeks old, in August 2008.

Peter with his wife, Morella, in San Marcos, California, in July 2008

CHAPTER 13

MORELLA ANZOLA

I met Morella Anzola out of the blue in Key Biscayne, Florida, partly as a political and economic consequence of the decision by the president of Venezuela to devalue the Bolivar and suspend foreign currency exchange. This move had left Morella, who was vacationing in Florida with her two children unable, to use a credit card since all Venezuelan credit cards were now invalidated in the United States.

It was August 1985 and I was visiting my mother and stepfather in Florida. My brother Antonio told me that a relative of ours needed to get a U.S. credit card and that he had assured her I could do that through Merrill Lynch. From the way my brother spoke I thought she must be sixty-five-years old. So I went to the apartment where she was staying in Key Biscayne and knocked on the door. This thirty-eight-year-old woman answered the door and I thought it might be the daughter. I asked, "Are you ... Morella?" She said yes.

We were both Anzolas, of course, so we talked about our relatives. In the back of my mind I had a faint memory of having seen her as a little girl at the Laguna Beach Club in the 1950s. She told me about her children. They were in another room so I went in to say hello. Her thirteen-year-old son, Victor, was busy flinging martial arts "throwing stars" at a board. I asked him, "Does your mom know you have those dangerous stars?" He said, "She buys them for me." Morella's daughter Mari was eleven and very attached to her mom.

After we had made arrangements for a credit card I suggested we go for ice cream nearby. We drove to Coconut Grove and walked into an ice cream place with only two other people in it. By an amazing coincidence they were my older brother Daniel and his son Danielito, who lived in Caracas. I didn't even know they were in Florida at the time.

I asked Morella if she and the children wanted to go sailing that weekend. The trip went well and we started dating. What struck me most about Morella was a quality difficult to describe. She was so kind to everyone she came in contact with. I thought immediately that she was like an angel. She loved her children dearly and I realized that my only hope was to win the kids over.

Morella's husband, Victor Baquero, had died in a tragic flight accident in Caracas. A trained pilot, he was taking supplemental lessons in instrumental flying. On the day of the accident the airport reversed the flight patterns due to wind conditions and Victor and his instructor crashed into a mountain. Morella was suddenly left with two children, six and eight years old at the time, no income, and no specific employable skills. She went to Miami to train as a dental hygienist and began to work back in Caracas. When I met her she was on vacation with the children at her parents' apartment in Key Biscayne.

We spent about a week together, seeing each other almost every day. Then she had to go back to Caracas and I went back to Berkeley. I started saving up to make the trip for her birthday in September. In Caracas I met Morella's parents and sisters. Morella's father, Cesar Anzola, is a direct descendant of Miguel Anzola. Two generations earlier, Morella's great-grandfather, Juvenal Anzola, served as the head of the Venezuelan Supreme Court. Juvenal and my great-grandmother Carmen were brother and sister; they were the grandchildren of Miguel Anzola.

Morella's mother, Ida Degwitz, is half German. An excellent golf player, she represented Venezuela in tournaments throughout Latin America. Morella has two sisters, Nancy and Helena. Like Morella, they both had two children each, a boy and a girl, and now a growing number of grandchildren. They all live in Venezuela. Morella's parents have been wonderful to me, and throughout Morella's life they have stood by her whenever she needed their help.

Later Morella visited me in Berkeley. My living conditions sort of shocked her. I had a small, rent-controlled apartment with two bedrooms, a total of three plates, old broken-down furniture, no microwave, and a little TV I could roll from the living room to the bedroom. One room had nothing in it but boxes of books. Hidden behind the couch in the living room was a mattress that Alan Hicks had placed there so when he was in the Bay Area he could stay at my place. Little did Morella know that I had actually bought a coffee table for ten dollars the day before she came to make the place look better.

Family

The children made a huge impact on me. It is a little hard for me to admit this, given my views on life and the world, but the fact that these children were my relatives affected me. Morella was so loving toward her children and they were always on her mind. Whenever she visited me the children would call, leaving messages while they were having a fight. I remember the two of us laughing together as we listened to their messages on the answering machine.

On a trip to Florida over the holidays, I asked Morella to marry me. My marriage proposal was kind of odd because I spent most of it warning her about how political I was and how that was a very important part of my life. We were married on August 2, 1986, in Boca Raton, Florida. We moved to Lafayette, California, and rented a house right across the street from the school that Mari would attend. I had no idea what being a father was all about, while Mari felt very threatened by the marriage, thinking that somehow I was taking her mom away from her.

We took our honeymoon in Maui, Hawaii, bringing along the children as well as their friend, my niece Chantica. Chantica, my brother Antonio's daughter,* tried so hard to convince Mari not to worry about my being her new dad. We had a wonderful time in Maui.

Morella had to take a course in Sacramento to get certified and pass her board exams in order to practice as a dental hygienist in California. On those days she would be gone overnight and I was left with the children.

---

* Chantica, at sixteen, was killed on Christmas Day of that year in a car accident in Venezuela. She was an incredibly talented artist and had great potential to become an actress. At the time of her death she was being considered for a leading role in the movie *Stand and Deliver* with Edward James Olmos, about teenage Chicanos in Los Angeles who against all odds succeed in learning calculus. In the credits the film is dedicated to Chantica and the last name of the main teenage female character is Camejo. Her death was very hard on my brother and Chantica's mom, of course, but also on all of us.

Every evening Mari leaned on her mom to help her do her homework. One evening when her mom was not there she leaned on me and I was so overjoyed that I was now accepted by her as a parent.

When Mari was in sixth grade all she had to do to get to school was cross the street. But all her friends had their parents drive them to school so she wanted me to drive her too. I would get her into the car, back the car down the driveway, and park on the other side of the street so her friends could see that her dad had driven her to school. When the children needed a note from a parent I would sign it "Peter Baquero" so they would not have to explain anything.

For a few years our family expanded to include my brother Dan Ratner, who came to live with us in 1987, when he was nineteen. The son of my mom and stepdad, Danny attended Merritt College in Oakland and worked with me for several years at Progressive Asset Management, Inc.

As time passed we moved to Alameda and bought a house at 116 Sherwood Lane. After Victor and Mari had graduated from the Alameda public school system we moved to Walnut Creek, into a house we absolutely loved, and discovered a small group of wonderful neighbors. Victor went to college at Berkeley where he met his future wife, Kelly Moreno. After they were married, Victor attended medical school in Virginia and became a family practice doctor. Kelly is a high school teacher in American history, following her family's tradition of being part of the educational system. They live in Folsom, California.

Mari attended UC Davis and subsequently earned two masters degrees. Today she is a school psychologist near San Diego. She married Charlton Lee, a high school friend, who works managing a computer system for a city near their home.

In 2002 when I ran for office I agreed to move to Folsom so Morella could be near two of our grandchildren, Daniel José and Andrew John, the children of Victor and Kelly. We now have a third grandchild who is only two months old as I write this. His name is Oliver James Peter Lee, our daughter's first child.

For me nothing could be more joyous than to have the grandchildren nearby. They have had a huge effect on me. During my campaigns I made many efforts to take them with me and get them on TV when I did interviews. I even had Daniel, the older one, vote for me. I asked permission and the workers at the polling place told me "Sure, go ahead." Andrew, who was born the day I announced for governor, and Daniel appeared on a special Channel 3 TV story about our home in Folsom, which is a "zero-energy" house.

Morella retired from dental hygiene and worked with me for many years in my business, but her true loves are painting and gardening, both of which she takes very seriously. Our life now centers on our family and grandchildren since my last run for office, for governor in 2006.

As I write this in 2008 we have been married for twenty-two years. I have been suffering from cancer for two years. During my illness her presence has been like having a nurse twenty-four hours a day. Morella is hard to describe in terms of the kind of love she exudes in our family. I remember how a leader of the New Zealand movement, my friend Matt McCarten, came to visit me in California and stayed with us. One day he said to me, "I feel such love in this home."

CHAPTER 14

PROGRESSIVE ASSET
MANAGEMENT, INC.

I worked at Merrill Lynch for less than two years. Toward the end of that time I came up with an idea called "The IRA That Cares." For every Individual Retirement Account (IRA) opened with Merrill Lynch, the firm would donate ten dollars* to the San Francisco AIDS Foundation. We could also extend the model to other not-for-profits, such as the American Heart Association. But I was specifically interested in helping the AIDS Foundation, since San Francisco in 1986 was in a crisis over the spread and impact of AIDS. My office manager loved the idea of "The IRA That Cares." He saw it as something charitable but also as a goodwill gesture that could bring business to Merrill. On the investment side the approach would be very conservative, since we didn't want anyone participating in the program to take any losses.

The plan, of course, needed to be approved by Merrill's national office in New York. Their response was that the idea was okay—but not for the San Francisco AIDS Foundation. I told my office manager that I wouldn't allow the program to go forward if Merrill discriminated against the AIDS

---

* It is against the law for a firm to offer people money to invest with them. An exception existed for IRAs in light of their tax-deductible status. According to the law a firm could spend up to ten dollars per IRA. With this idea I was essentially proposing that it be donated to charity instead.

Foundation. The foundation had been working closely with me on this idea and was very disappointed that Merrill Lynch refused to do it.

I immediately signed with a headhunter and began seeking another major firm that would launch the program. The first to respond was Prudential Bache. The head of their IRA department came out to see me in San Francisco and said that they would do the program for any nonprofit. With that offer I agreed to transfer my business and go to work for Prudential Bache (now called Prudential). They also offered me a signing bonus of $40,000 to shift firms, since I would be bringing business they wanted.

I moved my business to Prudential's office in Orinda, a town east of Berkeley. The Prudential office was much smaller than Merrill's; coincidentally, one of the brokers who worked there at the time was Suze Orman, who later became incredibly successful as a television personality. I don't think I ever spoke to her, but today she has a TV program that offers carefully thought-out, prudent investing advice aimed at the average person.

To make a long story short, after I had transferred all my business to Prudential Bache the firm reneged on its agreement to do the program for the San Francisco AIDS Foundation. I received notice of their decision in an overnight package.

Progressive Asset Management, Inc.

I was invited to meet with a small group of Series 7 brokers (holders of a General Securities license), and we started discussions about setting up our own firm. The initiator was Jerry Dodson, who had launched his own socially responsible mutual fund. Many of the people involved were new to the industry and were not managing large amounts of assets; my production was probably greater than all the others combined. Also interested in the idea was John Harrington,* who had been the president of Working Assets, the first socially responsible money market fund.

Dodson pulled back at the last minute, concerned about the liabilities and challenges. I drove up to Napa where John Harrington lived and asked

---

* When John was young he did something so brave that it is really worth mentioning. He joined the U.S. Air Force when he was nineteen and was doing electrical work on B52s in Guam. One day they asked John to work loading bombs that were going to be dropped on Vietnam. He refused by simply not showing up for work. They gave him a thirty-day sentence, demoted him to the lowest rank, and sent him back to Travis Air Force Base in California.

him if he wanted to go ahead with the project. He said yes, he would help me. I arranged that John would be the founding chairman of the board and the two of us would work together to raise the initial working capital of $500,000, which for this kind of venture was really quite a small sum. Later we raised another million dollars.

We opened the doors for business at our new firm, Progressive Asset Management, Inc. (PAM), in October of 1987, right during a stock market crash. PAM started with only seven people. Cathy Cartier, who had worked with me at Prudential Bache as what is called in the industry a "sales assistant," came with PAM and eventually took charge of operations.* The other person from the original group who evolved into a central leader in PAM was Eric Leenson, who had been active politically in Latin America and helped start La Peña Cultural Center in Berkeley. He later became the Chief Financial Officer (CFO) and when I started running for office took over as CEO, expanding PAM through continuous recruitment.

As part of his social commitment Eric supported the landless workers movement in Brazil. At one point he came to me and said, "I want to raise some money for the landless workers in Northern Brazil so they can buy cars for their organizers." I think he needed $50,000 in total. He assured me we would be repaid. I didn't think there was any realistic chance we would see the money again but I agreed anyway and contributed, if I remember correctly, $10,000. Amazing as it may sound we were repaid for every penny and Eric raised the entire sum that they needed. He has worked tirelessly for this cause and many other similar projects through the years.

We gradually assembled a fantastic group of people, each with a special interest in environmental, social, or political issues. By 2005–2006 the assets with which we were involved totaled more than a billion dollars. Many finance workers passed through PAM and went on to set up their own firms. Not everything went smoothly, of course. Over time I learned that you must not be too trusting or make assumptions about people. When we set up PAM John Harrington instructed me to be very careful and to have zero tolerance for anyone violating regulations or doing anything that seemed inappropriate. A few bizarre experiences led me to fire some of our brokers. One individual got leads from our advertising and passed them along to

---

* Today Cathy is really my partner in the Camejo Group with its office in Oakland, California.

another firm where his wife worked as an independent contractor and thus received a higher payout. In another case, two brokers were sent to do due diligence on a small firm for which we were considering raising some capital. One of them cut a separate special deal for himself, did not report it to us, and still tried to appear objective as to whether we should invest with them. Fortunately the CEO of the company called me and told me what had happened. That was two more brokers fired.

In our early days PAM got involved in financing low-income housing in California through a new tax credit program. We were helped by Ed Kirschner from Berkeley, who was very knowledgeable and helped put together those early deals. His programs were rather amazing as investments— the investor made a return of as much as 20 percent per year, tax free; and after fifteen years the low-income housing would pass to a not-for-profit and remain low-income housing forever. Eventually the larger firms realized how profitable this program could be and PAM could no longer find investments safe enough for our clients. In my book *California Under Corporate Rule** I suggested that the program should have been structured differently to maximize how much low-income housing could be built.

The Eco-Logical Trust

In 1990 Merrill Lynch launched two Environmental Technology Unit Trust funds. The term "unit trust fund" means that an investment firm selects a group of companies and puts them together in a fixed portfolio ("trust") for five years. The firm then sells the fund as an investment option to the public and the purchasers get a profit or take a loss at the end of the five-year period. A recent wave of media on environmental issues had resulted in tens of millions of dollars being invested in these two funds.

I wrote a letter to Merrill protesting their use of the word "environmental" to describe funds that included some major polluters. I had no particular purpose in doing this except perhaps to be able to say that I had sent them a letter and they never responded. To my surprise I received a call from Stanley Craig, vice president of national sales for the Merrill Lynch Unit Trust Department. (Merrill Lynch prepared the unit trusts and five of the largest brokerage firms participated in selling the units, so this department represented more than just Merrill Lynch.)

---

* Peter Camejo, et al. *California Under Corporate Rule* (Published by author, 2006).

Stan turned out to be a remarkable person. In many ways we were exact opposites—he was religious and a conservative Republican, but he also had a core of real honest morality. Stan was concerned that they had made no checks at all on the companies included in these funds, and asked me what I thought they should do. In truth, he caught me off guard. I hadn't given any thought to what Merrill should do, so I gave an obvious, idealistic answer, knowing it was likely impossible. I said to Stan, why not launch a fund that included only companies whose products and behavior were pro-environmental? To my astonishment he replied, "Peter, get on a plane and come out and see me. I want to talk to you about this." I thought I might have talked myself into a trap and either Stan was much smarter than I was or else he was just an incredibly decent, honest person. As it turned out he was both.

I flew to New York and we talked. At that time no major Wall Street firm had ever put together a fund with social or environmental screens. If anything, that was considered an absurd and losing investment strategy. I pressed Stan to let PAM choose the companies and, I added, part of the profits had to go to the environmental movement. After talking with his colleagues Stan came back with an agreement that we would do a pro-environmental fund as a joint project between PAM and Merrill. PAM would pick a large pool of companies that met our screens on the environment and Merrill Lynch would winnow down that list to about twenty based on estimates of their potential financial performance. We also planned for a percentage of the profits to be donated to Earth Share, a coalition of all the major environmental groups in the United States.

Stan coined the fund's name: "The Eco-Logical Trust." For the final presentation to Merrill Lynch in New York, a special meeting was scheduled that included representatives from the Unit Trust Department, the CEO of Merrill, and top corporate attorneys. Stan and I went over at length how he should present the proposal. Working together we had become friends and I was pretty emphatic with him to take a stand that this was the right thing to do and that the fund would perform well financially. I asked him to call me the minute the meeting ended.

He called me about an hour and a half later with a marvelous story. The meeting room was packed. They let him make his presentation. Afterward the CEO said, "I can think of a hundred reasons we shouldn't do this." In other words, just about every firm PAM had screened out did business with Merrill, including some that had been included the two other "environmental" funds. Then one of Merrill's head lawyers took the floor and replied, "I can think of a hundred reasons we shouldn't do this but I can't go home and tell my wife we didn't do it." The whole room broke out in laughter. Here was evidence of the impact of the environmental movement having penetrated right to the top of the brokerage industry. The CEO of Merrill Lynch turned to Stan and said, "Okay, let's do it."

Two fascinating things happened with the Eco-Logical Trust. One, it became the second-best-performing fund of all unit trusts at Merrill at that time; second, hardly anybody wanted to invest in it. According to common wisdom a fund that cared about the environment was destined to under-perform financially. Stan did everything he could to try to get people past their prejudices. He even began explaining to people our moral obligation to begin taking the environment seriously, emphasizing that we as a people had to take a stand.

While Stan was in San Francisco for a conference we went to have a cup of coffee and he said, "Peter, I'm out of ideas for new unit trusts. Have you got some recommendations for me?" I thought for a minute and replied, "I know something that will work out financially almost for sure and will be easy for you to market, but it isn't 'social.'" He said, "Okay, let me hear it." I laid out an idea widely known in the industry called the Dogs of the Dow. The concept is simple. Each year you take the five worst per-forming stocks in the Dow Jones index (thirty stocks) and you invest in them, selling the ones from last year. Over time you outperform the Dow Jones index.

What I suggested to Stan was that a unit trust, despite its fixed portfolio, could make changes as long as they were automatic and could be performed by a computer. He agreed, made note of the idea, and said to me, "I think this might work." My mistake was not quickly writing down a contract stat-ing, "And I get 1 basis point [one percent of one percent] of whatever Mer-rill makes off my idea." Soon Merrill launched the idea and the five firms involved sold billions of dollars' worth of the investments. A broker even cold-called me at home one day to solicit me to invest in it. I am still waiting for my thank-you note from Merrill.

Helping Create Employment

Through the work of John Harrington PAM helped raise funds for the Ecumenical Development Cooperative Society (EDCS), a group in Europe that provided loans to workers' cooperatives, which they often helped establish. For example, the EDCS might get a group of poor people involved in fishing and then provide a loan so the group could buy a modern boat. As the new cooperative gained income, they would repay the loan and EDCS would move on to help another group. The EDCS also required that half the leadership of each cooperative had to be women. They had a very high rate of success; almost all the loans were repaid. John drove this project forward and helped raise millions of dollars for the EDCS, some of it from major foundations.

PAM aimed to set up a foundation using the EDCS approach to create jobs in the poorest communities in the United States. James Nixon of our staff suggested we solicit major banks to contribute toward a $100 million fund for making these kinds of loans, to be administered by EDCS in the United States. Every bank by law had to invest 1 percent of their funds in what were called community investments, but few banks ever met the criteria.

James succeeded in getting the major banks in California to meet with our tiny firm to discuss this plan. Bank of America agreed to put up $10 million but demanded that PAM have at least one major insurance company, which would not have been under the same legal obligation, on board as a contributor. James tackled this seemingly impossible task—the California Public Employee Retirement System (CalPERS), with more than $200 billion in investments, agreed to take part but then pulled out at the last minute and we weren't able to launch the fund for EDCS.

Earth Trade

The best thing PAM ever did was to create a firm called Earth Trade, which was formed in 1992 as the civil war in El Salvador ended. The goal of the firm was to aid the Salvadoran peasants, especially those who had been involved in the struggle to end the dictatorship, by helping them shift to organic farming. The key roles Earth Trade played was to find a market for the products in the United States, and to establish advance contracts so the peasant cooperatives could be certain of the price they would be paid for their crop. Earth Trade also extended to Nicaragua, which had great agricultural potential because farmland needs to lie fallow for five years to rid the soil of pesticides before crops can be considered organic. Due to the U.S.-backed civil war much of Nicaragua's land had not been farmed for years.

When we started Earth Trade I asked Mike Davis, the author and social activist, to head it up. He had been a leader in the Committee in Solidarity with the People of El Salvador (CISPES), the solidarity group backing the Salvadoran movement for independence and democracy. We went down to El Salvador, where I got a chance to meet with FMLN leaders and to see units of the guerrilla army built before they were dissolved after the peace agreement.

In El Salvador we discovered one of the small farmers' greatest needs was to break the stranglehold on imports maintained by the most reactionary companies, controlled by the super-rich; for instance, a monopoly on fertilizer, for which the peasants were overcharged. We stepped in and made a very gutsy move. We set up a firm in El Salvador, went to a bank, and asked for partial financing to import fertilizer from Colombia. The bank consented but required that we put down $250,000 against a loan for a total purchase of one million dollars' worth of fertilizer.

We completed the agreement with the bank, ordered the fertilizer, and signed a contract with the Colombian source. Without warning the bank in El Salvador suddenly told us we would have to put up $500,000. Mike and others from CISPES working for Earth Trade did an astonishing job and raised another $250,000 to meet the bank's request. As soon as we had done that they said we would have to deposit $800,000—for a $1 million loan. This was clearly an effort to break up the firm and destroy our efforts to have a peasant-owned and -controlled company do its own importing. Incredibly, Mike and the others succeeded in raising all the funds needed.

In Nicaragua, Earth Trade was more successful, turning Nicaragua into the world's largest producer of organic sesame. Earth Trade signed contracts for the sale of the organic sesame with American companies and then with the cooperatives in Nicaragua to deliver their crop. The quality of the Nicaraguan sesame was the best in the world and we found great demand for it in the United States.

I had told Mike, whatever you do, do not lend money against crops in Central America. Other groups, mainly religious organizations, had tried to do this. I told him that lending money in developing countries—as North Americans without any legal recourse—was like throwing water in a desert. You would lose the money. If a peasant cooperative didn't repay us what could we do? Take their horses? Confiscate their land? Any of that would be impossible, not only from our social objectives, but also because we would lose the case in any Nicaraguan court. Thus any loan would need to be non-collateralized.

Mike got caught in an impossible position trying to make this work and started lending some of our capital to peasant cooperatives. The price of sesame rose; competitors from Guatemala offered higher prices than we had agreed to and bought the organic sesame crop out from under us. Some FSLN-led cooperatives refused to sell and lived up to their agreement but many sold. When Mike asked the cooperatives to pay back their loans they just said they couldn't. Short on cash, Earth Trade, through our contacts in PAM, raised about a million dollars in loans, backed up by actual crops already in containers. But once problems had developed they just got worse. In short, Earth Trade went broke.

This was very for me as I tried to handle the situation. We hadn't allowed anyone to invest more than 2 percent of their net worth, so if Earth Trade went under it wouldn't create a major loss for those clients. But the loans were different. PAM brokers had assured investors making loans that their funds would be collateralized. We decided to give up and dissolve Earth Trade, but I proposed that PAM, over time, repay the loans that had been made to Earth Trade. There was no legal obligation to do so but I felt this was the morally right thing to do.

PAM repaid the loans by giving a small percentage of our revenues each year to the lenders until they had recouped all their funds. Some lenders told us it was okay for us not to pay them back; they understood and were supportive of what we had tried to do. Those admirable gestures notwithstanding, slowly over almost ten years PAM paid back all the investors in the Earth Trade loan program.

Crisis in PAM

At the end of the 1990s we hit a major crisis in PAM. The Earth Trade failure certainly affected our creditability and put a financial burden on us, but two other major events hit us hard. The worst was a raid by a large firm that offered a group of our brokers a total of about $500,000 to transfer their business away from PAM. That left us weakened and in negative cash flow. Then John Harrington, for various legitimate reasons, concluded that it would be better for his money management business to move his accounts to Schwab. John had been invaluable to PAM for about ten years.

These three events left us in a very difficult position. We feared that if any other brokers left we would probably go under. In light of our reduced cash flow we decided to restructure PAM, naming another firm, Financial West Group, as our broker-dealer, where the brokers' licenses would be held and our back office transactions executed, leaving PAM as a network of SRI (socially responsible investing) brokers that received an override based on each one's production. With this restructuring we were able to stabilize PAM financially.

Soon after I began getting active with the Green Party and running for political office. Eric Leenson took over as CEO of PAM, I became chairman of the board of directors, and Cathy Cartier remained the chief operations officer. PAM slowly began to grow again, over time expanding to between sixty-five and seventy brokers. After I got cancer I tried to push to make PAM more outgoing—more involved with overseas investments—but differences between the major producers indicated the need for a generational transition. A threatened hostile takeover led us to an agreement with the president of Financial West Group, Todd Melillo, to buy 50 percent of PAM shares and become its CEO. In effect I retired from involvement in PAM and sold my PAM shares to Todd at book value, that is, at a minimal price. Other founders of PAM did the same. This shift was concluded in August of 2008.

Serving on a Pension Board

In the late 1990s I was approached with a request to serve on the Board of Trustees of the Contra Costa County Employee Retirement Association (CCCERA), a $4 billion pension fund. They needed to select two new board members. I knew this would be a substantial time commitment without compensation, but I really wanted to learn how pension funds function.

Upon being selected I was fascinated to learn how it was structured. There were nine board members. One, Helen Shea, represented the retirees and was elected by them. Three came from the participants in the fund, including unions: Bob Rey from the firefighters, Richard Cabral from office workers, and Brian Hast from what was called "safety"—police and other, mainly white-collar occupations. Four were chosen by the county supervisors. These included myself, Paul Katz, Maria Teresa Viramonte, and James Lee, who had worked for a short time at PAM. The elected county treasurer, Bill Policeck, also served as a trustee.

Throughout California the supervisors tended to choose as their trustees retired businesspeople, especially from the investment or banking community, thinking that was beneficial. The county treasurer tended to be from the same background. This amounted, generally speaking, to giving conservative, pro-business, anti-union people majority control of the workers' pension funds. The workers contributed monthly to the pension fund, the retirees depended on the fund to meet their economic expenses, and their money was controlled by people essentially hostile to their unions and often to their interests. Although the retirees and union representatives learned a great deal serving on the board, they did not come from a financial background so the anti-union forces could intimidate them to some extent.

Most people on the board or the staff didn't realize for a while who I was. But the dynamics of a normal pension board had now been altered. The union board members and the retiree representative quickly recognized that I was different and on their side—plus I knew about investing. That left the board's direction up for grabs. A progressive pro-labor current now had a chance of winning board votes. Since I was in a new, unfamiliar framework I had to go very slowly. I started by becoming friends with two union representatives: Richard Cabral, the most militant of the reps, and Bob Rey from the Firemen's Union, one of the most patient, committed, pro-labor members of the Board of Trustees. Gradually I began to understand the dynamics of the pension fund and how it was administered.

The first thing that struck me was how the retirees were abused. The fund had done well in the market and had accumulated a large surplus—about $500 million—beyond what was needed to meet the pension obligations at that time and into the future. Yet I soon learned that the oldest workers were not hedged for inflation, so the retirement funds that they depended on for survival were cut each year by inflation until some were left with next to nothing to live on. I saw cases where retirees were receiving four hundred dollars a month. The retirees were demanding something be done with the huge surplus to benefit them. Slowly I began to understand how this played out with the county board of supervisors, which included a couple of progressive Democrats who privately expressed pro-labor views.

Here is the way the corporate world, through its control of the two-party system, played all these people. The counties were starved by the state so the county supervisors had very little discretion over funds; in our case they had control over only $100 million out of a $1 billion budget, or just

10 percent. Therefore the counties were always desperate to try to meet the electorate's demands for critical services such as children's programs and health care. This was of strategic importance because the county—from its taxes, in a contractual agreement with its employees—made an annual contribution to the pension fund. The county supervisors were driven to try to lower that commitment whenever the fund made a surplus, rather than increasing the pension pay to the workers.

Before making any moves I wanted time to understand all the issues. Given my nature I would go home after board meetings and tell Morella what I saw and how it upset me. Consider what often happens in corporate takeovers. When a corporation seeks to take over another, one aim is commonly to destroy their unions. They hire a Wall Street investment firm to arrange the deal, which then uses a labor pension fund like ours to help pay for destroying the unions. The workers never even know this is happening. Such takeovers sometimes invest in projects that drive old people out of low-rent apartments, make token renovations, raise the rent, and make out like bandits. Proposals like these were actually presented to us to invest in. They were not hard for me to block with the support of the labor delegates, but they provide a snapshot of the level of conflict between pension funds and who they supposedly represent and what they actually do.

The members of the board of trustees were obligated to act as "fiduciaries," that is, to look out for the interests of the workers whose pension money they were administrating. In my opinion the whole system was in direct conflict with their fiduciary responsibility.

Community Bank

Out of its billions of dollars, the pension fund was required to maintain about $30 million to $40 million in short-term certificates of deposit (CDs) or other safe short-term investments. In Oakland there was a Community Bank whose mission was developing low-income housing and helping create jobs for the poor. The Community Bank was always starved for more funds. If our pension fund invested in a CD at the Community Bank there was no risk, since the investment would be guaranteed by the federal government for both principal and interest.

I proposed that we put a little of our money in the Community Bank because it was in the interest of working people. I arranged to have the leaders of the bank, African Americans, make a presentation to our board about their projects. The attitude of some of the conservatives on the board was outrageous. They started talking about risk when there was no risk of any kind for the pension fund, desperately looking for any excuse not to help the Community Bank.

Initially I didn't know that pension funds could buy CDs so I proposed that the relatively minuscule amount of $100,000 be placed in the Community Bank to establish the precedent. I got that proposal passed, plus arranged for a letter to be sent to twenty other California pension funds, urging them to follow our lead. Of all twenty pension funds we contacted, not a single one followed suit.

The trustees' attorney, Ed Lane, a political conservative with no connection with the labor movement, then attempted to carry out an illegal act over this $100,000 investment. Without my knowledge, Lane called the county district attorney general and asked him to investigate me—his own client—to see if I had any interest in the Community Bank. He meant to find out if I had any shares in the bank, or had invested in it in some way, so he could bring me up on charges of having made this proposal with a clear, unrevealed conflict of interest; thus I would be in violation of my fiduciary responsibility. One of the trustees, my friend Brian Hast, happened to work at the county district attorney general's office. So the district attorney asked Brian to investigate. Brian called me and asked if I owned any shares of the Community Bank or had any other relationship that could be a conflict of interest. I told him no. He wouldn't tell me why he was asking but I figured it out.

At the next board meeting I read Ed Lane the riot act and told him he should be immediately fired and disbarred for carrying out something that violated his fiduciary responsibility to the board members as well as other regulations, including attorney-client privilege. Lane didn't know how I knew but realized immediately that he was caught in an impossible situation. He confessed and resigned his position. Yet after committing this crime and resigning Lane was offered his full retirement benefits—and then he was rehired by the county government, giving him two incomes. So he benefited financially from having committed a crime.

The board of trustees had to hire a new lawyer. I proposed Bill Sokol, a well-known pro-labor lawyer. Precisely because he was a pro-labor attorney there was a lot of opposition from both the fund's staff and a few trustees. It is astonishing how they thought hiring lawyers from pro-corporate firms was perfectly legitimate but not a lawyer whose experience was in defending workers, the people who owned the pension fund and whom we were obligated by our fiduciary responsibility to protect. In the end we won and Bill Sokol became the first and only labor attorney hired by a public employees' pension fund. The news about this went to the very top of the AFL-CIO.

Socially Responsible Investing

Soon after I was elected to the CCCERA board of trustees, Richard Cabral started pushing me to present the case for socially responsible investing (SRI). Through my work at PAM I had learned a great deal about SRI. Among other things I had found that, surprisingly, environmental groups with endowments were among the least socially responsible. At the time, most of them opposed putting any screen on their investments. While they advocated opposing pollution they invested in polluters, from Exxon and Enron to Waste Management, Inc. I had meetings with leaders of many of the major environmental organizations and they all rejected caring about the environment in how they invested their endowment funds.

There was one major exception: John Wood "Woody" Bolton of the Nature Conservancy. After I had met him and urged him to consider investing with us he asked us to recommend money managers. He chose a very aggressive manager and placed, I think, about $10 million dollars to start and later added some more. This investment became the Nature Conservancy's most successful, making them something around $100 million.

For the board of trustees I suggested we hold a one-day conference and bring in some top experts to make presentations, primarily on the performance comparison between SRI and non-SRI. Our fund invited trustees from other pension funds and about a hundred people came. After the conference I pressed forward and got the trustees to vote unanimously to divest from tobacco. Then they approved a proposal I made always to vote our shares pro-environment and pro-labor.

The voting policy we established was the first and only one of its kind in the United States. Titled "CCCERA's Social and Environmental Issues Voting Policy," it included working to eliminate child labor, sweatshops, slave labor, discrimination because of race, religion, national origin, or sexual orientation, and to eliminate or reduce toxic emissions. The policy aimed to promote equal employment opportunities, diversity for management and boards of directors, corporate respect for laws both national and international, disclosure of environmental liabilities, product and marketing integrity, respect for environmental laws, and a smoke-free environment in company facilities. All this was achieved in a relatively conservative county in California.

The Contra Costa county supervisors, in their battle to get their hands on the surplus and in their opposition to helping the retirees, came into direct conflict with what I was advocating for the pension fund. I fought hard to assert that the pension fund money did not belong to the county and that the fund should not be used in any way, shape, or form to try to balance the county budget. As a trustee I would not go along with them even though I knew they would eventually remove me from the board, which is what they did. The retirees, of course, loved me for standing up for them. After my three-year term I was not renominated.

During this period I edited and wrote sections of a book titled *The SRI Advantage—Why Socially Responsible Investing Has Outperformed Financially*.* The book explained why the labor movement must fight for control of its money and ensure that all labor pension funds are invested in their interest. With historical data I tried to show that investing in a pro-labor, pro-environmental manner had led to increased financial performance. From there I made the rather simple point that insisting on investing in polluters, criminals, and anti-labor firms—in order to earn *less*—constitutes a clear violation of fiduciary responsibility.

Shortly after it came out I received a surprise package from Taiwan containing six copies of my book, unexpectedly translated into Chinese.

---

* New Society Publishers, 2002. Kate Gifford was an enormous help to me getting the book's data organized as well as solving other problems. My close friend Steve Hiatt edited the manuscript.

CHAPTER 15

POLITICAL ACTIVITY
DURING THE 1990S

The work I was doing through PAM was complemented by my other political activity, including international efforts in Venezuela and New Zealand as well as in the United States. Please bear in mind that all this was done while I had a full-time job managing money for clients. Looking back I don't know how I did it. But once I was no longer in the SWP, caught up in sectarian politics, I began to take an interest in learning about and helping social, political, and environmental movements I thought were playing positive roles.

Earth Share

Soon after I created the Eco-Logical Trust with Merrill Lynch and PAM I got a call from Kalman Stein, the president of Earth Share, the environmental coalition that we had written into the trust to receive a donation from the profits. Kal was curious as to how the arrangement had come about. We met in Berkeley and talked over lunch. By the end of our meeting Kal asked me if I would serve on Earth Share's board of directors. He wanted to bring some outsiders, people not representing any environmental group, on board to get help and new ideas. Headquartered in Bethesda, Maryland, Earth Share was founded in California and later retained Kal to develop it into a successful national venture. Environmental groups and other not-for-profit currents that were not included in United Way needed to set up their own federation in order to participate in workplace giving campaigns, programs through which workers automatically donate a portion of each paycheck to charity, with the donation being tax deductible.

It took a couple of meetings before I began getting a feel for what Earth Share was all about. I found the opportunity to meet people involved with all the major environmental organizations enlightening in many ways. One initial thing that struck me was that our meetings, with about forty people, were essentially all white. All the environmental groups participating in Earth Share were led primarily if not exclusively by European Americans. I asked Kal to let me try to find a way to overcome this situation so that environmental groups tied to African Americans, Latinos, Native Americans, and Asian Americans could get a seat at the table.

To be a member charity with Earth Share a group had to be established in at least fifteen states and meet other strict eligibility requirements. No single environmental organization led by people of color could meet these requirements, so the idea came to me to unite them into a group, which we eventually called the Environmental Justice Fund, in order to get a place on the Earth Share roster. I got on the phone with all the environmental groups led by people of color to explain what I was trying to do.

It took some time for people to entertain the possibilities. On one hand, there was some fear among these groups that the major environmental organizations were simply not concerned about their communities. On the other hand, some of the larger, white-led groups had set up special projects to work on issues related to minority communities and wanted to know why these projects couldn't also be included in the Environmental Justice Fund. It took effort for me to explain that it was vital for those who had suffered discrimination to have their own groups that they controlled and to be treated as equals, not as a department of somebody else's group.

At one meeting, organized with the help of Peggy Saika, the director of the Asian Pacific Environmental Network, I was explaining how I thought the chances of getting funding, not just from Earth Share but from some of the major foundations, would increase if they unified. After a while Richard Moore from New Mexico, who represented the Southwest Network for Environmental and Economic Justice (SNEEJ), looked at me as one Latino to another and said, "Peter, what do you get out of this?" It was as though he thought I was withholding something. I had never thought about how to answer such a question. Surprised, I told him, "Richard, I don't want anything. Once this is set up you all will have a board and run it. I will be completely out of the picture."

Richard was well known throughout the country for his tireless confrontation of environment abuses in minority communities. Like all the other people-of-color-run groups, Richard's SNEEJ functioned with little to no support from the established environmental organizations. Also participating in this process was my old friend Baldemar Velásquez, president of the Ohio-based Farm Labor Organizing Committee, whom I first met during my 1976 campaign. Tom Goldtooth represented the Indigenous Environmental Network. There were several others who played a role in getting the Environmental Justice Fund established whose names I regret I can't recall.

The unified Environmental Justice Fund began receiving funding from Earth Share and also succeeded in getting some contributions from major donors like the Ford and MacArthur Foundations. Unfortunately after I left the Earth Share board the Environmental Justice Fund was dropped from the roster due to eligibility issues. They have continued to exist as a fund for the people of color environmental movement, but I did not solve the issue of trying to integrate Earth Share.

Idea of the Millennium

I conceived what I thought was one of the world's best ideas to raise money for all the environmental organizations in Earth Share. I really thought I could raise a billion dollars for Earth Share. The idea was simple. About seven years away from the new millennium, saving the planet had become a popular goal for the year 2000. So I proposed that I would get Merrill Lynch, through my contacts at the Unit Investment Trust Department, to create a financial product that all ten thousand Merrill brokers could offer the public. The idea was to use remainder trusts. Remainder trusts are a way for an individual to leave a university, environmental, or any not-for-profit group a large asset. The donor names the particular charity as a recipient, gets a tax advantage, pays no capital gains tax—sometimes a huge savings—and receives income from the full value of the trust for the rest of his or her life. In my millennial proposal a person would establish a remainder trust for, just as an example, ten thousand dollars. It would be invested in 100 percent–safe financial instruments and then, in 2000, the investment would be dissolved, producing a money-market-rate return between income and tax advantages to the contributor, and would also result in about two thousand to three thousand dollars going to Earth Share.

It was a way to give without giving. The funds would be put in a trust run by Merrill Lynch, with their support, and the interest would go each year to Earth Share. We planned to market this with environmentally minded celebrities urging people to participate in what would be essentially "parking funds" for seven years, making a money-market rate, yet resulting in the creation of a very large endowment fund that would continue giving to environmental groups forever. The loose figure of the total number of all Earth Share contributors was about 15 million people, so a marketing effort by Merrill could result in possibly tens of thousands of "giving without giving—forever" investments to create the endowment.

I presented my plan to the executive committee of Earth Share. They voted unanimously to back the proposal and told me to go ahead and try to set it up with Merrill Lynch. So I went to Merrill Lynch and explained my idea to them, starting with my friend Stan Craig. They were intrigued. Stan asked me if I was sure that Earth Share with its forty groups and fifteen million–strong donor base was really going to go through with this project. I said, "Of course, I have the unanimous vote of their executive board. Why would they throw such a possibility away?"

I was naïve to assume that, with zero financial risk and a potential for massive income, the executive committee would stay convinced. Kal Stein called me one day to alert me that the largest five environmental groups in Earth Share, led by the National Wildlife Federation, had met together to ask that we kill the program. I was stunned. Kal explained to me that they feared this program would lead Congress to change the remainder trust law, since it would be used for a purpose different from its original intent.

The largest environmental organizations had a monopoly on the use of remainder trusts and it was a major source of income for them. They didn't want anything that could mess with the existing law. I also think the larger environmental groups were wary that the smaller ones were about to step onto their turf and benefit from a fund-raising mechanism that the small groups had hardly ever used. Kal said, "We can't go against these five. We have no choice, I'm sorry." Their decision destroyed my relationship with Merrill.

In retrospect I do feel there was some validity in the major environmental groups' concern: it would be impossible to know how the Democrats and Republicans in Congress would react to seeing a law they had written to benefit the rich being used to save the planet.

New Zealand

In 1989 Jim Anderton, a Labour Party member of the New Zealand parliament, stood up in parliament one day and denounced the Labour Party as having sold out to big business. He formed the New Labour Party. At the end of 1991 it fused with the Green Party, Mana Motuhake (the Maori party), and two other small parties to form the Alliance. Matt McCarten, a Maori involved in both the Labour and Maori parties, joined with Anderton, becoming the Alliance's president. Matt proposed that a proposal be put on the ballot for creating proportional representation, which would assure seats for the new Alliance in parliament. Of course the two major parties, the National Party and the Labour Party—just as in the United States—opposed allowing for the expansion of democracy.

I heard of this development in its early stages and learned about Matt from Australian friends. I flew down to New Zealand and spent days talking with Matt and later to all the other leaders of the new Alliance. Matt told me I was the first and only person internationally that had shown such interest in what they were doing. Matt and I had come from very different experiences but had arrived at similar conclusions about the two-party system, the left, and how to build a political force that could win the people. Later he came to the United States and stayed at my home, taking some time off from our political discussions to visit Yosemite and other sights.

I returned to New Zealand to give the keynote address at the founding convention of the Alliance Party. The results of their battle for proportional representation came in the 1993 elections. Despite opposition from both major parties, from most if not all of the major media, and of course from corporate money, the Alliance referendum for proportional representation passed with the support of the majority of voters. New Zealand took an important step toward allowing truly free elections, something we could not even dream about today in the United States. The new law didn't take effect until the next election, in 1996, but even without it the Alliance won 18 percent of the vote and two seats in parliament. In 1996 with proportional representation in force the Alliance won thirteen seats in a parliament of 121.

As the years passed the Alliance, under the pressure of political events, began to unwind. First the Greens decided to leave. In 1999 the Alliance joined a coalition government with the Labour Party, with Jim Anderton as prime minister. Later the issue of whether to back the U.S. invasion of Afghanistan divided the two central leaders. Anderton split and formed his own small Progressive Party. But proportional representation still exists in New Zealand and new alliances among the Maori people, young progressive movements, and trade unions organizing the poorest people in New Zealand are in the process of formation. My friend Matt McCarten remains at the center of all these new efforts.

Venezuela

In Venezuela a group called Causa R (Radical Cause) was making headway in the unions, in the poorest communities, and in elections, gaining a strong base in the parliament. I decided to try to meet with them. I went to Venezuela, contacted the Causa R leadership, and asked for a meeting. They were intrigued by my story as a Venezuelan living in the United States. Some of the Causa R leaders had been FALN guerrillas in the sixties and they were excited to learn that a film had been made about their activities—by my brother, in fact—that they had never seen.*

I was stunned as they told me of their founder, Alfredo Maneiro, who in the 1970s had developed a new approach for building a movement in Venezuela. The Causa R people explained to me that Alfredo had fought as a guerrilla leader associated with the Communist Party but had changed his mind. He had a small group of followers, maybe twenty, and he convinced them that it was insane to support a totalitarian society like the Soviet Union and that they would never win the Venezuelan people for social justice without defending liberties and full democracy. He insisted that they stop using terminology that no one understood or that led to confusion. They took a name that was simple generic for change, "Causa R," with the letter "R" (reversed in their logo) meaning any number of things, that is, it could mean simply "change" or rebellion or revolution. Alfredo was opposed as a principle to ever supporting either of Venezuela's two pro-corporate parties and he was against all the leftists who did this. I am probably one of only a handful of people in the United States who have some of Alfredo Maniero's writings. What I would have given to have met him, but he died in December 1982.

---

* See chapter 4 for details regarding this film and Daniel's arrest in Mexico.

Starting with a small nucleus in 1971, Causa R began to grow as the rest of the sixties left declined. Gradually, through enormous effort, they won elections in some of the major unions, which was extremely difficult to do given the utter corruption and violence of the pro–Acción Democrática (AD—think U.S. Democratic Party) union leadership. As Causa R grew in membership they developed influence in the poorest neighborhoods. In 1992 they elected the mayor of Caracas. Their candidate, Andrés Velásquez, a leader of the steelworkers union, became governor of Bolívar province. In the 1993 presidential election Causa R ran Velásquez, who officially got 22 percent of the vote in an election with heavy fraud by the major parties.

I invited representatives from Causa R to come to the United States to speak about the political activity in Venezuela. Few people here were interested; Venezuela was not in the news. Causa R sent some of their central leaders to speak in California in June 1992, including Bernardo Alvarez Herrera, a deputy in their congress who is now Venezuela's ambassador to the United States. Bernardo stayed at my home for a week and also spoke at the conference launch of the Progressive Alliance of Alameda County. The Causa R representatives explained to Americans that in order to make a difference, learn to talk in a way the people will understand. They combined this with unconditional advice never to vote for the Democrats.

I also learned that Causa R had developed support inside the Venezuelan Army, including Hugo Chávez, who was a secret member of the group. Chávez's position was that the whole Venezuelan government, from the Supreme Court to the parliament, was utterly corrupt and should be removed to allow for free elections. Chávez suggested to the Causa R leadership that he could mobilize some army units to take control of the government and call for a popular uprising. At first Causa R agreed but just prior to the uprising, set for February 1992, they backed off and only a small sector tried to mobilize workers to support the uprising. The military revolt was quickly defeated but overnight Chávez became a massively popular hero for his attempt to drive the two-party dictatorship out of office. He was imprisoned.

The 1993 presidential elections were won by former president Rafael Caldera, who was my next-door neighbor when I was a child. He belonged to COPEI, the equivalent of the Republican Party, but in the 1993 election he ran as an independent and promised to free Chávez. With Caldera in office Chávez was freed. He waited for Caldera's term to finish and then announced for president. With little funding and the complete opposition of the entire media, corporate world, and pro-corporate trade unions, Chávez was elected with 56.2 percent of the vote. The rest is now history.

The Progressive Alliance of Alameda County

Throughout the 1990s there was a lot of interest in the notion of third parties but nothing much had developed. After talking to people on the left in Oakland I thought we should experiment by forming a coalition of all progressives who were open to forming an independent political movement. Mike Wyman from the North Star Network joined me and between us we put up $100,000 to launch the movement. We set up an office on the first floor of the building housing PAM.

The founding conference of the Progressive Alliance of Alameda County was held June 1 and 2, 1996, at the Federal Building Auditorium in Oakland. Gus Newport, the former mayor of Berkeley, opened the conference. Among the major presenters were two international speakers, Jeanette Fitzsimons, a Green Party leader from New Zealand, and Bernardo Alvarez Herrera from Causa R in Venezuela. The conference included many progressive-minded registered Democrats, such as supporters of the New Party and Berkeley Citizens Action, as well as Peace and Freedom Party and Green Party supporters.

The goal that came out of the conference was to make endorsements primarily for local and county elections, to back people who were truly progressive and favored creating a force independent of the Democrats and Republicans. As time passed I saw that I had misjudged the sentiment. The number of people who truly understood the need to fight the two-party system was limited and when it came to endorsements they immediately started compromising.

The Alliance was dissolved about two years later. That is, not long before Ralph Nader appeared with the first real mass break challenging the two-party system.

CHAPTER 16

RALPH NADER—THE END OF THE ICE AGE

I first met Ralph Nader in 1996. He was testing the waters to see what support there would be if he were to run for president in opposition to the two parties—his platform would be pro-labor, anti-imperialism, antiracist, in favor of independent political action, and green. I was intrigued. No person with his popularity and public standing had ever made a move in this direction in my lifetime.

Greg Jan, a leading Green Party activist* who had been working with me on other activities, told me about his involvement with Ralph's effort. Greg was helping to coordinate the outreach on a national scale. At PAM we had an empty office, so I rented the office from our firm and let Greg use it for his Nader work.

Greg worked incredibly hard, so much so that I sometimes worried about him because of the absolutely relentless way he dedicated himself to the movement. I was always impressed by his deep commitment. He had a unique style of organization, which around the office we called "Greg's filing system." This involved covering every square inch of his space with stacks of paper, mail, newspapers, and assorted other chaos. We sometimes amused ourselves by peeking into his office when he wasn't there just to behold the mess.

---

* Greg was also one of the original founders of the Green Party in California.

When Ralph was coming through the Bay Area Greg arranged for me to meet him. Politically I liked what I saw. I didn't press him or ask a lot of questions. I just listened. Greg suggested to Ralph that I go out to raise money for his campaign. But Ralph didn't want anyone to raise money at that time—he didn't want to deal with the electoral laws that would then kick in. At that initial meeting it seemed to me that he had not yet made up his mind to commit to a campaign for the presidency. It was clear to me that Ralph was still evolving in his thinking. I couldn't tell exactly where it would lead but I was impressed with what I heard and how carefully he was thinking through his approach.

Of course I had known of Ralph Nader since the 1960s. I had always thought of him as a well-intentioned, dedicated advocate for consumer rights but not as a person who understood fully the nature of our society or its two-party system, how it defended the interests of money over people or—as I would have phrased it in the 1960s—defended the interest of a ruling class. I was surprised by the depth of his commitment to American workers and to all exploited or oppressed people. Looking back it is obvious what he had to consider. He knew that if he told the truth about our two-party system, it would mean a permanent break with the Democrats and a loss of much of the support he had received in the past.

Dan Hamburg and the Green Party

I had registered Green in 1992 just as the party made statewide ballot status through its voter registration campaign—to qualify for ballot status they had needed to register about eighty thousand people. I was very impressed with this accomplishment and the fact that the Greens had about thirty organized chapters in the state. In the early 1990s I attended my first Green Party meeting, in Berkeley, and was turned off by what I saw. It was clear to me that they had no intention of confronting the Democrats. Most of the leaders at that meeting favored not running in partisan races. They aspired only to nonpartisan positions such as those on the city council or board of education. There were also a lot of countercultural types in attendance who did not seem not interested in class or race issues.

Then an important change occurred. Dan Hamburg, a committed social and environmental activist, elected to Congress from Northern California as a Democrat in 1992, became disgusted by the corruption he saw in Washington. He was defeated for reelection in 1994 and subsequently joined the Green Party. Dan and I had worked together on some projects and I started urging him to run for governor of California in 1998 (a bit misguided on my part, as I completely overestimated the party's ability to support a campaign.) My interest in the Green Party began to grow as I saw the potential for candidacy of people like Ralph Nader and Dan Hamburg, candidates who in my eyes understood the critical issues of our time and were aligned with the long-term goals I supported.

Dan decided to run for governor and slogged through a campaign in which he got very little grass-roots support from the Green Party. The media paid him little attention despite his having been a congressperson. One highlight was that with the help of my old friend Antonio Gonzalez, the leader of several major Latino organizations, Dan got the opportunity to debate the Democratic candidate Gray Davis in front of a thousand Latinos. As Dan laid out a platform of social justice for Latinos and for the rights of working people, the audience was clearly surprised and elated, having assumed that Greens were only good on support for the environment. The overwhelming response shocked Gray Davis as Dan received a standing ovation and emerged completely victorious before such a large audience of Latinos.

Dan's effort opened the door for Greens to consider running in more partisan races, even though his campaign was unable to generate the rank-and-file support he deserved. Along with Dan the Green Party ran two other statewide candidates in the 1998 elections, Sara Amir for lieutenant governor and Glenn Bailey for one of the State Board of Equalization spots. The Greens also contested five California congressional seats and two seats in the State Assembly.

I had originally considering running with Dan for treasurer of California or another statewide office. Due to a crisis at PAM, however, there was opposition to my getting involved in a campaign. Over the next years I worked to reorganize the company to enable me to run for office.

The Ice Age Ends

On February 21, 2000, Ralph Nader announced his campaign for president in Washington, D.C. All three major networks and *The NewsHour with Jim Lehrer* were in attendance. None of them ran any coverage of Nader's campaign announcement.

Nevertheless, before that campaign ended all of America would be talking about it. Nader's rallies drew more people than those of either Gore the

Democrat or Bush the Republican, even though Gore and Bush had all the advantages of mass corporate media coverage and endless funding for their campaigns. Nader even had a handicap. To make the mass rallies possible the campaign charged twenty dollars per person to attend; the Democrats and Republicans charged nothing, and more people still came out to hear Nader.

Nader's 2000 campaign was an historic event. It showed that progressives no longer were forced to support the Democratic Party. The power of Stalinism to sideline progressives had finally come to an end: remnants of the once-strong Stalinist currents were still busy supporting the pro-corporate Democratic Party, but they were now irrelevant. The political ice age had ended.

Nader returned America—in a totally new context—to a time when movements for social justice had a reflection in the electoral arena, posing the question of who should rule, money or the people. Just as the Liberty Party of the 1840s appeared a decade before a massive wave of sentiment for social change hit the nation, Nader's 2000 campaign was the precursor of the inevitable wave that will engulf America for all the reasons he posed in his campaign.

Super Rallies

Ralph's book about the 2000 campaign, *Crashing the Party: Taking on the Corporate Government in an Age of Surrender*,* provides a detailed account of the entire process. In the book Ralph notes that three members of his campaign staff, Greg Kafoury, Mark McDougal, and Laird Hastay, came up with the idea of renting large arenas to hold huge rallies. They were convinced it would work and that people would pay twenty dollars to attend. For their first rally they set out to fill the Portland Memorial Coliseum with more than ten thousand people. The campaign team in Portland had only twenty days to promote the event, set for August 25, 2000. As of the day of the rally six thousand tickets had been sold. This was viewed as quite a success and, as Nader explains, they did not expect to sell out the whole Coliseum. To their amazement thousands of tickets were sold at the entrance, and every available seat was filled.

The power and success of the event forced the media to take note. The following is Ralph's summation of his speech at that rally. I assure you that

---

* Quotes in this section are from Ralph Nader, *Crashing the Party: Taking on the Corporate Government in an Age of Surrender* (New York: St. Martin's Press, 2002).

Ralph did not get his idea from me. It was his natural instinct and, to me, it is obvious why it worked.

> On such occasions I find it essential to run through some American history and remind the audience about their heroic forebears who raised the levels of justice against powerful odds. Brief recountings of the antislavery abolitionists, the women's suffrage drive, and how workers and farmers threw off some of the corporate yokes on their backs—all ordinary people producing extraordinary history ... Next I made connections between the economic stagnation boom of the past twenty years and the chronic American poverty that plagues millions of people and children.

Nader argues in exactly the kind of formulations I believe are essential for reaching working people. He stands solidly in opposition to the two-party system: "Both parties are weakening our democracy and furthering the concentration of economic and therefore political power."

The winner-take-all system, by not allowing for runoffs, aims to forever leave people who dissent thinking that there are only a few people who agree with them. The ideological trap is set and—as has been repeatedly demonstrated—it works. Ralph noted the following about the Portland super rally: "One of the reason the rally was so high-energy was that the participants hadn't realized there were so many other people sharing their views."

I attended just one of these rallies, one of the smaller ones, in Oakland, California. I sat near the back and watched, thinking to myself, this is the beginning. But I thought a storm was coming to crush this movement. I was struck by how little most Greens understood the Democratic Party and what it would do to silence such a force.

Madison Square Garden

The largest of the super rallies was at Madison Square Garden in New York City. The Nader campaign was daunted by the attempt to fill the 15,500 seats with a charge of twenty dollars at the door. The decision to forge ahead was made just nine days beforehand. Campaign workers handed out 200,000 flyers. Well-known Nader supporters Michael Moore, Phil Donahue, Bill Murray, Susan Sarandon, Tim Robbins, and many more were doing radio interviews urging people to turn out.

At the beginning of the rally master of ceremonies Phil Donahue announced that the Garden was sold out. Ralph Nader described the success at Madison Square Garden: "It was as if a drought over such politics for years had been suspended by a good spring rain and the flowers were sprouting."

Labor Day

On Labor Day 2000 Ralph joined workers in the Labor Day parade in Detroit, where the union bureaucrats had as their speaker anti-labor, pro-war Senator Joe Lieberman of Connecticut, Al Gore's vice presidential running mate and probably the most right-wing, anti-labor Democrat in the U.S. Senate. Nothing could embody more perfectly the betrayal of labor and what the marriage of the unions to the Democratic Party meant than having Senator Lieberman speak at a Labor Day rally.

Ralph's commitment to the labor movement went back to the 1950s. His achievements of the Coal Mine Safety Act and the Occupational Health and Safety Agency (OSHA), to name but two, helped bring about improvement in the deplorable conditions that had resulted in more miners dying since 1890 than all the U.S. deaths in World War II combined. Slowly some unions began to endorse Nader. These included the United Electrical, Radio and Machine Workers; the California Nurses Association; AFSCME local 1108 in Los Angeles; and Postal Workers and Teamsters in Seattle.

Capitulation

As Nader's campaign gained exposure it began to get more media coverage. Well-known personalities joined Ralph as speakers. Among them was filmmaker Michael Moore, famous for his excellent films exposing injustices in our society. In 2000 while campaigning with Ralph, Moore said, "If you start now, caving in your conscience and not doing what you know is right, you're going to have a miserable life. Because it starts in little tiny increments, doing things that you don't really want to be doing, like voting for Gore instead of who you know you should vote for. And you start chipping away at your conscience and you start settling for less and less and less and less."

By 2004, Moore had himself capitulated and done exactly what he had urged people not to do. He endorsed, campaigned for, and falsely depicted John Kerry as though Kerry were not a pro-war, pro-corporate politician. He turned on Nader and—I actually saw him do this—on television called Nader crazy for running. Often when people capitulate under social pressure they become exceptionally angry at those who refuse to join them, since something deep inside them says, "This is wrong." Once they capitulate, unless they are very young, it is extremely rare that they will ever stand up again. Michael Moore is now owned by the Democrats. He now has to be careful what he says about them in his films. He will of course make a passing criticism as cover for his capitulation but they can now add him to the list of the people that will serve their rule as "progressives."

The same can be said for many other people who campaigned with Nader. But in 2000 they were different people. A whole layer of liberals from the Democratic Party crossed over and began expressing great hostility to the two-party system and to the Democrats in particular. Democrat Jim Hightower from Texas said, "We've got an old saying in Texas, 'If you've found that you've dug yourself in a hole, the first thing you do is to quit digging.' If we don't quit digging in 2000 we're going to be in a hole in 2004, 2008, 2012. We're going to dig deeper and deeper. Let's get out of the hole." Hightower is now so deep in his hole of capitulation I doubt we will ever see him again.

One last example is Howard Zinn, author of the very popular and informative *A People's History of the United States*. In 2000, supporting Nader, Zinn said, "They can give me all the arguments they want about the lesser evils, about being realistic, about being practical, but I refuse to surrender my conscience to the moneyed interests. . . . It seems to me that an election where the candidate needs 150 million dollars or 200 million dollars to run is not a free election." Zinn added, "Every month a million children die in the world for lack of food and medicine while these candidates and their parties support this obscene military budget and more and more money for jet fighters and nuclear weapons. They have supported a class war against the poor here and in the rest of the world. And I cannot bear to pull a lever on Election Day in support of that."

In 2004 Zinn capitulated. I was on a radio program on KPFK in Los Angeles with Zinn when he asked me if I didn't agree that we had to vote for Kerry. I said no, I would not vote for Kerry. After a bit Zinn said he had to go and excused himself from the conversation. In 2004 he could "bear to pull a lever" for everything he said he opposed in 2000.

Nader and the Debates

The presidential debates are run today by the equivalent of a private corporation owned and controlled by the Democrats and Republicans, funded by a group of the largest corporations in America. This not-for-profit corporation calls itself the Commission on Presidential Debates (CPD).

The corporate-backed CPD had no intention of allowing a pro-labor candidate to participate. They were scared of Nader and wanted to let the Nader campaign know they wouldn't tolerate dissent. Nader was not just barred from the debates; he couldn't even be present in the audience. If he were in the audience, the reasoning went, that could lead to the media giving him coverage.

In Boston the presidential debate was held in the athletic center of the University of Massachusetts. A large meeting area, removed from the debate location, was set up for students to come and watch. A student who had a pass gave it to Nader. So Ralph went to watch the debate at this separate location. Waiting for Ralph was a representative of a security firm hired by the CPD along with regular police officers. They told Ralph he could not attend even though he had an invitation. In blatant violation of the law, the police officers took orders from the security representative. They physically pushed Nader back out of the entrance, at a public university, ejecting him from an event to which he had an invitation. The CPD acted as though it were a government agency with the right to determine access to a public building and to use the police to enforce its decisions.

The corporate control over the United States and its two parties keeps increasing, to the point that the whole debate process is now completely out of the hands of the public. In the 1970s and '80s the League of Women Voters sponsored the presidential debate process. Even though the League also discriminated against dissent they were removed by the Democratic and Republican parties after they called the 1988 debates a "fraud." The debates are now orchestrated by the two parties, which control what will be asked by whom. The entire process is in turn backed by the corporate media, which refuses to allow discussion of certain issues, facts, or dissenting opinions. During this whole charade the media, the educational system, and the churches join in maintaining the illusion that this is all "democracy," in fact the greatest "democracy" ever.

The Vote

All counted, almost three million people voted for Nader. If the electoral laws in the United States had allowed for runoffs and the "spoiler" issue had not been a factor, that total would have been much larger. After the election, the Democratic Party launched a massive campaign to try to stop the phenomenon Nader represented: a political movement outside the control of money. The Democrats, with the full backing of the press, started a very successful campaign to associate the election of George W. Bush with the fact that Ralph Nader had run for office. What no newspaper, television network, or radio station pointed out was that this charge was predicated on one simple fact—no runoffs are held in U.S. elections. It is no accident that the "spoiler" issue does not occur in Europe.

The charge that Nader helped elect Bush is empirically wrong for a series of reasons. Let me mention a few:

- Two hundred thousand Democrats voted for Bush in Florida. The headlines could just as easily have read "Democrats elect Bush."

- Most people added to the voting base by Nader eventually voted for Gore. Without Nader, Gore would have lost by a larger margin and might have lost some states that he ended up winning.

- The conservative Pat Buchanan's presidential campaign "spoiled" the election for Bush, leading to victories for Gore in Oregon, Iowa, Wisconsin, and New Mexico. This fact, of course, was not mentioned by the corporate media since the whole spoiler issue was intended to silence the pro-working-class political current that Nader was creating.

- The media did its own review that showed Gore won in Florida.

- The Republicans stole the election by running a computer program that took away the right to vote from thousands upon thousands of voters, primarily in the African American community, who would most likely have voted for Gore. This was accomplished by denying any citizen the right to vote whose birth date and name matched those of a convicted felon—without any proof the person excluded from voting was actually the felon in question.

This last issue, the abuse of African Americans' right to vote, is of critical interest because the Democrats blocked an investigation of the abuse and did nothing to fight for a new election in Florida. In other words, they joined in covering up for Bush's stealing of the election. This issue devolved into farce as African American members of Congress demanded an investigation but couldn't get it approved because not a single Democrat in the Senate would back it, as was required by law. The Senate included all kinds of "progressive" Democrats like California's Barbara Boxer and Minnesota's Paul Wellstone, not to mention Gore himself, Lieberman, John Kerry, and John Edwards. Not one supported investigating this violation of the law, which had resulted in the stolen election.

In my opinion all the African American congresspeople who protested were actually in on the fact that there would be no investigation, because they knew the Democrats had decided not to have any of their senators support them. But demanding an investigation looked good to African Americans back in their home districts. Why do I make this assertion? If they had truly believed in their protest they would have been outraged and publicly denounced their own party for betraying their people.

During the summer of 2000 Ralph called me and asked me to join him at the home of environmentalist David Brower to talk about our strategy in regard to the Sierra Club. I was so glad to finally have the chance to meet Brower, one of California's most dedicated, principled defenders of the environment. David endorsed Ralph and often spoke about how Clinton and Gore had done more damage to the environment than Reagan and Bush, another untold story of the truth about the Democrats.

David died on November 5, 2000, at the age of eighty-eight. He had cast his absentee ballot for Ralph the day before. I was so glad that before he died David Brower saw the rise of a candidate who truly fought to defend our planet.

Understanding Ralph Nader

Having now known Ralph for more than a dozen years, I think I have grown to understand him and the unusual political approach he represents. He perplexes people. He has fought for national health care, better conditions for workers, consumer protection, environmental protection, equal rights for women and African Americans, and much more. The question about his decades-long efforts on behalf of consumers and the public is, why did he succeed? Why did he have such a huge impact? Where were the much larger forces represented by unions, for instance, in protecting workers' rights or safety?

People have not focused clearly enough on how Ralph approached these issues. He mobilized people, usually young people, to begin a campaign of bringing out publicity, winning public opinion, and putting people into action, combined with lobbying elected officials—usually Democrats but also Republicans. That is, every group Ralph has formed has been independent of the two parties and has enlisted people to take action to win a reform. Meanwhile he refuses to join any party. He always remains an independent.

Throughout his career he has also remained separate and apart from what has been called the left, in particular the "socialist" left. He is polite to everyone but has carefully avoided entanglement with all the "left" currents. I doubt he ever wrote anything about it but he saw the "left" as a dangerous involvement that would limit the building of effective, mass independent citizen actions that could reach millions of people. He is clearly for civil liberties and democracy and thus has no association with the totalitarian Maoists or Moscow Stalinists. He refuses to use "left" language that people will not understand. He is much closer to the culture and manner of those who fought for the rights of workers, farmers, slaves, minorities, Native Americans, and women during the nineteenth century. This is true in his language, method of organizing, and theory of how change can be won.

He is friends with some Democrats and has often said kind things about some of them, especially those who have helped get bills passed for the movements he has organized. However, there is very little "quid pro quo" with elected figures, often none at all. Ralph's basic approach is that of mobilizing average American working-class people and youth into active independent efforts for change.

In our recent history, even at the same time as Ralph was building these grass-roots movements, there have been many others that came forward and worked on similar projects or had methods that approximated many of his. But those all became tied to the Democrats and lost their effectiveness, or became tied to the sectarian "left" and became isolated from the people.

There is something peculiar about Ralph. As he became famous, back in the '60s and '70s, the Democrats began to approach him. They considered running him for office or giving him a cabinet post. Nader turned them down. As it became clearer and clearer to the Democrats that Nader was different, that he would not sell out the people, would not compromise and accept "playing the game," their attitude hardened. Their willingness to let him pressure them for changes began to lessen. When Bill Clinton entered the White House Nader's influence declined. The Democrats closed the door.

By 1996 it was evident that Ralph was trying to find a way to talk to the American people about the failure of the two-party system. When he ran seriously for president in 2000 the Democrats were caught off guard at first, as Ralph held rallies with larger crowds than they could ever draw. They had never heard a candidate speak so clearly, with such a mass impact, for democracy and social justice. The Democrats had not in their lifetimes experienced the kind of challenge Nader presented in 2000. The hate toward him as a threat to their existence as servants of the corporate world grew day by day. They had to find a way to crush him and to enlist their liberal friends to act as their agents to keep the two-party system untouched.

Large numbers of people think his decision to run for president was in conflict with his past, that it made him less effective. On the contrary, I believe it was the greatest and bravest thing he did in his entire life.

Nader's decision to challenge the two-party system in 2000 was an historic moment and a grand conclusion to all his other struggles. This was the most important contribution to social justice he made in his life. Had he not done so, he would be regarded as a wonderful reformer who tried to make changes but never understood how America was ruled. Future generations will respect this critical and courageous stance.

CHAPTER 17

RUNNING FOR GOVERNOR

After Nader's 2000 run I told my wife that before I died I thought I would run for office one last time. She said okay, but that she wanted us to move to Folsom, California, so she could be near our grandchildren. I agreed, in part because I liked the idea of moving to Folsom as well. For me having grandchildren was one of the greatest joys of my life.

The very day I announced my campaign, November 14, 2001, my second grandchild was born. A reporter from the *San Francisco Chronicle* wanted to know the name of my new grandson so I called my daughter-in-law Kelly, who was in labor in the hospital. She said the baby's name would not be revealed until he was born, even for the *San Francisco Chronicle.** I also had my right arm in a sling because of an operation on my shoulder. The sling and my newborn grandson got more attention than the platform I laid out. But as it turned out my candidacy was at the right moment in the right place and it began to get momentum thanks to Governor Gray Davis, a Democrat whose popularity was in free-fall.

---

* His name is Andrew. Our first grandson's name is Daniel, and we now have a third grandson, Oliver, who was born as I was writing the chapter on Nader's 2000 campaign.

Gray Davis

Davis had been widely accused of selling legislation. One well-known example was that when a representative from the teachers' union went to the governor's office to lobby for some legislation, Governor Davis allegedly said, "That will be one million dollars." The state attorney general was a friend of the governor's as well as a Democrat so nothing was done about it. I used the term "pay to play" to describe the governor, which caught on. The media started repeating it as did Bill Simon, the Republican candidate for governor.

The frustration among Democrats—unhappy with their increasingly unpopular governor yet unwilling to vote for a conservative Republican—began to create media interest in my campaign. When I gave a talk at Berkeley to a small audience of about fifty people, Carla Marinucci, a leading reporter for the *San Francisco Chronicle*, came out to hear me. Afterward she said that it was far more interesting to listen to me than the other candidates. Her report, which covered the key points as well as some of the humor, ran on page three of the *Chronicle*.

Soon afterward another *Chronicle* piece on my campaign ran on the front page.* Many of the daily papers began doing interviews with me that were fairly accurate, even supportive in comparison to my opponents. The only paper that was negative toward me was the *L.A. Weekly*, the alternative newspaper, which was edited by a liberal Democrat, Harold Meyerson. Television and radio coverage also increased. There was a huge difference between KPFK, the Los Angeles progressive station, which gave me continuous coverage, and KPFA, the Berkeley station, which essentially refused to cover me. Whenever they felt obligated to say something they asked me whether I would be a "spoiler." Of course they never said to a Democratic candidate, "Why do you oppose runoffs and instead maintain a spoiler system?" The difference between the two was that KPFK was run by more independent-minded people and KPFA was in the hands of liberal Democrats. I finally told KPFA that I was opposed to spoiling and since they never asked that

---

* The very positive and friendly reports in the *San Francisco Chronicle* suddenly halted near the end of the campaign. Upper management finally stepped in and cut any reference to me in the last weeks before the vote. Carla Marinucci was on a public TV show with my campaign manager, Tyler Snortum-Phelps, after the elections and she explained that my name was taken out of articles in the last period of the campaign.

question of Democrats or Republicans I would refuse to talk to them about it. Liberal Democrats never protest if a conservative third-party candidate runs, only if a pro-labor, pro-peace candidate appears.

Our Slate

Larry Shoup, who had initially asked me to run, said he was interested in running for secretary of state. Donna Warren, a leader in the work against California's "three strikes" law as well as other issues, ran for lieutenant governor with me. It was a great joy to listen to her speeches, especially when she was winning over the young people in a crowd. Donna was very outspoken about breaking with the two-party system and how proud she was to be in the Green Party. Greg Jan helped to complete the other positions in our slate: Jeanne Rosenmeier for treasurer, David Sheidlower for insurance commissioner, and Laura Wells for controller. All of us worked together and often one of the "down-slate" candidates would come with me to speak at campaign events.

My campaign was run out of my office with Tyler Snortum-Phelps as the campaign manager. Tyler was a member of the Green Party County Council in Contra Costa County. He knew all the Greens statewide and was very effective at organizing meetings for me throughout California. After a while we noticed that the more isolated counties where the population was a bit more conservative seemed to be far more supportive of the campaign than the more progressive centers such as San Francisco, Oakland, and Santa Monica. Gradually I began to realize that where the Democrats were more "progressive," the Greens were less interested in our statewide campaigns because their Democratic friends would complain about the spoiler issue.

Throughout the campaign I was not invited to speak by the San Francisco Greens until the campaign became so popular that they wanted me to come in order to attract more people to hear their local candidates. In fact when my campaign first started I got a call from Ross Mirkarimi, a Green leader from San Francisco who had been Nader's California coordinator. He told me in an insulting manner that it was crazy for me to run and that he wanted the Greens to support a Democrat. Later when the campaign had become quite popular he called me demanding to know why we had not asked him for advice. I put the phone on speaker and Tyler and I both tried not to laugh. This shift in attitude directly corresponded to the level of media coverage.

Tyler and I decided early on to make contact with the Republicans as a way to try to get into the debates. We met the coordinator of Bill Simon's campaign, who was very courteous to us—we assumed because they figured our campaign could help their chances of winning. But after I met Bill I developed a different opinion about him. He is quite conservative in his views and we differed strongly on a series of key issues but he was very polite and respectful.

The Debates

New California Media, an association of non–European American ethnic news outlets, sought to sponsor a gubernatorial debate. The majority of California's population is now non–European American and polls indicate that a very large percentage of this population gets their information from media specifically aimed at their ethnic and/or racial group. They invited Davis, Simon, and me. Davis refused to attend. I assumed he was following the usual example, as candidates leading in the polls commonly refuse to debate. I also thought that my being a Latino might be a factor since the debate audience would be mainly Latino and African American.

The report I got from friends who had spoken to the governor was that he was very hostile toward me and felt I was doing him great damage by attacking him from the left. I suspect that he feared having to deal with issues that disproportionately affected Latinos and African Americans, such as the death penalty, the three-strikes law, the inadequate minimum wage, regressive taxes, and the right to driver's licenses for undocumented workers. On these issues he was a hard-core reactionary. Davis opposed every request for clemency that came his way. He was openly pro-corporate and gave away state funds to help corporations while he opposed raising the minimum wage in any meaningful way or taxing rich people or corporations.

In California the rich pay the lowest tax rate—7.3 percent of their income for state and local taxes—while the poorest people pay the highest rate, 11.2 percent. The tax structure is totally regressive, with the average person paying 9.2 percent. In education California once spent six hundred dollars per student above the national average. As time passed and the state became wealthier, the amount per student dropped until California was spending six hundred dollars per student less than the national average, adjusted for inflation. I think Davis was reluctant to debate me on these issues, seeing it as a dangerous thing to let me get a hearing. Few people in California are truly aware of the regressive tax structure and the Democrats' policies on taxes favoring the rich and corporations.

At the New California Media event Bill Simon and I debated without the governor. Davis spent that day in Los Angeles near the debate location, which was openly insulting since he was making it clear that he could have attended but he would not show respect for the minority-oriented New California Media.

As might have been expected I received a great deal of support on the issues from the debate audience. At the same time I was struck by Bill Simon's honesty in a forum where his positions on many issues were unpopular. There was one remarkable incident in this debate. I was asked a question that I knew nothing about. I replied, "I don't know. I am not able to answer the question." The response was a burst of applause and laughter at that kind of frankness coming from a political candidate.

Davis Hands Me a Media Coup

Gray Davis agreed to one debate but only with the Republican, Bill Simon. It was to be held in Los Angeles and sponsored by the *Los Angeles Times*. A poll indicated that more than two-thirds of Californians wanted me in the debate, but the governor had made it a condition of his participation that I be excluded. Bill Simon protested. He told me that he was considering refusing to debate if I were not included. Later he explained that something had come up that made it crucial for him to take part. I said I appreciated his efforts and asked him if he would put me on his list of invited guests so I could be present at the debate. He agreed to do so and I was sent a formal invitation.

When Davis heard I was to be a guest he told the *Los Angeles Times* that if I were in the building he would leave. Of course this led to immediate front-page coverage. The media asked me what I would do and I answered, "I have an invitation to attend and I have no control over the governor. He will do whatever he wants."

Davis wasn't finished with his unintentional efforts to promote my campaign. He hired forty unionists to stand outside the *Los Angeles Times* building to try to shout me down so I couldn't talk to media as I arrived for the debate. Most media people who witnessed this had great sympathy for me. The paid demonstrators were told to chant "Four more years." I told the press it should be "Four to ten years." The reporters liked that. I noticed that a few individuals, mainly Latinos, had come with homemade signs saying "Let Peter Debate."

When the time came I told the growing press contingent that I would now enter the building. As I went in there was a table with a representative of the *Los Angeles Times* sitting behind it and police standing between me and the hallway leading to the debate area. A woman from the *Times* said to me, "You can't enter, please leave." I told her, I have a formal invitation, on what grounds are you asking I leave? Her answer was, "You cannot enter, please leave." I explained to her that there was a specific California law that prohibits excluding a person from any event based on their race, religion, or their political views—legislation that was written to end racial discrimination but that also applied to the exact circumstances I was in. The answer remained the same words. Finally I asked her if she knew any other words. She answered, "You cannot enter, please leave."

Latino Media

During the campaign I was invited to speak to a small group of Latino workers in Los Angeles. One young person told me it was important that I meet Miguel Araujo, who had been involved in progressive politics in Mexico but was now living in Northern California and leading a movement for Latino rights. I called Miguel, who owned a restaurant in San Bruno, and set up a meeting. We spent many hours talking. He was very frustrated about how the Democrats had repeatedly betrayed Latinos. He focused on how the denial of driver's licenses—a motion made and passed by Democrats—had forced undocumented Mexican workers to get false papers in order to be able to feed their families, which left them vulnerable to criminal charges.

I assured Miguel of my full support on this and other issues, from raising the minimum wage, which when adjusted for inflation was now lower than in 1968, to legalization for undocumented workers. Miguel was connected with all the Spanish-language stations and he started setting up interviews for me.

Soon our campaign and Miguel's work began to support each other. His group was organizing demonstrations of Mexican Americans demanding the right for driver's licenses. Greens started showing up at the demonstrations, sometimes in small numbers but occasionally more. Before long the demonstrators started carrying signs, "Vote Green" or "Vote Camejo," chanting "No to Davis, Si to Camejo." Through Miguel I met my friend Gil

RUNNING FOR GOVERNOR   239

Cedillo, a member of the state legislature who had been fighting for the right to driver's licenses for all people living in California.

Antonio Gonzalez invited me to speak at some meetings of the Willie Velasquez Institute, which included many leaders from Latino nonprofits. At the first meeting he invited all three candidates but only Bill Simon and I showed up. I pointed out that *La Opinión,* the major Spanish-language newspaper in Los Angeles, had not written one word to cover the first Latino in years to run for governor and the only candidate that favored legalization for all undocumented workers and the right to driver's licenses. The owner of *La Opinión,* Democrat Monica Lozano, was upset at my reference to her paper's failure to cover my campaign and pulled Antonio aside to vent her anger. Antonio diplomatically assured her I was a good person and all she needed to do was cover my campaign. The editor of *La Opinión,* Pilar Marrero, invited me to speak with members of her staff. They understood that I was fighting for the very things they supported as Latinos. Pilar made sure afterward that my campaign received coverage.

Antonio also invited me to Southern California to be the keynote speaker at a conference of the Southwest Voter Registration Education Project. The meeting was full of young people who were working to register Latinos to vote. A reporter from the *San Diego Union,* the local major paper, was smiling throughout my speech, enjoying the jokes I made about the campaign. The next day the paper printed this one: How do you get Governor Davis to change his position 180 degrees in one second? Tell him the check bounced.

My final tally came in at 393,036 votes or 5.3 percent. This was the largest vote in decades for a progressive third-party gubernatorial candidate. In the triangle between Santa Cruz to the border with Oregon and to the border with Nevada at Lake Tahoe my vote was about 10 percent. We called this the Green triangle. In the inner Bay Area, including all of San Francisco where I received 17 percent and parts of the East Bay, I came in second, beating the Republican. The highest percentage of my vote came from Latinos and young people.

Political Money

During the campaign I had two peculiar meetings, which I will describe without giving names of the persons involved. The first was an offer by the Republicans to fund my campaign with substantial donations. My campaign manager Tyler, probably the most principled person on the planet, got nervous that I didn't say no instantaneously. The reason was that I was trying to learn as much as I could exactly why this was being offered and from whom. I considered the messenger a friend and a well-intentioned person. Of course I said no thank you.

The other meeting was even stranger. It was with a Democrat who had been involved in the leadership, according to him, of one of the major Democratic presidential candidates. He told me that this race was unusual due to Davis's unpopularity and said he thought I could be elected if I agreed to let a committee of Democrats run the campaign. I would have to agree to say only what I was told to say; they would raise money and then begin an all-out effort to get me elected. Again Tyler was nervous that I just sat there and let this person speak. In the end I thanked him for considering me but that I couldn't do what he proposed and that it wouldn't work even if I did agree.

Both these meetings amazed me with regard to the power of money. Here I was, radical as hell, a principled person that no one could buy, period, and yet here was money trying to get control of me. Imagine what happens to popular candidates who are not so principled, whose main goal is just to get elected, and you are on the way to understanding how the electoral system in the United States really works.

I recall telling my Dad, who is very conservative, about this experience. He said to me, you did the right thing. Never accept money from politicians.

The Recall Election

No sooner had the election ended than the Republicans took note of Davis's low approval ratings and entertained the possibility of removing him through a recall campaign. California's law on a gubernatorial recall was rather strange. A very large number of signatures was required to hold a recall election. No governor had ever been recalled in California. The ballot for a gubernatorial recall had two parts: in the recall part voters would choose "yes" or "no" on the recall itself. In the second part they would vote for their choice to replace the current governor in case the "yes" vote won.

At first the prevailing opinion of the media was that the nearly one million signatures would never be collected. The pro-recall forces, led by the Republicans, ended up getting about two million—probably the highest number of signatures ever collected on any issue.

As the Republicans set out to gather signatures and campaign for the recall they received large donations from a couple of wealthy conservatives. The Democrats blasted the recall as a Republican coup to undo the previous election. But polls showed some remarkable facts that did not get much publicity. The poorest people in California were the most in favor of the recall. A majority of union members favored the recall even though the entire union leadership, who were almost all Democrats, opposed it. Middle-class people, students, and almost every other demographic group indicated that they were in favor of removing Davis.* There was only one group that opposed his recall: the wealthiest people in the state.

The requirement to enter the gubernatorial race to replace the governor was simple: collect sixty-five signatures and pay $3,500. All candidates were in a nonpartisan-style race. The candidate with the highest vote would win. No runoff structure was in place, so if many candidates entered, a candidate could win with a small vote. My reaction upon watching the recall process unfold was what an incredible opportunity this could be to get across the need for electoral reform, the need for runoffs, and the power of the best form of runoffs—instant runoff voting, called IRV—which respects the will of the people and can be accomplished within one election. People simply select their first, second, and third choices. If no candidate emerges with a majority, the candidate receiving the lowest vote is removed and the second choice of those voters is factored in. This process continues until one candidate has a majority and is declared the winner. This system makes it possible for people to vote for the candidate they really favor with no risk of a spoiler effect, and no candidate can get elected who is not the real choice of the majority.

Greens and the Recall Election

I e-mailed Susan King, who was the director of the Green Party statewide committee on elections at the time, and asked that a meeting of the committee be called to discuss how the Greens should respond to the recall situation. King's reaction was to dismiss my request and instead, without even contacting me, she sent out an e-mail to Greens throughout the state giving her opinion as though it were a decision. Her e-mail stated that the Greens should

---

* Even after massive pounding by the Democrats against the recall, exit polls would show 45 percent of Latinos voted for the recall as did 48 percent of people living in union households.

have nothing to do with the recall race. In other words we should keep our mouths shut and leave the recall to the two corporate parties.

At a statewide conference the state Green Party leadership asked me to make a presentation on the recall. The Greens were divided three ways. Some said we should recall Davis, some said we should vote "no" on the recall, and some in the middle were not sure exactly how we should handle it. I proposed that we accept our divided opinions and allow all Greens to organize and argue for their views on this issue. I made it clear in my report that I was seriously considering entering the race and why. My proposal of respect for all points of view and full freedom of expression passed almost unanimously.

Over One Hundred Candidates

Once the requirements for the recall had been met, the date of the election was set for October 7, 2003. Then the registration of gubernatorial replacement candidates began. The threshold was so low—only the sixty-five signatures and $3,500—that the ballot was swamped. The system led to 135 candidates being on the ballot.

The Democratic Party leadership put out an official call, led by Dianne Feinstein, that no Democrat should run. They proposed that everyone vote against the recall; if it passed, the governorship was to be handed to the Republicans. I think their rationale was that by turning the recall into a "yes" or "no" vote on the Republicans there might be a chance that Davis could survive. Most of the Democrats who were considering a run backed down and announced that they would not enter the race.

I announced that I would run and took the public stance that Davis should not only be removed but tried for corruption and given jail time if the accusations in the media turned out to be true. Given my 2002 vote within a spoiler framework of 5.3 percent, the media immediately presented me as one of the major candidates that could make the difference as to who would be elected.

Online publisher and public figure Arianna Huffington, who called herself a progressive independent, also announced her intention to run. I called her and suggested we get together and talk. She agreed and I went down to her home in Los Angeles. Talking was difficult. All I could do was sit and listen. She told me her life story and listed off all the books she had published. Then some political friend of hers dropped by and could hardly contain his annoyance that I was there.

As I moved to leave I said to her, "Let's try to see if we can still be friends at the end of this." She started pushing for me to drop out and support her. I argued that having both of us run gave us two voices to address the many issues we agreed on. Not only that but I spoke Spanish and could get on Spanish-language stations. In the early polls we both had low but respectable numbers; she was a few percentage points above me. I told her that given the power of the two major parties neither of us could win but we could bring attention to important issues.

She seemed to believe she could win. Her campaign offered me a co-chair position if I didn't run. I got the feeling that she had no idea who I was or what I believed in. People started walking up to me to thank me for taking a supportive stance toward Arianna. She was immediately declared by the media to be a major candidate.

The lingering question was whether a Democrat of standing would enter the race after the Democratic Party leadership came out with the no-one-should-run policy. The media began interviewing Democrats, some of whom said they were going to vote "no" on the recall but would vote for me just in case. I took the public position that such a policy was wrong, that they should not defend a governor who was under a cloud for alleged corruption and that Democrats should enter the race to debate the issues of what California needed instead of trying to avoid the debate.

Some Democrats who respected me told me that Cruz Bustamante, the Latino lieutenant governor, was considering breaking the ban on Democrats running since he was the next in line to become governor if Gray Davis were removed. Miguel Araujo and I went to talk to Cruz. We agreed on some issues and not on others—Cruz had voted to take away the driver's licenses from undocumented workers but he had changed his mind and admitted he had made a mistake.

Cruz announced that he would run and became the leading Democrat in the race. At first he was leading in the polls by 30 percent to Arnold Schwarzenegger's 25 percent.* The most prominent Republican to announce turned out to be Schwarzenegger, a conservative on most issues who, thanks to his celebrity, had the high visibility that would be necessary to win.

---

* Peter Schrag, *California: America's High-Stakes Experiment* (Los Angeles: University of California Press, 2006), 180.

The First Debate

Immediately the main issue that developed was which candidates to allow in the debates, of which about five were projected. Public interest in the recall was enormous. The election became a bit of a show as the entire country's media poked fun at California. The media now had the power to pick the candidates they would allow in the debates.

It is a challenge to describe the atmosphere that resulted once the normal pattern of one Democrat and one Republican was broken. Many Republicans entered the race, not just Arnold. Among the best known were Bill Simon, Tom McClintock, and Peter Ueberroth. The first debate, in early September, was sponsored by Channel 2 in Oakland and featured three Republicans; one Democrat; one independent, Arianna Huffington; and me from the Green Party. Schwartzenegger was invited but he chose not to participate.

I prepared for the first debate extensively. I spent two days working on my one-minute summary that fortunately turned out to be two minutes. I had the speech memorized so I could deliver it clearly and cover all the crucial points.

At every debate in which Arianna also participated I made sure to say something positive about her. She never recognized my existence publicly at any time. I also went out of my way, when any candidate said something I agreed with, to point out that we agreed. Such an approach helped make me likable to enormous numbers of people watching the debates. Taking this stance made it easier for me to hit on the key class, race, and environmental issues I stood for.

During the debate when asked about driver's licenses for undocumented Mexicans I answered that European Americans had been in California for 150 years and we should give them driver's licenses. The audience laughed, understanding immediately where I was going. Then I noted that Mexicans have been on this continent for twenty thousand years so obviously they have every right to a driver's license.

I focused on California's regressive taxes, pointing out that taxing the rich at the rate that an average person pays (9 percent) would balance the budget. At the end of my presentation I mentioned that in other countries if a party gets 20 percent of the votes they get 20 percent of the seats but not in America; they get zero. When the debate concluded the moderator repeated what I had said, as if to say, "That certainly sounds logical." Of course without me in the campaign these issues would never be heard.

Huffington's approach was very different. She attacked Bustamante in a very personal manner for accepting funds from gambling firms. While I agreed with her point and even stated so, I felt uncomfortable with the vicious way she condemned him.

In Los Angeles the committee working to repeal the three-strikes law, led by Geri Silva, organized a press conference and invited all the major candidates to attend. My running mate from 2002 Donna Warren was there with me as were many other leaders of the movement against three strikes. The presenters included spokespeople who had a family member, usually a father, doing life in prison for a nonviolent crime, usually a drug-related offense. During the press conference I had tears in my eyes as I heard the testimony of children who had lost a parent to this ridiculous law, which sentenced people to life in prison for nonviolent crimes.

I was the only candidate there. I was surprised at how Arianna presented herself as a progressive but carefully avoided controversial issues on which it is crucial for progressives to speak out.

Not only was I doing media work geared to the Latino community in general, I also campaigned before groups of undocumented workers. In Stockton, California, I gained the support of a worker advocacy group led by Luis Magaña. With Luis's assistance, I took a team of news reporters to a large farm in Stockton to interview its undocumented employees.

I spoke in Spanish to the workers, who thanked me for fighting to reinstate driver's licenses for all who live in California as well for other issues, such as raising the minimum wage. In order that the TV crews could film the conditions these workers' families live under, we walked around the farm a bit, stopping to talk to the young wife of one the workers next to their tiny mobile home. At that moment the Anglo farm manager discovered us and ran up, shouting. Randy Shandobil, the political editor of Channel 2 in Oakland, tried to talk to him. The angry farm manager threatened to hit Randy. I asked the man if he realized who he was talking to. Behind me the cameraman was filming the whole exchange and it dawned on me one second too late that a really good, dramatic story was in the making and I was messing it up by giving this racist jerk a warning.

After we had left I apologized to Randy for spoiling his story. He just laughed. Channel 2 gave a very supportive report on their news that evening, pointing out additionally that I was the only candidate campaigning among Californians who couldn't even vote.

Agha Saeed, my Pakistani friend whom I met back in 1976, has played a leadership role in the Muslim community for many years. He invited me to the annual family gathering of Muslims in San Francisco, which takes place in Golden Gate Park and draws thousands of people. I was asked to speak as the one candidate who defended the rights of Muslims and opposed the discriminatory policies they were confronting. It surprised me how deep among Muslims the support for the Green Party had grown. Polls showed more than 20 percent of Muslims citing their party as the Green Party.

The Second Debate

The second debate, focusing on people of color, was sponsored by the Greenlining Institute of San Francisco and the New California Media on September 9, 2003. This debate received the least media coverage, although it was in a way the most important. It focused on issues the other debates didn't touch, and if I hadn't been part of the debates they would have gone unmentioned. These included the death penalty, three-strikes law, and the minimum wage, as well as the high cost of home ownership and other obstacles confronted by lower-income people.

Only three of us attended, Bustamante, Arianna, and I. I had much less speaking time than the other two due to the format, in which a group of media people asked whatever questions they wanted to whichever candidate they chose. Their main agenda was to get Bustamante pinned down on some issues. I actually raised a complaint about the method, although I am sure there was no intention to deny anyone equal time.

The Largest Debate

The California Broadcasters Association (CBA) proposed sponsoring a debate in Sacramento. They were only inviting five candidates; I was not on the list. Arnold agreed to attend, assuring the debate massive media and public interest because of his fame and his rapidly growing support. Tyler and I couldn't figure out how to get me into the debate so we called Bill Simon's advisor, who suggested we see Stan Statham, president/CEO of the CBA.

Stan agreed to meet with me. He was very friendly, explaining that he respected my candidacy but that they could pick only five for what would be a huge debate in terms of the listening audience. He mentioned that stations all over the United States and in Europe and Japan were going to air the debate. I asked him what I needed to do to convince them that I should be included. Stan had a smile on his face while we talked that I couldn't figure out. At the end of the meeting he told me to go home and not to worry about it.

It turned out Bill Simon had decided to pull out of the race, opening up one seat in the debate. But Stan couldn't tell me at the meeting since the information was not yet public.

There was great excitement among the Greens that we would be included, that in fact for the first time in American history a nationally televised election debate would include a candidate of a party to the left of the Democrats. That had never happened before. It gives me great pride that I was the first; there will in time be many more. The media coverage was intense, with pictures of the five candidates on the front pages of the daily newspapers. It is ironic that the story was picked up by some of the mainstream media but none of the "progressive" news outlets gave it any importance.

The question for me was how to handle a five-way debate in front of a TV audience of tens of millions of people, 98 percent of whom would not know who I was. My instinct was to work up some comments as a way to go after Arnold, who was leading in the polls. But my wife Morella advised me to take a different approach. She pointed out that when people turn on the TV to watch a debate they think of it as though the participants are actually in their living room. They dislike attacks, especially anything that sounds personal. Morella told me, stick to what you stand for and continue to be polite and kind to all the others and you will make more headway.

There were about five hundred people in the live audience and a large media turnout. Stan Statham as the head of the CBA was moderating and calling on candidates for comment.* He told us he would allow some back and forth so it would not be so dry. Arianna Huffington and I had exactly opposite strategies for the debate. She went on the attack against Arnold, which I believe helped Arnold because he was able to avoid the real issues by playing a game with Arianna. She never actually answered the questions asked her but instead simply accused Arnold of being pro-Bush. This was not so hard for Arnold to deflect since the primary focus of this race centered on California's budget deficit.

---

* About two years later Stan Statham sent me a beautiful picture of the debate that I have in my office. With it he sent me a short personal note that said, "You were the only one who didn't spin your message."

For instance I pointed out that the rich in California paid the lowest tax rate and that the budget would be in a surplus if they were to pay the same rate as the poor. I turned to Arnold and asked him and State Senator Tom McClintock, both sitting to my right, whether they would agree that it was wrong for the rich to pay the lowest tax rate. Both were silent as the media and the millions watching waited for what they would say. Then Arnold said something provocative to Arianna, avoiding my question. Instead of Arianna's responding, "Answer Peter's question," which would have put Arnold on the spot—on the key issue of the debate, how to balance the budget—she fell for his maneuver and responded in kind as Arnold used her to get laughs from the audience while a key class-issue was dropped.

Because I did not interrupt any of the other candidates I felt I had spoken the least when we were about two-thirds through. To try to get Stan the moderator to call on me more often, I began my answer to a question with these words, "I have tried to be polite to all the candidates this evening." The audience in the hall immediately interrupted me with a huge burst of applause. I realized right there that Morella's strategy of being extra-polite had been effective. She was right.

After the debate* each candidate got a ten-minute interview with the large contingent of reporters. To my surprise no one asked me the usual "spoiler" question. They mainly focused on the issues with a couple of hostile questions about taxes. One was whether I was donating money to help overcome the deficit. My answer was no.

The next day, a nonscientific e-mail poll by the *San Francisco Chronicle* on who had won the debate put me in first place with Arnold coming in second. Arianna Huffington came in last.

Switching Sides

Soon after the main debate Arianna's campaign director called to let me know they had decided to end her campaign. I asked why they would

---

* Near the end of the event I mentioned that the League of Women Voters along with the *San Diego Union* had decided to exclude me from future debates. I asked the audience to protest this decision. The *San Diego Union* had to close down their website because of the flood of e-mail protests they received. Then a few days later at an election event both Tom McClintock and Cruz Bustamante publicly protested my exclusion and pointed out that my participation was helpful in raising issues. I especially want to acknowledge Bustamante's stance—it was extremely rare for a major figure in the Democratic Party to stand up for a third-party progressive in regard to a debate. The League of Women Voters switched their criteria and allowed me to participate in the last two debates.

do such a thing when there were two more televised debates coming up. Their response was that they needed to have an exit strategy and feared going to the end and getting a very small vote.

I was shocked to learn what they had really decided. Arianna came out in support of Gray Davis, our shady governor. She reversed everything she had done up to that moment, switched sides, and joined his campaign. There was TV coverage of her flying with Davis in his private airplane.

At the next debate they announced that before the candidates spoke the governor's representative would be given time to speak on his behalf. That was nothing unusual but what was surprising was that the Democrats sent Arianna Huffington as their official representative. I was sitting next to Cruz Bustamante and asked him why his own party would choose a person that had been criticizing him in such a strong, personal manner. Cruz turned to me and said, "How many times do I have to tell you they tell me nothing. I knew nothing about this."

My vote came in right behind the three major candidates, Arnold, Cruz, and Tom, but the total was only 2.8 percent, or 242,247 votes. I thought it would be higher but it showed how support does not reflect itself in the votes in a single, winner-take-all race. As we reached the end of the campaign McClintock got a major lesson about the spoiler system when his supporters started declaring that they were voting for Arnold. Repeatedly he asked people to vote for the candidate they really wanted. McClintock now understands why Greens favor holding runoff elections through IRV.

Green Party Endorsement

By the end of the campaign 91 percent of the Green Party county organizations had endorsed my campaign. Thousands of new people joined the Green Party and an important shift appeared. The single largest percentage of Green votes came from African Americans; second was Latinos. Given that the Democrats were running Bustamante, a Latino, my percentage among Latinos dropped a bit but still remained relatively high. Another important discovery was that my vote was heavily from young people and lower-income people. The Green Party was changing in terms of who was voting Green.

Another major lesson I learned from that campaign was the power of television. Wherever I went people came up to me. I couldn't eat in a restaurant without somebody stopping by my table. I was on an airplane when a young woman saw me and yelled out so just about the whole airplane could hear, "Oh my God, I'm on the same plane with Peter Camejo!" I shook her hand and said something genial. But most amusing to me was that the guy sitting next to me was clueless and asked me if I was a rock star.

CHAPTER 18

MATT GONZALEZ: THE 2003 RACE
FOR MAYOR OF SAN FRANCISCO

One night in early August 2003 I got a call on my cell phone from Matt Gonzalez. He said, "Where are you? I need to meet with you." At thirty-eight, Matt was an incredible development within the Green Party. He had graduated from Stanford Law and worked for years as a public defender. He had run for district attorney as a progressive Democrat, opposing the three-strikes law and the death penalty while supporting the need to promote environmental prosecutions.

In 2000, still a Democrat, Matt ran for the Board of Supervisors of the City of San Francisco from a progressive district that included the famous Haight-Ashbury area. He became the favorite to win the nonpartisan race. Late in the campaign Matt attended a KRON-TV senatorial debate between the Democrat Dianne Feinstein and the Republican Tom Campbell while Medea Benjamin, the Green Party candidate, had been excluded. It dawned on him that he didn't agree with much of what the Democratic Party stood for and how it acted. Just before the first round in the elections for supervisor, Matt switched his registration to the Green Party. He wrote an op-ed in the *Bay Guardian* titled, "Why I Turned Green." He made it into the runoff as a registered Green and then proceeded to win, becoming the highest elected official in California for the Green Party.

When I got Matt's call I was in a hotel in San Francisco because the next morning I had to do a TV interview for the recall election. As it turned out Matt was only two blocks away at his girlfriend's apartment. The three of us sat together in the tiny kitchen, drinking port and coffee, as Matt explained that he was going to enter the race for mayor of San Francisco. I remember my initial response: "What? Jesus, you should have decided that months ago. There's very little time. [Gavin] Newsom's been campaigning for a year."

Matt said, "I think I could win."

I responded, "No, the Democrats have San Francisco locked up."

He said, "Well, in any case we'll get a good showing and stop Newsom from having a mandate."

I told him, "Okay, if you decide to do this I will back you 100 percent and do what I can to help you."

I had met Matt in 2000, soon after his election to the board of supervisors, at a Green Party meeting where he gave a talk. I walked up to him, introduced myself, and told him I really liked the talk he gave. I sensed immediately that he was a very principled person, not a calculating politician looking to see what could promote a career.

Matt's election demonstrated a shift to the left among the Democrats. Mayor Willie Brown's more rightist Democratic current lost its majority on the board of supervisors and a progressive wing on the board started working together. Matt was included in this informal bloc without alienating the more conservative members. His demeanor was polite and honest—he told people up front if he disagreed with them, but always respectfully.

After two years when it was time to choose a new board president Matt's name was raised as a possible candidate who could both represent the progressive majority and work with the others effectively.

After a few deadlocks around other candidates enough supervisors shifted to Matt to give him the presidency. A board of supervisors dominated by the Democrats elected Matt, the Green, to the second-highest position in the city. The pro-corporate Democratic Party establishment, especially people like Nancy Pelosi, Dianne Feinstein, and most of all Mayor Willie Brown, were not happy.

Few people realized how effective and principled Matt was. Through his work as president of the board of supervisors he began promoting legislation that would make a difference to working-class people. He raised the minimum wage and tied it to the cost of living so its gradual erosion through inflation ended, at least in San Francisco. He helped support strikes and looked out for the interests of the poorest workers in the city. He stood up for animal rights and opposed gentrification by stopping the introduction of major chain stores that would destroy small family businesses.

Matt proposed instant runoff voting (IRV) for San Francisco and won, setting an example to help promote electoral law changes. San Francisco's pro-corporate politicians, naturally, opposed it. But thanks to Matt the law was changed.

I cannot emphasize strongly enough how important this issue is. The rule of money over people needs to maintain a two-party monopoly. IRV threatens that because it removes the spoiler issue and establishes the right of people to vote for their candidate of choice, regardless of party. In the end, if IRV were established along with proportional representation—meaning every vote would count and every citizen would have representation—the door would be open to a wave of change. It would inevitably mean the breakup of the Democratic Party's unprincipled coalition. I say "unprincipled" because those who vote Democratic are in their majority Latinos, African Americans, unionized workers, the poor, environmentalists, and progressive-minded people, while the policies that are implemented by the Democrats are pro-corporate and beneficial to the rich. With truly free elections this coalition would become a potential electoral base for people who favor democracy and the rule of people over money.

In June 2003, before he had decided to run, Matt and I along with Jo Chamberlain, chair of the San Mateo County Green Party, had marched together at the Gay Rights Parade, leading a small contingent of Greens. As we marched we noticed that block after block the people enjoying the parade broke into applause as we passed. I leaned over to Jo and said, "Do you see what is happening?"

Keep in mind, even in a "spoiler" framework, 17 percent of the people of San Francisco had voted for me for governor in 2002 and they were pleased by Matt's rise to president of the board of supervisors. There was definitely the potential to build an alternative political force in this city. Proof of that would come over the next several months.

Last-Minute Candidate

With the support of Mayor Willie Brown and some of San Francisco's big financial interests, a pro-business economic conservative Democrat, Gavin Newsom, had begun campaigning for mayor more than a year before the election. Newsom later became famous for standing up in favor of a very progressive policy issuing marriage licenses to same-sex couples. To his credit, after being elected mayor Newsom championed this cause, which made him popular among people who would have otherwise been turned off by many of his policies. What few people know is that prior to his election Newsom was the only candidate running for mayor who opposed gay marriage. Even the Republican police chief running for mayor, Tony Ribera, favored marriage equality.

The progressive current on the board of supervisors began looking for a candidate to run against the pro-corporate Newsom and conducted a poll to see who among them might be the strongest possible candidate. The poll showed strong support for Matt. Up to that point Matt had no plans to run.

On August 8, 2003, Matt became an official candidate for mayor. His decision was so late in coming they had to gather $10,000 on short notice so he could qualify for the ballot, since there was no time to collect signatures. The first round in the elections was set for November 4 with the runoff on December 9. In the first round Matt needed to come in at least second among a group of well-known, relatively well-financed, established progressive and liberal Democrats, who had been campaigning for months. He needed to raise funds and organize volunteers quickly.

To get the Green Party's endorsement Matt had to appear before a county meeting. Unfortunately the rank and file of the party, especially the youth, tended not to be among those who attended the county meetings—if a Green didn't show up regularly at the rather boring monthly meetings, they weren't allowed to vote. Matt and I went together to ask the Green Party of San Francisco to endorse him. Matt made a presentation on what his campaign would mean and why the party should support his running in the election, and I gave a short but emotional appeal to those present to vote for Matt. A two-thirds majority was needed. To my shock the San Francisco Greens did not vote to endorse him. Matt won the endorsement of the Deputy Sheriffs' Association and the Bicycle Coalition before the San Francisco Greens finally came around to support his campaign. Eventually they called a second meeting to reconsider. Matt got their endorsement by only one vote.

Matt's campaign took off immediately upon his announcement, making the events within the Green Party leadership largely irrelevant. Dozens, then hundreds of people turned out to volunteer. At the beginning his campaign had only a small office in Matt's home district, in the Horse Shoe Café on Haight Street. Among those volunteering were many rank-and-file Greens, of course, but also independents and registered Democrats. Later Matt moved to an enormous office that I believe could fit close to a thousand people. I remember driving one night at about 11:00 p.m. through the Mission and deciding to take a look at his new office. To my surprise about thirty volunteers were still in there working. In the primary race they raised about $150,000, the lowest among the leading six candidates. In the runoff they raised about $750,000, way behind the millions Newsom had but the highest ever for a Green mayoralty candidate.

Democrats Divide

The rapid and amazing growth of Matt's campaign can be explained in good part by a split in the Democratic Party leadership. Gavin Newsom clearly represented the pro-corporate right wing of the Democrats. The more progressive-minded and, I would even say, radical local Democratic Party leaders were upset, since they felt—correctly—that the majority of Democrats stood by them, not Newsom. They bolted and began endorsing Matt Gonzalez. They could care less that he was registered Green.

Supervisors Aaron Peskin, Chris Daly, and Jake McGoldrick endorsed Matt and soon it would be 6 to 3 backing Matt on the board of supervisors. Matt's platform was clearly pro-labor, antiwar, anti–corporate domination—in clear opposition to official Democratic politics, yet a majority of elected Democratic Party leaders on the board of supervisors were shifting to support him. Many Democrats, even elected leaders, loved the fact that Matt stood his ground and did not bend on his pro-labor positions.

Matt's support among youth spread rapidly. Even though there was little time before the elections there was a jump in registrations among young people. In the Latino sections of the Mission, Matt's support was overwhelming, as high as 80 percent. Working people in general were becoming interested in Matt. He combined elements that no other Green candidate possessed. He had credibility as a high elected official and had succeeded in getting important legislation passed. His personality was charismatic and appealing. His character was flawless. What he lacked was the organizational structure of a strong party behind him.

The Greens were too weak. With fifteen thousand San Francisco members we should have had local chapters in all the supervisory districts and membership involvement at a much higher level. But that would have required an experienced leadership team and—more critical—political clarity on our objectives. The problem was that two slightly conflicting currents were passing through the Greens.

In the 2002 campaign for governor I had been strongly pro-labor. I had taken economic and racial stances not common in the party, in addition to holding the ecological positions more typical of Green candidates. The positions I advocated were popular among young Greens but were not so well received by the older generation, which tended to be more countercultural than progressive. The more conservative wing of the Greens remained open to fusion with the Democrats, a current that clearly controlled the national Green leadership.

If a third party the size of the Greens with a clearer leadership, platform, and organizational structure had been behind him, Matt's campaign could have opened up a different dynamic.

The Primary

In the primary many Greens felt Matt couldn't win and they had to pick the best of the other progressives. However, the reports coming in from Matt's campaign were very hopeful, though the odds were against him. Matt booked a meeting hall for the primary results that could fit about five hundred people. When I got there on election night the crowd was overflowing. I squeezed my way around to get a feel for it. The supporters were of all ages but a lot were youth. Suspense was in the air; no one knew how this might turn out. When the votes started coming in, Newsom was way ahead but not with the 50 percent majority necessary to end the race. For the runoff position it went back and forth but Matt was always either in first place or a close second. As time ticked away Matt developed a lead that gradually grew. The room went electric. People were amazed that the lowest-funded, latest entrant had made the runoff.

Newsom's vote came in at 41.92 percent and Matt's was second at 19.57 percent. Even though the percentages seemed lopsided most of the other votes had gone to candidates whose votes could shift to Matt. I inched my way toward the front for Matt's victory announcement. The excitement was tremendous. All I can remember, which made such an impact on me, was that he said, "Now you will hear a lot about me, I just want you to know none of it is true." Applause thundered in response. Everyone understood that Matt's opponents—the corporate media, Newsom, Mayor Willie Brown—would want to talk about anything but the real issues. Willie Brown was quoted as having said of Matt, "Too far left, out of touch, from outer space." The media focus even got down to how Matt combed his hair.

The Runoff Campaign

Endorsements kept coming in to Matt's campaign. Art Agnos, the former mayor of San Francisco from 1988 to 1992, stepped forward and endorsed Matt. He put no pressure on Matt to alter his views, just said he preferred Matt for mayor. In fact he gave Matt five of his suits for the campaign. It was a joke among the staff that Matt was just trying to get the suits back to the mayor's office.

A pollster told Matt that they had just finished a poll, to be published the next day, which showed him in first place. The margin of difference was very small and the poll had to be considered a tie. This, of course, created a panic in the Newsom campaign. But even more revealing was the panic it created in the Democratic Party as an institution. Were they about to lose San Francisco, a Democratic Party fortress, to a pro-labor independent ... a Green? What message would that send to the nation?

Amazing events began to take place. Bill Clinton, the Democratic former president of the United States, took off three days from his schedule to come to San Francisco to campaign against Matt. The fear this reflected was astonishing. This should be a lesson to all progressives of the underlying power of a mass break from the two parties.

The Nader phenomenon, which the Democrats thought had been buried by their relentless "spoiler" campaign, had raised its head in a new place and manner. A city assumed to be completely controlled by the Democrats—where a challenge had never even been considered a possibility—was in play to a Nader supporter.

Quickly following Clinton was Al Gore, the former vice president, who came to plead with the Democrats to stand fast behind their party's nominee. Never mind that Newsom had been on George Bush's voter cards in the 2000 election when Newsom was running for board of supervisors. Never mind that Newsom was essentially also the nominee of the Republican Party. Did Gore or Clinton argue the issues? Of course not. Jesse Jackson was next in line, making robo-calls urging a vote for Newsom. Nancy Pelosi and Dianne Feinstein also got in on the act. Here was a clear class lineup. San Francisco Republicans and Democrats joined forces, with the Democrats reaching for their biggest names, to try and stop an unknown Green Latino from becoming a pro-labor mayor of a major U.S. city.

The Labor Movement

The AFL-CIO in San Francisco understood perfectly that this electoral fight was between a pro-business and a pro-labor candidate. They also knew that if they dared break with the Democratic machine it would create a fight within the unions, as the Democratic machine would go to work to eliminate the rebels. They decided to continue in their submissive role. Today they know very well they threw an election that could have brought labor to power in San Francisco and changed the dynamic of the city.

Matt felt terrible that after he had fought for so many of these unions they closed the door on him. Here he was pressing for the highest minimum wage in the country and found himself opposed by the union leadership. One union stood up for Matt: Local 2, representing the hotel workers and other primarily Latino workers. Matt had also hoped for the endorsement of the janitors. He had marched with them and helped them at every turn. Sadly, they capitulated and endorsed Newsom.

I Speak for Matt

During the campaign I rarely spoke at Matt's events. Near the end of the campaign he asked me to come and speak with him at one event, which I regard as having been symbolic. The crowd was primarily young people, numbering about five hundred. Supervisors Aaron Peskin, Chris Daly, and Jake McGoldrick gave talks, which were quite good and clear, posing the main issues for the city and urging a vote for Matt. They all received strong support from the crowd.

Just before Matt was to speak he told the moderator to put me on. As I rose to speak there was an ovation. I gave a five-minute talk, combining politics with history and the commitment to be true to yourself. I raised the idea of values greater than simply who would win this race, and spoke about Matt Gonzalez the person and what he represented. When I finished I got a long standing ovation. It was as though the youth were saying, "This is what we believe; this is what we want." Then all three of the supervisors ran up one at a time to hug me. To some this might appear as though the progressive Democratic supervisors observed the audience's response and decided that they wanted to be associated with me. I don't think so. I think deep down they actually agreed with what I had said and all three felt moved. They wanted to thank me for having the courage always to speak the full truth. It was a great moment of joy for me and I have had only the most positive feelings toward all three of them.

The Debates

There was only one televised debate in the runoff. Even though the polls were now even, the Newsom people, with much more money to buy TV exposure via advertisements, did not want to agree to televised debates. I have noticed this throughout my life. Get a Democratic or Republican candidate with an advantage in the polls or in funds and they don't want the people to hear the other candidates firsthand. They back out of debates with one excuse or other.

Newsom tried to shift the focus of the debate to dealing with panhandling, an issue that can be approached from two vantage points that of those suffering from utter poverty or those molested by the endless requests for funds on the streets. Which votes Newsom wanted was pretty transparent and it wasn't the panhandlers'. These issues of homelessness and extreme poverty are not easily dealt with, as they often interrelate with unemployment, mental illness, drug addiction, lack of education, and depression. They are not easily solved. Newsom, knowing there was a desire by higher-income voters to see the beggars removed, played it as a major focus, promising all would be done in a humane and helpful manner. He proposed to take away from the homeless what little funds they received from the city in return for a promise of services. When the supervisors pushed him to agree to specific services he refused.

By making this his main focus he could avoid dealing with other pressing issues for the people of San Francisco, such as the impossible cost of housing for working people, the drop in educational services, the long-standing decline in the minimum wage, and an endless list of others vital to the average San Francisco citizen.

Matt tried to maintain a balanced approach to the problems confronting the city, including homelessness but also the tax structure favoring the rich, which undermined education and other desperately needed city programs. Undoubtedly this is the reason Matt polled his lowest, about 20 percent, in the wealthiest districts of the city while he polled the highest in the poorest areas such as the Mission. People in the middle, often impacted by the pro-business media, were influenced to vote for Newsom. More educated and progressive-minded people sided with Matt, along with working people and youth.

In the one debate Matt's thought-out and charismatic presentations won people over. It was the relentless pounding of radio and TV ads, due to Newsom's financial superiority and media backing, that allowed him to introduce confusion around Matt's positions and in that way win some votes. But on election day Newsom lost the majority of registered Democrats to Matt by a small margin, a stunning defeat.

Final Vote: December 9, 2003

I arrived at Matt's campaign headquarters about 9:00 p.m. the night of the election. I had to park many blocks away, near Mission Street. As I walked toward the office I saw hundreds of youths come pouring outside, chanting "Matt Gonzalez!" and other slogans. They had so much energy they couldn't stand the wait and ran outside to stage an impromptu demonstration. Everyone was hoping they were about to witness a great moment in the history of San Francisco and, really, the nation.

As I entered the headquarters I was impressed by how packed it was. I sat and talked to people, noting the intensity in the room. I left Matt alone, as he was busy with media and all kinds of other things. I felt the tension and anticipation. Could we win?

Believe it or not, that evening we did win; more people voted for Matt than for Newsom. But the mail-in absentee ballots, especially an 80 percent landslide vote from the Republicans, tipped the scales so that when all the votes were tallied, we lost. Newsom received 133,546 votes to Matt's 119,329 or 52.8 percent to 47.2 percent. The Republicans elected Newsom. All other sectors voted in their majority for Matt.

All around me people were crying, literally crying, men and women of all ages. I was actually overjoyed. I hadn't believed that we could do this well against all the odds. I sat alone, thinking, what does this mean? I tried to tell a few people, "We did great." It was useless. The moment was too deep. Soon it got to me too and I felt tears coming, not so much that we had lost but what it could have meant if we had won.

No one left. They all wanted to wait for Matt to speak. The audience was so packed they couldn't move. Young people had climbed up the walls to be able to see. One after another the leaders of the campaign spoke, including former Mayor Agnos, the supervisors, and many others. All spoke briefly. I had no plans to say anything. But Matt looked around and saw me and waved, asking the moderator to call me up to the front.

I tried to say that we had won. That this was a victory for our movement and the battle had only begun. I don't remember the rest but Matt kids me about it and claims I said, "We start tomorrow to continue this struggle."

Finally Matt rose to speak. The ovation was overwhelming. He thanked all those who had worked for him and stated so beautifully how this was a campaign of the people of San Francisco for a new beginning. He talked in his careful, measured way.* The response was immense, along with all the tears. People cheered him for having come so close to writing a chapter in American history at a time when no one believed it possible.

The truth is Matt did write a chapter. He showed what could happen. Although this was in San Francisco and only an electoral rebellion, it was possible. The power of money over people will not rule forever, and with courage, commitment, and mass action—thoughtful action—the people can change this world. This campaign will go down in the history of San Francisco and of our nation as a flash of lighting, a glimpse of what will come in time.

I hugged a lot of people, especially Matt, and went home very late, my mind tormented by what I had witnessed.

Epilogue

A few days after the election Matt called and said, "Come have dinner with me." I met him near his place and we went out to talk about what would happen now. He came right to the point. "I'm not going to run again for the board of supervisors." I wasn't expecting that at all. My reaction was, "Why?"

Matt pointed out that he was now so popular that he represented a threat. The media, the union leaders, all the major institutional structures

---

* See Appendix 2 for the transcript.

were ready to try to destroy his popularity and high standing with the people, which they were already starting to do by monitoring every piece of legislation he worked on and keeping tabs on the meetings he was holding in city hall. As one example, Matt had called a meeting of taxi cab companies and drivers to discuss the taxi industry. The next day Newsom announced he was assembling a "blue-ribbon commission" to investigate taxi matters. It came as a total surprise to the people Matt was meeting with and it was obviously rushed to undermine his efforts. The "blue-ribbon commission" never met.

His establishment opponents would do it slowly. The *Chronicle* would start to criticize this and that, the TV stations would run little snippets of negative news on him, and so forth. But if he were to step down, after a first ripple of surprise they couldn't touch his popularity. When the right moment came we could move on what we had built.

Slowly I began to understand. Matt Gonzalez is one of the most intelligent people I have ever met. Even now, some five years later, when Matt walks down the street in San Francisco, people wave at him and thank him. Matt's standing is still there; he was right. But the moment has not yet come. For a time reporters would call me to ask if I knew what Matt's next move was. All I can say is, he will win.

CHAPTER 19

THE 2004 PRESIDENTIAL ELECTIONS AND THE GREAT CAPITULATION

In 2004 I ran for vice president with Ralph Nader. It made me, I believe, the first person in American history to run for president and later for vice president. Each campaign also gave me the distinction of being the first Latino to run for either office.

To describe what happened in 2004 is difficult and devoid of the ease and joy with which I have written about the explosive antiwar movement of the 1970s or Matt Gonzalez's wonderful campaign in 2003. This chapter is the story of Ralph Nader's courage in the face of violent abuse and the utter capitulation of people who are considered, and who consider themselves, to be progressives.

Many progressives launched a fight to prevent Nader from even running for office. They were the "liberal" cover for a criminal campaign by the Democratic Party to disrupt and undermine Nader's right to run and people's right to vote for him. These progressives were complicit in the Democrats' criminal activity, in part because they openly supported it or kept their mouths shut when they heard about the relentless harassment.

Today, four years after these events, twelve leading Democrats in Pennsylvania, elected officials and their staffs, have been charged with felonies for their party's criminal activity in 2004. Evidence has revealed that Democrats in the Pennsylvania House of Representatives used several million dollars of state funds to pay hundreds of people to harass the 2004 Nader campaign and a Green Party campaign two years later. Those who did the best job of trying to prevent Nader from being on the ballot not only had their salaries paid to do this illegal work, but were also given bonuses from state funds.

The July 15, 2008, *Philadelphia Inquirer* reported that a grand jury found "a 'massive' effort by House Democrats to oust the independent presidential candidate Ralph Nader from the ballot in 2004." The account continued:

> The grand jury report, released by Attorney General Tom Corbett last week, alleges that former House Minority Whip Michael Veon of Beaver County ran a statewide political operation out of his Capitol and district offices involving hundreds of legislative workers on the House Democrats' payroll.
>
> One of the House Democrats' most visible targets was Nader, who in 2004 was seeking to challenge Democrat John Kerry as well as President Bush. As many as 50 Pennsylvania House staff members worked on a challenge to Nader's ballot petition, and more than half received state-funded bonuses, in part for their 'Nader efforts,' according to the report.*

The Democrats claim these scores of paid agents were merely checking the validity of the tens of thousands of signatures on Nader's petitions for ballot status. To the contrary, I suspect the Democrats sent agents into the Nader campaign, stole petitions, and put fake names on them. These were then submitted to state election functionaries, who were in on the conspiracy yet acted shocked to discover the falsified signatures.

Four Democrats subsequently appeared as "citizens" to bring personal charges against Nader in regard to the disputed petitions. The Common- wealth Court ruled for the Democrats, and the Democratic Party–controlled Pennsylvania State Supreme Court upheld the ruling that we had engaged in criminal activity. Nader and I were fined more than $80,000. Our crime was that we tried to get on the ballot in Pennsylvania. This was the first time in American history that candidates were personally fined for attempting to get on the ballot. That this ruling was upheld in court could have a major chilling effect on independents running for office.

---

* Amy Worden, "National Tie to Pa. Bonus Scandal," *Philadelphia Inquirer*, July 15, 2008.

THE 2004 PRESIDENTIAL ELECTIONS AND THE GREAT CAPITULATION 265

Of course, Nader and I preferred to refuse to pay the fines, since to us it was clear this was all part of the Democrats' criminal activity. Unfortunately for me what then would happen was that the Democrats handed the fines over to collectors, who would then put a lien on my home. So if someone did an Internet search of my name, they would discover that there was a lien on my home because the Supreme Court of the State of Pennsylvania had found me guilty of criminal activity. Such a possibility presented a direct threat to my livelihood, which centered on the trust people put in me to manage their money.

This harassment campaign reached the point that I had to pay the Democrats $20,000 through John Kerry's law firm so a lien would not be put on my home. Matt Gonzalez's law firm handled the negotiations in order to curtail the risk this presented for me. Nader has stood his ground and refused to pay them a penny. The Democrats took actions to freeze some of his bank accounts. With the 2008 felony indictments of the Pennsylvania House Democrats, we are now very hopeful that at least some of these people will go to jail for their crimes, the legal action against Nader will be overturned, and I will recover the $20,000 stolen from me.

The Great Capitulation

I want to explain what I mean by "great capitulation" and very carefully lay out the politics involved, since I will name names and tell the full truth of what was perpetrated by people who are self-proclaimed progressives and who claim to support democracy and free elections. The campaign to silence Ralph Nader was, in its essence, an effort to win an election by preventing people from voting for their candidate of choice and, in turn, manipulating people to vote for the pro-war candidate favored by the Democrats, John Kerry. The antidemocracy operation began with a massive political attack on Nader by progressives, which was heavily publicized by the corporate media.

These "progressives"—Michael Moore, for example—were given major TV exposure to attack Nader, to call him crazy and other slights. Often the corporate media featured these individuals describing how they had once supported Nader or once respected him, with the intent of lending more credibility to their subsequent attack on him for daring to run against the two-party system. There proved to be no lack of willing accomplices. The Democrats' campaign against free elections involved the

Nation,* the *Progressive*, MoveOn.org, Medea Benjamin, Noam Chomsky, Ben Cohen, Norman Solomon, Howard Zinn, and thousands of others.

MoveOn.org was originally a brilliant idea, touted as a Web-based forum for progressive independents to combine their efforts in order to try to affect policy. Their effective e-mail fundraising campaigns enabled them to run advertisements that aired positions not usually heard in the pro-corporate media. But slowly MoveOn.org evolved into an organ of the Democratic Party. Today this is openly recognized. They are no longer really independent. They play a role in boosting the Democrats, defending them as the answer to our problems, and thus reinforcing corporate control through the two-party system.

With the progressives as their front-line soldiers the Democrats then launched a multimillion-dollar onslaught of disruption against Nader. They brought more than twenty frivolous lawsuits simultaneously against the Nader campaign to tie us up in litigation we could not afford. The Democrats spent millions upon millions of dollars to do this. It never could have taken place without the approval of the top leadership of the Democratic Party and of Kerry himself.

Lawyers went to the homes of Nader campaign supporters and made false threats of possible arrests for backing Nader. They harassed petitioners, threatening them with legal actions. In Ohio they forced Nader volunteers to go to city hall to prove where they lived. The Democrats organized people to interfere with Nader meetings, sent agents into the campaign to disrupt, stole petitions, and tried in every way possible—including clearly criminal actions—to deny American citizens the right to vote for the candidate they wanted.

Criminals in Oregon

In one of the most brazen interventions the Democrats organized their operatives to pose as Nader supporters in order to sabotage a Nader nominating conference in Oregon. Under Oregon law to obtain ballot status a

---

* I find it interesting that the *Nation* magazine, published since 1865, participated in another mass capitulation of an even greater degree and importance. Almost 140 years earlier the *Nation* led the efforts to turn former abolitionists against African Americans. The *Nation* carried out a relentless, racist campaign—aimed at progressives—to support crushing Reconstruction in the South and instituting the Jim Crow system. See Peter Camejo, *Racism, Revolution, Reaction, 1861–1877: The Rise and Fall of Radical Reconstruction* (New York: Pathfinder Press, 1976).

candidate was required to hold a gathering at which one thousand registered voters signed petitions for the candidate. The Democratic infiltrators came early and packed the hall, which had a limited capacity. The rest of the turnout couldn't fit so Nader's staff told the later arrivals, "Thank you but we have enough people to qualify." While the petitions for Nader were being circulated the Nader volunteers suddenly realized the room was full of Democrats, who not only refused to sign but also put on a show of how proud they were to have obstructed the right of Americans to vote for their preferred candidate. Some even lifted their shirts so to display their "Kerry" T-shirts beneath. These acts, while not involving violence, nonetheless befit a fascist mentality that enjoys crushing other people's rights.

Scandals such as this were reported by Nader supporters on the Internet and at public meetings across the country. Not one of the so-called progressives protested the actions of the Democratic campaign of disruption. Instead they intensified their efforts against Nader and stepped up their ads urging people to vote for Kerry and the Democrats, the very people carrying out these totalitarian attacks, who continued to vote for everything Bush asked them to—supporting the war in Iraq, the Patriot Act, and so on.

During this whole sorry business not a single elected Democrat protested the party's criminal activity or spoke out in any way to defend the voting rights of the American people. What an historical condemnation of the Democratic Party and what it stands for. Consider all the Democrats who posture as progressives, alleged advocates of the Bill of Rights, such as Barbara Boxer or Dennis Kucinich. When they were put to the test every last one took a stance against free elections and against the First Amendment to our Constitution.

I should add that just because someone got caught up in this operation doesn't mean everything they have done in their life is without merit. Michael Moore has made some outstanding films both before and after his participation in the campaign against free elections.

Remarkably, Nader treated all these people during the attacks and since with great respect. He never responded in kind. Personally, I think the truth has to be stated, these people should be named, and the full meaning of their capitulation to the rule of money should be spelled out as a political reflection of opposition to free elections. The antidemocratic operation against Ralph Nader in 2004 in my opinion constituted the capitulation of a generation of older "progressives."

Thus my mentioning Medea Benjamin's participation is to indicate that she is a contradictory person who has engaged in many progressive activities and yet participated in this totalitarian effort. These are not personal attacks. My comments are a political condemnation of people who through their actions became complicit in a pro-corporate antidemocracy campaign.

The Logic of Capitulation

From their standpoint the capitulators followed a logical train of thought to justify their actions. Their position was this: George Bush is a terrible president, a criminal who is causing people to be murdered, who has no respect for the rule of law, and must be removed. In their view voting for Kerry was the only way to remove Bush. Therefore, they argued, everyone who disagreed with Bush should join with them in supporting Kerry. They then drew the illogical conclusion that no one could disagree with them and not, in fact, be an agent of Bush. This was the tone and approach of their campaign.

Certainly people have the right to their opinions no matter how wrong they may be. I have no objection to the *Nation*'s running editorials stating, "Kerry may be for war, oppose democracy, support the Patriot Act, and destroy our environment, but we think you should vote for him for the following reasons." Then they could explain their support of Kerry in terms of the need to remove Bush. This strategy is commonly known as "voting for the lesser of two evils" or "lesser-evil voting."

Lesser-Evil Voting

Let me reiterate that people have every right to support any candidate they want for whatever reason. However, in my opinion the arguments for lesser-evil voting are utterly wrong even though it represents a very large current among progressives and liberals. It actually has the opposite impact of what they think it has. Lesser-evil voting (and its relative, lesser-evil promotion) shifts all politics to the right. The anti-Nader campaign actually served to strengthen Bush.

Behind the lesser-evil strategy lies a complete misunderstanding of the nature of our electoral system and how the two parties reinforce the rule of money over people. American elections are heavily influenced by the completely corporate-controlled media, which not only determines who can get each corporate party's nomination, but also reacts to the needs of the rich. Candidates of the two parties tend to modify their views and policies as they feel the pressure and control of money. If they step out of line, the media can isolate them in short order.

Often money wants the most conservative candidate to win so its policies have the authority of having been "elected." But if masses of people are in the streets protesting government policies and the stability of the nation is in question, such as during the Vietnam antiwar movement, the media will consider giving the "liberal"—the one speaking as though sensitive to the feelings of protest—better exposure in order to demobilize any independent force of the people.

It is in that context that money needs the Democrats, especially "progressive" Democrats, to contain struggles and set the framework to get the Republicans elected and press their platform forward while the people think it was their own decision. The role the Democrats always played during the Vietnam War era was to ask that all demonstrations stop while elections were held. Such a policy makes it easier to get the Republicans elected. In 2004 the liberals leading the antiwar movement called off all demonstrations except one, which was held at the Republican national convention and ended with no rally or speeches. I think one of the things they feared was that a speaker might point out that the organizers were supporting the pro-war candidate Kerry, who had called for more troops to be sent to Iraq.

Kerry's campaign was a model of how to support the right as the "opponent." In the debates he basically agreed with all of Bush's policies but said he could do them better. Even Kerry's murder of a young Vietnamese patriot during the war in Vietnam was touted as a reason for people to vote for him as a "war hero." Such propaganda by the Democrats simply reinforced the reactionary positions of the pro-war, pro-corporate forces. This approach completely undermined the mass feelings of opposition to Bush and made it more feasible for the power of money to promote retaining Bush as president.

Lesser-evil voting does not lead to a lesser-evil result. It leads to a greater evil because it undermines people's understanding of our electoral system, it weakens opposition, and helps the Democrats carry out the very policies the lesser-evil voter is supposedly trying to oppose.

The Bush Myth

The lesser-evil current and American liberals in general lack an understanding of how the power of money actually rules the country. George

Bush's open violations of the law, attacks on the Bill of Rights, and illegal wars were all policies promoted and defended by the media and the power of money. If Bush had gotten out of hand or taken positions clearly hurting the interest of money he could have been crushed by the media in thirty days. If the media were to make such a turn the Democrats would have suddenly started talking differently about Bush and sought to impeach him. This system works via a very flexible self-correcting mechanism whose electoral laws are written to keep everything under control and prevent the rise of a Nader or any voice representing the people.

The Campaign Against Nader

Lesser-evil politics may have the opposite impact its promoters expect, but it still falls under the definition of opinion. The attacks on Nader, the campaign to prevent his being heard and getting on the ballot, and the promotion of falsehoods about his views were something of a different nature.

I am not exaggerating when I say the Democrats wanted Kerry to win through a lie. When they met for the Democratic national convention in Boston I was in the city trying to hold a press conference against the policies of war. I saw firsthand how they operated. Democrats had rented every hotel within a certain radius of the convention and hotels had to ask their approval if any room were to be rented out for a press conference. We were forced to move far from the convention to be able to hold a media event critical of their pro-war policies.

The newspapers had reported a poll indicating that 95 percent of the Democratic delegates opposed John Kerry's position on the Iraq war. Yet these same people gave Kerry standing ovations as he presented his pro-war policies. Consider the level of moral corruption of those delegates, who pretended to care about the interest of the people. They were prepared to do whatever they were told to secure this small participation in power and the money that came their way. Inside the convention if anyone dared to hold up a sign calling for peace—what most rank-and-file members of the Democrats favored—they had their signs torn out of their hands.

Dennis Kucinich

Dennis Kucinich, the so-called progressive who had campaigned during the primaries as being antiwar and against the Patriot Act, was told to shut up and to tell his supporters to shut up, which he did. He was told to declare for Kerry and I assume he, too, was there at the convention giving a standing ovation for war when ordered to do so. After the election these "progressives," led by Kucinich, formed the Progressive Democrats of America (PDA), which works to keep progressively inclined Americans contained within the two parties of war while the organization presents itself as being for peace.

Kucinich had asked during the primary to use Nader's campaign list to raise money. Ralph had given his okay, since Kucinich was talking against the war and taking other progressive stands. After the primaries Nader asked for Kucinich's list. Kucinich not only said "no," but also proceeded to lead the Democrats' attack on Nader and said that he would campaign against Nader while supporting pro-war Kerry.

Earlier in the campaign I had talked to Kucinich for about an hour in California while sharing a car ride with him from one meeting to the next. I told him that the meaning of his campaign would be determined by what he did after the primaries. I don't think he had any idea what I meant.

I also asked him if he would remove a section from a campaign video in which he called on all Greens to go back to the Democratic Party. He agreed to do so. The person driving the car later became Kucinich's campaign manager and many months later, after he had left the campaign, called to tell me that when the issue of removing that part of the video had come up, Kucinich had argued with his staff to keep it. One thing Kucinich understood is that you do as you're told in the Democratic Party otherwise they will organize to remove you from Congress or take away any other privileges you might have.

Battle Within the Green Party

The antidemocratic campaign against Nader was also reflected inside the Green Party. Led by David Cobb,* who announced early on that he was seeking the Green Party's nomination for president, some Greens began an anti-Nader campaign. A group of well-known Greens signed a statement that advocated lesser-evil voting as the right thing to do, that is, voting for Kerry. These leaders rallied to Cobb's campaign against Nader.

As of late 2003 it was still unclear if Nader were going to run again. Forrest Hill—a leading California Green, head of the coordinating committee—

---

* Cobb had served as general counsel for the Green Party and ran for Texas attorney general in 2002.

set up a website that asked people to urge me to run for president. I had told Forrest I would not run against Nader and, beyond that, I had no intention of running for president at all. Ralph and I spoke a few times about what was happening; I assured him I was not behind the website and that if he ran he would have my full support.

Nader was already on the Green Party's primary ballot in California but withdrew his name at the last minute because he was considering running as an independent. It dawned on me that without Nader on the ballot David Cobb might win the California primary by default, and California Greens—numbering around 150,000—represented close to 50 percent of all Greens nationwide. That could put Cobb in a position to represent the Greens on a national level.

I rushed to get my name on the ballot as a "favorite son," planning to turn my delegates over to Nader when the time came. The secretary of state, Kevin Shelly, was a great help and called me to say "Okay, Peter, I got you on by a minute." Once I was on the ballot for primary I entered the one Green Party debate in California. Months before Cobb had said at a meeting of Greens that if I entered the race he would withdraw. Now he had to debate me and no longer offered to drop out.

In front of about a hundred Greens I debated Cobb in Los Angeles. During the exchange Cobb made it clear that he believed the United States should continue to occupy Iraq for about two more years. What disturbed me more than Cobb's declaration in support of U.S. imperialism was the lack of shock or outrage by the Greens present. Cobb's position was one no Green candidate had ever taken. The lack of reaction worried me as an indication of how far the rightward shift in the Green Party had manifested itself. When it was my turn to speak I said I opposed the U.S. occupation of Iraq and favored an immediate withdrawal; moreover, I added that Cobb's pro-war position completely changed the focus of the internal debate in the Green Party.

On June 23, 2004, the first day of the Green Party national convention, I debated Cobb again, this time on *Democracy Now!*, the national public radio show. I made it clear I was for immediate withdrawal from Iraq. Cobb responded, "We can't just cut and run and leave the mess for the Iraqi people to deal with. We have a responsibility in figuring how to work with the Iraqi people ..." This sort of rationale, of course, is what is referred to as "the white man's burden." The United States or Europeans invade and occupy third world countries and are then obligated to stay on indefinitely as a ruling power, given that third world people can't take care of themselves.

How I Became the Vice-Presidential Candidate

I had assumed Nader would choose a woman for vice president as he had with Winona La Duke in 2000. The notion that I might be asked to run with Nader didn't cross my mind until the Green Party national convention was drawing near. Some Greens had asked Ralph to name me as his running mate. When this happened I told Ralph that I would prefer not to run, but given the hate campaign against him it was imperative that he have a vice-presidential candidate able to withstand the pressure. His previous running mate, La Duke, had already capitulated and endorsed John Kerry. In another discussion Ralph asked if I would accept if he offered me the second spot on the ticket. I told him I had one condition: I wanted his assurance that no matter what happened we would run to the very end. Ralph laughed a little and said, "Yes, you have my word."

The official call came while I was up in Seattle speaking at Green Party meetings where the capitulation to Kerry was pretty advanced. I am not certain of the date but I do remember the hour, because I couldn't believe Ralph would call me at 2:00 a.m. his time. On or around June 10 I got a conference call from Ralph and his staff at 11:00 p.m. while I was in a car with two hard-working Nader supporters. The staff asked me a long series of questions; finally Ralph just said, okay, we want you to run for vice president. The announcement was set for June 21 in Washington, D.C., only two days before the national Green Party convention in Milwaukee. The media turnout for the VP announcement was quite large, although they covered very little of what I said, focusing more on the fact that Nader had picked a Latino who was bilingual and a leader of the Green Party.

The Green Party Convention

The national Green Party nominating convention was held in Milwaukee June 23–28, 2004. Running as an independent, Nader sought the formal endorsement of the Green Party. By that time most of us thought Nader couldn't lose, having won three of the five primaries and enough state convention delegates without even campaigning. The key state, California, had gone overwhelmingly for pro-Nader candidates. The vote was 75.9 percent

(33,753) for Peter Miguel Camejo, 11.5 percent (5,086) for David Cobb, 10.6 percent (4,759) for another pro-Nader supporter, Lorna Salzman, and 2 percent (913) for an independent Green, Kent Mesplay. In New Mexico, Carol Miller, a Nader supporter, had won the primary. In all primary states except Rhode Island, where fewer than two hundred Greens even voted, Cobb had not received a majority of the votes.

From a one-person, one-vote perspective, the California vote alone should have settled the issue. Cobb had campaigned throughout California and got the endorsement in San Francisco of the *Bay Guardian*, a pro–Democratic Party alternative paper. I hadn't campaigned at all. The total landslide vote against Cobb reflected the will of the Greens' rank and file. State by state, mostly through nominating conventions but in a few states through primaries, Nader was doing fine without any campaign. Cobb had tried to attend all the state conventions, spreading his anti-Nader point of view. But as each state reported its votes it was clear that Nader should win the formal endorsement he was seeking.

Gradually news started reaching us that the right current in the Green Party was looking to alter the results by stacking the national convention. I tried to talk to David Cobb to come to an agreement. If his supporters were to succeed in overriding the membership's vote, the bad blood would be toxic. I offered Cobb a major concession. Both groups would support a joint endorsement by the convention and leave it to each state to choose which candidate they wanted on the ballot. We would run as two different factions within the Green Party and try to keep the hostility down so it would appear to be more of a friendly debate within the currents of the Green Party.

Cobb refused to meet with me. I think his people were confident that with artful manipulation they could carry the vote. For instance, the Maine nominating caucus had voted 33 percent for Nader and 26 percent for Cobb, with the remainder split in smaller percentages among several other candidates. When the Maine delegation arrived at the convention, however, the right had packed it so there were no delegates for Nader and 18 out of 19 went for Cobb.

The key ended up being the California delegation. The enormous lead Nader had among the party ranks made it impossible for Cobb to win at the convention unless he could alter his 9 to 1 defeat in California. If the system were one-person, one-vote there would have been no issue; Nader would have been nominated as the choice of the membership. But the Green

Party followed a whole set of undemocratic, bureaucratic rules that served to weaken the impact of large states and gave huge power ratios to small states with next to no members. The Cobb people had created party units in these borderline states. Iowa, in particular, had so few members that the state's Green Party had dissolved in 2002, yet there were nine Iowa delegates at the 2004 convention. Even with this maneuvering, if the California delegates voted with respect to how the membership had voted—or even according to their own declared preferences—we couldn't lose.

Unfortunately, according to Green Party rules, the only requirement for being a delegate was being able to attend the convention. The pro-Nader people had not demanded the right to appoint our individual delegates so that we could count on their actually voting for us. At a California state meeting of counties the pro-Cobb/Kerry people, especially out of San Francisco, had declared they were Camejo supporters and wanted to be counted as part of our delegation. They had already secretly agreed to oppose Nader and support Cobb. I believe, as events will show, Medea Benjamin was in on this effort to throw the membership's vote away and deliver the Greens to the Democrats.

As the second round of voting* started I noticed that California delegates pledged to me were voting for Cobb. I said to Medea, "Do you see what is happening?"—thinking that perhaps, regardless of our differences, she respected democracy. She smiled and said, "Maybe they changed their minds." I watched as states like Maine, in complete violation of its membership's vote, went for Cobb almost 100 percent and all the delegates from borderline states with next to no membership also voted for Cobb.

In the second round of voting, if the delegates' votes had reflected the will of the membership, the figures would have been as follows: 62.4 percent for Nader,† 24.1 percent for Cobb, 10.8 percent for uncommitted, and 2.9 percent for other. To take Cobb from 24.1 percent—his preconvention support among the national Green membership, after campaigning with no organized opposition—to over 50 percent required a massive manipulation.‡

---

* According to Green Party rules, multiple rounds of voting were conducted until one candidate had attained a majority.

† Because Nader was asking for an endorsement, not a nomination, the vote for Nader took the form of "no nominee" and if that category won the party would proceed to endorsements.

‡ Howie Hawkins, ed., *Independent Politics: The Green Party Strategy Debate* (Chicago: Haymarket Books, 2006), 286. This book provides a detailed study of how the convention was stolen. Percentages were provided by Forrest Hill. See also Forrest Hill and Carol Miller, "Rigged Convention," available at http://www.greens.org/s-r/38/38-13.html.

When it came to California the exact number of votes needed by Cobb—twenty-two—shifted from my delegation and voted for Cobb in the second round of voting. I was stunned by this brazen act, utterly disrespectful to the membership. Medea Benjamin was overjoyed. Cobb would have the Green Party's nomination and her Democratic Party friends and donors would doubtless thank her for having helped deliver the Green Party to their pro-war candidate.

Several hundred delegates were in a state of fury that could hardly be contained. The Green Party had just capitulated through an openly undemocratic party maneuver to rob the membership—who clearly wanted Nader—of its choice. We immediately called a caucus. It was agreed that our current would take the majority of Green activists to support Nader and let the rest of them run their pro-Kerry campaign. And so it transpired that Greens everywhere went to work for Nader while a miniscule number backed the sham Cobb campaign.

We called an opening rally for the Nader/Camejo campaign in San Francisco. At a packed meeting of about a thousand people I gave a speech hard as nails against Kerry and received a standing ovation. Ralph followed with an outline of the major issues and reinforced our opposition to war and corporate domination. He also received an overwhelming standing ovation. Later David Cobb held his first campaign rally in the Bay Area. From the convention vote, one would have thought Cobb was backed by the majority of the Bay Area Greens. The turnout for his first rally was twenty-eight people, and some of those were from our campaign who had gone over to take notes. Cobb represented only a tiny layer of pro-Kerry Greens. Once he had been nominated the Democrats thanked him and forgot him.

At the end of the campaign Cobb went to the national convention of the Progressive Democrats of America (PDA), where they gave him a standing ovation. He and Medea Benjamin joined the Democrats at that conference through the PDA and become spokespeople for that pro-Democratic Party organization. They both kept their voter registration in the now housebroken Green Party.

The Congressional Black Caucus

One of the first events I participated in with Ralph was a meeting with the Congressional Black Caucus. It was as if they had requested the meeting just to yell at him. One after another they got up to denounce Nader. It was interesting to watch. Not one person who spoke was aware that by being in a party that supported a pro-war, pro–Patriot Act, pro-corporate candidate they were in fact supporting Bush and his politics. They had conveniently forgotten how, after many African Americans were denied the right to vote in Florida in 2000,* not one Democratic Party senator— not Barbara Boxer, John Kerry, or any other liberal Democrat—had supported them.

One of the caucus members stood up and said that the Democrats had sacrificed the South to oppose racism. Another said, "Anything within the Democratic Party, nothing outside." Finally I asked Ralph's permission to say something. I mentioned that 38 percent of the American people state that they support neither of the two major parties, and that it should not come as a surprise that people run for office who are not Democrats or Republicans. Then I started to say, "You are supporting a candidate that is pro-war, pro–Patriot Act, pro-corporate—" but I could not continue. The congresspeople in the room started screaming, actually screaming, with such hostility they couldn't hear anything, certainly not the truth.

Ralph Nader had always defended full rights for African Americans yet those present from the Congressional Black Caucus showed him nothing but utter disrespect. Nader remained kind and polite throughout. As we walked out I told some of the people with us from the Nader campaign, "The Democrats are dead. There is no hope for this party." One exception was Barbara Lee, the congresswoman from Oakland, who said nothing during the exchange and came up afterward to shake my hand and show some courtesy. There may have been others who were embarrassed by the spectacle of hate. Later Ralph received a message of apology from Congressman Jesse Jackson, Jr., Jesse Jackson's son, who had not been in attendance.

Campaigning as the VP

We set up a campaign office in Oakland where my schedule would be coordinated and hired three full-time people, Forrest Hill, Rachel Odes, and Todd Chretien. Rachel Odes was a Berkeley student whom I had gotten to know from antiwar struggles on campus. She had worked for me in my of-

---

* Fifty-four percent of all the rejected ballots in the state had been cast by African Americans, who were only 11 percent of the electorate.

fice and transferred over to work on the campaign. Rachel was also a member of the International Socialist Organization (ISO). Todd Chretien had led Nader's campus campaign work in California in 2000 and was the central organizer of the ISO in California.

I had first learned of the ISO when Todd approached me during the final phase of the 2003 recall campaign. I had assumed the ISO was just another sectarian group, but Todd was calm and supportive. I was very impressed with the base they had built on campuses and the commitment level of their student activists. Even though the ISO and I had some differences of opinion we shared many fundamental areas of agreement and quickly started working together. The other socialist group supporting Nader was Solidarity. Their members in the Bay Area all supported Nader, but some in Los Angeles favored voting for Kerry. We worked with Solidarity in many cities, especially in Oakland and Detroit.

I began to get extensive media coverage, doing radio interviews just about every day and newspaper and TV interviews as well. I spoke at campaign meetings starting in California and later extending across the nation. Forrest Hill traveled with me on these national speaking tours. On the East Coast ISO supporters played a major role in organizing many of the meetings and the Greens also helped build them. I remember two in particular, in Albany, New York, and Burlington, Vermont, that made lasting impressions on me.

I was struck by the intensity of the young audiences on campus. They had seen the endless anti-Nader TV ads and read the newspaper op-eds by the endless lists of older people telling them to vote for war, to vote against democracy, to vote for the Patriot Act, and so on. But when I showed up they wanted to hear the other side. It was amazing to see in their eyes that they understood what older people could not. Sometimes at the end of the day I got teary thinking, maybe today I helped some young person to understand why they must not capitulate to the power of money, the two-party system, and all the corruption around them. And perhaps twenty years from now that person will be helping to lead a massive struggle of our people for democracy.

The Myth of Republican Money

In early July 2004 Carla Marinucci from the *San Francisco Chronicle* asked to interview me. I had considered her a friend, but on this particular occasion what she did was quite insidious. She asked me if I would accept money from the Republicans. As I understood the question at the time I thought she meant an organized move by the Republicans to finance a progressive current with the intent of altering the electoral results. I told her no, I would not. I also related the story from 2002, when I was offered money during my campaign for governor. She was very interested in learning more. I told her everything she needed to know, but remained firm that I was not going to reveal the "messenger" and have her and others beat up on him in the press. I had no idea what Carla was up to and she didn't tell me.

The reporting staff had found that a few Republicans had donated money to the Nader campaign and they planned to use this information to tarnish Nader, claiming he was financed by Republican money. The article ran on the front page of the *Chronicle*. The story was then picked up and promoted not only by other newspapers but by the "liberals" on the warpath against free elections. It was completely inaccurate.

Republicans, especially those who run corporations, donate money to both corporate parties. John Kerry received millions upon millions of dollars from Republicans. That fact was not reported. But a few Republicans had donated to Nader's campaign and the press thought they were on to something big.

As it turned out some Republicans voted for Nader in 2000 and 2004 and some have been contributors to him throughout his career. Certainly at some time or other a Republican might have sent money to Nader in the hope that it would help Bush. There was no way to be sure since party affiliation is not listed on donations. But we saw no patterns. Donation lists can be compared to those from previous campaigns and we could see that the bulk of our money, most of it in small amounts, had come from working people, primarily from people registered independent or Democrat. The *Chronicle*, of course, did not point out that for every dollar a Republican may have donated to Nader $100 had been donated by Democrats. Such facts were not allowed to interfere with a political objective disconnected from the truth.

I immediately went public with a simple proposal: if Kerry returned the multiple millions of dollars he had received from Republicans, we would return the few thousand we had received. My proposal did not get one percent of the coverage the misrepresentation by the *San Francisco Chronicle* got. It should go without saying that Kerry never returned a penny from

Republicans. The whole affair was utter hypocrisy, smoke and mirrors generated by people looking to fight Nader on anything but the issues.

Campaign Snapshots

Just for one day, but repeating about every ten minutes, CNN ran a clip of me, making a statement along these lines: "The Democrats love Bush. They gave him thirty standing ovations in one hour at the State of the Union address." I was waiting to catch a flight when I noticed the clip. That made my day, seeing the truth on TV for a moment.

In September Ralph and I attended the annual national gathering of Muslims in Chicago, an event drawing tens of thousands of people. Once again my friend Agha Saeed played a major role in getting both of us invited. Also included in the invitation was Jo Chamberlain, a national co-chair of the Green Party and Nader supporter, who coordinated the Green Party's relationship with the Muslim community in the Bay Area.

While campaigning in California I invited Marsha Feinland, the senatorial candidate of the Peace and Freedom Party, to join me. The Greens had not run a senate campaign against Democrat Barbara Boxer, who voted repeatedly for war and voted for the Patriot Act, so Marsha accompanied me and we spoke jointly at events.

Matt Gonzalez had me over for dinner with Sean Penn, Peter Coyote, Tim Redman, editor of the *Bay Guardian,* Todd Chretien, and a few others. The purpose of the meeting was that Sean Penn wanted to plead with me to stop our campaign. In the short time we spent talking about an issue on which we disagreed, I developed a good impression of Sean. Being as famous as he is one would think he would reflect some of that when meeting with people. The opposite was the case. I left that meeting with great admiration for him. He was one of the first people I met who opposed our running yet discussed the issue with real respect and no hostility. I had previously met Peter Coyote, whom I also respect. We all sat around and had dinner, mostly cracking jokes.

The 2004 campaign with Ralph ended in San Francisco where it had started. The Nader vote was about 500,000, a sharp drop from the 2000 figure. Taking into account our exclusion from the ballot for about half the U.S. population, due to the efforts of the Democrats and their "progressive" friends, one could estimate that about one million citizens stood against the campaign of lies to vote for peace, social justice, and democracy. I consider that vote quite good, given the extent and viciousness of the Democrats' efforts to undermine Nader.

When the campaign ended I felt really good that I had the chance in my life to be part of something akin to defending the Liberty Party in 1840, when only a few thousand people had voted against slavery. For a brief moment in time I had the opportunity to tell the truth to young people. I had stood with Ralph Nader to oppose the hypocrisy and capitulation of so many, even many of my old friends.

Postscript

During the campaign I noticed that I quickly became very tired. For instance, when Ralph was in California we were scheduled to do five meetings in one day. I told the staff I would do only three because otherwise I would become too tired. Sometimes while walking with Morella I suddenly needed to hold on to her, as I felt a little faint. At the time I had no idea what was wrong. Morella and I both thought it was exhaustion from the never-ending campaigning, which had been almost continuous for three years.

As I would learn two years later, there was something wrong with my heart. It was not beating correctly and that made me feel dizzy. In 2006 I also had a stroke. That was the year in which I ran my last campaign, once again for governor of California. I kept the information about my heart and the stroke private until the campaign ended. A month later I was diagnosed with cancer, lymphoma. The doctors told me I had had it for the previous six months.

CHAPTER 20

2006 DEMONSTRATIONS
AND ELECTIONS

In December 2005 the U.S. House of Representatives passed the draconian Border Protection, Antiterrorism, and Illegal Immigration Control Act of 2005 (H.R. 4437), aimed at undocumented workers. Among dozens of extreme and punitive provisions, the bill made it a crime to assist or provide services to undocumented workers, denied them due process, and called for seven hundred miles of border fence. Grass-roots committees cutting across all existing Latino NGOs began organizing outraged protests around the country.

The calls for action were able to develop mass support due to a loophole in the corporate control of the media. Spanish-language radio, with its many commentaries and hosted shows, traditionally had some room to express the views of the Spanish-speaking community. Once demonstrations had been called on this wide-ranging issue the Spanish radio stations began not only to inform the public, but also to endorse taking action. Local ad hoc committees of activists came together and took the initiative. Suddenly the largest demonstrations the United States had ever seen were taking place.

I went to Los Angeles on Saturday, March 25, 2006, to take part in the march and rally. The turnout was estimated by the *Los Angeles Times* to be five hundred thousand and by the organizers to be around a million. It was our community—families with children in strollers, people of all ages, very young and elderly, documented and undocumented workers together, Salvadorans, Mexicans, Chicanos, Colombians. On the East Coast huge numbers of Puerto Ricans, Dominicans, and others came pouring into the streets.

During the L.A. march I became concerned that we had no monitors. The demonstration was much larger than had been expected and the streets were completely jammed. As the crowd approached the rally point there was the potential for real danger if anything were to happen and people needed to move quickly. I climbed up to the stage. to see if anything could be done to protect the participants. As the organizers were not equipped to address the issue, we all were praying nothing serious would occur. Fortunately there were no incidents.

This immense expression of working-class protest was absolutely amazing. In almost every major U.S. city a new coalition appeared to lead the protests. Equally remarkable was the silence from the union leadership and so-called progressive Democrats.

The original wave of protests in many cities led to a call for nationwide mass marches on May 1. As might be expected competing proposals began to emerge but the May 1 call started to catch on and build momentum, in part because it had the support of the L.A. ad hoc committee, including my old friend Nativo Lopez, who had called the March 25 action. In the Bay Area I took the initiative and caucused with organizers of the ISO. We began assembling a coalition to coordinate the local response.

The ISOers really kicked in and did much of the thankless work to make the May 1 action a reality. The Salvadorans immediately came in to help and a Peruvian activist stepped forward to start coordinating media. I called Miguel Araujo, who had just had an eye operation and couldn't even walk unassisted yet, but he came up to San Francisco regardless. Coalition meetings were growing rapidly. We were in close contact with Nativo and the L.A. committee, and with Antonio Gonzalez and his broad network across the Southwest.

Miguel organized several sessions at a church in the southern Bay Area to bring in more Latino groups and individuals. Slowly a coordinating structure developed for the effort, although a lot of people were also working independently. The Spanish radio stations backed us all the way. Leaflets were pouring out. The coordinated effort we were putting into place was beginning to exceed its resources. I became concerned that too many commitments would be made in the name of the coalition and we would never be able to meet the expenses.

Todd Chretien of the ISO handled the negotiations with the city of San Francisco; a very difficult task. He did a fantastic job in getting what we needed at a reasonable price. Miguel, bless his heart, could not be contained. He ordered tens of thousands of additional leaflets. I tried to slow him down but that was impossible. Mariana Wong, vice president of Unite Here! Local 2, the hotel and restaurant workers union, threw the support of her union behind us and we started holding our ever-expanding coalition meetings at their office. Meetings now involved more than a hundred people. As more and more groups and individuals joined the action, organizational life got a bit more complicated. One of the familiar crises arose over who would speak at the event. Tensions developed between groups and individuals, all of whom meant well but some of whom thought they should take charge. All kinds of petty conflicts were happening at the level of work committees, control of posters, and of course the speakers' list. Aside from these typical minor problems we came out fine; there were no major political rifts.

I was desperately trying to ensure we included everyone, gave full respect to all the currents participating, and made it through the mass action without negative incidents. The broader community had no idea who was actually organizing the event. Many recognizable names were involved but no one individual or group wielded overriding influence. What made the whole project possible were the Spanish-language radio stations.

The day of the big event I ran into a group of Green Party leaders from San Francisco who were watching the demonstration but had nothing to do with it. They stopped me to say hello and then stated that they thought the Green Party should have nothing to do with demonstrations of this kind. What a revealing comment—large numbers of left-wing Greens were actually helping to organize and lead the demonstration.

On the actual day in San Francisco my concerns were, first, to avoid a blowup between personalities and groups among the leadership, and second, to try to raise the funds to cover our expenditures. I took charge of setting up collection barrels in which we asked everyone to make a donation. A large group of volunteers, almost all very young, monitored the barrels. A small group of Venezuelans carrying a Venezuelan flag had come down from Sacramento and I grabbed them to help me with the barrels. They were great, shouting slogans and asking everyone to pitch in.

We set up a sound system near the barrels and I got up there for a while urging people to donate. When it was time for me to address the rally I went up to the main podium. The crowd was immense, with enormous, sky-high morale. I planned to raise the issue of Santos Reyes, the undocumented worker who, for taking a driver's license test on his cousin's behalf, was sentenced to twenty-six years to life in prison. A violation on a driver's license application is a misdemeanor, but the prosecutor changed the charge to perjury, making it a felony. Since Santos had two previous felonies, one for stealing a radio as a teenager and the other an alleged robbery attempt in his early twenties, this third felony charge led to a life imprisonment conviction. The jury was unaware of what they had been manipulated to do.

I went to a friend, Richard Abbott, a sign maker in Concord, and asked him to make two huge banners, one for Anthony Soltero, a fourteen-year-old from Ontario, California, who committed suicide when his teachers castigated him for leaving school to join the protests, and the other for Santos Reyes. The workers at the sign-making shop in Concord would not accept pay for the banners as their way of showing solidarity with the effort. We had hung the two banners over the main speakers' platform.

Like most of the speakers I addressed the crowd in Spanish. I went quickly to the issue of Santos Reyes and the injustice being done him. Explaining that only the governor could free him, I asked that everyone who demanded that the governor free Santos raise their hands. The crowd shouted their approval, raising tens of thousands of hands. I continued, "No, not one hand. Let the governor know what this means to us. Raise both hands." The response was a massive roar with everyone's hands reaching in the air.

As this happened I thought to myself that this was the largest protest meeting in the history of the United States to demand the freedom of a political prisoner like Santos; yet, as I feared, not a single TV station or newspaper covered that fact.

At the end of the event with a few volunteers I took the collection money first to the ISO office in the Mission and then across the street to a Latino community bank. We spent hours trying to count it and had to come back the next day. In round figures we collected only about fifteen thousand dollars and had spent twenty-five thousand. I gave this situation some long, hard consideration and decided to make up the difference so no one would be held responsible nor would internal issues flare up among the coalition. So I donated ten thousand dollars to cover the deficit. Later some right-wing radio stations hostile to immigrant rights tried to spread rumors that I had taken money.

After the demonstration we sent a delegation to meet with the *San Francisco Chronicle* to address their failed coverage. The *Chronicle* leadership was very polite; they listened to our concerns and tried to explain some of their difficulties, such as having no independent way to judge the size of the crowd. They also admitted that they didn't have a single Spanish-speaking reporter covering the demonstration.

No one knows the exact numbers but we estimated that a hundred thousand people participated in the May 1 demonstration in San Francisco. In Los Angeles it was again between five hundred thousand and a million. These demonstrations were an enormous show of the power of the Latino community and the largest worker protests in American history.

Rise of the Right among Greens

As the 2006 state elections neared I noticed the continued rightward shift among many Green leaders, reflecting the 2004 capitulation. Mike Feinstein, the Green former mayor of Santa Monica, at a plenary of the state Green Party suddenly announced that he now favored fusion with the Democrats. He had figured a way around the laws to create fusion tickets, he said, and had two Democrats ready to run with dual endorsements as Democrats and Greens. As was generally the case with the right in the Green Party, he had written nothing to explain why he thought this might be a good idea.

I was a bit surprised but relieved to hear Mike call for fusion. It had become increasingly clear to me that, behind a series of undemocratic organizational and administrative moves designed to take over the California Green Party leadership structure, Mike must have had a political objective. Now that he had made it clear just how far to the right he had shifted it would be possible to challenge him without getting his usual response—that people were attacking him personally. If the internal debate could be put on a political level and get off the level of personal attack and rumor it would be a step forward.

It was arranged that I would debate Mike Feinstein on the issue of fusion at a Green Party plenary in Oakland. Matt Gonzalez chaired. Mike presented some of his thoughts as to why fusion would work to build the Green Party. I argued strongly that to follow the logic of his views would be to give up our independence from the two corporate parties. I explained how fusion had destroyed other third-party efforts. At least a hundred or more county delegates were listening to the debate. I kept referring to the antifusion current as representing the majority. One Green yelled out, "Peter, what gives you the right to claim your view against fusion is a majority?" Immediately I asked everyone in the room to take a vote. The result was 80 percent for independence and 20 percent for fusion. Mike looked at me and said, "Well, what if I just drop it?"

I responded that he should not be ashamed of his views but should run against me for governor so we could go around the state and debate this issue before the Green Party membership and let the membership express what they thought. But that was the last thing Mike wanted. He lived in a world of political and personal intrigue and gossip. I was surprised that he had agreed to the debate at all.

The Avocado Declaration

In January 2004, during the lead-up to the 2004 elections, I published the Avocado Declaration, a sociological and political analysis of the two-party system (see Appendix 3). The title referred to being "green on the outside and green on the inside." Howie Hawkins and Todd Chretien, among others, helped edit the document, which quickly became the political statement of the left in the Green Party. The Avocado Declaration was published on the Web and reprinted by Green chapters.

The right current in the party never tired of responding. The only position they took, however, was that lesser-evil voting was the correct choice. They gave no analysis nor did they offer a political, historical, or sociological basis for their views. The level of political discourse within the Green Party leadership unfortunately was weak and tended toward political impressionism (i.e., a fuzzy approximation of reality) and organizational intrigue.

Mike Feinstein's method of operation tended to maximize a cliquish approach to politics that can be found in most organizations. Instead of political discourse and unity based on compromises around differing approaches, his aim was always clique-building in the interest of organizational control. For the right wing in the party this was important because, in many cases, if the issues were to be presented to the membership and put to a vote, the right would lose. Fearing the membership they maneuvered to gain organizational control.

Mike was full of energy and put it toward some outrageous behavior. He secretly initiated attack e-mails, making it appear they were coming from a different sender, which accused Greens of all kinds of things. For some time Mike maintained a relatively successful campaign of innuendo and slander against a few California leaders, such as Jo Chamberlain, Michael Borenstein, and Peggy Lewis, as he worked to get control of the state leadership.

At a bank in Los Angeles Mike had opened a personal account under the title "Green Party." This move was not under the jurisdiction of any elected body. It was his own private bank account. Starting as early as 2000 he then proceeded to deposit checks made out to the Green Party into this personal account. When Nader spoke at a fundraiser in Santa Monica, the people in attendance thought they were making donations to the Green Party, but Mike and a couple of accomplices stole some fifteen thousand to twenty thousand dollars in contributions and deposited the money into Mike's private account.

Eventually this scandal hit the press in Santa Monica, hurting the credibility of the Green Party. The *Santa Monica Daily Press* of February 5, 2003, reported "accusations that [Feinstein] allegedly misappropriated more than $30,000 in campaign contributions to the Green Party," and that he ignored requests to explain why he deposited this money in "a private bank account."[*] The biggest problem, indicative of where the Green Party leadership stood, was that they didn't expel Feinstein and move quickly to recoup the money. Instead the issue was allowed to devolve into charges that anti-Feinstein forces were twisting the facts to hurt him personally. Mike quickly gained support among the more conservative elements, like the San Francisco Greens. Once again the right was able to out-organize the left and, despite being censured by the party, Mike succeeded in getting enough of his supporters on the key state committee that he was exonerated of charges. The money was never returned.

The growing division between left and right, accelerated by the 2004 election disaster, resulted in a decline for the Green Party. Fewer people volunteered to set up tables or participated in activities. Attendance at county council meetings began to drop off. Cat Woods and others led enormous

---

[*] Andy Fixner, "Feinstein Haunted by Party Accusations," *Santa Monica Daily Press*, February 5, 2003.

efforts to reform the national party to establish a one-person, one-vote policy, but these reforms were blocked. The leadership knew that to democratize the Green Party, allowing decisions to be made by the broad membership, would lead to a victory for the left.

The 2006 Campaign

An important development in California was to strengthen the left. The fact that the Green Party voters were shifting toward the working class, people of color, and youth was something many of us wanted to build on. The ISO, which had worked hard for the Nader/Camejo campaign in 2004, had gotten its members to register Green. They were very interested in putting together a principled, statewide slate of candidates for the 2006 elections, and were open to discussing what else to do.

Given the factional atmosphere within the party I put out a call for us to launch a slate of Green candidates with pro-working-class, antiwar positions and with a firm stance of independence from the Democrats. The aim was to try to draw out the right wing of the party to run against us so the Greens' membership could participate in the discussion and voice their opinions. The right, of course, realized that in an open, pro-democratic process their views would be resoundingly defeated.

In Oakland we held a meeting of Green leaders in agreement with the call and put together a slate. In the spirit of the slate and with contributions from several of our candidates I wrote a book, *California Under Corporate Rule.** This was the first book of its kind, written from the vantage point of a state Green Party, posing the major issues facing the state and offering specific solutions.

There was one additional issue we needed to confront. The Peace and Freedom Party (PFP), in existence since 1967, had been threatened with loss of their ballot status. As polls got under way we learned that the Green Party was outpolling the PFP and if the PFP didn't get 2 percent of the vote for one of their state candidates, they could lose their line on the ballot. All of us on the Green Party slate didn't want to damage the PFP so we left one seat on the slate empty, for controller. The PFP leadership discussed this with us at the Green Party state conference and appreciated our efforts to protect

---

* Camejo et al., *California Under Corporate Rule.*

their ballot status. The announcement that the PFPers were there to work with the Greens met with a very positive response from the Green delegates. Polls showed that in the race for U.S. Senate the Democrat, Dianne Feinstein, was so far ahead that there was no spoiler issue. Our Senate candidate, Todd Chretien, hoped that we would muster a large protest vote against war and suggested that we call our slate "One Million Votes for Peace."

Editor's Note

The manuscript breaks off at this point. A few days later Peter Camejo went back to the hospital for the last time. He died on September 13, 2008. Peter left an outline of topics he intended to add to this chapter. From public sources we have added a brief factual summary of the points he listed, though of course we do not know precisely what he meant to say about them. Peter did complete the chapter that follows this one, the intended final chapter in the book.

- The 2006 gubernatorial race pitted incumbent Republican governor Arnold Schwarzenegger against Democratic state treasurer Phil Angelides for the two major parties. During the primary period Peter Camejo helped create a California political action committee called Green IDEA to support Green candidates for party and public office who would work for political independence, internal party democracy, membership empowerment, and accountable leadership. One of its goals was to run candidates for California Green county councils, the local leadership bodies of the Green Party. In particular there was a battle over the Los Angeles County Committee in which Mike Feinstein refused to recognize an election that replaced incumbents loyal to him and his fusion perspective.

- During the statewide election campaign that fall, in an interview in the August 9, 2006, *San Francisco Chronicle*, Peter said, "The Democrats have re-elected Arnold Schwarzenegger. They are handing it to him, and they can't take him on, because they rely on the same special interests ...

There's no vision ... there's no enthusiasm for the Democrats, and [the party] is unable to articulate what people want," Camejo said. So "you're free to vote for me. It's over. Send a message ... for once, progressives, stand up for what you believe in."

- On October 8 the only debate of the campaign was held, at California State University, Sacramento, between Schwarzenegger and Angelides. Peter Camejo was excluded from the exchange. In the last week of the campaign the Green Party aired a radio message in which Peter Camejo declared, "A vote for the Democrat will send no message, but a vote for the Green Party, which opposes war, the Patriot Act ... would be a powerful message to vote for peace."

- In the November 7 election Peter Camejo received 205,995 votes, or 2.3 percent. There were ten minor party candidates. Only one other, the Libertarians, got more than 1 percent; their candidate, Art Olivier, came in at 1.3 percent. Peter polled 5.4 percent in San Francisco County and 6.9 percent in Santa Cruz County.

- On August 2, 2008, in his last public appearance, Peter attended the California Peace and Freedom Party convention, at which he spoke for and won that party's endorsement of Ralph Nader for president. A video of Peter's speech was later widely circulated on YouTube.

CHAPTER 21

THE NORTH STAR

The North Star is one of the greatest symbols for justice stemming from the history of our people. "The North Star" was an expression that meant heading toward freedom as slaves tried to escape northward. It has become a symbol in my life of both the goal and the guiding light on the road ahead.

In this final chapter I would like to offer some of my views as to how we can change our nation and the world. These ideas have developed gradually throughout my politically active life. As I have mentioned they began shifting more definitively in the 1980s but I have rarely written down my thoughts.

Change

The world is changing at an ever increasing rate. Human knowledge is rapidly expanding. Computer technology has completely altered the nature of our society, economy, and ability of our species to function into the future. Almost anything anyone says about the future will, as usual, be in good part wrong, but now their predictions will be tested faster than ever.

Yet human knowledge has made little or no progress in finding ways of stopping the destruction of the planet or of ending the vast inequalities that leave the majority of our species living in poverty, with huge numbers dying needlessly from hunger and disease. Even one simple solution, making contraception widely available, is opposed and obstructed by major organizations and governments, including that of the United States, in favor of "abstinence." This contradiction between the potential of human society, based on knowledge and productivity, and its reality is the most striking feature of our time.

No issue is more vital than saving our Earth, the basis of all life. Even though a considerable movement is developing in support of saving the planet, the world economy as a whole continues moving toward the destruction of the oceans, air, and topsoil, while contributing to global warming at an increasing tempo.

I am convinced that whatever I write here, someone reading it forty years from now will say, "Well, of course, there was no way Camejo could have known about what has happened in countries X, Y, and Z, which has made it a lot easier now to understand how to solve these issues." So the first piece of advice I have for young people is to think for yourself and recognize that having an understanding of how to change society is a moving target. It is a science, not a ritual.

Was Marx Right?

Of course Marx was right. Marx said human history can be understood like any other scientific process. He applied the most advanced, progressive, and scientific knowledge of his time to social issues and rejected all the silly superstitions that were commonplace—and still are—as to how to explain human history, why some people are poor and others rich.

Marx connected changes in human history—primarily the changes in how humans survive, otherwise referred to now as the economy—to material causes. He thought the standard opinion of those at the top, that things won't change or can't change, was wrong and will continue to be wrong. He believed that humans can establish a far more egalitarian existence than the class societies that appeared when agriculture made food surplus possible. Marx raised the idea that humans can transcend the brutality, violence, and abuse that have characterized most of human society for at least the past few thousand years. He laid out a view that attempted to tie society's past evolution to how it might evolve in the future.

Poor Marx. Over time his views grew so popular that distortions became commonplace. He was turned into a sort of "god" who had discovered the truth, and a priesthood was required to interpret his discoveries and profound truth correctly. If we think of Marx as a scientist and revolutionary who was trying to comprehend human society in order to change it, we will be much closer to an accurate appreciation of the role he tried to play.

Was Marx ever wrong? Not according to some of those who have tried to turn him into a religious figure. Yet it is inevitable that scientists who make important discoveries are in time superseded by others. Was Newton wrong because Einstein's theories supplanted some of his? Well, to a degree. As we learn more about human beings and our societies, and as concrete events help bring a deeper understanding, our views on social change will alter. That does not mean that Marx was "wrong" for working to make our understanding of human history a science rather than a superstition.

Did Marx ever say stupid things? Of course. One in particular that amuses me because it touches on Venezuela is his statement about Venezuelans being lazy and British troops having to do the fighting to get rid of the Spaniards.* I don't give this much credence. For someone fighting all the prejudices of his era about human nature Marx did pretty well at presenting his views in a scientific manner. A slip into this kind of comment in his time is wrong and lamentable but easily dismissed since it runs in contradiction to most of what he said.

It's similar to the case of Thomas Jefferson. The Declaration of Independence was an amazing step forward for humanity in many of the concepts it raised. The fact that the author himself, in complete contradiction, owned human slaves does not completely negate the positive nature of what he wrote, said, and did.

There are no gods. The people we admire, learn from, and look to for inspiration, were just that—people. They were all human beings, mammalian primates, and reflected in infinite ways their own time and surroundings just as we do.

So the fundamental point I want to make—and repeat and repeat—is that you have to think for yourself. When theory comes into conflict with reality it is best to drop or adjust the theory, not deny the reality. Human society is full of contradictions. Sometimes trying to explain things through formulas will simply separate you from reality. That is another fundamental

---

* "But, like most of his countrymen, [Bolivar] was averse to any prolonged exertion ..." Karl Marx, "Bolivar y Ponte" *The New American Cyclopaedia*, vol. III, 1858. Available at http://www.marxists.org /archive/marx/works/1858/01/bolivar.htm.

lesson from Marx, a lesson he drew from the ideas of others—that reality is always in flux and is full of contradictions.

The science of social change is permanently evolving. We will learn what works—that is, what is "true"—through the inevitable conflict of ideas and by testing those ideas against reality. This is a challenge, to say the least, because we are all influenced by the contradictions and conflicts in society. But this struggle is not over some abstract arguments; it is a battle for the physical survival of humanity.

To create a just society and end thousands of years of violence and exploitation is not simple. Generations upon generations of humans have tried to move in a more just, egalitarian direction. It is essential that we respect and learn from these people. The history of all positive social gains has been the product and effort of millions upon millions of humans working together. It is a science, not superstition. Superstitions come from a mystical, unchangeable source. Science is the product of a massive, collective, ever-changing effort of our species.

The Cost of Stalinism

In this book I have explained that the movement for positive, egalitarian social change was derailed for a period of history by the rise and dominance of Stalinism. Those opposed to change in an egalitarian direction, toward human justice, try to claim that Stalinism was the natural outcome of the mass progressive social movement of the 1800s. I think the evidence shows exactly the opposite. Stalinism was a terrible defeat for the progressive movement. It is only now that we see that era of Stalinist distortion coming to an end throughout the world. The struggle for social justice never stopped. Millions of people continued struggling for equality and progressive change. But Stalinism in its time was able to block, exploit, disorient, or destroy many of the mass social movements impacting the world.

During the era of Stalinism the so-called left became splintered and sectarian, each group distinguished by specific rhetoric that was incomprehensible to the average person. This issue needs to be understood and confronted. The goal of people fighting for social change is to succeed, not to win a theoretical argument or to sound more radical than someone else. Empty rhetoric is a form of capitulation.

Content versus Form

Those of us trying to reach people to oppose war, injustice, and exploitation must recognize the need to speak in language and with symbols that people will understand. The concept of communal life—or in its politicized word form, communism—originated with some progressive elements in the ideology of the early Christian religion. The word was later used in the mid-1800s to describe a totally egalitarian society. For most people in the United States today "communism" invokes horrible totalitarian regimes and has become shorthand for government-run economies that deny all civil liberties and human rights.

In many cases spending one's time trying to argue the correct meaning of a word is about as productive as arguing with people who call themselves Chicanos by informing them that "Chicano" was once a derogatory racist term for Mexicans in the Southwest, or insisting that "monster rally" does not refer to a rally of monsters but a large demonstration.

The word socialism now has a series of associations that are completely different from 150 years ago. If you were to stop ten average Americans and ask for the meaning of "socialism" you would get about fourteen different answers. Some think it means government ownership; some connect it with government services, such as "socialized medicine"; others think it refers to an economic system that can lead to totalitarianism as in the Soviet Union. Still others might think of a bureaucratic system that paralyzes economic growth. The word's definition even depends on the country in which it is used—"socialism" in Europe or Latin America has different connotations than in the United States.

Many people who consider themselves socialists use a definition separate from the various meanings promoted by our educational system and mass media. They think of socialism as an economy based on democracy, not benefiting a small rich minority but instead benefiting all the people. Wouldn't it be helpful if those people were to express this idea in understandable terms—such as "economy based on democracy"—instead of getting into arguments over terminology or confusing others as to what is being advocated? Among some socialists, however, there is a grave fear that to omit the word "socialist" is to betray the great ideals of social justice born in the 1800s.

Saying the word "socialist" repeatedly may allow some people to think they are very radical but the truth is that sectarian language and actions that isolate people politically are a form of capitulation. Having lived through this phenomenon I am more convinced than ever that we will not build a movement in the United States with a mass base until we learn two things. One of them is to ground our language and movement in our own history, traditions, language, and culture. The second is to have an understanding of how our society works. By this I mean not harboring illusions about those who have chosen to favor money over people and understanding fully how the power of money controls our media, education, religion, government, military, and political parties.

The Third American Revolution

The United States is ripe for a third revolution. The First American Revolution, which ended British control over the United States, raised some astoundingly progressive positions for that time, such as separation of church and state, the right of assembly, free speech, and the establishment of an elected government—although only 10 percent of the people had the right to vote. This revolution inspired people all over the world. For more than two hundred years the Declaration of Independence has been used as an example by people fighting for their freedom.

The United States was born as a country that allowed and promoted human slavery. The second revolution, the Civil War, ended chattel slavery and deepened the concept of democracy. Out of that revolution came explosions of workers' struggles seeking the right to unions, women demanding the right to vote, and most profoundly, Reconstruction governments in the South that opposed racism, sought equality, and promoted all kinds of progressive social legislation and rights for working people.

Just as the first revolution, in complete contradiction to the goals stated in the Declaration of Independence, had left untouched the system of chattel slavery, the Second American Revolution left the country controlled by a small minority opposed to the very ideas of democracy and equality that had come out of the revolution.

Deep social changes like the first two revolutions of our nation take a long time to mature. Today the contradiction of a society that is supposedly of, by, and for the people but instead is of, by, and for an extremely wealthy minority cannot sustain indefinitely. It is unlikely, in spite of all the handicaps, that the majority will never mobilize itself to end the rule of a minority and finally create a democracy in the United States.

The political structure of the United States is rooted in a lie. The rulers have to give the appearance that the people rule. Their manipulated elections, control of the media, influence through religion, and falsifications in education have allowed them to weather one potential social explosion after another. In good part their success is rooted in the triumph of U.S. imperialism and the maintenance of a relatively higher standard of living for large sections of working people. But that era appears to be coming to an end.

The average American worker has not experienced any gain in wages, adjusted for inflation, in thirty-five years. This is the first time in American history that the average person has not gained for that stretch of time. Now, with the fall in home values, for many families their actual well-being is in decline. The need for the rich to maintain the illusion of democracy is a sign of weakness to begin with and could become a major problem for them. The pending battle for free elections, runoffs, and proportional representation will have a different meaning in the United States than it has had in Europe. In any case I would think that opening up the electoral system may soon appear as a major issue in American history.

The vacuum of leadership in the trade unions, their utter corruption, and failure to fight corporate domination—although these are now negatives—may turn out to be beneficial, because these same unions would be useless against a sudden political explosion. The main instrument effectively blocking the development of a mass movement for change is the Democratic Party. But the success of the Democrats in derailing and co-opting movements requires that the party be able to offer some concessions, which may be coming to an end on some levels.

Whatever happens, it will take everyone by surprise. It is like water running downhill—when stopped temporarily by obstacles in its course, the water eventually finds a way around the blockage and keeps moving, usually in an explosive new channel or by removing part of the obstacles.

The culture of the left tends to expect forms similar to those from the past. But the world is moving so quickly that the formulas understood to be "the way" change occurs are changing too. In fact, events may prove so complicated and misleading that many people waiting for an explosion or revolt to bring about social change may not recognize it when it occurs, or may even oppose it. The process is likely to be very contradictory. That is, a movement might not appear at first to be progressing toward a confrontation with the rule of money, but it will either develop splits that move in that direction or the movement itself will veer. Such a possibility might be borne out precisely because of the enormous success of the two-party system and the wealth in this nation. The fact that there exists no real "left" force with preconceived ideas or other objectives (as with Stalinism) leaves very little to get in the way once a mass movement unfolds.

Will there be splits in the Democratic Party? Of course, once a mass movement develops all kinds of possibilities will appear. One thing is sure, an explosion of opposition to the Democrats could open the door for a sharp move toward revolution because the entire system is set up with the Democrats as the main roadblock to change. The culture of the Democratic Party is so corrupt that a split, unless driven from its ranks and clearly hostile to the Democrats, would likely not be much of a help but rather act as another roadblock. One example is the small Working Families Party, which tries to attract people alienated from the two-party system, only to offer another way to vote Democratic.

I am convinced the struggle will appear as a fight for democracy and will develop around very concrete issues of a defensive nature. The form may be deceptive because mass mobilizations and electoral explosions are often narrowly focused on a specific law or specific events, yet they can transform quickly into a broader challenge to the ruling system.

Can the Third American Revolution occur without a visionary leadership having been formed? I think the answer to that is no. But such a leadership can develop very quickly if currents exist that have broken with the rule of money, such as electoral oppositions whose politics and culture simply will not vote Democratic. If one studies the Second American Revolution one sees such developments in play. They appear chaotic, but over time they were laying the groundwork for a political explosion.

The Forty-Year Wave

There appears to be a pattern of successive waves of mass struggle, about forty years apart, throughout the history of our nation. Each takes a different form, fighting to improve people's conditions and for increased democracy. In 1849 you see the flare-up of the battle against slavery. Forty years later came the huge populist eruption after 1889. Everyone recognizes the date 1929 with the rise of the labor movement and the creation of the industrial unions that followed. Forty years later in 1969 we were already in the mass rise of a youth rebellion, antiwar struggle, the beginnings of a new wave of feminism, and the gay rights movement. Today we might just be at the beginning of a new wave.

Why this seems to hold true remains elusive. The empirical evidence has been noticed by many people and disputed by just as many. Some have raised the idea that the forty-year period corresponds to technological cycles in our economy.

I lived through one of these waves. I want to relay to you how fast people can suddenly change their minds. When it seems hopeless that the American people will ever understand what is happening around them, question what the media is saying, and fight back—spontaneously it seems to happen. Looking back it becomes much easier to see that these struggles were actually percolating prior to the explosion. Certainly the massive civil rights struggles of the 1950s and 60s set the framework and started the process that found broad expression at the end of the 1960s. I watched in the late 1960s and early 1970s as what had been a small minority point of view—opposition to the war in Vietnam—rapidly expanded into a resounding majority.

Change Is Inevitable

Although we cannot completely rule out apocalyptic scenarios such as our species failing and the world being destroyed or some sort of fascist society arising that annihilates all the gains of the past, I believe there is very little indication that such outcomes are likely. Change will be difficult, that is certain; possibly very violent, since the resistance to democracy and justice is deeply embedded in our society. But I believe that victory will occur. Preparing the way for future generations and fighting to create currents of thought to see through the lies and manipulations can help usher in a victory when a wave hits. Mass defeats such as the rise of Stalinism can derail the process for a generation or more but humanity still appears to be moving forward.

Sometimes changes are occurring beneath the surface that are not fully understood. Even within the two parties of money the roles of women and African Americans are changing, after more than two hundred years of only white men as leaders of our nation. The new wave that is coming will probably accelerate these developments, moving women, Latinos, African Americans, and other minorities closer to the center of our history.

Guiding the social movements back onto the path of scientific thought, shedding the anti-materialist, "idealist," neo-religious concepts that penetrated the left during Stalinism's chokehold, and refusing to get caught in sectarian schemas that isolate us will all be important steps toward the creation of a revolutionary current to fight for the Third American Revolution. Just as important, if not even more so, will be to develop movements that draw the line on capitulation and refuse to sell out to the power of money.

Temporary setbacks are inevitable. It is sad to see us move forward, as with the Nader campaign in 2000, and then have the forces opposed to democracy push back for a period. Setbacks often serve to solidify an ever more committed layer of leaders with the insight and patience to endure, making the next rise even stronger. This is part of the process through which leadership is created for social change.

This is far easier to describe than do. Our movement will always be full of conflict and divisions. That is not just the unfortunate reality; on the contrary, it is a dynamic essential for success. How to build a movement, where to draw the lines, is a process of discovery that occurs in real time as ideas are checked out against material fact. The debate on these issues takes the form of a conflict of ideas. We must never fear democracy, differences, and conflict within our movement for social change.

Internationalism

The Third American Revolution will be part of a world revolution. Saving our planet is not a national but an international issue. The U.S. economy, unlike at the time of our first two revolutions, is now completely interlinked with the rest of the world. Referring to the Third American Revolution is not hidden nationalism or the notion that we are different from the rest of the world. As long as humans are still grouped in nation-states the dynamics of our people will in great part be tied to the history and culture created within our national boundaries. But the coming struggles will consist in part of the dissolution of those boundaries. There is nothing more revealing of the failure of the leaders of our country than when they talk of being "competitive" in the world. Why would we want to compete with and defeat other members of our species? The idea is fundamentally absurd. Such phrases have a purpose, to convince working people to view other humans as the enemy and the ruling class of their own nation as their defenders. The truth is exactly the opposite. The formation of international movements can offer an enormous benefit for everyone.

We are one species. We are one planet. Our success for justice and democracy in this world, for creating a world without hunger or poverty, depends on our species comprehending this simple yet all-encompassing truth.

All these movements—the struggle for women's rights, an end to racism, an internationalist outlook—will come together in time. The Third American Revolution will have as a central aspect of its ideology the end of the nationalist, racist superiority that has characterized so much of U.S. history.

The corporate rulers can co-opt such positive developments for their own purposes to make it easier to move capital and exploit across borders. We are now living in the beginning of the era of the unification of our planet as one economy and one people. We are very far from the day when the people living in India will have the standard of living of the people in the United States. But that must be our goal. The only real solution is to have a peaceful planet where all humans can live in harmony.

APPENDIX 1:

GUS HOROWITZ ON STUDENT DAYS WITH PETER CAMEJO

I first met Peter Camejo around a poker table in September 1958, during freshman orientation week at MIT. His playing style, like his personality, was mercurial. Mine was more pedestrian, more by the book. Poker, some say, is about life. Yet we were both, I think, good poker players.

Although we met each other frequently during the first couple of months of school, it was only while playing poker. I knew nothing of Peter's socialist ideas and activities. That changed in the second semester.

Peter and two other students were the lucky residents of a very large dormitory suite, a quadruple with only three inhabitants. I knew the other two students as well, one from playing pool and the other from the kosher kitchen. Poker, pool, and keeping kosher—the three vices I brought with me from high school—were personified right there in that dorm room.

The pool player soon dropped out of school. The other two, fearing that the school authorities would deluge them with strangers, took preemptive action by inviting me in to fill the third slot and limit the suite's population to only three.

Thus began months of discussion and argument—about socialism and capitalism, about God and atheism, about ethics, morality, sex, and the meaning of life. I am happy to report that we resolved all of these issues, at least for a time.

Peter was a year and a half older than I, and much more worldly-wise. So he had a big influence on me, and not merely in the realm of ideas. We went out on double dates, and he also introduced me to my first non-kosher hamburger.

Joining many of these dorm room discussions was Barry Sheppard, a senior, who worked with Peter to try to get some socialist activities going in those still-conservative times, the last years of the 1950s. The three of us were to become political comrades for the next twenty years as members and leaders in the Socialist Workers Party.

Peter's political biographers sometimes mention his perfect 800 score on the mathematics SATs, the college entrance exams. That wasn't very impressive to me. Many students at MIT had high scores. It may have puffed up our egos as high school hotshots. At MIT, however, we were just faces in the crowd. There were certainly a few really brilliant minds among the students, but not very many.

Neither Peter nor I was particularly studious or exceptional academically. But there was something about his way of thinking that I remember. The occasion was a physics exam, a tough exam, with one question that stood out for its difficulty. Afterwards we were all discussing the proper, textbook solution to the problem, using the various tools provided by calculus. Peter, it turned out, had completely bypassed the standard approach and solved the problem by a simple appeal to symmetry. His solution was obvious and intellectually elegant. Although I have long since forgotten the problem, I have always remembered Peter's ingenious way of solving it. Peter is a creative thinker, a talent that served him well over the years.

When we were together later on Peter and I sometimes reverted to our old dorm room personas. On a couple of occasions in Europe, at meetings of the International Executive Committee or World Congress of the Fourth International, we were assigned to the same lodgings. So, when the meetings adjourned for the evening, Peter and I would while away the time competing in mathematical and logical puzzles, as we used to do in the old school days.

Peter and I became good friends that first year in college, and although we drifted apart as time went by, we still remain friends.

Gus Horowitz
March 20, 2007

APPENDIX 2:

MATT GONZALEZ'S CONCESSION SPEECH IN THE 2003 SAN FRANCISCO MAYORALTY RACE

December 9, 2003

Thank you very much. [crowd noise, applause] Thank you very much. You've been a great group of people to be in a campaign with. [crowd chanting "Whose city? Our city!"] Thank you. Thank you so much. It's been a great campaign. It really has been.

I want to offer my sincere congratulations to Supervisor Newsom, who was elected Mayor of San Francisco tonight. [crowd begins "booing"] No, no. Cut it out, cut it out. You know, we live in a democracy and people get to vote. They vote for the society that they want. And Supervisor Newsom won that contest tonight. And let me just say [crowd booing] No, no, no, no, no, no, no. Listen, let's be good sports about this. [applause]

I have been trying to articulate during this race that a campaign like this is really bigger than one person. There's a certain inevitability to what it is that we are trying to accomplish. It doesn't matter whether or not we win one particular race in this city. It really matters whether or not we can regroup, and whether or not we come back. And whether or not when Mayor Newsom is wrong, we're there to oppose him. [applause] But I want to emphasize the opposite as well. When Mayor Newsom is right, we have

307

to get behind him and support him. Because there are a lot of issues in this city that really need our attention and cooperation. [applause]

I think that it's sort of natural at the end of a campaign, when you don't win, to look at the things that you did wrong or the things that might have turned a little differently. But I want to tell you that this has been a hell of a campaign. [applause] The people in this campaign have been fantastic. It's been my pleasure, really. You know, if I could have spent four months getting such little sleep, I can't think of any group of people I would have rather of done it with. [applause]

In a lot of ways this race was cast as a Green vs. Democrat contest. And there is a lot of truth to that division. But I also want to emphasize this: This is a city with 3 percent Greens and look what we went and did. [applause] We had 47 or 48 percent of the electorate voting for a Green candidate. [applause] And I think what this really means, that the Democratic Party and other parties have to acknowledge that people voted for a candidate outside of their party because that candidate represented the values of democracy. [applause] That's really what we've accomplished here.

I also want to pay my respects to the many elected officials who are Democrats who were willing to cross that line, and who will likely suffer for it. [applause] You've heard from them tonight and they're righteous people, they're glad to be here, they're proud to be here. But you know what? We've got to take care of them, because they had the courage to step forward and to do the right thing. [applause] And they're now going to get targeted for that and we have to be there to support them. [applause]

I want to also say that unlike any other campaign that has happened in this city certainly during my adult life, while I've been watching—you know, there is a tendency as the candidates run, that the candidates start trying to water down what it is that they represent so that they can try and win more voters that way. And let me just say that I am really proud of having run a progressive campaign. From the outset I was saying that this is a progressive city. [applause] This city really represents the most American of American values. [applause] There are folks in other parts of the United States, and they want to think that what's going on here is unusual. Well, it might take five or ten years but we're going to catch up with them. [applause] What I tried to do here, what you helped me to do, what we did together, was that we essentially said, let's break out of the traditional sense of watering down our opinions and instead let's go out and persuade people that we're right. [applause]

A political contest ultimately gets decided by who turns out to the polls. Let me tell you, we had enough supporters to win this election. We didn't win it, but we didn't lose it either. [applause]

I look forward to working on the next progressive campaign in this city. We've got some campaigns that will be coming up in November. They tend to be races that don't get a lot of attention: school board, community college board races, some of the supervisor races. The only way that the context can be created to have a mayoral victory like the one we tried to accomplish today, is if we fight those battles and win some of those seats. That's what we have to do. [applause]

[Audience member shouts "Matt for president!" Matt replies "I'm already the president." more applause]

There have been some great folks in this campaign doing tremendous stuff. It's just been amazing. I'm not going to name names because there are so many people. Just to be in this space and the energy we got working together has been phenomenal. It really speaks to the inevitability that I was speaking about earlier.

Let me close by saying again, I really do want to congratulate Supervisor Newsom. He is a colleague of mine on the board of supervisors. [booing and applause] Really, if there's anybody that can't handle this, then they should just leave. The man won this election.

Part of what it is to run against someone and to challenge them is to try and educate them. [applause] I hope that he has learned something from us. And like I said before, I hope we will be able to work together. And if we have to be on opposite ends of fights, well then, certainly that's where we'll be. [applause]

Thank you so much. You're all very beautiful. Thank you.

APPENDIX 3:

THE AVOCADO DECLARATION

[Peter Camejo initiated the Avocado Declaration on January 1, 2004, as part of the Avocado Education Project to explain how the Green Party of the United States needed to adopt a firm and uncompromising identity to promote its values and combat opposition from the more powerful Democratic and Republican parties in the United States. The name Avocado Declaration references the ideal of party members being like the avocado: "Green on the inside; green on the outside." The declaration is the principal document of the group Greens for Democracy and Independence.]

Introduction

The Green Party is at a crossroads. The 2004 elections place before us a clear and unavoidable choice. On one side, we can continue on the path of political independence, building a party of, by, and for the people by running our own campaign for president of the United States. The other choice is the well-trodden path of lesser-evil politics, sacrificing our own voice and independence to support whoever the Democrats nominate in order, we are told, to defeat Bush.

The difference is not over whether to "defeat Bush"—understanding that to mean the program of corporate globalization and the wars and trampling of the Constitution that come with it—but rather how to do it.

We do not believe it is possible to defeat the "greater" evil by supporting a shamefaced version of the same evil. We believe it is precisely by openly and sharply confronting the two major parties that the policies of the corporate interests these parties represent can be set back and defeated.

Ralph Nader's 2000 presidential campaign exposed a crisis of confidence in the two-party system. His 2.7 million votes marked the first time in modern history that millions voted for a more progressive and independent alternative. Now, after three years of capitulation by the Democratic Party to George Bush they are launching a preemptive strike against a 2004 Ralph Nader campaign or any Green Party challenge. Were the Greens right to run in 2000? Should we do the same in 2004? The Avocado Declaration, based on an analysis of our two-party duopoly and its history, declares we were right and we must run.

Origins of the Present Two-Party System

History shows that the Democrats and Republicans are not two counterpoised forces, but rather complementary halves of a single two-party system: "one animal with two heads that feed from the same trough," as Chicano leader Rodolfo "Corky" Gonzalez explained.

Since the Civil War a peculiar two-party political system has dominated the United States. Prior to the Civil War a two-party system existed which reflected opposing economic platforms. Since the Civil War a shift occurred. A two-party system remained in place but no longer had differing economic orientations. Since the Civil War the two parties show differences in their image, role, social base, and some policies, but in the last analysis they both support essentially similar economic platforms.

This development can be clearly dated to the split in the Republican Party of 1872 where one wing merged with the "New Departure" Democrats that had already shifted towards the Republican platform, which was pro-finance and industrial business. Prior to the Civil War, the Democratic Party, controlled by the slaveocracy, favored agricultural business interests and developed an alliance with small farmers in conflict with industrial and some commercial interests. That division ended with the Civil War. Both parties supported financial and industrial business as the core of their programmatic outlook.

For over 130 years the two major parties have been extremely effective in preventing the emergence of any mass political formations that could challenge their political monopoly. Most attempts to build political alternatives have been efforts to represent the interests of the average person, the working people. These efforts have been unable to develop. Both major parties have been dominated by moneyed interests and today reflect the historic period of corporate rule.

In this sense United States history has been different from that of any other advanced industrial nation. In all other countries multiparty systems have appeared and to one degree or another these countries have more democratic electoral laws and better political representation. In most other countries there exist political parties ostensibly based on or promoting the interest of noncorporate sectors such as working people.

Struggles for Democracy and Social Justice

In spite of this pro-corporate political monopoly, mass struggles for social progress, struggles to expand democracy and civil rights, have periodically exploded throughout United States history.

Every major gain in our history, even pre–Civil War struggles—such as the battles for the Bill of Rights, to end slavery, and to establish free public education—as well as those after the Civil War have been the product of direct action by movements independent of the two major parties and in opposition to them.

Since the Civil War, without exception, the Democratic Party has opposed all mass struggles for democracy and social justice. These include the struggle for ballot reform, for the right of African Americans to vote and against American apartheid ("Jim Crow"), for the right to form unions, for the right of women to vote, against the war in Vietnam, the struggle to make lynching illegal, the fight against the death penalty, the struggle for universal health care, the fight for gay and lesbian rights, and endless others. Many of these struggles were initiated by or helped by the existence of small third parties.

Division of Work

When social justice, peace, or civil rights movements become massive in scale, and threaten to become uncontrollable and begin to win over large numbers of people, the Democratic Party begins to shift and presents itself as a supposed ally. Its goal is always to co-opt the movement, demobilize its forces, and block its development into an alternative, independent political force.

The Republican Party has historically acted as the open advocate for a platform which benefits the rule of wealth and corporate domination. They argue ideologically for policies benefiting the corporate rulers. The Republicans seek to convince the middle classes and labor to support the rule of the wealthy with the argument that "What's good for General Motors is good for the country," that what benefits corporations is also going to benefit regular people.

The Democratic Party is different. They act as a "broker" negotiating and selling influence among broad layers of the people to support the objectives of corporate rule. The Democratic Party's core group of elected officials is rooted in careerists seeking self-promotion by offering to the corporate rulers their ability to control and deliver mass support. And to the people they offer some concessions, modifications on the platform of the Republican Party. One important value of the Democratic Party to the corporate world is that it makes the Republican Party possible through the maintenance of the stability that is essential for "business as usual." It does this by preventing a genuine mass opposition from developing. Together the two parties offer one of the best frameworks possible with which to rule a people that otherwise would begin to move society towards the rule of the people (i.e., democracy).

An example of this process is our minimum-wage laws. Adjusted for inflation, the minimum wage has been gradually declining for years. Every now and then the Democrats pass a small upward adjustment that allows the downward trend to continue, but gives the appearance that they are on the side of the poor.

Manipulated Elections

Together the two parties have made ballot access increasingly difficult, defended indirect elections such as the Electoral College, insisted on winner-take-all voting to block the appearance of alternative voices, and opposed proportional representation to prevent the development of a representative democracy and the flowering of choices. Both parties support the undemocratic structure of the U.S. Senate and the Electoral College, which are not based on one person, one vote, but instead favor the more conservative regions of the nation.

Elections are based primarily on money. By gerrymandering and accumulating huge war chests—payoffs for doing favors for their rich "friends"—most officeholders face no real challenge at the ballot box and are reelected. In the races that are "competitive," repeatedly the contests are reduced to two individuals seeking corporate financial backing. Whoever wins the battle for money wins the election. Districts are gerrymandered into "safe" districts for one or the other party. Gerrymandering lowers the public's interest and involvement while maintaining the fiction of "democracy" and "free elections." The news media goes along with this, typically focusing on the presidential election and a handful of other races, denying most challengers the opportunity to get their message out to the public.

Corporate backing shifts between the two parties depending on short-term, and even accidental factors. In the 1990s, more endorsements from CEOs went to the Democrats. At present the money has shifted to the Republican Party. Most corporations donate to both parties to maintain their system in place.

No Choice, No Hope

The Democratic Party preaches defeatism to the most oppressed and exploited. Nothing can be expected, nothing is possible but what exists. To the people they justify continuous betrayal of the possibility for real change with the argument of lesser evil. It's the Republicans or us. Nothing else is possible.

Democracy versus Co-optation

Democracy remains a great danger to those who have privilege and control. When you are part of the top 1% of the population that has as much income as the bottom 75% of the people, democracy is a permanent threat to your interests. The potential power of the people is so great that it puts sharp limits on what corporations can do. The ability of the Democratic Party to contain, co-opt, and demobilize independent movements of the people is a critical element in allowing the continued destruction of our planet, abuse, discrimination, and exploitation based on race, gender, sexual preference, and class, and the immense misdistribution of wealth.

As we enter the 21st century there is no more important issue than saving our planet from destruction. The world economy is becoming increasingly globalized. Corporate power is now global in nature and leads to massive dislocations and suffering for most people. The planet is overpopulated and the basis of human life declining. The greatest suffering and dislocations exist in the third world but there is also a downward trend in the

United States as globalization leads to a polarization of income and wealth. This shift is making the United States each day closer to a third-world country with an extremely wealthy minority and a growing underclass. This polarization adds further fear of democracy for the elite.

The Growing Shift against the Rule of Law

The shift away from the rule of law has accelerated in recent years. This process will be a factor in the 2004 presidential elections especially if a Green candidate is involved in the race. The shift away from our Constitution is proceeding with the complicity of both parties and the courts. The changes are made illegally through legislation rather than the official process by which the Constitution can be amended because to do otherwise would awaken a massive resistance. A similar process is under way regarding the rule of law internationally.

The reason given for these steps since September 2001 is the terrorist attack within the borders of the United States. An attack made by forces originally trained, armed, and supported by the United States government. The so-called war on terrorism does not exist. The United States Government has promoted, tolerated, and been party to the use of terrorism all over the world. The United States has even been found guilty of terrorism by the World Court.

The terrorist attacks against U.S. targets are important, but they need to be countered primarily in a social and political manner. A manner which is the opposite of that taken by the USA PATRIOT Act, and the occupations of Afghanistan and Iraq. On the contrary, by aggravating inequality, injustice, disrespecting the rule of law and its military interventions and occupation, the present policies of the U.S. government add to the dangers faced by U.S. citizens throughout the world and in the United States. Especially dangerous are the promotion of nuclear, chemical, and bacteriological weapons, and the open declarations of the intention to once again use nuclear weapons.

This recent shift, while rooted in bipartisan policies over the last decades, has been accelerated by the present Republican administration. Its ability to carry out these actions has depended on the Democratic Party's support, and its ability to contain, disorient, and prevent the development of mass opposition.

Amazingly, in December of 2003 General Tommy Franks, the recently retired head of U.S. Central Command was quoted as stating that he thought the people of the United States may prefer a military government over our present Constitutional Republican form, if another terrorist attack occurs. Such a statement is so far off base one must wonder why it is being made. The people of the United States are solidly opposed to any consideration of a military dictatorship in the United States. In fact, polls have repeatedly shown they favor increasing our democratic rights such as limiting campaign contributions and allowing more points of view in debates.

Never in our history have top military leaders or ex-military leaders spoken openly of ending our Constitutional form of government. No leader of the Democratic Party has protested Franks' comments. How many officers in the armed forces have such opinions? If there are any, they should be immediately removed from the military.

Democrats: Patriot Act and Unequivocal Support for Bush

The Democratic Party leadership voted for the USA PATRIOT Act. In the United States Senate only one Democrat voted against the Patriot Act. Democrats considered "liberal" such as Paul Wellstone and Barbara Boxer voted for the USA PATRIOT Act. Huge majorities have repeatedly passed votes in the Congress against the United States Constitution. In one case only one Congresswoman, Barbara Lee, voted against the abrogation of the Constitution's separation of powers as stated in Article 1, Section 8. Democratic Party politicians, when called upon to support the Republican Party and their corporate backers, repeatedly comply and vote against the interest of the people and against the Constitution they have sworn to uphold.

The Democratic Party leadership as a whole gave repeated standing ovations to George Bush as he outlined his platform in his January 2002 State of the Union address, a speech that promoted the arbitrary decision to occupy sovereign nations through military aggression in violation of international law. The ovations given the Republican Platform by the Democratic Party were done on national television for the people to see a unified political force. The effect is to make people who believe in peace, support the U.N. charter, the World Court, and the rule of law feel they are isolated, powerless, and irrelevant.

A resolution was passed in March of 2003 calling for "Unequivocal Support" to "George Bush" for the war in Iraq. It had the full support of the Democratic Party leadership. Even Democratic "doves" like Dennis Kucinich would not vote against the resolution. Only a handful (eleven) of congressional representatives voted against the motion for "unequivocal support" to George Bush.

The Role of the Democratic Party

The Democratic Party with its open defense of the Republican Platform and its attacks on our Constitution and the rule of law internationally would be of little value to those who favor the present policies if it allowed the development of a mass independent opposition. The failure of such forces to exist in sufficient strength permits the Democrats to be more open in their support for antidemocratic policies.

Nevertheless some voices outside the Democratic and Republican Parties are beginning to be heard. Massive antiwar street demonstrations, and the voice of a new small party, the Green Party, have gained some attention and respect. In no case did the Democratic Party as an institution support, call for, or help mobilize popular forces for peace and respecting international law. Yet large numbers of its rank and file and many lower-level elected officials participated in and promoted antiwar protests.

Many lower-level elected officials among the Democrats and even some Republicans who defend the Constitution of the United States are voting to oppose the USA PATRIOT Act at the local level. Even many middle-level Democrats have conflicting views and sometimes take progressive stances in concert with the Green Party's platform. These individuals live in a contradiction with the Party they belong to. While we can and should join with them behind specific issues, we do not adopt their error of belonging to a party that is against the interest of the people, that is pro-corporate and is against the rule of law.

Democrats Attack the Green Party

The Democratic Party allows its lower-level representatives to present themselves as opposed to the war. Some of its leaders have begun to take on an appearance of disagreeing with "how" the policies of Bush are being implemented. The Democratic Party has unleashed a campaign to divide and conquer those opposed to the pro-war policies. On one hand it tries to appear sympathetic to antiwar sentiment while on the other it tries to silence voices opposed to Bush's policies.

Soon after the 2000 presidential election the Democrats began an attack on the Green Party on the grounds that since there is no runoff system, that is, since the Democrats in partnership with the Republicans do not allow free elections, the Green Party's existence and its candidate for President Ralph Nader in 2000 should be declared responsible for George Bush becoming president.

Progressive Democrats Join Attack

This campaign against the Greens has been heavily promoted by the corporate media. It has achieved success in part because of the support it has received by the more liberal wing of the Democratic Party and some of the "progressive" journals controlled by liberal Democrats, such as the *Nation* and *Mother Jones*.

Their political message is simple and clear: "no voice truly critical of the platform of the Republicans may be permitted; only the Democrats must appear as 'opponents' to the Republicans." They have no objection to rightist, pro-war third-party candidates entering the race and promoting their views. They only oppose a voice for peace and the rule of law like that of Ralph Nader in 2000.

Never in the history of the United States has a magazine claiming to favor democracy run a front-page article calling on an individual not to run for president—until the *Nation* did so against Ralph Nader running for president in 2004. The fact that polls show 23% of the people favor Nader running (extrapolated to the total voting population this would represent about 40 million people) and 65% favored his inclusion in debates is of no concern to the *Nation* as it seeks to silence the only candidate who in 2000 opposed the premises of George Bush's platform.

The Conspiracy against the Voters

The *Nation*'s editorial board is free to campaign for the Democratic Party and urge people to vote for the Democrats in spite of their support for the USA PATRIOT Act, their votes for "Unequivocal support to George Bush," etc. That is their right. But they want something else. They want the Greens to join with them in a conspiracy to deny the voters a choice.

All voters are fully aware there is no runoff in a presidential race. Many who support the platform of the Greens will vote against their own principles by voting for the Democratic Party. Each voter will make that decision. But the *Nation*, along with many others, is calling on the Greens to disenfranchise voters who disagree with the *Nation*'s preference for the Democratic Party. It wants these voters to have no choice and be unable to express their electoral wish. The *Nation* and those it represents want to silence the voices of these voters, not to allow it to be registered, as a way to try and force them to vote for their party, the Democrats.

The passage of the USA PATRIOT Act, the undemocratic electoral laws, the manipulation of electoral campaigns by the corporate media, and the campaign to silence the Greens are all part of the same campaign against democracy. They are just another example of how the two-party system is set up to repress and silence those who favor democracy.

Lesser Evil Leads to Greater Evil

The effectiveness of the "lesser evil" campaign has penetrated within the Green Party, where a minority supports the concept that the Green Party should not run in 2004. Behind this view is the concept that politics can be measured in degrees, like temperature, and that the Democrats offer a milder and thus less evil alternative to the Republican platform. This view argues that to support the "lesser evil" weakens the greater evil.

Such a view fails to grasp the essence of the matter. Political dynamics work in exactly the opposite way. To silence the voice of the Green Party and support the Democrats strengthens George Bush and the Republican Party because only the appearance of forces opposed to the present policies, forces that are clearly independent of corporate domination can begin to shift the relationship of forces and the center of political debate. Despite the intention of some of its promoters, the anti–Green Party campaign helps the policies pursued by Bush as well as his re-election possibilities.

Although some claim that George Bush's policies represent only a small coterie of neo-conservative extremists, the reality is otherwise. Bush and his friends serve at the will of the corporate rulers. His standing with the American people can be crushed in a moment if the corporate rulers so choose—just by the power of their media, which today is concentrated in the hands of a half dozen giant conglomerates.

It is in the interests of the corporate effort toward a new colonialism to have Bush reelected in 2004, thereby legitimatizing his government before the world. In order to safely achieve that, the voices that truly oppose Bush's policies need to be silenced.

Opposition Is Rising

Opposition is rising against Bush. The massive overwhelming majority of the world is against Bush's war policies. The resistance to the occupation in Iraq and Afghanistan, and the inability of the U.S. media and government to prevent the world from hearing the truth about these events, is weakening Bush's standing. The corporate interests and their media apparently want to make a great effort to get Bush elected, but if this becomes too difficult, the Democratic Party will be prepared to appear as an "opposition" that will continue the essence of Bush's policy with new justifications, modifications, and adjusted forms.

The only force that could upset the general direction of the bipartisan policies put in place over the last few years would be a destabilizing mass development inside the United States, along with world public opinion. This occurred during the war in Vietnam and forced a reversal of U.S. policy.

In the case of Vietnam, the Republicans under Eisenhower initiated the direct U.S. intervention by sponsoring the Diem regime in the south of Vietnam when the French withdrew in the mid-1950s. With U.S. encouragement, his regime refused to abide by the peace accords and hold talks and elections to reunify the country. The Democrats under Kennedy sent ground troops in the early '60s. The U.S. force expanded massively from 16,300 under Kennedy to more than half a million by 1967 under Lyndon Baines Johnson, Kennedy's vice president, who won reelection in 1964 as the supposed "peace" candidate.

The rise of a massive uncontrollable opposition within the United States and around the world became a critical brake on the pro-war policies. An entire generation was starting to deeply question the direction of the United States in world affairs. The Democrats and Republicans, reflecting the opinion of the major corporate leaders and strategists, decided they had no choice but to pull back and concede military defeat in Vietnam because the developing division in U.S. society threatened to result in the emergence of a massive independent political force. This change in policy was carried out under Republican Richard Nixon.

Saving Bush from a backlash is now on the agenda, and the positions of the Democratic Party help Bush in several ways.

First, they seek to prevent even a small but independent critical political development, that is they try to silence the Green Party, and they orient those opposed to the new colonialism to stop demonstrating and focus instead on the electoral campaigns of their Party.

Second, they seek to convince the people that what was wrong with the invasion of Iraq was just that the United Nations—meaning the undemocratic Security Council dominated by the wealthiest countries—did not lend it political cover, or that NATO was not the military form used, or that the United States did not include France and Germany in stealing Iraq's resources, or that not enough troops are being used, or some other question about how things are being done rather than what is being done.

They promise that all will be well if the Democrats can take charge and handle the matter better. With this orientation the Democrats free the hands of corporate America to give their funding and support to Bush. With the exception of a relatively few isolated voices they offer, not real opposition, but only nuances.

And those isolated voices of opposition within the Democratic Party (Kucinich, Reverend Al Sharpton, and Carol Moseley-Braun), no matter how well-intentioned, have a negative consequence: they give legitimacy to the Democrats as the "opponents" of the Republicans.

These exceptions to the general rule are allowed on condition that after the primary campaigns these individuals will urge a vote for the Democratic nominee. This must be done no matter how different that nominated candidate's positions are from the positions taken during the primary campaign. The cover for their political sellout is the winner-take-all system that allows them to posture as just "opposed to Bush" as they support the very party that has supported Bush.

Those are the dues you have to pay to "play" in that game; otherwise they will be eliminated and driven out of the House, the Senate, or a governor's office.

For the Green Party there is nothing more important or effective, long term and short term, in the efforts to stop Bush than to expose how the corporate interests use their two-party system and the role of the Democrats in that system. We must let all Americans who question the policies of Bush, who favor the rule of law, peace, and our Constitution and Bill of Rights see the Democratic Party's hypocrisy, how they support the war and the USA PATRIOT Act.

Democrats Help Institutionalize Bush's Platform

It is transparent that the Democrats' objective is to help institutionalize the USA PATRIOT Act and its break with our Constitution and Bill of Rights. They do this by proposing amendments and adjustments to the law that will disorient, divide, and weaken the opposition to the USA PATRIOT Act, and give the appearance that public concerns have been corrected.

The Democrats are making interesting suggestions for how to pursue the war effort. Some are calling for a more extensive commitment and the sending of more troops to suppress any resistance to U.S. domination in Iraq and Afghanistan. Others are suggesting more flexibility in forming alliances with European nations that had made capital investments to exploit Iraq's oil wealth under the Saddam Hussein dictatorship. These proposals are all aimed at continuing the denial of self-determination for the people of Iraq, which means continuing war and continuing violation of international law.

The Democrats and Republicans both supported Saddam Hussein and the Baathists in Iraq before 1990 when it served their interests. Now they argue with each other over how best to oppress the Iraqis as they try to fool the American people into thinking they are actually trying to bring the Iraqis democracy and freedom.

Self-Correcting Mechanism

The role of these two parties is not a conspiracy. Boxer, Wellstone, and many other Democrats did not vote for the USA PATRIOT Act consciously seeking to assist Bush. Being Democrats, they become part of a system that will have them removed if they do not follow the rules of support when corporate America insists. To rise in the Democratic Party there is a process that results in compliant people unable to question, who remain silent before betrayals or criminal acts. Cynthia McKinney is an example of a Democrat who refused to go along, stepped across the line within the Democratic Party and was driven out of office by the combined efforts of both the Democratic and Republican parties and the corporate media.

The Fourth Amendment to the Constitution prohibits searches without probable cause and a judge's order. Voting for a law that abrogates this amendment, as the USA PATRIOT Act does directly, is an illegal act. The Democrats and Republicans who voted for this law were fully aware of what they were doing. It is an insult to the intelligence of people like Wellstone and Boxer to say that they didn't fully understand the choice they were making. The Green Party differs; it defends the Fourth Amendment and seeks to defend the Constitution and respect for the law, which provides the only method by which the Constitution can be amended, requiring the consideration and vote of the states.

It should be said that there are many issues where Greens agree with Democrats like Boxer and Wellstone, and even admire positions they have taken and efforts they have made. But to go into denial, and refuse to recognize the obvious—that the Democrats have joined in passing and promoting the USA PATRIOT Act against the Constitution with the support of people like Boxer—is to deny the true framework we face politically in our nation.

The self-purging process of the Democratic Party is an ongoing balance between allowing, even welcoming, voices of opposition in order to co-opt, but not allowing those voices to form a serious challenge, especially any challenge that favors the development of political formations not dominated by corporate money.

Success of Democratic Party

The Democratic Party should be seen historically as the most successful political party in the history of the world in terms of maintaining stability for rule by the privileged few. There is no other example that comes near what the Democratic Party has achieved in maintaining the domination of money over people.

Through trickery, the Democratic Party co-opted the powerful and massive rise of the Populist movement at the end of the 19th century using precisely the same lesser-evil arguments now presented against the Green Party.

They blocked the formation of a mass Labor Party when the union movement rose in the 1930s. They derailed, co-opted, and dismantled the powerful civil rights movement, anti–Vietnam war movement, and women's liberation movement. They have even succeeded in establishing popular myths that they were once for labor, for civil rights, and for peace. Nothing could be further from the truth.

One quite popular myth is that Franklin Delano Roosevelt was pro labor. Continuing the policies of Woodrow Wilson who oversaw a reign of anti-union terror, including blacklisting, and deporting immigrant labor organizers, FDR's administration sabotaged union drives every step of the way. When workers overcame their bosses' resistance and began winning strikes, FDR turned on them and gave the green light for repression after police killed ten striking steel workers in 1937. As FDR said himself, "I'm the best friend the profit system ever had." After WWII Truman used the new Taft Hartley Anti-Labor Act to break national strikes more than a dozen times.

The Democrats have not abandoned "progressive" positions they once held, as some Democrats repeatedly claim but have simply shifted further to the right as world globalization has advanced, leading to the lowering of democratic rights and the growth of wealth polarization within the United States. If a massive opposition develops, if the Greens begin to win races and their following grows, the corporations will put more money behind the Democrats, the media will become more sympathetic to the Democrats, promote their more "progressive" voices. The media would also become more critical of the Republican lack of sensitivity, all in an effort to maintain the two-party system. That is, a shift towards the Democrats will occur if the Democrats cannot control the people.

The two-party system is a self-correcting mechanism that shifts back and forth between the two parties, and within different wings of those parties, to maintain corporate political control. Loyalty to the two-party system is inculcated in the educational system, and our electoral laws are rigged to discriminate against third parties.

Green Voice Must Be Heard

Those who call for a "lesser evil," which is still a call for evil, will unfortunately succeed. The call for a "lesser evil" is what makes possible the greater evil. Those voices who say Ralph Nader should not run, that the Greens should consider withdrawing, that the Greens should not campaign in states where the vote is close are unconsciously helping Bush's reelection by weakening the development of an opposition political movement which could shift the balance of forces. Nothing is more important than the appearance of candidates and mass actions that tell the full truth, that call for the rule of law, respect for the Bill of Rights, and speak out for peace and social justice.

There is nothing more threatening to the rule of the corporations than the consolidation of a party of hundreds of thousands of citizens, especially young people, that fearlessly tell the truth to the American people. Only such a movement can in time become millions, then tens of millions and eventually win. But it is also the best strategy for the short term, to force a shift away from the direction being pursued today.

Short Term versus Long Term

The idea there is a conflict between the short term and the long term is a cover for capitulation. It has been the endless argument of the Democrats against challenges to their policies. When independent movements appear they call on people to enter the Democratic Party and work from within. There is no time to go outside the two-party framework, they argue. This argument was made 100 years ago, 50 years ago, 25 years ago and, of course remains with us today. Millions have agreed there's no time to do the right thing. Very powerful groups, like the AFL-CIO, have followed this advice. As a result, the number of workers in unions has dropped from 37% of the work force to 12% as they politically subordinated themselves to the pro-corporate Democratic Party.

Rather than success, these movements have found the Democratic Party to be the burial ground for mass movements, and of third-party efforts that sought to defend the interests of the people throughout American history.

If we follow the advice of the "left" Democrats who call on Greens to return to the Democratic Party, the Green Party will collapse like the New Party did for fear of confronting the Democrats.

The exact opposite is needed. We need to encourage those Democrats who are opposing the policies of their party to follow the lead of Congressman Dan Hamburg and break with the Democrats and join with us in developing an alternative force, fighting for democracy, social justice and peace.

All people who believe in democracy need to call on the *Nation* and others to stop their campaign against the Greens, a campaign at the service of corporate America. Instead they should join with the Greens in a battle for democracy in the same manner in which many progressive Democrats in San Francisco rejected their party's nomination for mayor and joined with the Greens to create a progressive alternative. We need to suggest to "progressive" Democrats that they should concentrate their attacks on the leadership of their party and its support for George Bush's policies, and not on the Greens for telling the truth and actually fighting for the ideals many of these Democrats claim to hold.

The Year 2004

The year 2004 is a critical year for the Greens. The campaign of the Democrats will be powerful and to some extent effective. Some will abandon us but others will be attracted by our courage and our principled stance. In California, the Green registration continues to rise even as the campaign against the Green Party grows. We may very well receive a lower vote than in 2000. But if we do not stand up to this pressure and hold our banner high, fight them and defend our right to exist, to have our voice heard, to run candidates that expose the two-party system and the hypocrisy of the

Democratic Party and its complicity with the Republicans, we will suffer the greatest lost of all.

The Green Party

The Green Party can and will win the hearts and minds of people when they see us as reliable and unshakeable, if we stand our ground. In time this leads to respect and then support. Those Greens who agree with the Ten Key Values but have disagreements with this Avocado Declaration need to be respected. We need to allow an open and honest debate as an essential part of our culture.

Truth can only be ascertained through the conflict of ideas. Thus democracy is essential for society but also for our internal process. The present discussion around the 2004 elections is one that will not end but will be with us for a long time. It finds expression in many forms because it is the most FUNDAMENTAL ISSUE of American politics in our epoch. Are we willing to stand up to the rule of corporate domination and its central political agent that has deceived and betrayed our people, the Democratic Party?

The Green Party Must Be a Pluralistic Organization

The Green Party seeks to bring all those who agree with its Ten Key Values into one unified political party. It welcomes diversity, debate, and discussion on issues of strategy, tactics, and methods of functioning. By its nature, a healthy organization that fights for the interests of the people will always have internal conflicts, sharp differences, personality difficulties, and all other things human. This is not only normal, it is healthy.

The Greens do not consider themselves a substitute for other movements or organizations, such as peace organizations and other specific issue groups that seek to unite people of all political persuasions around a specific platform. We welcome diversity with other groups that seek to move in the same direction with us but are not agreed to join us. We will try to work with such organizations where common ground exists. Thus the AVOCADO DECLARATION includes a call for the Greens to accept diversity and maintain unity as we seek to build an effective mass organization.

Let those that agree with the AVOCADO DECLARATION help protect and build the Green Party as a vehicle for democracy, freedom, liberty, and justice for all.

APPENDIX 4

ORIGINS OF THE TWO-PARTY SYSTEM

The two-party system in the United States is not the product of a conspiracy. It developed as a product of this nation's peculiar history. Although there are many systems of two-party rule in other countries the U.S. version, which is substantially more undemocratic, came about in a very different manner than most of the others.

Slavery

From the earliest days of the United States of America the sector of the economy dominated by the use of human slave labor was a minority. The slave owners feared entering a government in which they could be outvoted. To protect them several arrangements were made, aimed at ensuring slave owners control over their own states and granting them extra representation in the federal government. For instance, the U.S. Constitution to this day provides that "Representatives and direct Taxes shall be apportioned among the several States which may be included within this Union, according to their respective Numbers, which shall be determined by adding to the whole Number of free Persons ... [and] three fifths of all other Persons." The "other persons" were the slaves, who were not permitted to vote but were each counted as three-fifths of a person to determine how large a representation slave states would have in the Congress of the United States.

A natural economic alliance developed between the Southern slave states and the states to the west of the Appalachian Mountains. In the areas now called the Midwest farmers produced food to be shipped down the Mississippi River to feed the South, whose agriculture focused not on food but on producing cotton for the world market, mainly for England. Labor was much cheaper in England than in the United States—labor costs were about a third less. Thus it was more expensive to build a plow in the United States. Labor was also in short supply as potential workers drained away to the West, where there was an abundance of cheap or free fertile land.

The cotton-oriented slave-based economy joined with the Midwest in seeking free trade with England for its supplies of manufactured goods and opposed any tariffs aimed at favoring national manufacturing interests in the United States.

The Democratic Party

The Democratic Party was born as a political consolidation of an alliance between the slave owners, some merchant interests, small farmers of the West, and some of the more plebeian voters of the Northeast. This coalition could offer support for Midwest farmers to buy cheaper equipment from England by maintaining free trade, while in return receiving support from these farmers for protection of the slave-based economy. In opposition to the Democrats stood the Whig Party, which reflected primarily the interest of businesses in the North, including commerce, banking, and the early development of industry, as well as small farmers along the eastern coast. Many within the Whig Party had mixed feelings about slavery, although they were somewhat tied to slavery through their involvement in shipping or financing for the cotton industry and slave importation from Africa and other parts of the world. Within the Whig Party a current known as the "Conscious Whigs" gradually developed, which harbored doubts about the future of human slavery. They were more open to trying to industrialize America and protect its economic well-being by keeping it independent of England.

The Democratic Party was born under the control of the most reactionary, antidemocratic current in America—the slave owners—but within a coalition that could not be maintained without a "populist" approach toward farming interests, including small farmers, and some workers' interests, in contrast to the exploitative relations with other wings of the ruling class.

The Democrats were also expansionist. Slave farming depleted the soil rapidly and thus the slavocracy was interested in adding more land. This won them the support of some small farmers but by the 1850s opposition grew rapidly as conflicts developed as to whether slavery should be allowed in the new territories. The anti-expansion sentiment was at first based primarily in the Northeast but later expanded throughout the Midwest.

The Erie Canal

The Midwest farmers sent their harvests south because it was too expensive and slow to transport goods eastward over the Appalachian Mountains. There was an immense market not only in the Eastern states but in Europe and England if the farmers could find an economical way to transport their crops. There was a huge demand for food in Europe—Midwest farmers had an advantage because of the fertility of the American soil. The transportation issue was a major obstacle to economic growth and profitability for the Midwest.

The construction of the Erie Canal altered the entire dynamic and helped to drive one of the nails into the coffin of slavery. Opened to barge traffic in 1825, the canal connected Lake Erie with the Hudson River. New York City was rapidly transformed into a major port and, before long, into the main city of the United States. The Midwest farmers became less dependent on the slave economy of the South for selling their produce, and the Midwest economy expanded with increased migration as well.

Before long the wheat crop being produced in the United States, a good percentage for export to Europe, surpassed cotton as the primary crop. The coalition upon which the pro-slavery Democratic Party had been built began to come under question. A growing sector of industrial capitalists, fighting the free-trade policies of the slavocracy, began to look for ways to weaken the Democratic Party.

The Liberty Party

The first truly national "third party" in the United States, the Liberty Party, was formed in 1839 during this process of transition. The Liberty Party positioned itself not only against slavery, but also against racism. The slavocracy immediately went into vicious opposition against the Liberty Party. But, amazing as it may sound, the Liberty Party received some of its most hostile reception from people who claimed to oppose slavery, including some committed and active abolitionists. They attacked the new party because of what they perceived as a "spoiler" factor that could take votes from the Whigs, allowing the Democrats to win in close elections. The Liberty Party responded by saying it was a matter of principle not to vote for political parties that supported slavery. They dared to raise the idea that abolitionists should seek to win control of the U.S. government to abolish slavery.

The attack on the Liberty Party by opponents of slavery was strikingly similar to the rancorous condemnation of Ralph Nader for running for president by self-proclaimed liberals and well-known "progressives." Nader dared to raise the idea that we should not vote for parties that favor the rule of money over people. Like the early antislavery forces the anti-Nader progressives of our time feared the "spoiler" issue. In both cases there was little discussion or understanding that the "spoiler" issue would be an easy matter to resolve just by having runoff elections. Quickly those at the top of U.S. society recognized the leverage to be gained by not having runoffs and maintaining a winner-takes-all system, which would serve to divide any political challenge and keep the masses from having alternative political choices.

In Europe, and in most of the rest of the world where elections are held, "spoiler" politics is blocked by allowing for runoff elections. In the United States the rejection of runoffs and of proportional representation played a major role in stopping the development of political parties representing popular movements. This form of elections proved to be very useful to the ruling class and became an ingrained tradition in U.S. electoral law.

Fear of the "spoiler" small-party candidate repeatedly became an excuse used by those in the popular movements who sought to sell out to the two parties of money. This current would become known as "lesser-evil" proponents or "fusionists," who in one way or another argue for ending independent political efforts and seek to back one of the two major parties. In many cases the fusionists would be rewarded with electoral positions or financial gain.

Prior to the appearance of the Liberty Party many abolitionists had set as their goal to end slavery by convincing the slave owners to allow their slaves to go free. The new party questioned that whole concept. It wanted to open a battle for political control to end slavery through governmental power.

Thus came about the first major use of what the Green Party and others would later call the spoiler system, that is, election laws couched in such a way that any third-party campaign is automatically subject to the accusation that it is acting as a spoiler by daring to run at all.

The presidential election of 1840 with progressives split as to how to relate to the Liberty Party was the first mass education for the rich in America on what a wonderful system it was to have two parties with no runoffs. It simply happened; no special backroom conspiracy was necessary. An electoral system was in place that they could count on to produce a most peculiar political phenomenon: abolitionists, their supposed enemies, became the most vociferous opponents of other abolitionists daring to enter the electoral arena. People opposed to slavery became the first line of defense in maintaining the status quo for slavery.

While the first vote for the Liberty Party was tiny—only 6,797 people voted for them in 1840—a core leadership appeared that would not capitulate. Four years later their vote grew to 62,103 and they were accused of having "spoiled" the election for president, allowing the Democrat James Polk to defeat the Whig Henry Clay by 39,490 votes.

The easily resolved issue of "spoiler" elections would be repeated generation after generation to protect the rule of a minority over the majority. In each episode "progressives" and "liberals" were on the front lines to defend the two-party system, urging people not to vote for their candidate of choice but to accept voting for candidates who opposed what the voters believed in.

The U.S. electoral system is a self-correcting mechanism. It is always in motion and shifting. Its power is based on its flexibility and its ability to prevent popular movements from entering the electoral arena, gradually developing into an alternative power, and posing the issue of who should rule.

The idea of such an alternative power is not new. It was championed by one of the greatest newspapers in American history, the *North Star,* the first paper to defend the rights of women, Native Americans, and labor, and to oppose slavery and racism. It was founded in 1847 by the former slave Frederick Douglass in Rochester, New York. In its early history the Liberty Party had the support of the *North Star* as it dared to challenge the two proslavery parties. In fact the *North Star* merged with the Liberty Party newspaper in 1851 and was renamed *Frederick Douglass's Paper.*

Economic Issues

The abolitionists in the late 1840s began to appeal to the American people that slavery was hurting the United States's economic well-being because free labor was in competition with unpaid slave labor. Another critical economic factor set in. As small farmers expanded westward they ran into resistance from the slave owners, who wanted new land open to slavery. This led to major battles, including the use of arms, and it had the effect of continuing to weaken the Democratic Party coalition. A new antislavery current appeared within the party, especially in New York, made up of disgruntled Northerners nick-named "Barnburners" by their opponents. The term was a joke referring to a farmer who, in order to get rid of rats, would burn down his barn—the par-allel being that, according to the pro-slavery contingent, the developing op-position to slavery was too extreme a solution for the economic issues under discussion. (After the Compromise of 1850, which included a law requiring all states to collaborate in returning fugitive slaves, a similar antislavery current appeared in the Whig Party, the aforementioned Conscious Whigs.)

The Free Soil Party

The U.S. war with Mexico from 1846 to 1848 under the Democratic president James Polk seized from Mexico all of California, Arizona, Nevada, and Utah, as well as parts of New Mexico, Colorado, and Wyoming. An op-position current calling themselves "advocates of free soil," aligned with the Liberty Party, began appearing in 1846 and 1847. The two groups fused in 1848 to form the Free Soil Party. To a great extent both the Liberty Party and its Free Soil successor were led by former Democratic Party Barnburn-ers. The Free Soil's first candidate, former U.S. president Martin Van Buren, won 291,501 votes in the presidential elections of 1848, or 10.1 percent (the country's population was so small at the time that the winner received just 1.3 million votes). The Free Soil Party ran presidential candidates in the 1848 and 1852 elections, trying to challenge the two-party system. Its main plank was against the expansion of slavery into new territories in the West.

In 1852 the antislavery forces held state conventions, most of which at that point had begun to call themselves the Free Democratic Party, and ran Senator John Parker Hale for president. Some histories still refer to Hale as the Free Soil candidate. The name change mirrored a broadening of the movement's concerns, as it was beginning to combine antislavery forces with radicals newly arrived from Europe who advocated socialism. The Free Democratic Party sought to win over the labor sector of the Democratic Party to a more radical platform that included opposing slavery.

Again the "spoiler" issue played a major role and the hopes of the Free Democrats were dashed. The party fell apart as quickly as it had come together. But while fear of "spoiler" candidates remained a critical one for keeping the electoral system safely controlled by the status quo, these third-party challenges began to change the psyche of the American people. A mood of rebellion was in the air. Divisions within the Whigs and Democrats around slavery, free soil, and tariffs continued to intensify. The interest in a new party kept growing, started by the Liberty Party and expanded by the Free Soil and Free Democratic parties.

The Republican Party

While the Free Soil Party was gathering its supporters, even broader forces, reaching deep into the ruling circles of commerce, finance, and the beginnings of industry in the North, were considering the formation of a new political party. Men in the top leadership of the Whig Party began a move to create a new political party opposed to slavery. It was to be less radical than the Free Soilers but with far wider support.

Integral to this new vision was a dynamic that is often oversimplified by the version of American history in textbooks. The abolitionists, Free Soilers, Conscious Whigs, and Barnburners were all being attracted into a new coalition. That coalition, which brought together the Midwest farmers and Eastern economic interests, saw as its enemy the rule of the slavocracy. Critical to this equation were events taking place within the Democratic Party. The shorthand version of American history states that the Whigs collapsed and a new party, the Republican Party, replaced them. This version has the virtue of maintaining the political mythology that a two-party system has been and will always be the way politics are run in our nation. What was really happening marked the beginning of the end of a genuine two-party system representing competing social and economic forces.

The key to understanding the developments of the early 1850s was the increasing rise of opposition to slavery and the beginning collapse of the Democratic Party coalition. In the North it was starting to be unpopular to be an out-and-out supporter of the slavocracy's leadership of the Democratic Party. Crucial to this equation was the growth of the Barnburners (antislavery Democrats). And it was the willingness of some of them to join the formation of at first the Free Soil Party, and then in much greater numbers the Republican Party, that set in motion the political shift ending the two-party system of that time.

The pro-agriculture, pro-slavery sector of America's ruling class was under siege. The rise of industry and finance not only challenged them for control of the national government but also attracted an alliance of small farmers, abolitionists, large sectors of the working people, and—most important of all, though in a delayed and nonelectoral form—the African American people. African Americans, 44 percent of the South's population, would be pivotal directly and indirectly in spurring forward a revolution to crush the slave owners by expropriating a huge sector of their capital—human slaves— and stripping the slave owners of much of their remaining capital by ending their ownership of the best lands of the South.

The Republican Party was rising to become the political arm of a new America seeking industrialization, expansion, and a battle for dominance in the world markets against Europe and more specifically England. To make this coalition strong enough to win what would become a revolution, the new political alliance needed to include masses of farmers, workers, and the African American people. By the end of the Civil War almost two hundred thousand African Americans had served as soldiers in the Union Army. But that is still not a complete picture. An unrecorded number of African Americans, estimated at three hundred thousand to four hundred thousand, served the Union forces in a myriad of occupations—as laborers, carpenters, fortification builders, teamsters, scouts, and spies. In addition there were the unpaid multitudes that accompanied the advancing Union armies doing volunteer work.

The rise of the Republican Party was not, as we are taught in most histories of the United States, a simple replacement for one of two existing parties. It was developing in a manner to end both parties that had supported slavery and had held back industrialization and the dominance of industrial and finance capital.

When the Republicans first launched their electoral campaigns many if not most of the candidates they put forward were former Barnburner Democrats. Combined with the entry of the abolitionists, this constituted a mass radical left wing backed by all the forces of the left as it existed at that time, including labor Democrats. The early socialists of the time nervously backed the rise of the Republican Party; I believe it was even a socialist who coined the name "Republican" for the new party. In Europe Karl Marx urged American workers to vote for the Republicans as he saw a revolutionary struggle to destroy human slavery unfolding.

Obviously this was a complicated process and I am overgeneralizing in the interest of being concise. The political turmoil of the 1850s was the stirrings of a revolution, disguised in the 1860s as a civil war because of the geographic division between the two conflicting forces. The rise of the Republican coalition and its electoral triumph forced the slave owners to make a desperate effort to survive by declaring the formation of a new country. At first the slavocracy tried to hold referendums on secession in many Southern states. They only carried one state, South Carolina. In other states they lost the vote for secession. They were forced to send troops from South Carolina to help pro-secession forces stage coups to take over all the Southern states they could. The Republicans at first offered them concessions if they would accept the new order. One of those was to allow human slavery to continue for an indefinite time in the deep South. Originally the Thirteenth Amendment to the Constitution, which ended slavery, was intended to retain slavery with geographic limitations. This offer collapsed as the slavocracy gambled on secession in the hope that their ally England could help them stop the unfolding revolution.

The Civil War ended the two-party system. A new system appeared afterward that was called a "two-party system" but it was quite different. In the pre–Civil War version the two parties were led by conflicting economic forces; they truly did represent two currents in America. The two-party system that developed after the Civil War constituted two political styles that expressed the same economic interests.

After the Civil War

With the end of the Civil War the Republicans immediately faced a new problem. They now completely dominated the nation and had grown dramatically in power as a consequence of the war. But to win they had built a coalition against slavery that included economic forces with a series of conflicting interests. The farmers, especially the Midwesterners, had joined the Republican Party not because they supported tariffs but to end the power of the slavocracy and to make all new Western lands "free soil."

The Republicans had included the African American people and their abolitionist allies in the struggle along with immense numbers of small farmers and workers. The African American people wanted land reform and democracy in the South. Working people in the North wanted better conditions, shorter hours, higher wages, and the right to unions.

As could be expected, at the end of the Civil War the Republicans faced problems ruling with such a diverse electoral coalition. In the South since only whites could vote and their economy was still primarily agricultural, a natural alliance with farmers in the North once again could develop. The Democratic Party, which, although substantially weakened, still formally existed at the end of the war, suddenly had its hopes for political power revived. Nationally the Democrats saw such an agrarian and commercial bloc as a possibility. They accepted the end of slavery but not equal rights for African Americans. They saw themselves and publicly campaigned as the "white man's" party.

The more conservative forces inside the Republican Party feared the radicalization on social issues that the Second American Revolution had unleashed. They now dreaded facing demands from the ex-slaves, small farmers, and workers. The first reaction tied to money of the Republican leadership was to allow elements from the old Democratic Party in the South, along with conservative ex-Whigs, to begin reorganizing the South politically, reducing the freed slaves to the status of second-class citizens in what amounted to a new caste system.

But reviving the Democratic pro-agricultural alliance was immediately recognized as a threat to the aims of the backers of industry-oriented finance capital. The move to the right in the South just as the war ended, with many of the same politicians taking control, elicited a massive reaction from the left in the Republican Party that quickly won major support among ruling-class Republicans and the population as a whole.

A radical, relatively unified, shift took place to put a stop to the potential revival of the old pro-agrarian Democratic Party alliance. This danger was eliminated by taking away the votes of about 10 percent of the Confederate sympathizers in the South, establishing military rule over the defeated Confederacy, and not granting those states representation in Congress until they passed the Fourteenth Amendment to the Constitution, which gave the right to vote to (male) ex-slaves. It is interesting to note that most African Americans got the right to vote first in the South and only later in the North. By passing Radical Reconstruction, for a short moment in America's history the Republican Party opened up in the South a period of relatively free elections. This move guaranteed that control of Congress would remain safely in the hands of the Republicans. In the South two "parties" appeared, both supporting the Republican Party nationally. One was called the Radicals and the other the Conservatives. The Radicals consisted largely of the new African American voters aligned with whites, often of a more radical inclination. The Conservatives were led by ex-Whigs, some elements of the new Northern businesses entering the South, and the remnants of the old Democratic Party.

With even a small percentage of whites in the South siding with the African American people, Republican control was assured in most former Confederate states. South Carolina's population was two-thirds African American; Louisiana, Florida, and Mississippi were majority or about 50 percent African American.

Within a decade democracy and relatively free elections in the South of the United States ended. In the South a one-party system controlled by the Conservative faction gained total control. In time they readopted the name Democratic Party, held corrupt elections, and remained in power for almost a hundred years. The South was to become the backbone of ignorance, reactionary antilabor policies, and an extreme system of racist apartheid.

African Americans were disenfranchised while most whites in the South stopped voting. Candidates were handpicked by the one political party that with few exceptions, such as North Carolina during the populist rebellion of the 1890s, always won the elections.

Taming the Republicans

The one-party Republican national rule consolidated after the Civil War was reflected in the fact that as much as 50 percent of all federal taxes collected never made it to the government but went directly to the Republican Party apparatus. The Republicans had grown into a very strong organization because of the demands of the war. Now they had developed a degree of independence as a bureaucracy, that is, they were to some extent independent of the ruling economic circles.

The congressional elections in 1866, which had threatened a revival of the Democratic Party pro-agrarian coalition, turned into a crushing of the Democrats and a massive victory for the left wing of the Republican Party. The racist, anti-industrial Democrats had one advantage: the assassination of Lincoln had brought a Democrat into the White House, Andrew Johnson, who fought for the revival of the old-line Democrats.

The Radical Republicans failed by one vote to impeach the racist President Johnson. Many years later, in 1955, the future president John F. Kennedy would write a racist historical evaluation of these events, *Profiles in Courage*, in which he attacked democracy in the South. He described Radical Reconstruction as a "black nightmare the South never could forget." Kennedy viciously attacked abolitionist leaders who fought for the rights of African Americans, such as Thaddeus Stevens, as "the crippled fanatical personification of the extremes of the Radical Republican movement."*

Since the class that had controlled and led the Democratic Party had been crushed economically, a rapid shift took place among the existing electoral pockets still in the hands of the old Democratic Party. Leaders of the Democrats, specifically in the North and Midwest, now sought to completely dissociate themselves from the old pro-agricultural Democratic Party led by slave owners, and instead sought to align with the growing economic power of the industrial and financial ruling circles. The majority of the leadership in the Northern wing of the remnants of the Democratic Party declared themselves "New Departure" Democrats. In doing so they began shifting the Democratic Party to support tariffs, industrialization, larger government, higher taxes, and against free trade—all the key economic points that defined the policy of the Republican Party.

The former slave owners had been decimated, first by the expropriation of their slaves, and second, because the massive investments they had made in war bonds for the Confederacy had been declared worthless. To pay taxes or meet other obligations they were often forced to sell their land to Northerners. A very rapid decline occurred in the South that left Northern financial interests dominant.

Campaign for Stability

Sectors of the wealthy became upset at the Republican Party's strength, especially since the party often required that bribes be paid in order to do business. The wealthy saw the development of democracy in the South, an area with a shortage of labor, as now being a problem. It was proving difficult to turn profits since the African American labor force was now free to negotiate its pay.

A campaign for stability by forces representing money rapidly won support from the upper-middle-class intelligentsia, including many former abolitionists. They campaigned for an end to Republican Party corruption and for "stability" in the South, a code word for ending democracy, promoting the rule of whites, and implementing racist laws that would disen-

---

* John F. Kennedy, *Profiles in Courage* (New York: Harper & Brothers, 1956).

franchise African Americans, take away their legal rights, and force them to serve as a cheap labor force. Surprising as it may sound to people who read the progressive magazine the *Nation,* that journal was at the forefront of convincing former abolitionists to join this openly vicious, racist campaign. Within the Republican Party the groups promoting stability became known as the Liberal Republicans. In the 1872 elections this issue dominated the nation's attention. The Republican Party split and two Republicans ran for president, the incumbent Ulysses S. Grant and the Liberal Republican standard-bearer Horace Greeley. The Democrats, seeing little hope of winning, did not run a candidate and instead declared support for the Liberal Republicans. A small group of Democrats tried to run a campaign, but it failed to get any support. The Republicans opposed to the Liberals were called the Stalwarts. They defended the party's power and were often politicians benefitting from the corruption of the day.

The Stalwarts won, reelecting Grant. After the elections the Liberal Republicans merged with the "New Departure" Democratic Party, assuring "new" Democratic support for the same economic interests and policies: for tariffs, hard currency, higher taxes, larger government, etc. Senator Charles Sumner, a long-term proponent of abolition, stated, "The Democrats have accepted absolutely a Republican platform with a lifetime abolitionist as their candidate." Horace Greeley, as editor of the *New York Tribune,* was famous for his support of many liberal and radical causes. For vice president, Greeley picked Gratz Brown, a well-known Radical Republican who, at that time, was governor of Missouri, elected on the Liberal Republican ticket.

The New Two-Party System

When leftist opponents of the two-party system speak of the Democrats and Republicans being two wings of the same party, they are historically correct. The new two-party system was completely different from the pre–Civil War two parties that had fundamentally different policies and represented two different sectors of the population. Both parties today derived from the party of the Second American Revolution, the Republican Party.

It is important to note that the name Democrat was kept and brought with it a tradition of being "populist," that is, claiming to represent poor farmers and workers, carried over from its days as the party of slavery. It also was known as the party of "white men." The rise of industrial and finance capital in the United States can in good part be explained by the effectiveness of the "populist" Democrats and their ability to adjust their appearance to co-opt all attempts at developing political instruments that represent the people.

The defeat of Radical Reconstruction in the South took place via the formation of terrorist militias that were specifically set up to overthrow, with military power, the democratically elected state governments. The national Republican government gradually began to support and even provide arms to these terrorist groups as they forcibly confronted and eventually defeated the official state militias. Many of the terrorist groups gave themselves colorful names, such as the "Red Shirts," but most came to be called the Democratic Rifle Clubs.

When the Reconstruction governments were overthrown the new governors were almost exclusively controlled by Northerners and their states' economies were ruled by Northern business interests. The way all of this is taught in our schools—that it was about "home rule," the problem of "corruption" under Reconstruction, and the nation coming back "together"— is racist and false, a cover-up of one of the most horrific chapters of our nation's history.

Soon after the election of 1872 a new current, the Half-Breeds, arose within the Republican Party, fighting to tame the party. They favored ending corruption as well as radical policies and aimed to turn the Republican Party away from being an independent force into a party at the service of the new economic rulers. The name "Half-Breed" came from their claim that they took a middle ground between the Stalwarts and the Liberal Republicans. Gradually this new current took over the party, bringing the Republicans and new Democrats into close political equivalency.

When the Half-Breeds finally got control of the presidency under James Garfield, a Stalwart, Charles Guiteau, assassinated Garfield at the train station in Washington, D.C., shouting, "I am a Stalwart of the Stalwarts and Arthur will be president!" Guiteau was referring to the vice president, Chester A. Arthur, who was a Stalwart. But in office Arthur largely followed Garfield's policies. The assassination didn't change the Republicans' direction and the Half-Breeds continued to take control of the party.

Today the Republicans tend to openly advocate the policies sought by the rule of money while the Democrats assure that no opposition develops from the people. The key to the stability of the one-policy, two-party rule is the ability of the Democrats to co-opt, assimilate, and demobilize any popular opposition that appears among the overwhelming majority that have no party representing their interests.

Farmers and Workers

With the new "two-party" system in place, the two major groups in the North without a party were workers and farmers, not to mention of course Native Americans and African Americans. As the new system consolidated, challenges to its authority began to appear. Mass actions by workers and farmers around numerous demands, such as wages and hours, spread throughout the North. Massive struggles by workers were crushed by the use of force. The ruling circles called for special armories to be built in case of any future uprising. To this day some of these armories still stand as old fortresses, but hardly anyone knows the story behind their origin.

Farmers were the largest group of people who felt betrayed by the results of the Second American Revolution and were the first to attempt to build electoral organizations to fight for their interests. The first electoral formation fighting the two parties was the Greenback Labor Party. The party not only sought to defend poor farmers and workers, but it also opposed the totalitarian end of democracy in the South, seeking to defend the rights of African Americans. Some of its members were murdered for their work in the South.

This was the first test of the ability of the new Democrats to co-opt an opposition. The Democrats maneuvered well, offering fusion. These blandishments worked and this first attempt after the Civil War to create a party of working people and farmers was eventually defeated despite the heroic efforts of many of its leaders and ranks.

The Populist Explosion

In the 1890s an electoral explosion took place around the formation of the People's Party. The roots of this upsurge are usually explained by the creeping expropriation of small farmers by corporate farming, the railroads, and the banks. Certainly this was a central aspect to how the People's Party was formed and why it developed such rapid mass support. But the populist explosion was more than that. It was a protest of all the oppressed people in America looking to establish more democracy, to open up the electoral system to the ranks of the people, to have a say in government. The populist movement was a struggle for democracy, for the right of the people to fight for a government that would defend their interests.

It is beyond the scope of this overview to describe how fusion killed the People's Party after the 1896 convention. In the case of the populists both Republicans and Democrats entered into fusion to co-opt them in different states. But it was the Democrats who eventually crushed the populists through fusion at the national level.

Native Americans

After the new industrial-finance rulers took power they waged a fight against the working people, farmers, and African Americans as well as denying the hopes of women for the right to vote. They also launched a war, using the new power of the U.S. Army, to crush the Native American people. This process stretched from 1865 to the turn of the century. The key to its success, which left the overwhelming majority of the people with no representative power, was the two-party system and its ability to prevent through its undemocratic laws the consolidation of any opposition.

While the people of our nation fought back in massive efforts of direct action and even armed struggles to defend their rights, the rule of money over people after giving some concessions consolidated itself absolutely.

The Socialist Party of America

The efforts to find a political expression to strive for social justice and expand democracy continued to reappear. At the turn of the century a new party was created, the Socialist Party of America (SPA) formed as a merger of the Socialist Labor Party and the Social Democratic Party, founded by Eugene V. Debs. Debs, one of this nation's great working-class heroes, had also founded the American Railway Union and helped lead the Pullman Strike of 1894. As the SPA's presidential candidate Debs received close to 900,000 votes in 1912 and, despite being in prison at the time for his political views, won nearly a million votes in 1920. The SPA was instrumental in founding the Industrial Workers of the World, the independent labor union commonly known as the "Wobblies."

The SPA split after the Russian Revolution and both wings, the social democrats and the Left Wing Section, which by the end of the 1920s became affiliated with the Stalinists—ended up giving their support to the

Democrats. Small oppositions within each current emerged that refused to support the Democrats.

The Woman's Party

As women fought for the right to vote the Democrats put up the greatest opposition, especially in their bastion of the South. Eventually some women decided they would no longer vote for a party that opposed the right of a woman to the vote and created their own party, the National Woman's Party, in 1917. Once again the courageous women who formed the National Woman's Party were treated terribly. Many of their leaders were imprisoned. When they went on a hunger strike protesting their imprisonment they were tortured by force-feeding. After decades of struggle, under the impact of the mass independent mobilization of women throughout the country, in the end, the rulers of America conceded to women the right to the vote.

The Period of Silence

With some minor exceptions, primarily at local state levels, efforts to build a political electoral alternative to the two-party system in the United States had come to an end by the 1930s. While great struggles for social justice continued, for instance, by working people for trade unions and democratic rights, no mass political expression arose. The domination of the left by the Stalinist Communist Party was critical in this historical betrayal; otherwise the potential for a massive new party that defended the rights of the people would have been an enormous possibility.

After World War II the powerful struggle for equal rights by African Americans and later by Latinos arose to challenge Jim Crow and racism in general. But with few exceptions, such as the rise of La Raza Unida Party in South Texas, no electoral expression of these mass movements appeared on the national level.

The short-lived Progressive Party of 1948 was a peculiar movement backed by the Communist Party, shocked that its alliance with the Democrats had ended overnight as the Cold War began. The CP quickly returned to the Democrats, self-chastened for having dared to consider any independent political action.

In this long period from the early 1920s through the rest of the twentieth century no opposition of national dimensions manifested. I call this the ice age of our people in terms of expressions of political alternatives to the money-controlled two-party system at the national level. As I have mentioned I believe that era, which is at long last over, was due to the rise of Stalinism and its domination of the left.

This long political ice age, challenged by small groups throughout the decades, was finally broken by the appearance of Ralph Nader's campaign for president in 2000, which resonated nationally. The campaign drew larger crowds to its public meetings than either of the two parties of money. The Nader campaign was the first national electoral campaign defending the rights of workers, women, minorities suffering discrimination, standing for peace and in defense of our environment, that reached millions of people across the United States.

INDEX

"Passim" (literally "scattered") indicates intermittent discussion of a topic over a cluster of pages.
Italic numbers indicate photographs.

ALSO FROM HAYMARKET BOOKS

Breaking the Sound Barrier
Amy Goodman, Edited by Denis Moynihan, foreword by Bill Moyers • Amy Goodman, award-winning host of *Democracy Now!* breaks through the corporate media's lies, sound bites, and silence in this wide-ranging new collection of articles. • ISBN 9781931859998

Essays
Wallace Shawn • In these beautiful essays acclaimed playwright and beloved actor Wallace Shawn takes readers on a revelatory journey through high art, war, politics, culture, and privilege. • ISBN 9781608460021

Hopes and Prospects
Noam Chomsky • The Americas, both North and South, have been in motion with elections and political shifts that Noam Chomsky explores here with his characteristic independence and insight. • ISBN 9781931859967

Independent Politics: The Green Party Strategy Debate
Edited by Howie Hawkins • Leading independent and Green Party activists ask: Can we break the two-party stranglehold on U.S. politics? Ralph Nader, Peter Camejo, and other Green Party members and allies assess the 2000 and 2004 presidential elections, and debate strategy for how to build a challenge to the Republicans and an increasingly corporate Democratic Party. • ISBN 9781931859301

No One Is Illegal: Fighting Racism and State Violence on the U.S.-Mexico Border
Mike Davis and Justin Akers-Chacón • *No One Is Illegal* debunks the leading ideas behind the often-violent right-wing backlash against immigrants, revealing deep roots in U.S. history. The authors also remember the long tradition of resistance among immigrants organizing in the factories and the fields. • ISBN 9781931859356

The Bending Cross: A Biography of Eugene V. Debs
Ray Ginger, introduction by Mike Davis • Orator, organizer, self-taught scholar, presidential candidate, and prisoner, Eugene Debs's lifelong commitment to the fight for a better world is chronicled in this unparalleled biography by historian Ray Ginger. • ISBN 9781931859400

The Democrats: A Critical History
Lance Selfa • Offering a broad historical perspective, Selfa shows how the Democratic Party has time and again betrayed the aspirations of ordinary people while pursuing an agenda favorable to Wall Street and U.S. imperial ambitions. • ISBN 9791931859554

Vietnam: The (Last) War the U.S. Lost
Joe Allen, foreword by John Pilger • Allen analyzes three elements that played a central role in the U.S. defeat in Vietnam: the resistance of the Vietnamese, the antiwar movement in the United States, and the courageous rebellion of soldiers against the U.S. military command. • ISBN 9781931859493

ABOUT HAYMARKET BOOKS

Haymarket Books is a nonprofit, progressive book distributor and publisher, a project of the Center for Economic Research and Social Change. We believe that activists need to take ideas, history, and politics into the many struggles for social justice today. Learning the lessons of past victories, as well as defeats, can arm a new generation of fighters for a better world. As Karl Marx said, "The philosophers have merely interpreted the world; the point, however, is to change it."

We take inspiration and courage from our namesakes, the Haymarket Martyrs, who gave their lives fighting for a better world. Their 1886 struggle for the eight-hour day, which gave us May Day, the international workers' holiday, reminds workers around the world that ordinary people can organize and struggle for their own liberation. These struggles continue today across the globe—struggles against oppression, exploitation, hunger, and poverty.

It was August Spies, one of the Martyrs targeted for being an immigrant and an anarchist, who predicted the battles being fought to this day. "If you think that by hanging us you can stamp out the labor movement," Spies told the judge, "then hang us. Here you will tread upon a spark, but here, and there, and behind you, and in front of you, and everywhere, the flames will blaze up. It is a subterranean fire. You cannot put it out. The ground is on fire upon which you stand."

We could not succeed in our publishing efforts without the generous financial support of our readers. Many people contribute to our project through the Haymarket Sustainers program, where donors receive free books in return for their monetary support. If you would like to be a part of this program, please contact us at info@haymarketbooks.org.

Order these titles and more online at www.haymarketbooks.org or call 773-583-7884.